Seeing the Face of God

Exploring an Old Testament Theme

Puttagunta Satyavani

© 2014 by Puttagunta Satyavani

Published 2014 by Langham Monographs
an imprint of Langham Creative Projects

Langham Partnership
PO Box 296, Carlisle, Cumbria CA3 9WZ, UK
www.langham.org

ISBNs:
978-1-78368-963-7 Print
978-1-78368-962-0 Mobi
978-1-78368-961-3 ePub

Puttagunta Satyavani has asserted his right under the Copyright, Designs and Patents Act, 1988 to be identified as the Author of this work.

All rights reserved. No part of this publication may be reproduced, stored in a retrieval system or transmitted, in any form or by any means, electronic, mechanical, photocopying, recording or otherwise, without the prior written permission of the publisher or the Copyright Licensing Agency.

The Masoretic Hebrew Pentateuch is used in this work. The biblical references are to the Hebrew Bible. Unless otherwise mentioned the translations of the Hebrew text are the author's own.

The English translation of The Septuagint by Sir Lancelot Charles Lee Brenton is used in this work, as found in the BibleWorks: Version 4.0.032c- Copyright (c) 1998 BibleWorks, LLC.

British Library Cataloguing in Publication Data
Satyavani, Puttagunta, author.
  Seeing the face of God : exploring an Old Testament theme.
  1. God--Face. 2. Bible. Pentateuch--Criticism,
  interpretation, etc. 3. Self-disclosure--Religious
  aspects--Christianity.
  I. Title
  231-dc23

ISBN-13: 9781783689637

Cover & Book Design: projectluz.com

Langham Partnership actively supports theological dialogue and a scholar's right to publish but does not necessarily endorse the views and opinions set forth, and works referenced within this publication or guarantee its technical and grammatical correctness. Langham Partnership does not accept any responsibility or liability to persons or property as a consequence of the reading, use or interpretation of its published content.

Contents

Foreword xi

Acknowledgments xiii

Abbreviations xvii

Chapter 1 1
The Subject and Approach
   1.1 Introducing the Subject of Study 1
   1.2 Stating the Problem 2
   1.3 Reviewing the Previous Literature on Seeing the Face of God 4
   1.4 Assessing Previous Approaches 13
   1.5 Significance of the Divine-Revelations in the Pentateuch 18
   1.6 The Different Functions of פנים "Face" in the Pentateuch 24
      1.6.1 The Function of פנים "Face" with Personal/Pronominal Suffixes 24
      1.6.2 Prepositional Phrases Developed with the Noun פנים "Face" 25
         1.6.2.1 The function of the phrase לפני "before" 25
         1.6.2.2 The function of the phrase מפני "from before" 28
         1.6.2.3 The function of the phrase מלפני 29
   1.7 A Brief Reflection on Methodological Issues and Approaches 30
   1.8 Methodological Approach in this Study 35
   1.9 Specific Method in this Study and the Chapter Outline 38

Section I: Chapters 2–3: Texts from Genesis

Chapter 2 43
The Self-Revelations of YHWH/God in Genesis
   2.1 Introduction 43
   2.2 Genesis 3:8–10: God Walks 43
      2.2.1 Canonical Context 43
      2.2.2 Divine Self-Revelation and Communication 44
      2.2.3 The Mode of Self-Revelation, Human Recognition and Response 48
      2.2.3 The Function/Significance of Divine Revelation 49
      2.2.4 Conclusion 50
   2.3 Genesis 12:1–8: YHWH Calls 51
      2.3.1 Canonical Context 51

- 2.3.2 Divine Self-Revelation and Communication 51
- 2.3.3 The Mode of Self-Revelation, Human Recognition and Response 53
- 2.3.4 The Function/Significance of Divine Revelation 53
- 2.3.5 Conclusion 54
- 2.4 Genesis 15:1–21: YHWH Appears in a Vision 54
  - 2.4.1 Canonical Context 54
  - 2.4.2 Divine Self-Revelation and Communication 54
  - 2.4.3 The Mode of Self-Revelation, Human Recognition, and Response 56
  - 2.4.4 The Function/Significance of Divine Revelation 56
  - 2.4.5 Conclusion 57
- 2.5 Genesis 16:7–14: YHWH Sees 57
  - 2.5.1 Canonical Context 57
  - 2.5.2 Divine Self-Revelation and Communication 57
  - 2.5.3 The Mode of Self-Revelation, Human Recognition and Response 59
  - 2.5.4 The Function/Significance of Divine Revelation 60
  - 2.5.5 Conclusion 60
- 2.6 Genesis 17:1–5: YHWH Appears 61
  - 2.6.1 Canonical Context 61
  - 2.6.2 Divine Self-Revelation and Communication 61
  - 2.6.3 The Mode of Self-Revelation, Human Recognition and Response 66
  - 2.6.4 The Function/Significance of Divine Revelation 67
  - 2.6.5 Conclusion 67
- 2.7 Genesis 18:1–8; 16–22: God Eats Food 68
  - 2.7.1 Canonical Context 68
  - 2.7.2 Divine Self-Revelation and Communication 68
  - 2.7.3 The Mode of Self-Revelation, Human Recognition, and Response 70
  - 2.7.4 The Function/Significance of Divine Revelation 72
  - 2.7.5 Conclusion 72
- 2.8 Genesis 28:12–22: God/YHWH Stands and Speaks 73
  - 2.8.1 Canonical Context 73
  - 2.8.2 Divine Self-Revelation and Communication 73
  - 2.8.3 The Mode of Self-Revelation, Human Recognition and Response 74
  - 2.8.4 The Function/Significance of Divine Revelation 75
  - 2.8.5 Conclusion 76
- 2.9 Concluding Remarks 76

Chapter 3 79
"I Saw God 'Face-to-Face' and My Life is Rescued": Genesis 32:25–32
3.1 Introduction 79
3.2 Canonical Context 80
3.3 Exegetical Study of Genesis 32:25–32 81
    3.3.1 Conflict and Conversation between the Man and Jacob:
    vv. 25–27 81
        3.3.1.1 Jacob stays alone (v. 25) 81
        3.3.1.2 A man touches Jacob's hip (v. 26) 82
        3.3.1.3 Conversation between the man and Jacob (v. 27)....83
        3.3.1.4 The name Jacob is changed to Israel (vv. 28–30) 85
    3.3.2 Jacob Sees God "Face-to-Face", and His Life is Saved:
    vv. 31–32 87
        3.3.2.1 Jacob calls the place Peniel (v. 31a) 87
        3.3.2.2 Jacob saw God face-to-face (v. 31b) 88
        3.3.2.3 Jacob's life is saved (v. 31c) 94
3.4 Mode of Self-Revelation, Human Recognition, and Response 96
3.5 The Function/Significance of Divine Revelation 96
3.6 Conclusion 97
3.7 The Question of Background of the Motif פני־יהוה/אלהים
"Face of YHWH/God" 98
3.8 Beyond the Present Text 100

Section II: Chapters 4–5: Texts from Exodus

Chapter 4 103
The Self-Revelations of YHWH/God in Exodus
4.1 Introduction 103
4.2 Exodus 3:1–12: YHWH/God Appears in the Midst of Fire 104
    4.2.1 Canonical Context 104
    4.2.2 Divine Self-Revelation and Communication 104
    4.2.3 The Mode of Self-Revelation, Human Recognition, and
    Response 109
    4.2.4 The Function/Significance of Divine Revelation 111
    4.2.5 Conclusion 111
4.3 Exodus 24:1–18: YHWH/God Appears in the Cloud and Fire 112
    4.3.1 Canonical Context 112
    4.3.2 Divine Self-Revelation and Communication 113
    4.3.3 The Mode of Self-Revelation, Human Recognition, and
    Response 120
    4.3.4 The Function/Significance of Divine Revelation 121

  4.3.5 Conclusion..121
 4.4 Concluding Remarks..122

Chapter 5 125
"You Cannot See My Face; No One Can See Me, and Live":
Exodus 33:12–23
 5.1 Introduction..125
 5.2 Canonical Context 128
 5.3 Exegetical Study of the Text..136
  5.3.1 The Divine Task Given and Moses' Needs Expressed:
  vv. 12–13..136
   5.3.1.1 Moses' dialogue with YHWH over the accompaniment
   (12a) 137
   5.3.1.2 Knowing by name, finding grace and knowing
   YHWH's ways, and knowing YHWH (12b–13) 142
  5.3.2 Moses' Requests Heard and YHWH's Presence Promised:
  33:14–17 146
   5.3.2.1 YHWH promises to accompany Moses (v. 14)............146
   5.3.2.2 Moses' continued insistence for the presence of YHWH
   (vv. 15–16)..150
   5.3.2.3 Moses found grace in the eyes of YHWH (v. 17) 151
  5.3.3 Moses' Continued Requests and YHWH's Responses:
  vv. 18–20..152
   5.3.3.1 Moses' desire to see the glory of YHWH (v. 18)..........152
   5.3.3.2 YHWH gives details of his self-revelation (v. 19) 155
   5.3.3.3 "You will not be able to see my face; for no man
   shall see me, and live" (v. 20)..158
  5.3.4 The Divine Revelation Promised and Moses'
  Desire Fulfilled: 33:21–34:10, 28–35. 169
   5.3.4.1 The details of the proposed divine revelation
   (vv. 21–23)...169
   5.3.4.2 YHWH reveals himself to Moses on the Mountain
   (34:1–7)...171
   5.3.4.3 Moses bows before YHWH and worships
   (Exod 34:8–10)..175
   5.3.4.4 The shining in Moses' face (Exod 34:27–29)...............177
   5.3.4.5 Fear generated by the shining in Moses' face
   (Exod 34:30–32)..180
   5.3.4.6 Moses puts a veil on his face (Exod 34:33–35).............182
 5.4 Mode of Self-Revelation, Human Recognition, and Response 185
 5.5 The Function/Significance of the Motif...186

5.6 Conclusion 187
5.7 The Question of Background of the Motif פני־יהוה
"Face of YHWH/God" 190
5.8 Beyond the Mountain 192

Section III: Chapters 6: Text from Numbers

Chapter 6 195
YHWH Makes His Face Shine upon and Lifts His Face toward Israel: Numbers 6:22–27
6.1 Introduction 195
6.2 Canonical Context 197
6.3 Exegetical Study of Numbers 6:22–27 205
  6.3.1 The Pronouncement of YHWH's Blessing to the Israelites:
  vv. 22–23 205
    6.3.1.1 YHWH blesses his people to keep/protect them (v. 24) ...206
    6.3.1.2 YHWH shines his face upon his people out of his grace
    (v. 25) 208
    6.3.1.3 YHWH lifts his face toward his people to grant peace
    (v. 26) 212
  6.3.2 Name of YHWH and Future Blessings: v. 27 216
    6.3.2.1 Putting the name (27a) 216
    6.3.2.2 The Name and the Blessing (27b) 217
6.4 Mode of Self-Revelation, Human Recognition, and Response 219
6.5 Function and Significance 219
6.6 Conclusion 220
6.7 The Question of the Background of
"Shining and Lifting YHWH's Face"..................................223
6.8 Looking beyond Numbers 6:22–27 224

Chapter 7 227
Conclusion
7.1 Conclusions in Summary...227
7.2 The Face of God and His Physicality 233
  7.2.1 The Face of YHWH/God 233
  7.2.2 The Physicality of YHWH/God and His Human Form.......234
    7.2.2.1 The Appearance of YHWH/God in Human Form:
    Normal Life Situations 234
    7.2.2.2 Appearance of YHWH/God in Human Form:
    Visions and Dreams 238
      7.2.2.2.1 Visions 238
      7.2.2.2.2 Dreams..238

7.2.2.3 Human Form and the Bodily Aspect in the
Appearance of YHWH/God 239
    7.2.2.3.1 Human Form 239
    7.2.2.3.2 Human Body...240

Appendices

Appendix I 245
Contribution of Canonical Context and the Interpretative Results of the Texts Studied
    I.1 In the Texts in Genesis 246
    I.2 In the Texts in Exodus..248
    I.3 In the Text in Numbers 6:22–27 251

Appendix II 253
Relevance, Usefulness and Future Scope of this Dissertation
    II.1 Relevance and Usefulness for Other Fields of Research 253
    II.2 Scope for Future Research..255
    II.3 A Closing Reflection 256

Bibliography... 259
    Web articles 277

Foreword

It is a pleasure for me to write a foreword to this very interesting study on the "face of God" in the Pentateuch. The author, Dr Satyavani, has been in Christian ministry in India for many years, and has now proved to be a diligent scholar who has dug deeply into the Word in an effort to determine the primary connotation of an important expression that relates to the divine self-revelation.

The expression in question, the "face of God", is a familiar one to Bible readers. It is evidently an anthropomorphism, but there has long been disagreement regarding its import. On the one hand, several scholars have summarily dismissed it as a mere metaphor, with no significance beyond that. Others have compared it with the face of gods and goddesses in the ANE religious context and contended that its significance is primarily cultic—that is, it represents devotees or worshippers seeking an audience with the divine king. This would be analogous here in South Asia to the darbar or royal court that used to be regularly held by royalty in days gone by.

However, the author has dared to disagree with previous scholarship and, on the basis of careful exegesis of several crucial passages in the Pentateuch, sought to establish that the expression "face of God" has to do not so much with the approach made by devotees or worshippers, as to the initiative of the Lord God of Israel to reveal himself to select individuals or groups among his people, Israel. The related expressions found in the priestly blessing in Numbers 6:22–27, "may the Lord make his face shine on you" and "may the Lord turn his face toward you" likewise have to do with God revealing his glory in the tabernacle and hence with his self-revelations to his people.

If this is indeed valid, it has interesting and important implications for our understanding of the incarnation of the Son of God, Jesus of Nazareth.

The preface of the fourth Gospel ends with the words, "No one has ever seen God, but the one and only Son . . . has made him known" (John 1:18). In a similar vein, Jesus tells the disciples, "Anyone who has seen me has seen the Father" (John 14:9). And in a very telling manner, the Apostle Paul compares hearing and believing the gospel of Christ, to God making his light shine in our hearts to give us the light of the knowledge of God's glory displayed in the face of Christ (2 Cor 4:6).

All in all, this is a most enlightening study and is warmly commended to all who seek to understand more fully the God of the Bible who revealed himself to his people Israel, and supremely through his Son, the Lord Jesus Christ.

Brian Wintle

Acknowledgments

At the outset, I would like to offer my praises and thanks to God, my heavenly Father, who has guided me to take up this research work and proven his faithfulness throughout those years, helping me to complete this study successfully in spite of many hurdles and ordeals.

I am deeply grateful to many who have supported me in various ways throughout the course of this study. In chronological order, my deep appreciation goes firstly to Dr Michael Biehl, Missionsakademie, Hamburg, for sponsoring my initial research in Hamburg for six months during which time I worked under the supervision of Professor F Hartenstein, then professor in the Department of Theology, University of Hamburg. I am particularly grateful to Professor Hartenstein for his guidance in pointing me to the German literature on "the Face of God". Those six months proved to be most fruitful for my further research.

I am thankful to Mr and Mrs Basil and Shirley Scott, who hosted me in their home and introduced me to Tyndale House. I am grateful to the former Warden of Tyndale House, Dr B. Winter, who permitted me to reside in the House, and work in the library for a few months; also to Dr S. Sherwin, whose encouragement helped me to continue my research in the UK. The Faculty of Divinity, University of Cambridge, graciously permitted me to use their library and attend seminars in Biblical Studies while in Cambridge, where I was able to meet such senior professors as B. S. Childs and R. E. Clements. I would also like to express my thanks to Sister Bridget of Margaret Beaufort Institute, where I stayed for a year. Her personal interest in my research made my stay there encouraging. My thanks to Drs Sekhar and Usha Vijjeswarapu, who were most helpful during my studies in the UK. My heartfelt gratitude to Dr Chloë Starr, who, with her constant friendship and encouragement, has made me stand firm whenever the ground under my feet seemed to be sinking.

My thanks to Dr N. MacDonald, then lecturer in the School of Divinity, University of St. Andrews, for his supervision of my MLitt thesis. I am indebted to Dr D. Shepherd, then teaching staff at the Institute of Theology, Queen's University Belfast, who supervised my doctoral work for the first two years; he was sympathetic to my interest in this subject, and gave me valuable suggestions, particularly with regards to the methodology I have adopted in my study. Dr R. Clutterbuck, Principal, Edgehill Theological College, was very kind and helpful during my one year stay at Edgehill. It was there that I wrote the final draft of my thesis and edited it before submission. My thanks to several friends in Belfast, particularly to William Corbett, who was kind and helpful in getting my thesis printed and bound; and Andrew and Charlotte Poots for providing me safe accommodation during my last term in Belfast.

My special thanks to Professor Hugh Magennis, Director of the Institute of Theology at Queen's University; it is no exaggeration to say that without his constant involvement in my academic life, this thesis would not have been successfully completed. I am also thankful to the Institute for granting me the TBF Thompson Ministries Scholarships for my final year.

I am greatly indebted to my thesis examiner, Professor R. P. Gordon, then Regius Professor of Hebrew in the University of Cambridge. His critical comments and suggestions have helped me in revising and improving my thesis.

Finally, I would like to express my heartfelt thanks to Dr Brian Wintle, Regional Secretary, Asia Theological Association, India, who has proved to be a faithful Christian brother over the years. I am grateful for the concern he has shown when I began my work on this subject and for his constant encouragement. My thanks to several of my Christian sisters and brothers in Andhra Pradesh (UESI and IEM circles) for their prayers for this study, particularly, I would like to thank Mr K. Yohan, the founder of Christian Truth Book Room (Tenali) and Christian Residential High School (Pallikona), who provided me with good accommodation in the school campus so that I could peacefully edit my draft before publication.

My heartfelt thanks to Langham Partnership and the team at Langham Literature for their efficient and generous help in editing the manuscript.

This book is dedicated to the memory of my parents, the late P. Rayappa and Suseela Chowdary, who sacrificed their meagre earnings to send me for higher education, and they also imparted God-conscious thoughts to me from my very childhood; and to my sisters and brothers—Sukavani, Manjuvani, Sudhakar Rao, Rama Koteswara Rao and Gowtham Buddha, who have shown continued love and sympathy for what I have been living for.

Praise the Lord! He has been on my side and made his face shine upon me, and strengthened me with his very presence, from the beginning to the end of this study.

Abbreviations

AB	The Anchor Bible
ABD	*Anchor Bible Dictionary*
ANE	Ancient Near East/Eastern
BA	*Biblical Archaeology*
BAR	*Biblical Archaeological Review*
BASOR	*Bulletin of the American Schools of Oriental Research*
BBR	*Bulletin for Biblical Research*
BDB	F. Brown, S. R. Driver and C. A. Briggs, eds. *HELOT*
BHS	*Biblia Hebraica Stuttgartensia*
BST	The Bible Speaks Today
CBC	Cambridge Bible Commentary
CBET	Contribution to Biblical Exegesis and Theology
CBOT	Coniectanea Biblica Old Testament
CBQ	*Catholic Biblical Quarterly*
CBR	*Currents in Biblical Research*
CD	Church Dogmatics
Ch.	Chapter
CJT	*Catholic Journal for Theology*
DB	*Dictionary of the Bible*
DCH	*The Dictionary of Classical Hebrew*
DDDB	*Dictionary of Deities and Demons in the Bible*
DSB	The Daily Study Bible
DSD	*Dead Sea Discoveries*
EAL	*Early American Literature*
EBC	Expositor's Bible Commentary
Eng.Vss	English Versions

FAT	Forschungen zum Alten Testament
fn.	Footnote
FOTL	The Forms of the Old Testament Literature
GKC	*Gesenius' Hebrew Grammar*
HTR	*Harvard Theological Review*
HALOT	*The Hebrew and Aramaic Lexicon of the Old Testament*
HB	Hebrew Bible
HCLOT	*Hebrew — Chaldee Lexicon to the Old Testament*
HELOT	*Hebrew and English Lexicon of the Old Testament*
HTR	*Harvard Theological Review*
HUCA	*Hebrew Union College Annual*
IB	*The Interpreter's Bible*
ICC	International Critical Commentary
IDB	*Interpreter's Dictionary of the Bible*
impv.	Imperative
Int	*Interpretation*
ITC	International Theological Commentary
JAOS	*Journal of the American Oriental Society*
JBL	*Journal of Biblical Literature*
JBR	*Journal of Bible and Religion*
JSJ	*Journal for the Study of Judaism*
JNSL	*Journal of Northwest Semitic Languages*
JPS	The Jewish Publication Society
JQR	*The Jewish Quarterly Review*
JR	*The Journal of Religion*
JSOTS	*Journal for the Society of Old Testament Supplements*
JTS	*Journal of Theological Studies*
KZHAT	Konkordanz zum Hebräischen Alten Testament
lit.	Literally
LXX	The Septuagint
LXXE	The Septuagint English Translation (Brenton)
MT	Masoretic Text
NASV	New American Standard Version

NAC	The New American Commentary
NBD	*The New Bible Dictionary*
NCB	*New Century Bible*
NCBC	New Cambridge Bible Commentary
NCBCS	New Century Bible Commentary
NDBT	*New Dictionary of Biblical Theology*
NEA	*Near Eastern Archaeology*
NIBCOT	New International Biblical Commentary on the Old Testament
NICOT	New International Commentary of the Old Testament
NIDOTTE	*New International Dictionary of Old Testament Theology & Exegesis*
n.d	No date/details
NIB	*The New Interpreter's Bible*
NIV	New International Version
n.p	No publisher
n.p.d	No publishing details
NKJV	New King James Version
NRSV	New Revised Standard Version
NT	New Testament
NY	*The New Yorker*
OBC	*The Oxford Bible Commentary*
OT	Old Testament
OTL	Old Testament Library
OS	*Oudtestamentische Studiën*
OTS	*The Old Testament Student*
OTT	*Old Testament Theology*
Ps	Psalm
Pss	Psalms
PW	Preaching the Word
RSV	Revised Standard Version
SBL	Society of Biblical Literature
SBLDS	SBL Dissertation Series
SBLSS	SBL Symposium Series

SBLSP	*Society of Biblical Literature Seminar Papers*
SEÅ	Svensk Exegetisk Årsbok
Sec.	Section
SOTSM	The Society for Old Testament Study Monographs
Sup. Ch	Supplementary Chapter
TB	*Tyndale Bulletin*
TCB	Theological Commentary on the Bible
TDNT	*Theological Dictionary of the New Testament*
TDOT	*Theological Dictionary of the Old Testament*
ThT	*Theology Today*
TOTC	Tyndale Old Testament Commentaries
TWBB	*A Theological Word Book of the Bible*
VT	*Vetus Testamentum*
VTS	Vetus Testamentum Supplements
WBC	Word Biblical Commentary
WEC	The Wycliff Exegetical Commentary
ZAW	*Zeitschrift für die alttestamentliche Wissenschaft*
ZTK	*Zeitschrift für Theologie und Kirche*

CHAPTER 1

The Subject and Approach

1.1 Introducing the Subject of Study

The "Face of YHWH/God" (פני-יהוה/אלהים) is an important expression in the Pentateuch[1] and its association with the verb "to see" (ראה) is significant.

The Hebrew term פנים "face" in association with human beings (with proper nouns or pronouns) often signifies the human face in a literal/physical sense;[2] likewise, פנים "face" in association with the divine Person (יהוה/אלהים)[3] appears to fall clearly into this same category. Of the 402 occurrences of this plural noun [4]פנים in the Hebrew Bible (HB),[5] more than

---

1. This motif/theme also plays an important role in the rest of the HB, particularly in the book of Psalms; similarly, in the NT, the Gk. term πρόσωπον "face" is used (semantically) similar to that of פנים in the HB. See E. Lohse, "πρόσωπον", *TDNT* 7, 768–780.
2. פנים means "face/s" in a biological sense, and it is used in this sense in several places. For example, פניו is used in a literal sense when Abraham fell on his face (Gen 17:3); Joseph washed his face (Gen 43:31); Moses covered his face (Exod 34:33–35); פנים also reflects emotions and attitudes (Gen 31:2).
3. פנים is associated mostly with יהוה, a few times with אלהים, and very rarely with אדני.
4. פנים always occurs in the plural, except in the proper name פניאל and פנואל in Genesis 32:31, 32.
5. See G. Lisowsky, ed. *KZHAT*, 1158–1174; cf. J. Reindl, *Das Angesicht Gottes im Sprachgebrauch des Alten Testaments* (Leipzig: St. Benno-Verlag, 1970), 8. According to Reindl, the noun פנים is used 121 times with God (which includes construct phrases and possessive suffixes); 246 times with living beings (includes animals); 35 times with objects. In total, the term פנים occurs about 3000 times in the HB (include the usage with ל, מן, אל, על, את) of which about 650 occur in the Pentateuch itself. For a detailed study on the usage of this term see A. S. van der Woude, "פנים", *TLOT* 2, 995–1014; S. Yofre, "פנים", *TDOT* 11, 589–615; H. F. Rooy, "פנים", *NIDOTTE* 3, 637–640.

one-quarter are used in association with אלהים/יהוה (YHWH/God); while this association occurs throughout the HB in various contexts, it occurs about 25 times in the Pentateuch itself.[6]

While the noun פנים "face" in connection with יהוה/אלהים (YHWH/God) signifies the divine presence,[7] its association with the verb ראה "to see" is particularly important as it signifies the physicality of YHWH/God, and this motif in the Pentateuch occurs in the context of divine self-revelations.

1.2 Stating the Problem

The motif "the face of YHWH/God" in the Pentateuch is normally placed in the context of divine self-revelations; the association of the verb ראה "to see" with the "face of YHWH/God" seems to signify the physicality of YHWH/God especially when different people had claimed that they had seen (the face of) YHWH/God. It is striking to read, for example, that Hagar claims, "I have seen (ראיתי) him who sees me"[8] (Gen 16:13); Jacob exclaimed, "I have seen God (ראיתי אלהים) face-to-face and my life is saved" (Gen 32:31). It is also stated that the elders of Israel saw[9] God and that he did not raise his hand against them (Exod 24:10–11). At the same time, Exodus 33:20, where YHWH had supposedly said to Moses, "You cannot see my face; for no man shall see me, and live", seems to stand in conflict with these texts. Furthermore, YHWH is said to have spoken פנים אל־פנים "face-to-face" (Exod 33:11) and פה אל־פה "mouth-to-mouth"[10] (Num 12:8a) with Moses, who also looked at YHWH's תמונה "form" (Num 12:8b). But, Deuteronomy 4:12, 15 states that when YHWH spoke out of

---

6. This includes construct phrases and possessive suffixes. E.g. Gen 32:31, 33:10, 35:1; Exod 33:11, 14, 15, 20, 23, 34:23, 24; Lev 9:24; Num 6:25, 26; Deut 34:10, etc. See Yofre, "פנים", 591–592.

7. Yofre, "פנים", 595.

8. LXX reads: γὰρ ἐνώπιον εἶδον ὀφθέντα μοι; LXXE: "For I have openly seen him that appeared to me".

9. The verb used in these texts is the qal form of ראה.

10. פה אל־פה "mouth to mouth" acts as a synonym with "face-to-face". See van der Woude, "פנים", 998.

the fire at the mountain (Horeb) people had only heard a voice (of words) and "saw no form".

Because of this, while the above-mentioned texts (i.e. Gen 16:13, 32:31; Exod 24:10–11) arguably imply a literal "seeing" of the "face" of YHWH/God, most scholars have concluded, primarily on the basis of Exodus 33:20, that the references to the visibility/physicality (seeing aspect) should be treated as metaphorical or with an abstract sense of "presence", rather than literal ("face"). Presumably, in these texts, both Hagar (Gen 16:13) and Jacob (Gen 32:31) made their assertions after they had an encounter with YHWH/God, who seemed to have appeared in a human form; the statement that the elders of Israel saw God was also made in the context of the divine appearance on the Sinai Mountain (Exod 24:10–11). In some sense, it seems that פנים "face" functions to signify the appearance of YHWH/God in the context of divine self-revelations. Some scholars have also taken the statement in Deuteronomy 4:12, 15 as a proof to argue against the corporeality of YHWH/God. Therefore, it seems appropriate to study the association of פנים "face" with YHWH/God and its association with the verb ראה "to see" in key texts in the Pentateuch with the objective of understanding the significance of the motif "seeing the face of YHWH/God" and to discuss these seemingly conflicting statements within the context of Israel's anthropomorphic traditions/divine self-revelations.

At this juncture, it seems appropriate to review the previous literature on the subject of "seeing the face of YHWH/God" and earlier approaches to this subject; to study the significance of the divine self-revelations and different functions of פנים "face" in the Pentateuch; to discuss methodological issues; and then to state the approach in this study.

1.3 Reviewing the Previous Literature on Seeing the Face of God

Given that scholarly analysis of the motif "seeing the face of YHWH/God" has not been particularly extensive,[11] this review will include the arguments from important works on Old Testament theology where these issues are raised.[12]

W. W. G. Baudissin, one of the earliest scholars to write on this subject, assumes that the expression "seeing the face of YHWH/God" (אלהים/פני־יהוה) was developed under Canaanite influence and that another cultic practice was adopted in Israel;[13] and he associates theophanies and visions with the places of rituals and sacral places. Making a distinction between the verb חזה (*schauen*) "to look at" and the verb ראה (*sehen*) "to see", he says that the verb חזה has a literal sense and involves the subject (viewer), while the verb ראה does not involve the viewer.[14] In light of Psalm 17:15, where חזה is associated with God's פנים "face" and תמונה "form", Baudissin understands that חזה meant "to look at God" in the temple[15] and equates "seeing God" (*Gott schauen*) with "visiting the temple".[16] However, lexically speaking, Baudissin's distinction of the verbs ראה "to see" and חזה "to

---

11. There has been relatively little attention given to this subject in Old Testament studies particularly in English. A few (primarily German) scholars have explored the concept of "seeing the face of יהוה/אלהים" and it is for this reason that German sources are reviewed in detail. Three of the German scholarly works reviewed here, namely W. Baudissin, F. Nötscher and J. Reindl were reviewed earlier in P. Satyavani, *The "Face of God" in Genesis and its Significance for Worship*. MLitt diss. (University of St. Andrews, 2006), 3–12.

12. Scholarly works are reviewed according to the dates of the works, so that the possible influence of earlier scholars on later scholarship may be discerned; exception to this is that Nötscher's work is discussed before Johnson's article, because of the extensive treatment of the subject in this work.

13. W. W. G. Baudissin, "'Gott schauen' in der alttestamentlichen Religion", in F. Nötscher, *Das Angesicht Gottes schauen: nach biblischer und babylonischer Auffassung* (Darmstadt: Wissenschaftliche Buchgesellschaft, 1969), 198–203. Reprint from *Archiv für Religionswissenschaft* 18 (1915), 173–239.

14. Contra Nötscher, *Angesicht*, 20–25.

15. Although Baudissin ("Gott schauen", 233–234) argues that in Ps 63:3 חזה meant "to look at God" in the temple and ראה meant an inner experience, he sees the difficulty in determining whether God was "seen" in a literal sense or in some inner sense.

16. Baudissin, "Gott schauen", 211. Baudissin also refers here to Babylonian prayers to Ištar ("ich blickte auf dein Angesicht") and to Marduk ("ich sehe das Angesicht Mardukus"), as parallels to "visiting the temple" in Israel.

look at" is not justifiable, because just as חזה has the literal sense, ראה also involves the viewer and has the literal sense of "seeing".[17] Baudissin also thinks that the *Gottesbegriff* "God concept" in theophanies was developed more towards transcendence during the later period in Israel and that it was different from the earlier texts (Gen 17:1).[18] But the idea of transcendence is also found in the earlier texts (e.g. Gen 28:12; Exod 19:20).

One can see that Baudissin's approach to the subject is from the perspective of *Religionsgeschichte*; he situates the Israelite beliefs in the religious context of the ANE and equates the expression "seeing the face of God" with visiting the temple.

F. Nötscher supports Baudissin in associating the theme of פני־יהוה/אלהים "face of YHWH/God" with the temple and in interpreting the theme in the context of the ANE;[19] but disagreeing with Baudissin that theophanies and visions should be associated with the places of rituals, he argues that YHWH was seen in a bodily presence even in non-sacral localities, and also in dreams (e.g. Gen 28:16).[20] While Nötscher acknowledges that in Genesis 3:8 God came to Adam and Eve in a human *Gestalt* "form", he argues that in Exodus 3:2 it was the storyteller who let Moses interpret the flame as an expression of "face of God"; and that in Exodus 24:10 Israel saw God without a face. He maintains that seeing פנים אל־פנים "face-to-face" did not signify a physical seeing (Deut 4:12), but believes that Moses saw the "form" of God (Num 12:6–8; Deut 34:10).[21]

Unlike Baudissin, Nötscher does not see evidence of Canaanite or Egyptian religious influence;[22] instead he suggests that the Israelite concept of פני־יהוה "face of YHWH" was influenced by the Babylonian

---

17. See D. Culver, "חזה", *TWOT* 1, 274–275; Culver, "ראה", *TWOT* 1, 823–825. Cf. Gen 32:31 where ראה is used for "seeing" God in a literal sense; Exod 24:10–11 (cf. Ps 63: 3) where both חזה and ראה are used as twin terms for "seeing" God.

18. This is because Baudissin (222–223) thinks that Jeremiah has no real vision and Amos has not described "seeing of God" in the visions. Baudissin uses "earlier" in the sense of canonical placement.

19. Nötscher, *Angesicht*, 1–10.

20. Ibid., 25–31.

21. Ibid., 33–47. He also refers here to Gen 17:1–4; פנים אל־פנים in Gen 32:31; Exod 24:10, 33:11; Num 12:8 (פה אל־פה), Num 14:14 (עין בעין).

22. Nötscher, *Angesicht*, 59 61. Although washing of the idols was practised and the Sun Amun (god) was worshiped in Egypt, Nötscher felt that in Egyptian religion there was no

religion and refers to a Babylonian prayer in which "to see Ištar's face" meant to seek Ištar's *Kultstätte* (cult statue)²³ and concludes that the expression ראה (את־) פני־יהוה "seeing the face of YHWH" was a parallel to "seeing the cult statue of YHWH". Although Nötscher supposes that there were "concrete ideas" behind the Israelite usage of פנים with YHWH, he rejects E. Kautzsch's argument that YHWH was represented *in Gestalt von Jahwebildern* (idol of YHWH) in the temple, and argues that in Israel the expression "seeing the face of YHWH" became a *terminus technicus* for "visiting the temple".²⁴

Nötscher then argues that although in the early Babylonian period gods were seen in the images, in the later period gods were increasingly equated with kings, and that in Israel also YHWH was identified as king and "seeing god" meant "seeing the king"; and the usage פני־יהוה "face of YHWH" and also עמד לפני "standing before" refer to having an *Audienz* before the king (cf. Gen 43:15).²⁵ He suggests that there was a development of the Israelite concept of "seeing" the face of God and that the concept in Israel also lost its concrete meaning. In the same vein, he argues that the MT's vocalization of the verb ראה (qal) to לראות (niphal) in Exodus 34:24 was influenced by Exodus 33:20's reticence of seeing God's face.²⁶ Because in Babylon, all the religious rituals (e.g. sacrifice) took place before the statue, he assumes that in Israel also the expression לפני יהוה "before YHWH" was primarily used in the context of the temple.²⁷

---

concept of the transcendence of the gods, and "seeing God" meant "seeing the king" and was pragmatic: "im Dienst des Königs stehen" (61).

23. Nötscher (*Angesicht*, 73–75) describes the prayer of a sick person who desires to see the face of Istar: ". . . o Ištar, der dein Antlitz schaut. Ich bin 'erkrankt'".

24. Nötscher (*Angesicht*, 54) citing E. Kautzsch, *Biblische Theologie des Alten Testaments* (Tübingen: J. C. B. Mohr, 1911), 94. Although Nötscher acknowledged the presence of idols in Israel (cf. Judg 18:13–24), he supposed that there was no iconic representation of YHWH in the official cult.

25. Nötscher, *Angesicht*, 53–57, 77, 87.

26. Ibid., 77–98. He refers to some linguistic similarities in the usage of *Gott schauen* "seeing the face" in Hebrew and Akkadian. Cf. W. von Soden, ed. *Akkadisches Handwörter Buch*. Band II (Wiesbaden: Otto Harrassowitz, 1972).

27. Nötscher, *Angesicht*, 94–109. He refers to the Psalms as a proof, which depicted God as king.

While Nötscher differentiates Israelite cultic practices from other traditions within the ANE, his heavy dependence upon non-Israelite religions prevented him from understanding the significance the motif "seeing the face of YHWH/God" played in ancient Israel. While he rejects the idea of YHWH's statue in the temple, and equates "seeing the face of God" with seeing the king for *Audienz*, he does not give any rationale why the Hebrew writers used the term פנים "face" in association with "YHWH/God" (פני־יהוה/אלהים). Since he rejected the presence of the idol in the official cult in Israel, he has to account for the usage of "the face of YHWH" which occurs frequently in the Psalms;[28] therefore, he perhaps brings the Babylonian idea of *Audienz* into the Israelite cultic context, but he does not reflect on the theological function and significance of the "face of YHWH/God" for the Israelite worship of God whom they believed as their creator (Gen 1–2). If one is persuaded by Nötscher, one has to imagine that "face" has no association with the "self-revelations of YHWH/God", and that it can only be associated with "seeing" ritual pictures or statues or with the secular idea of audience with the king.

A. R. Johnson suggests that the expressions פני־יהוה "face of YHWH" and לפני יהוה "before YHWH" should be understood as idiomatic, and that they became "mere figures of speech";[29] he assumes that the phrases such as לפני were used in the HB in a prepositional sense, and that it was the secondary use of the term פנים which had "arisen through the employment of synecdoche (*pars pro toto*)".[30] Johnson also suggests that when used with a suffix, פנים "face" serves as a personal pronoun and that "to see my face" is an emphatic way of saying "to see me".[31]

If Johnson admits that "to see my face" is an emphatic way of saying "to see me", this could well involve a physical seeing of the person. Since seeing the person normally involves seeing his or her face, "seeing a person"

---

28. Where the term פנים (as noun/pronominal suffix/prepositional phrase), in association with YHWH/God, occurs about 40 times.
29. A. R. Johnson, "Aspects of the Use of the Term פָּנִים in the Old Testament", *Festschrift O. Eissfeldt*. Ed. H. J. Fück (Halle an der Saale: Niemeyer Verlag, 1947), 155–159.
30. Johnson, "Aspects", 157, citing E. König, *Stilistik, Rhetorik, Poetik in Bezug auf die biblische Literatur* (n.p.d. 1900), 57.
31. Johnson, "Aspects", 158. He refers to Gen 32:21; 33:10; Exod 23:15; 34:20.

and "seeing the face of that person" cannot be easily separated. Contrary to Johnson's argument that פני יהוה "face of YHWH" and לפני יהוה "before YHWH" are to be treated as idiomatic and as figures of speech, there is ample textual evidence in the Pentateuch to confirm that these expressions are associated with the anthropomorphic person of YHWH in the context of the divine self-revelations.[32]

Johnson also thinks that the expression of seeing a person פנים אל־פנים "face-to-face" (as in Gen 32:31) was used "quite simply and with a perceptible weakening of its literal meaning to denote the enjoyment of personal contact with someone else (especially one's social superior)".[33] It is worth noting, however, that one searches in vain for any evidence of such "weakening" in Genesis 32:23–31, where the context on the contrary supports rather a more literal interpretation of Jacob's claim that he saw God face-to-face.[34]

W. Eichrodt argues that the expression seeing/seeking "the 'face' of YHWH/God" was "originally thought of in a completely naïve and concrete way", because the face of the statue in the temples in the ANE (especially Babylon) was a reality in front of the worshipers.[35] He finds this concrete conception of פנים in Jacob's claim that he saw God פנים אל־פנים "face-to-face" (Gen 32:31), but then sees Exodus 33:20 as an expression of later reticence regarding the possibility of seeing the divine face.[36] At the same time, Eichrodt acknowledges that "the realistic significance" of the expression "face-to-face" in several texts is "incontestable".[37]

However, he understands that "'seeing' the face of YHWH" is used only in a metaphorical sense to mean entering of the sanctuary; and in keeping with earlier scholars, he thinks that the expression of "seeing the face" is introduced into Israelite religious vocabulary from the ANE where gaining

---

32. This aspect can be seen in chapters 2–6 below.
33. Johnson, "Aspects", 158.
34. See ch 3, 81–87 below.
35. W. Eichrodt, *Theology of the Old Testament*. Vol. 2 (London: SCM Press, 1967), 39. He refers to the female Tanit who acts as pᵉnē baʻal (face of Baal).
36. Eichrodt, *OTT* 2, 35–36. He refers here to niphal pointing in Exod 23:15, 17; 34:20, 23; Ps 42:3.
37. Ibid., fn. 7, 20. He refers here to: Gen 32:31; Exod 4:24; 24:9; Num 12:8; Judg 6:22.

an audience with "one's superior" is described as "seeing" the countenance of the person in question.³⁸ He insists that in Exodus 33:11, פנים אל־פנים "face-to-face" is only a "heightened metaphor" and that it is "the direct personal meeting and speaking with the invisible God". However, referring to the usage of the phrase פני ילכו "my face shall go" in verse 14, Eichrodt says that "it is almost impossible not to conclude that we have here *another form of self-manifestation of the transcendent God,* by means of which his presence is . . . guaranteed to them".³⁹

Although Eichrodt admitted the usage of "face of God" as "incontestable", in line with Baudissin and Nötscher, he too placed this expression in the ANE religious context because he followed the *Religionsgeschichte* approach. Since he did not place the Hebrew texts in their own context, he could not see the theological significance of the expression of "seeing the face of God" and concluded that it was only speaking with the invisible God.

J. Reindl acknowledges that פנים אל־פנים "face-to-face" implies an unbroken and intimate relationship between God and Moses in Exodus 33:11, but he assumes that this phrase was used only in a metaphorical sense⁴⁰ and that it cannot be taken literally because of Exodus 33:20; in Jacob's case (Gen 32:31) פנים אל־פנים "face-to-face" was used as an "aetiological" expression; and the "face" was used only as *pars pro toto*.⁴¹ Reindl also suggests that this motif never became a *theologumenon* and was only an idiomatic or proverbial expression and stylistic way of speaking,⁴² and that this "anthropomorphic image of God" ("Gottesvorstellung") was used only as a means to make God more intelligible.⁴³

If this expression "face of God" was used only as an "anthropomorphic image" and as an idiomatic expression, one wonders how it would have

---

38. Ibid., 35–36. He refers to Baudissin and Nötscher (cf. discussions above) in support of his views.
39. Ibid., 37, 38.
40. Reindl, *Angesicht*, 10, 74–75, 163.
41. Ibid., 70–73. Cf. Johnson, "Aspects", 157.
42. Ibid., 198, 200. For similar views on idiomatic expressions see J.M. Babut, *Idiomatic Expressions of the Hebrew Bible* (N. Richland Hills: Bibal Press, 1999), 28, 56. Like Nötscher (fn. 34), he too refers to MT's vocalization of qal form of ראה to niphal.
43. Ibid., 200–201.

helped make God more intelligible. Because Reindl approached the text merely from a linguistic and form-critical point of view,[44] he could not see any theological significance in the Israelite expression of "seeing the 'face' of YHWH/God".

S. Terrien, interpreting the term פנים "face" in two different ways as "presence" (in Exod 33:14) and "face" (in v. 23), suggests that the term פנים "presence" was used metaphorically in prepositional constructions such as לפני to mean "a sense of immediate proximity",[45] but פנ־יהוה/אלהים "the 'face' of YHWH/ God" was specifically used "to designate the innermost being of God" which (he thinks) was not accessible even to Moses. The weakness of Terrien's suggestion is that there is no lexical basis for the semantic distinction he makes between פנים "face" as "presence" and "innermost being"[46] in contradiction to the "external face".

In line with Johnson's and Reindl's views, Terrien argues that the phrase פנים אל־פנים "face-to-face" is only an idiom that refers "to the direct, non-mediated (i.e. immediate) character of a manifestation of presence; it describes a 'person-to-person' encounter, without the help or hindrance of an intermediary",[47] an idiom that was often used with verbs of auditory rather than visual perception (cf. Exod 33:11; Deut 5:4) and Jacob's claim that he saw God פנים אל־פנים (Gen 32:31) "face-to-face" should not be treated as visual perception for it belonged to the aetiological *legenda*.[48] If the usage פנים אל־פנים "face-to-face" refers to the direct and immediate character of a manifestation, and if it describes a "person-to-person" encounter, as Terrien admits, there is no reason why it could not have involved visual perception. Perhaps, Terrien's critical views did not allow him to associate the expression "seeing the face" with the self-revelations of YHWH/God in the Pentateuch.

---

44. Unlike his predecessors, Reindl does not associate this concept with the temple.
45. S. Terrien, *The Elusive Presence: Toward a New Biblical Theology* (New York: Harper & Row, 1978), 65.
46. פנימי "inner" is only used of buildings, even that of the temple (e.g. Ezek 40–46).
47. Terrien, *Elusive Presence*, 90–91.
48. Ibid. Cf. Reindl, *Angesicht*, 70–73.

M. D. Fowler suggests that לפני יהוה was used to express "direct and personal communication";⁴⁹ however, he also argues that the phrase לפני יהוה "before YHWH" often has the nuance "in the estimation of YHWH" rather than "in the presence of YHWH";⁵⁰ he follows Eichrodt in maintaining that לפני יהוה was used in a "heightened metaphorical sense"; and that the expression לפני יהוה entered into the religious vocabulary of ancient Israel from the ANE where "gaining an audience with one's superior was commonly described as seeing the countenance of the person in question".⁵¹ Such a conclusion again invites the question of why לפני יהוה could not have indicated a literal physical manifestation, given that Fowler admits it as direct and personal communication.

F. Hartenstein, accepting most of the conclusions of Nötscher's thesis, endorses the view that the expression *Das Angesicht JHWHs* "face of YHWH" had its origins in the cultic realm. His study, with a particular focus on Psalm 27, is an attempt to establish that the idea of royal and cultic audience was the background of the expression "face of YHWH".⁵² Assuming that it is closely related to the idea of God as king, he argues that the "face of YHWH" expresses *Anthropomorphismus* (comparison is made with the face of a king); and that "the face of YHWH" had its roots/origins in the cultic realm, specifically in Jerusalem Temple in the analogy of "God's kingship" ("Königtum Gottes").⁵³ Since gods/goddesses in Egyptian religion had a human form and also played a social role, Hartenstein assumes that the "face of YHWH" expresses *Soziomorphismus*.⁵⁴ However, he attempts to show that the divine image in the ritual context neither represents the body of a deity nor the deity itself, but provides a room for the imagination of God's presence, the appearance of God.⁵⁵

---

49. M. D. Fowler, "The Meaning of *lipnê* YHWH in the Old Testament", *ZAW* 99 (1987), 386. Fowler refers here to Joseph's brothers presented לפני Pharaoh (Gen 47:2).
50. Ibid., 384–386, 390.
51. Ibid., 386–387. Fowler thinks that it was in this sense that Abraham stood (Gen 18:22; cf. 19:27) and Moses spoke לפני־יהוה (Exod 6:12, 30).
52. F. Hartenstein, *Das Angesicht JHWHs* (Tübingen: Mohr Siebeck, 2008).
53. Ibid., 10–14.
54. Ibid., 22–25.
55. Ibid., 37.

Although Hartenstein compares YHWH with the king, and agrees with the idea of anthropomorphic form, surprisingly, however, he argues that the reference to divine *Angesicht* "face" was only the devotee's imagination of praying before the "form" of YHWH ("Gestalt JHWH").[56] Supporting the view of aniconic tradition in Phoenicia and Mesopotamia,[57] he rejects Niehr's[58] assumption of the cult statue/idol in the Jerusalem Temple.[59] Interestingly, however, he compares the expression "to behold YHWH's 'beauty'" (בנעם־יהוה in 27:4) with the king Yehavmilk having "audience" with the Lady of Byblos.[60] If one associates the "beauty" with the monarch that involves a physical seeing, the question is why it cannot also be taken to indicate the physicality of YHWH/God.

Hartenstein assumes that the usage "to see/behold the 'face of YHWH'" has the pragmatic idea of *Audienzvorstellung*[61] in the analogy of meeting with the king for an audience (Ps 27:7–13);[62] he interprets "hiding place" (בסתר in Pss 27:5, 31:21) as a reflection of entering into the realm of protection in "the area of YHWH's throne" ("Thronsphäre JHWHs").[63] It is in light of these conclusions that Hartenstein discusses the expression "face of YHWH" in Exodus 32–34 and concludes that the idea that no one can see the "face of YHWH" (33:20) is antithetical to the idea in Psalm 27 where "face of YHWH" indicates audience and protection.[64]

Hartenstein's approach to the subject of "face of YHWH" is from the traditional-historical perspective, and he has situated the Israelite usage

---

56. Ibid., 140.
57. T. N. D. Mettinger (*No Graven Image? Israelite Aniconism in its Ancient Near Eastern Context* [Stockholm: Almquist & Wiksell International, 1995], 173–204; 540–549) first argued that aniconic worship was a more general West Semitic feature.
58. H. Niehr, "In Search of YHWH's Cult Statue in the First Temple", in *The Image and the Book*. Ed. K. van der Toorn (Leuven: Peeters, 1997), 91.
59. Hartenstein, *Angesicht*, 26–52.
60. Ibid., 103–118; cf. 139.
61. Ibid., 53–61, 205–209.
62. His assumption is based on the linguistic expressions used for the people approaching the king (for an audience), and for the worshipers approaching God, which were the same; hence Psalms were the proof which depicted God as king.
63. Ibid., 142–171.
64. Ibid., 277–282.

of the "face of YHWH/God" in the ANE religious and secular context.⁶⁵ Although he arrives at his conclusion that the motif "face of YHWH" had its origins in the cultic realm of the Jerusalem Temple,⁶⁶ he does not explain the reason why the expression "seeing the face of YHWH/God" was employed in terms of the divine-revelations, because he did not place Psalms in the context of divine revelations, and his association of "seeing the face of YHWH" with having a royal audience brings him to an impasse for his own interpretation of Exodus 33:20.

1.4 Assessing Previous Approaches

The approaches adopted by Baudissin and Nötscher, followed by Eichrodt and Hartenstein, in their attempt to understand the association of פנים with יהוה/אלהים YHWH/God in the HB is that of the (old) literary and historical criticisms, particularly that of the *Religionsgeschichte* and *Traditionsgeschichte*.

Working on the assumption that the Israelite association of פנים with God had developed under the influence of ANE religions, these scholars placed the Israelite concept of "seeing the face of YHWH/God" in the ANE religious context and compared it with seeing the face of Ištar's *Kultstätte* in the temple (of Ištar) or with the idea of audience before the king, and concluded that in Israel also it implied visiting the temple⁶⁷ or that seeing the "face of God" meant visiting the king for *Audienz*. The methodological difficulties of these scholars are: on the one hand, the adoption of the *Religionsgeschichte* and *Traditionsgeschichte* approach leads them to the conclusion that Israelites associated פנים "face" with יהוה/אלהים YHWH/God because of the influence of iconic ideas prevalent in the ANE; and on the other, they believe that there was no "idol/image" of YHWH in

---

65. Hartenstein's views from his unpublished dissertation were briefly discussed in an earlier work in Satyavani, *Face of God*, 13–15.
66. Cf. J. K. Kuntz, *The Self-Revelation of God* (Philadelphia: The Westminster Press, 1967), 11–175. Kuntz also suggests that the *Sitz im Leben* of "the face of YHWH/God" was the Jerusalem cult.
67. See also Baudissin, "Gott schauen", 198; Nötscher, *Angesicht*, 53–54, 73–75; Hartenstein, *Angesicht*, 230–233; cf. Eichrodt, *OTT* 2, 35.

the Jerusalem Temple.⁶⁸ Failing to reconcile these two conclusions, they need to account for the motif of seeing/ seeking the face of YHWH" in the Psalms; therefore, they locate the notion of "seeing the face of YHWH/ God" in the context of the ANE and hence bring the Babylonian secular idea of *Audienz* into the Israelite cultic context.

Hartenstein (in line with Baudissin and Nötscher) took Psalms as a proof that the motif "face of YHWH" was rooted in the cult, specifically in Jerusalem Temple in the analogy of YHWH as king. While the idea of God's kingship within the HB, as W. P. Brown suggests, has a "powerful illocutionary force: worship and praise were designated the proper responses to God's sovereign rule",⁶⁹ it is questionable if Hebrew writers had ever equated the motif "seeing the face of YHWH" with "seeing the face of a king" for audience; kingship in Israel was never given a divine status,⁷⁰ and ancient Israel understood God/YHWH as the King of all the earth.⁷¹

While Eichrodt thinks that פנים אל־פנים "face-to-face" (Exod 33:11) signifies a "direct personal meeting", he also thinks that it involves the metaphorical sense, that is, speaking with the invisible God;⁷² Fowler too admits that direct and personal communication was involved but follows Eichrodt in believing that it was in a metaphorical sense. Similarly, while Terrien suggests that פנים אל־פנים "face-to-face" with YHWH/God" signifies a direct, non-mediated, a "person-to-person" encounter, he also suggests that the term פנים "face" in association with YHWH/God has to be treated metaphorically and that it did not involve any visual perception.⁷³

One might query the intelligibility of a "direct personal" meeting with an "invisible" entity; and a direct "person-to-person" encounter without visibility of the persons involved. Although most of these scholars have

---

68. Nötscher, *Angesicht*, 1–10, 53–75; Hartenstein, *Angesicht*, 158–160.
69. W. P. Brown, *Seeing the Psalms* (London: Westminster John Knox Press, 2002), 188. Cf. Pss 10:16, 72:11, 96:10.
70. One may recall that asking for a king was seen as a rejection of YHWH (1 Sam 8:7), and the earthly kings in ancient Israel were not always helpful in guiding the people in the ways of YHWH/God. See R. P. Gordon, *1 & 2 Samuel* (Exeter: The Paternoster Press, 1986), 26–37; 109–110.
71. See Pss 47:8, 74:12, 95:3.
72. See above, 9.
73. See above, 12.

associated the concept of "seeing the face of YHWH/God" with the temple worship, their adoption of the historical critical approaches have not given them the scope to study it within the biblical context where anthropomorphic appearances of YHWH/God are described.

If it is maintained that the Israelites borrowed the usage of the "face" of YHWH from the cultic face of Ištar; if seeing the "face of God" also meant seeing the king for *Audienz*, as these abovementioned scholars argue, they have to give a rationale why the Hebrew writers had employed the term פנים "face" in association with "YHWH/ God" in the worship context in the temple. While previous attempts to understand the association of פנים "face" with YHWH/God in the HB have produced interesting insights, their particular methods of inquiry led to a limited range of conclusions which owe much to the comparative study of religions in the ANE,[74] comparatively they gave little attention to the study of the biblical text itself. The primary dependence upon non-Israelite religions prevented them from understanding the significance the theme of seeing "the face of YHWH" (פני־יהוה/אלהים) had enjoyed in ancient Israel.

To summarize, while most scholars have associated the term "face" with the statues and the worship in the ANE worship or secular context of *Audienz*, others have treated it as metaphorical/idiomatic.[75] Surprisingly, however, none of them has reflected on the theological implication of the "face of YHWH/God" in terms of the divine self-revelations described in the Pentateuch, and Reindl even concludes that this motif never became a *theologumenon*.[76] Despite the long history of such an understanding, the above approaches may be probed at various points:

1. If this expression denotes the enjoyment of personal contact and was used to express direct and personal communication between God and man in an idiomatic or metaphorical sense, as several scholars think, then the burden of proof should rest on those who would read it as anything

---

74. One may recall that this was due to H. Gunkel's "form critical" approach that began reconstructing the texts in light of the parallels in the ANE religions; and this approach opened a way to British and Scandinavian Myth-and-Ritual school with its interest to study the history of comparative religions.

75. Johnson, "Aspects", 155–157, 158; Fowler, "*lipne* YHWH", 384–386; Reindl, *Angesicht*, 70–73.

76. Reindl, *Angesicht*, 75, 163, 200.

other than the biblical representation of the literal manifestation of the divine face.

2. In the Israelite traditions, the noun פנים "face" occurs in association with יהוה/אלהים YHWH/God in a variety of particular canonical contexts focusing on divine revelations which bear no obvious relation to the iconic contexts in which the association appears in the ANE.

3. While there is some evidence in the HB that people made idols and images in their worship at times, it was never encouraged within the official Israelite tradition.[77] Since ancient Israel shared a common culture with her neighbours in the ANE,[78] one may expect linguistic affinity, but the detection of similarities of language must not preclude the identification of potentially very different theological assumptions behind common vocabulary and phraseology. How is it that the term "face" can only be associated with "seeing" ritual pictures or statues or with the secular idea of audience with the king? Why cannot the concept of "seeing the 'face' of YHWH" be associated with the "self-revelations" of YHWH/God whom the Hebrew writers described as appearing in human "form"?

Since the *Religionsgeschichte* approach to the Hebrew texts is limited in its capacity to focus on the significance of the Israelite usage of פנים "face" in association with יהוה/אלהים YHWH/God, it seems sensible to begin with a study of this motif in the context of the pentateuchal traditions, which seem to distinguish sharply from the religions of its environment, as G. E. Wright understands.[79] As S. Yofre confirms, "it is impossible to trace any direct dependencies of the biblical expressions with respect to the meaning or setting of corresponding expressions in ancient Near Eastern usage".[80]

Furthermore, an approach which does not begin with the HB itself cannot deal meaningfully with tensions within the biblical texts in relation

---

77. For an iconographic presence in Jeremiah-Deuteronomic texts, see R. Doyle, *Faces of Gods: Baal, Asherah and Molek and studies of the Hebrew Scriptures*. Ph.D. diss. (University of Sheffield, 1979).
78. Cf. J. H. Walton, *Ancient Israelite Literature in its Cultural Context* (Grand Rapids: Zondervan, 1989), 60.
79. G. E. Wright, *The Old Testament Against its Environment* (London: SCM Press, 1957), 12–16.
80. Yofre, "פנים", 606.

to the visibility of פני־יהוה/אלהים "the face of YHWH/God". For example, some of the above discussed scholars, for instance Nötscher and Terrien, had taken Exodus 33:20 and Deuteronomy 4:12–16 to argue against the corporeality of YHWH/God. While hearing YHWH's voice also has some association with fear of death (Exod 20:19; Deut 5:24–26), these scholars seem to stress the negation as stated in Exodus 33:20, in terms of "seeing" the "face of YHWH", without referring to the context in which the statement in Exodus 33:20 is made.

Lack of attention to the biblical context also fails to situate this important expression "seeing the face of YHWH/God" in the wider context of the anthropomorphic traditions. The challenge before this present study is, then, to understand the reason why the Hebrew writers have depicted יהוה/אלהים ("YHWH/God") in association with פנים ("face") and with the verb ראה ("to see") in the Pentateuch. Did they understand that the divine "face" was seen in a literal sense when YHWH/God revealed himself in human form? In light of this challenge, it is believed that a brief discussion on the significance of the self-revelations of YHWH/God in the Pentateuch will provide understanding of the expression "the face of YHWH/God". In addition to this, it seems also necessary to clarify whether or not פנים "face", when used with personal/pronominal suffixes and prepositional particles and in association with YHWH/God, retains its nominal/literal sense. In order that this aspect may be clarified, it is hoped that a brief discussion on different functions of פנים "face" in the Pentateuch might help. Therefore, both the significance of the self-revelations of YHWH/God and the different functions of פנים "face" in the Pentateuch will be discussed in the following two sections.

1.5 Significance of the Divine-Revelations in the Pentateuch

The earliest point of reference for understanding "who God is" in his relationship with humankind, as portrayed in Genesis traditions,[81] is that God is the creator (Gen 1:1) and that he created humankind in his image (Gen 1:26–27). Vivid anthropomorphic language and expressions are used in describing the actions of YHWH/God[82] in that he walked in the garden, and spoke to the first couple in a (human) language that was understood by them (Gen 3:8–10)—these descriptions seem to help in understanding the nature of "divine appearances"[83] in the Pentateuch. The noun פנים "face" is used in association with יהוה/אלהים (YHWH/God) from the very outset of Genesis traditions (3:8), and as Yofre articulates, פנים "face" being part of the human body, and hence of the person, seems "most capable of manifesting differentiated appearances".[84]

Pentateuchal traditions clearly portray a definite continuity between God, the creator, and the people, and this continuity is made possible because of the divine self-revelations.[85] Surprisingly, the Hebrew term גלה ("to uncover/reveal") is not used in association with the revelation of YHWH/God except once in the Pentateuch (Gen 35:7; cf. Deut 29:28).[86] It seems that for some reason, the Hebrew writers had associated the verb ראה ("to

---

81. The term "tradition" is used in this work simply to mean the stabilized canonical text (final form).

82. Genesis (e.g. chs. 1–3) associates יהוה/אלהים with human eyes, ears, hands, mouth and feet, and he does many things as humans do—he sees, speaks, walks and converses with Adam and Eve.

83. The term anthropomorphism (Gk. ἄνθρωπος + μορφή) is also used to mean the divine appearances in human form.

84. Yofre, "פנים", 606; cf. S. E. Balentine, *The Hidden God: The Hiding of the Face of God in the Old Testament* (Oxford: Oxford University Press, 1979), 17. Balentine sees even God's hiddenness as an integral part of his activity in the world.

85. Although the term "theophany" is commonly used to mean the divine appearances in the Pentateuch, the usage "self-revelations" seems more fitting, because the Gk. term θεοφάνεια (θεός + φαίνειν = "appearance of God") "theophany" had its original association with the images of "gods" which were shown to the people. For a comprehensive understanding of self-revelations/theophany, see Kuntz, *Self-Revelation of God*; R. B. Chisholm, Jr. "Theophany", *NDBT*, 815–816.

86. The writer uses the verb גלה, while narrating that Jacob built an altar at Bethel because God "revealed" (גלה) himself to him there, when he fled from his brother (Gen 35:7).

see") with the self-revelations of YHWH/God.[87] Could that reason be that the Hebrew writers wanted their readers[88] to know that YHWH/God appeared in a human (anthropomorphic) "form" and different people had seen his פנים "face"? It will be argued in this work that the question may be answered in the affirmative.

Since the noun פנים "face" is associated with אלהים/יהוה (YHWH/God) in the context of divine self-revelations, one may assume that some kind of "human form" was ascribed to the divine appearances. E. Jacob rightly insists that it is faith in a "living God" that achieved its best expression in anthropomorphic language,[89] and also argues against the view that the concept of "living God" is of later date.[90] Although the term אל חי (living God) is not used frequently in the Pentateuch, God is seen acting as a living entity from the very beginning of the Hebrew traditions,[91] and Deuteronomy 5:26 confirms Israelite belief in the living God, in that it was the "voice of the living God" (קול אלהים חיים) that spoke to them out of the midst of the fire which they heard.[92]

Israelites seemed to think that their God was both transcendent and immanent and was involved in their life situations; God was real to and active in the lives of ancient Israelites.[93] As R. E. Clements notes, "God was not the object of speculative thought" for them;[94] and the traditions describing the anthropomorphic appearances of YHWH/God are found

---

87. Whether the verb ראה ("to see") is used in qal stem or niphal stem, it does not minimize the reality of the manifestation/revelation of YHWH/God. Sometimes, קרא is translated to "reveal" (e.g. NRS in Exod 5:3) in the sense of "encounter". For a discussion on the concept of "revelation" see J. Barr, "Revelation", *DB*, 847–849; A. Richardson, *TWBB* (London: SCM Press, 1950).

88. In this work, "readers" meant those readers in ancient Israel who would have read the final form of the Pentateuch in the same canonical order (i.e. Genesis to Deuteronomy) for the first time.

89. See E. Jacob, *Theology of the Old Testament* (London: Hodder & Stoughton, 1958), 37–39, 42.

90. Jacob (*OTT*, 37) refers here to W. Baudissin, *Adonis und Eshmun* (Leipzig: n.p, 1911), 450.

91. God was understood as uttering words (Gen 1:3) and speaking to people (3:8–10).

92. Cf. Josh 3:10; Pss 42:2; 84:2.

93. Cf. Gen 35:3; Exod 3:8.

94. R. E. Clements, *Old Testament Theology* (London: Marshall, Morgan & Scott, 1978), 67.

throughout the Pentateuch (and the HB as a whole). But, surprisingly, W. Brueggemann says, "these theophanic narratives are rare indeed and occur only seldom in the long narrative account of Israel's faith".[95] However, as R. P. Gordon maintains, "the extent to which God is depicted anthropomorphically" in the HB is striking.[96] Undoubtedly, anthropomorphic divine appearances are found almost in every aspect of Israelite religious life and faith.

While the anthropomorphic appearances of YHWH/God are found throughout the HB, some scholars, for instance M. C. A. Korpel, assume that originally Israelites spoke with much less concern about the physical appearance of God, believing that God could reveal himself with a human face but that later metaphorical expressions were introduced and did not imply any visible form of God.[97] In Korpel's opinion, Deuteronomy 4:12, 15 "sternly affirms" that God did not reveal himself in any תמונה "form" lest the Israelites were tempted to make graven images after this "form".[98] Based on this very statement, one may argue that this is more of an affirmation that YHWH manifested himself to them but people (at Sinai) were not allowed to see God directly or from close vicinity (lest they made images).

A brief reflection of Deuteronomy 4 shows that Moses, in his recapitulation of past experiences, had reminded people that when YHWH spoke to them out of the midst of the fire they only heard his voice/words

---

95. W. Brueggemann, *Reverberations of Faith* (Louisville: Westminster John Knox Press, 2002), 216. He further adds: "on the grounds of rarity, we may be suspicious of contemporary religious claims of frequent experiences of divine intimacy, for this God is not easily, readily, or frequently accessible or intimate". However, contemporary claims of frequent experiences of divine intimacy has justification and foundation in the incarnational theology which signifies that God came to this world to be Immanuel and is accessible to everyone and at all times (Isa 7:14; cf. Matt 1:23; 28:20). See D. Ford, *Self and Salvation* (Cambridge: Cambridge University Press, 1999), 193–215. Ford sees connections between the usage of פנים in association with God in the Pentateuch and the face of Jesus in the NT.

96. R. P. Gordon, *Hebrew Bible and Versions* (Aldershot: Ashgate, 2006), 190.

97. M. C. A. Korpel, *A Rift in the Clouds. Ugaritic and Hebrew Descriptions of the Divine* (Münster: Ugarit-Verlag, 1990), 88–97; 103–104.

98. Ibid., 94; Since in Exodus 20:4 the term תמונה "form" was linked to the shape of the pagan idols, she assumes that it is highly unlikely that the term תמונה "form" would have been used for the form of God at a later date.

but saw no "form" (ותמונה) lest they made פסל תמונת כל־סמל "a graven image" and corrupted themselves (Deut 4:12–16). Moses also reminded them that when YHWH spoke with them פנים בפנים "face-to-face" (on the mountain), he stood between YHWH and them, communicated YHWH's words to them because they were afraid of the fire (5:4), and this seems to be an allusion to Exodus 24:17 (כבוד יהוה כאש אכלת) and the circumstance that the glory of YHWH on the top of the mount was like devouring fire. Previously, Moses told them that God came (בא) to them; although they were afraid of approaching God on the mountain, they witnessed his coming (Exod 20:18–20) and heard his voice (ואת־קלו שמענו: Deut 5:24); the Hebrew writer understands that YHWH spoke with the people "face-to-face" (פנים בפנים) from the midst of the fire on the mountain (Deut 5:4). Therefore, one may argue that the readers of Deuteronomy 5:24–26 were aware that the manifestation of YHWH/God in the midst of fire was a physical manifestation in human form,[99] because they were told earlier that YHWH/God gave Moses the two tablets of the covenant, inscribed by the finger of God (Exod 31:18).

Eichrodt rightly observes that it is in the context of self-manifestation that "God's connection with the world can be most clearly observed".[100] Whenever God appeared, there was some visual and audible evidence of his presence in such a way that people had unmistakably realized that it was God who spoke to them and understood the language used in the divine conversation.[101] J. A. Dearman suggests that Genesis 1:26–28 provides help in understanding anthropomorphisms as a means to the divine-human relationship "rooting the significance of the relationship in creation itself".[102] The "image of God" seems to play a most significant role in the

---

99. For a detailed discussion on God's appearances in "human form", see T. E. Fretheim, *The Suffering of God* (Philadelphia: Fortress Press, 1984), 79–106.
100. Eichrodt, *OTT* 2, 15. Although Eichrodt argued that the expression "seeing the face of YHWH/God" is to be treated as metaphorical, he saw the significance of the divine manifestations.
101. E.g. Gen 3:8.
102. J. A. Dearman, "Theophany, Anthropomorphism, and the *Imago Dei*: Some Observations about the Incarnation in the Light of the Old Testament" (Oxford Scholarship Online: *The Incarnation*, 2002), 31–35.

context of divine-human communication.[103] Whatever arguments one may have in interpreting "the image of God" in man, whenever God/YHWH appeared to humankind, he was supposed to have taken a human form; as Barr affirms, "the central truth in this is the ability of God to assume a form and to let this form be seen by men".[104]

While J. L. McKenzie argues that because of the prohibitions of representation, one cannot assume that ancient Israelites conceived of YHWH as spiritual/immaterial or invisible, he also thinks that there is a theoretical inconsistency between the prohibition of images and the anthropomorphisms of biblical language.[105] However, it may be argued that there is no theoretical inconsistency between the prohibition of images and the anthropomorphisms in the HB, rather, anthropomorphisms are associated with YHWH/God, who by virtue of being the creator, was able to take on a human form; and the "form" and "face" may well be associated not with any idol, but with the anthropomorphized divine person of YHWH/God. It seems that the possibility of meeting/seeing God was made possible because he was willing to reveal himself as per his own freedom and initiative, not "conditioned by human effort", as Barr understands;[106] and he lets himself be seen by means of his "anthropomorphic form".[107]

While the Hebrew writers did not depict their creator God by any image or idol, they did not hesitate to depict the appearance of YHWH/God in a human "form". How did YHWH/God manifest himself when he appeared and spoke to different people? Scholarly opinions may be discussed here: H. W. Robinson articulates that "the conception of God as formless spirit would be difficult to prove".[108] H. H. Rowley states that in the HB, "God is nowhere conceived of as essentially in human form. Rather he is

---

103. For more details on the image of God in man, see chapter 2, 50–52.
104. J. Barr, "Theophany and Anthropomorphism in the Old Testament", VTS, 7 (1959), 32–33.
105. J. L. McKenzie, *A Theology of the Old Testament* (Garden City: Doubleday, 1974), 48–51.
106. Cf. Barr, "Revelation", 847.
107. Cf. E. A. Martens. *God's Design: A Focus on Old Testament Theology* (Grand Rapids: Baker Books, 1994), 89.
108. H. W. Robinson, *The Theology of the Old Testament: Record and Revelation* (Oxford: Clarendon Press, 1938), 309.

conceived of as pure spirit, able to assume a form rather than having in himself physical form".[109] Whether or not God is conceived as pure spirit, the Hebrew traditions seem to believe that YHWH/God was able to assume a "form" and to let this form be seen by humans;[110] when he appeared to people, he is described in a vivid anthropomorphic language as though he was in human form and acted as a human and presumably he appeared in a human body.

Brueggemann suggests that the concept of an embodied God is absent from the Hebrew Bible;[111] and Wenham, referring to Deuteronomy 4:15–16, where Moses mentions that people saw no form when YHWH spoke to them at Horeb, expresses that the HB stresses "the incorporeality and invisibility of God".[112] However, the HB does not seem to advocate an incorporeal or invisible God; and it is difficult to imagine a disembodied God in the HB, given that the HB understands that YHWH/ God appeared in human form, which was visible to the human eye, as discussed in the beginning of this chapter. It may even be that all the divine appearances, as described in the HB, were in human form and there is no appearance which was "incompatible with an appearance in human form", as Fretheim argues.[113] It is also worth noting that when YHWH/God appeared, people generally responded either by falling (נפל על/אל) on their faces or bowing (שחה) before the divine person who appeared to them and this action probably indicates a literal aspect.[114] This leads, then, to the question of "body" of God when he appeared in human form.

What was that human form like? S. D. Moore understands that "the God of the Hebrew Bible is, by and large, a corporeal God".[115] R. S. Hendel

---

109. H. H. Rowley, *The Faith of Israel* (London: SCM Press, 1956), 75.
110. Cf. Barr, "Theophany", 32–33.
111. W. Brueggemann, *Theology of the Old Testament* (Minneapolis: Fortress Press, 1997), 302. He adds to it that the "'notion' of the incarnation is a major step beyond pathos, a step that the Old Testament does not take".
112. Wenham, *Genesis 16–50* (Dallas: Word Books, 1994), 30; see above, 22.
113. Fretheim, *Suffering of God*, 93.
114. The verb שחה ("to bow down/prostrate oneself"), עבד ("to serve"), נפל or קדד ("bow down"), may have a similar sense of indicating reverence before someone in view.
115. S. D. Moore, "Gigantic God: Yahweh's Body", *JSOT* 70 (1996), 115.

thinks that "Yahweh has a body, clearly anthropomorphic".[116] Of late, B. D. Sommer, in light of his comparative study of the other ANE religions, has come up with his thesis that people had a fluid view of divine embodiment and that YHWH/God has many bodies.[117] However, the body concept in the ANE seems very different from the biblical understanding of the body;[118] and Sommer himself rightly observes that biblical religion distinguishes itself from other religions of the ANE in its understanding of one God as the creator of the world.[119] It seems necessary that one understands the aspect of "human 'bodily' form" in light of the biblical texts, which describe divine self-revelations, and this aspect will be further discussed later in chapters 2–6.

1.6 The Different Functions of פנים "Face" in the Pentateuch

1.6.1 The Function of פנים "Face" with Personal/Pronominal Suffixes

The noun פנים "face", when used with personal/pronominal suffixes in association with any person, signifies that person, and takes the place of the personal pronoun; likewise, when used with personal suffixes in association with YHWH/God, פנים "face" signifies YHWH/God himself. For example, when Jacob says אראה פניו "I will see his face", this means "I

---

116. R. S. Hendel, "Aniconism and Anthropomorphism in Ancient Israel", in *The Image and the Book* (Leuven: Peeters, 1997), 223.
117. B. D. Sommer, *The Bodies of God and the World of Ancient Israel* (Cambridge: Cambridge University Press, 2009), 1, 17.
118. See T. Jacobson, "Formative Tendencies in Sumerian Religion", in *The Bible and the Ancient Near East* (London: Routledge & Kegan, 1961), 267. Jacobson notes the anthropomorphic phenomenon in Sumerian Religion, where deities are said to be little more than active principles and powers with some specific forms like reeds, animals; and they do not seem to act and only appear and vanish. See also Wright, *OT Against its Environment*, 26; Hendel, "Aniconism", 206–209; J.B. Pritchard, *Palestinian Figurines in relation to Certain Goddesses known Through Literature* (New Haven: American Oriental Society, 1943), 83–87; J.B. Pritchard, ed., *ANET* (London: Oxford University Press, 1969), 522, 537; I. Cornelius, "The Many Faces of God: Divine Images and Symbols in Ancient Near Eastern Religions", in *The Image and the Book*, 28.
119. Sommer, *Bodies*, 173.

will see him" (Esau), and here פנים "face" acts as a pronoun "him" (Gen 32:21); when YHWH/God says, פני ילכו "my face shall go", this means "I shall go" (YHWH himself)", and here פנים "face" acts as a pronoun "I" (Exod 33:14).

However, there are instances where פנים "face" does not signify the person as a whole, but rather signifies the countenance. For example, when Moses is said to have יסתר פניו "hid his face" (3:6) or put the veil על־פניו "on his face" (34:35), the noun פנים "face" means the front part of the head in a literal sense. In these texts, whether the pronominal suffixes with פנים "face" are used to signify the person or the front part of the head, פנים "face" seems to exhibit its literal sense.

1.6.2 Prepositional Phrases Developed with the Noun פנים "Face"

By virtue of the combination of the construct form of the noun פנים "face" (פני־ "face of") with particle prepositions such as ל, על/אל, which give the sense of "moving toward" the object/person, and with מן, which give the sense of "moving away" from the object/person, certain phrases such as לפני, מפני, מלפני, על־פני and את־פני are developed. While these phrases function as prepositional phrases, the nominative sense of פנים "face" in these phrases does not necessarily disappear, unless the temporal or adverbial sense is made obvious.

1.6.2.1 The function of the phrase לפני "before"

The phrase לפני (ל+פני[120]) has the sense "before/in the presence of", and in some contexts can mean "in the view/opinion/estimation of";[121] when used in a general context, פנים "face" in the phrase לפני retains its nominal sense. For example, in Genesis when men (Joseph's brothers) stand לפני "before" Joseph (43:15–16); when they sit לפניו "before him" (43:33), when Joseph takes his brothers לפני "before" Pharaoh (47:2–6); when he makes Jacob stand לפני "before" Pharaoh (47:7–10)—in all these texts,

---

120. ל ("to/in reference to, at, by" etc.) by itself is ambiguous". See van der Woude, "פנים", 1002, Reindl, *Angesicht*, 19; Nötscher, *Angesicht*, 6–7.
121. Fowler, "*lipne* YHWH", 384; BDB, 816h, 817a; Yofre, "פנים", 608; Clines, *Dictionary*, 479, 484.

one can only think that a literal interpretation of לפני "before" is possible, since Joseph and his brothers, Pharaoh, and Jacob are understood to be physically present in a literal sense, and a direct (face-to-face) conversation is described in these texts.[122] In Exodus, when Aaron casts down his rod לפני "before" Pharaoh and לפני "before" his servants so that it will become a serpent (7:10); when Moses and Aaron take ashes and stand לפני "before" Pharaoh (9:10); and when Moses and Aaron perform wonders לפני "before" Pharaoh" (11:10)—in all these instances לפני "before" gives a literal sense and understandably, Moses, Aaron, Pharaoh and his servants are understood to be physically present and the actions described (casting of the rod, etc.) are understood as being performed in a literal/visible sense.

When the phrase לפני "before" is used with YHWH/God, the meaning of לפני "before" does not necessarily differ from its general usage and signifies "in the presence of YHWH/God", and, depending upon the context and the verb used, it may also mean "in the view/opinion"/or "in the "estimation of" YHWH/God. In Exodus, several texts seem to understand YHWH to be physically present in Egypt, as the context of the text and the conversations between YHWH, Moses and Aaron show. For example, when Moses speaks לפני יהוה "before YHWH" (6:12) complaining to him of his problems in Egypt, then YHWH speaks (וידבר יהוה) to Moses and Aaron (6:13) and Moses says לפני "before" YHWH (6:30); when YHWH says (יאמר)[123] to Moses and Aaron, "Take your rod and cast it (לפני) 'before' Pharaoh" (7:8–9); when YHWH says to Moses, " . . . present yourself (לפני) 'before' Pharaoh" (Exod 8:16; 9:13)—in all these instances לפני "before" is understood in a literal sense, and YHWH, Moses, and Aaron are believed to be physically present in a literal sense. In light of these texts, one may also argue that when the text describes that YHWH went לפניהם "before them" in a pillar of "fire" (אש) to guide the people (Exod 13:21), YHWH is envisaged as present there as the giver of the light in a literal sense;[124] when the Israelites are told to draw near לפני יהוה "before YHWH", the glory of YHWH (כבוד יהוה) is seen (נראה) in the cloud in the desert, and, arguably,

---

122. Cf. Gen 41:46; 42:6; 43:26; 44:14.
123. The verb אמר "to say" used with God signifies his self-revelation. See chapter 5, fn. 88, 137.
124. Cf. Deut 9:3: "it is YHWH your God who goes before you like a consuming fire".

YHWH is understood to be present in his glory (Exod 16:9–11) in a literal sense, as he speaks (דבר) to Moses from the cloud.

The expression לפני יהוה "before YHWH" is frequently used in association with the tabernacle/tent of meeting, particularly in Leviticus and Numbers, signifying the localized presence of YHWH, and the majority of acts connected to the worship are seen taking place לפני יהוה "before YHWH". In a general context, bringing a bull לפני "before" the tabernacle (Exod 29:10) and presenting oneself or presenting the animal לפני "before" the priest involve the action in a literal sense (Lev 27:8, 11); likewise, since the activities at the tabernacle are associated with the divine self-revelations, לפני יהוה "before YHWH" seems to signify the localized presence of YHWH/God in a literal sense. The acts connected to the worship at the tent—"wave offerings" (תנופה),[125] "peace offerings" (שלמים);[126] the ritual of atonement,[127] consecration of the Levites (Num 8:10–11, 21), and gathering of the people—all are understood as taking place לפני יהוה "before YHWH"; sacrifices were offered לפני יהוה "before YHWH", and the priests sprinkled its blood on the altar לפני יהוה "before YHWH".[128] The reason why animal sacrifices are offered in the tabernacle and why it is described as taking place לפני יהוה "before YHWH" (Exod 29:10–12) is perhaps because of YHWH's promise that he would be before the mercy seat and would meet (lit., be met by)[129] Moses there (Exod 30:6). In all these texts, לפני יהוה "before YHWH" signifies an association with YHWH's divine self-revelations in the tent, where YHWH/God would reveal himself/dwell temporarily from time to time (Exod 25:8, 22; 29:42b).

In these texts, while the phrase לפני gives the prepositional sense "before", the nominal sense of פנים "face" does not disappear, and in light of the textual evidence, it may be argued that "the direct presence of" YHWH/God in the tent is to be understood in a literal sense. Significantly, out of 236 occurrences of לפני יהוה "before YHWH" in the HB, the Pentateuch itself has about 150 occurrences, and all 62 occurrences of לפני יהוה "before

---

125. E.g. Lev 7:30; 8:27, 29; 9:21; 10:15; 14:12, 24; 23:20; Num 6:20.
126. E.g. Lev 3:1, 5, 7, 12; 5:26; 9:2, 4; cf. Num 6:16.
127. Lev 5:26; 10:17; 14:18, 29, 31; 15:15, 30; 19:22; 23:28; Num 15:28; 31:50.
128. Lev 1:5, 11; 3·8; 4:4, 6, 15–18; 16:3, 18; cf. Exod 24:6.
129. The verb here is אועד (niphal impf. of יעד "to meet")

YHWH" in Leviticus are used in association with YHWH in the tent.¹³⁰ This may be an indication that the Hebrew traditions believed in the self-revelations of YHWH/God in the tent. In his study based on Deuteronomy, I. Wilson rightly argues that in most of the instances לפני יהוה "before YHWH" is used in its literal sense and that it implies YHWH was present at the tent.¹³¹ By employing this particular phrase לפני יהוה "before YHWH", the writer seems to convey that several activities connected to worship took place "before" the anthropomorphized person of YHWH. The phrase את־פני (את + פנים) "face of" with YHWH (פני־יהוה) also signifies his direct presence, and sometimes it is used in the same sense as לפני "before".¹³²

1.6.2.2 The function of the phrase מפני "from before"

The phrase מפני (מן + פני) "from the face of/presence of" signifies physical distance, in terms of "going away from" a person; and when used in a general context and in association with YHWH/God, פנים "face" retains its nominal sense.

For example, Jacob fled מפני עשו "from (the face of) Esau"¹³³ (35:1); when Esau went away מפני יעקב "from (the face of) Jacob" (36:6); Moses fled מפני פרעה "from (the face of) Pharaoh" (Exod 2:15); Moses fled מפניו "from the (face of) the/a snake (lit., from it: 4:3); when Adam and Eve hid themselves מפני יהוה אלהים "from YHWH God" (Gen 3:8)—in all these texts, פנים "face" in the phrase מפני retains its nominal sense, in that those from whom/whose presence (מפני) the separation took place (i.e. YHWH God, Esau, Jacob, the snake, Pharaoh); and those who "went away" (i.e. Adam, Eve, Esau, Jacob, Moses and Aaron) are understood to be present in

---

130. The number of occurrences of לפני יהוה in Genesis– 12, Exodus– 24, Numbers– 38, Deuteronomy– 21 (includes suffixes); מפני יהוה occurs once in each Gen 3:8 and Exod 9:30; מלפני יהוה –8; and in Leviticus and Numbers combine 7. See also Fowler, "*lipne* YHWH", 384–387.

131. I. Wilson, *Out of the Midst of the Fire: Divine Presence in Deuteronomy* (Atlanta: Scholar's Press, 1995), 147–148; 161–171; 191–194; 206–215.

132. E.g. Gen 19:13, 27; Exod 34:23; cf. Ps 16:11.

133. מפני עשו "from the face of Esau" means from Esau himself, and similar pattern is seen in other texts discussed here.

the scene in a literal sense.[134] In Exodus 14:19, both the phrases לפני and
מפני are used in a contrasting way, in that the angel of God, who ההלך לפני
"went before" the camp of Israel, moved and וילך מאחריהם "went behind
them", and the pillar of cloud moved מפניהם "from before them"[135] and
יעמד מאחריהם "stood behind them"—in this text, arguably לפני and מפני
are used in a literal sense, and both "the angel of God" and the people are
believed to be physically present. In these phrases, the nominal sense of
פנים "face" may be discerned, although מפני has a prepositional (causal)
sense "because".[136]

1.6.2.3 *The function of the phrase* מלפני

The phrase מלפני (מן +לפני) "from before/the presence" has a similar sense
to that of מפני. In a general context, when Jacob goes out מלפני "from before" Pharaoh (Gen 47:10); when the Israelites go out "from before" Moses
(Exod 35:20), the nominal sense of פנים "face" is retained; and Jacob,
Pharaoh, Moses and the Israelites are understood to be physically present in a literal sense. Likewise, when associated with YHWH, מלפני "from
before" gives a similar sense. For example, Moses takes the rod מלפני יהוה
"from before YHWH", who tells him to take it (Num 20:7–9), and that
YHWH, Cain and Moses are understood to be present in a literal sense.
Interestingly, מלפני "from before" also reflects another notion in association
with YHWH. For example, fire (Lev 9:24; 10:2) and anger (Num 17:11)
come out מלפני "from before/the presence of" YHWH/God, which means
YHWH/God is the source of fire and anger.

In light of this discussion, one may conclude that although these phrases (לפני, מפני and מלפני) exhibit a prepositional sense, the noun פנים "face"
retains its nominal sense, even when used with YHWH/God. It is the canonical context, in which פנים "face" is used with different suffixes and perhaps a verb used with it, which would help determine whether or not the

---

134. Contrary to Yofre's suggestion ("פנים", 611), that מפני emphasizes the prepositional sense of" מן and that the nominal meaning of פנם "vanishes almost entirely", the texts here reflect nominal sense.

135. At times מפני is used a synonym to לפני (cf. Exod 10:3; 34:24; Lev 19:32).

136. For example, מפני in Gen 45:3 may mean "because of" or "from" his presence; in Deut 5:5 מפני האש may mean "because of/from" the presence of the fire.

literal sense of פנים "face" is retained in the given text. This aspect will be further affirmed later in the study of the selected texts in chapters 2 to 6.[137]

In light of the above discussions and previous methodological approaches, this study will begin with the "extant canonical text" (i.e. final form of the HB), and attempt to interpret selected texts from the perspective of Israelite religious traditions and in their own context.[138] Prior to studying the selected texts, a brief discussion of methodological issues and approaches is warranted.

1.7 A Brief Reflection on Methodological Issues and Approaches

It goes without saying that the nineteenth century saw the birth and growth of "old literary and historical criticisms". Old Testament scholars, who have come under the influence of historical criticisms, have also studied the final form of the Pentateuch. However, they have dissected the biblical text on the basis of sources, even on the basis of minute linguistic and thematic variations;[139] and the Pentateuch has been treated more as a combination of sources than a unified piece. Although old literary criticisms offered some solution for the composite nature of the biblical texts when it was explained on the basis of sources, they have been challenged more recently in different ways;[140] and even some of the critical scholars have realized

---

137. These selected texts may also include the pronominal suffixes used with the prepositional phrases (לפני, מפני and מלפני). For example, לפנך (Gen 13:9); לפני (לְפָנַי: 17:1); לפניהם (18:8); מפניהם (Exod 13:21; 14:19); מלפניך (23:28), etc.
138. Cf. Childs, *Introduction to the Old Testament as Scripture* (London: SCM Press, 1979), 73.
139. Source critics have dissected the biblical text based on even minute linguistic and thematic variations. For example, they ascribed the pronoun אנכי to JE and אני to P; and the texts which describe the divine revelations are ascribed to different sources, that is, the text where God speaks directly is ascribed to J, dreams and angels to E, and divine speech from heaven to P. For counter arguments on JEDP source theory, see U. Cassuto, *The Documentary Hypothesis* (Jerusalem: The Magnes Press, 1961), 15–41, 99–100. See also J. C. L. Gibson, *Canaanite Myths and Legends* (London: T. & T. Clark, 2004), 28, 123. D. Kidner, *Genesis* (Illinois: Intervarsity Press, 1982), 1–23.
140. For a discussion on these approaches, see J. H. Hayes, *An Introduction to Old Testament Study* (Nashville: Abingdon Press, 1979), 123–130; 153–194; R. Rendtorff,

that the Pentateuch in its final form has become a unified piece.[141] The Pentateuch, as it appears now, is a comprehensive and continuous account from the creation up to the arrival at the border of the Promised Land.[142] G. von Rad has rightly suggested that exegetes must work with this existing (complex) unity and should understand it "as a whole with a consistent train of thought.[143]

As mentioned earlier, H. Gunkel's "form-critical" approaches went beyond "source criticism" and developed *Traditionsgeschichte* (traditio-history), attempting to study the pre-literary stage of the text; these approaches placed every unit of assumed *Gattungen* ("oral traditions") behind the text in a *Sitz im Leben* ("life situation"), and since then, form-critical methodologies have been influencing Pentateuchal research. While these form-critical methodologies have given some understanding of the tradition's history of the biblical text, the undue importance given to the ritual practices, beliefs and the folklore in the ANE in interpreting the biblical texts has opened the way to the British and Scandinavian Myth-and-Ritual school which began studying the history of comparative religions (*Religionsgeschichte*)[144] from the first part of the nineteenth century. Since the form-critical methodologies began reconstructing the biblical texts in light of the parallels in the ANE religions,[145] and since theological significance of the biblical texts was given less attention, this led some biblical scholars in the 1960s to raise their voices in this regard.

While acknowledging the necessity of "form critical" methodology, J. Muilenburg argued that the biblical text cannot be reduced to *Gattungen*

"The 'Yahwist' as Theologian? The Dilemma of Pentateuchal Criticism", *JSOT* 3 (1977), 2–9; R. N. Whybray, *The Making of the Pentateuch: A Methodological Study* (Sheffield: JSOT Press, 1987), 26–35; 133–173; 221–242.

141. See M. Noth, *History of Pentateuchal Traditions* (Englewood Cliffs: Prentice-Hall, 1972), 250.

142. Westermann, *Handbook to the Old Testament* (London: SPCK, 1980), 15; cf. D. J. A. Clines, *The Theme of the Pentateuch* (Sheffield: Sheffield Academic Press, 2001), 27–64.

143. Von Rad, *Genesis* (London: SCM Press, 1972), 75.

144. See above fn.74; it almost meant that the traditions in the HB were influenced by and borrowed material from different religious beliefs in the ANE. See S. H. Hooke, *Babylonian and Assyrian Religion* (Oxford: Basil Blackwell, 1962).

145. For example, H. Gunkel, *Genesis: A Commentary* (Macon: Mercer University Press, 1997).

and proposed rhetorical criticism with his famous declaration: "Form Criticism and Beyond".[146] Muilenburg's proposal for rhetorical criticism opened the way to a host of modern/new literary criticism(s)[147] which began to regard the Pentateuch as a single literary unit, to understand the text in its received "final form" by using techniques drawn from linguistics. There has been growing interest among the OT scholars for the past forty years in preferring the theology of the texts over their history, and the new literary approaches to biblical interpretation, by and large, have been concerned with the "final" form of the text, and their interest seems to be more with "literary" interpretation of the final form of the canonical text[148] with a focus on what it "means" rather than with what it "meant".[149] While the advantage of literary interpretation of the HB is that it engages with the "final form" of the biblical text, there have been controversies over the understanding of the theological intentionality (author's intention/what the text "meant") in the biblical texts.[150]

Literary critics, particularly narrative critics, have explained their method saying, "by narrative we mean all those literary works which are distinguished by two characteristics: the presence of a story and a storyteller".[151] However, just as there is no evidence within the HB to support the theory

---

146. J. Muilenburg, "Form Criticism and Beyond", *JBL* 88 (1969), 1–18.

147. New literary approaches to biblical exegesis range from formalism (studying the form of the Hebrew literature) and structuralism to deconstructionalism. The terms "New Criticism" and "Close Reading" are also used to represent narrative critical approaches. See V. P. Long, "Reading the Old Testament as Literature", in C. C. Broyles, ed. *Interpreting the Old Testament* (Grand Rapids: Baker Books, 2002), 85–123; H.G. Reventlow, "Modern Approaches to Old Testament Theology", in L. G. Perdue, *The Blackwell Companion to the Hebrew Bible* (Oxford: Blackwell, 2001), 227.

148. Long, "Reading the Old Testament", 85–123; for a survey on the modern literary study of the Bible, see T. Longman III, "Literary Approaches and Interpretation", *NIDOTTE* 1, 103–124.

149. This is in line with reader-response criticism rather than discerning the original author's intention. See S. E. Porter, *Dictionary of Biblical Criticism and Interpretation* (London: Routledge, 2009), 375.

150. See L. G. Perdue, *The Collapse of History: Reconstructing Old Testament Theology* (Eugene: Wipf and Stock, 2002); S. A. Cummins, "The Theological Interpretation of Scripture: Recent Contributions by Stephen E. Fowl, Christopher R. Seitz, and Francis Watson", *CBR* 2 (2004), 179–196.

151. Reventlow, "Modern Approaches", 227, citing R. Scholes and R. Kellogg, *The Nature of Narrative* (New York: Oxford University Press, 1966), in *The Blackwell Companion to the Hebrew Bible*, 227.

of the storytellers, as advocated by the form-critics,[152] there is no evidence if the narrative critic's theory of the story-tellers can be proved. Even when new literary approaches consider the "final form" of the texts for their interpretation, it seems that the immediate canonical context in the "final form" is not always given importance. A few examples may help in understanding the complication in new literary critical approaches.

Explaining that the Pentateuch is literature, and that the books are construed as works of literature, J. H. Sailhamer states that "they have, in fact, proved themselves to be classic works of literature" and suggests that a close study of narrative sheds light on the final shape of the work.[153] However, he interprets Genesis 3:8 in the context of Sinai tradition (Exod 20:18–21) and concludes that the "wind" in Genesis 3:8 was intended to resemble the "powerful wind" similar to that of Sinai and that just as people fled to a distance at the mountain, so also Adam and Eve fled at the "first sound" of YHWH.[154] Arguably, it was not the first time that God spoke to Adam and Eve, and the (narrative) context of Genesis 3:8 gives no clue whatsoever to identify the wind with that of Sinai theophany.[155]

R. W. L. Moberly in his study of Exodus 32–34, which is based on the final form, interprets the text as a literary narrative. However, he interprets the association of פנים "face" (in 33:14) with YHWH as "shrine" (cf. Exod 29:42–46), and as he sees it, "the shrine is movable that it is possible to speak of Yahweh's פנים 'going'".[156] One can see that this interpretation has not placed the text (33:14) in the context of the divine self-revelations within Exodus 32–34, and thus has identified פנים "face" with the shrine rather than with the revealed anthropomorphic person.

M. D. Wessner also approaches פנים אל־פנים "face-to-face" expressions in the HB from a literary perspective. While it may be argued that the "man" who met Jacob was God himself in his anthropomorphic "form", given that Jacob himself was supposed to have claimed this (Gen 33:31), Wessner concludes that "careful reading" of the text suggests that איש

---

152. See Whybray, *Making of the Pentateuch*, 158–175.
153. J. H. Sailhamer, *The Pentateuch as Narrative* (Grand Rapids: Zondervan, 1992), 3.
154. Sailhamer, *Pentateuch*, 35.
155. See also, chapter 2, 46.
156. R. W. L. Moberly, *At the Mountain of God* (Sheffield: JSOT Press, 1983), 74.

(man) in Genesis 32:23–31 was only a man sent to Jacob on behalf of God (אלהים). This is because Wessner placed the expression "face-to-face" merely in its literary context.[157]

As V. P. Long reflects, lack of clarity on what a "literary approach" should be like seems to have led to divergent ways of dealing with the final form of the text;[158] and even when the "final form" is considered, new literary criticisms have their own limitations.[159] Furthermore, the new literary approaches with their focus on what "it means", have opened many doors to a kind of approach to biblical interpretation that focuses on contemporary context.[160] According to this, a text's meaning is assigned by its receivers;[161] and this also means the narrative is to be assessed without any relation to the intentions of the author.[162] However, as R. Rendtorff stressed, "the most important task of exegesis is to understand the intention of the text" and "exegetes must therefore be concerned to understand this context and give it a due place in their interpretation of the text".[163] The major purpose of the biblical writers/compilers seems theological[164] rather than exhibiting linguistic excellence, although the texts are written in a literary manner, that is, with thought to the manner of expression.[165]

Although, technically speaking, descriptive and historical approaches are limited in their theological focus of the biblical text,[166] it seems, as Childs argued, "what the text 'meant' is determined in large measure by its relation to the one to whom it is directed" and "when seen from the context

---

157. M. D. Wessner, *Face to Face:* פנים אל־פנים *in Old Testament Literature*. MA diss. (Regent College, 1998), 35.

158. See Long, "Reading the Old Testament", 86.

159. Some scholars rightly caution against the danger of a literary approach to biblical interpretation and of the possible imposition of modern literary categories on the biblical text. See L. Ryken, *Literary Guide to the Bible* (Grand Rapids: Zondervan, 1993), 16–24.

160. See F. Watson, *Text, Church and World: Biblical Interpretation in Theological Perspective* (Edinburgh: T & T Clark, 1994), 1–5.

161. Porter, *Dictionary*, 375.

162. See Reventlow, "Modern approaches", 227.

163. R. Rendtorff, *The Old Testament: An Introduction* (London: SCM Press, 1985), 1.

164. Cf. Clines, *Theme*, 107.

165. The Hebrew writers perhaps had not planned to write as a novel writer would plan today.

166. Cf. G. F. Hasel, *Old Testament Theology* (Grand Rapids: Eerdmans, 1991), 40.

of the canon both the question of what the text meant and what it means are inseparably linked and both belong to the task of the interpretation of the Bible as Scripture".[167] In other words, an attempt to discern "what the text 'meant'" does not mean that it belongs to the historical critical approaches.[168] This dissertation will take the "final form" of the biblical text (i.e. canonical context) seriously. However, it will not follow new literary approaches, rather it will attempt to understand what the theme of "seeing the face of YHWH/God would have "meant" to the Israelite readers, when the text was read in the extant canonical ("final form") context.

1.8 Methodological Approach in this Study

The methodological approach taken in this study is the exegetical study method. The texts, selected from the "received form"[169] (final form) of the Pentateuch in the HB, will be approached exegetically, in the hope that this approach will help to derive the possible meaning the writers intended to communicate to their readers. It may be naïve to think that one particular method/approach to studying the Hebrew texts can be put above every other method. However, exegetical study method, it is hoped, will give protective measures not to deviate much from the authors' purpose, but to have a meaningful engagement with the text,[170] and to discern how the first readers,[171] who would have read the completed Pentateuch (i.e. the final form), probably by now in a proto-Masoretic form, for the first time; and how they would have understood the motif "seeing the 'face' of YHWH/

---

167. B. S. Childs, *Biblical Theology in Crisis* (Philadelphia: Westminster Press, 1970), 141; also *Introduction*, 72–74.
168. "What the text meant" is not associated with "historical critical treatment", rather "what it meant" to those readers (in history), who would have read the final form of the Pentateuch in its canonical context.
169. Moberly prefers to use "received form" (i.e. final form) because of the role of the biblical text in relation to Jewish and Christian communities that have received it. See his *Old Testament Theology: The Theology of the Book of Genesis* (Cambridge: Cambridge University Press, 2009), fn. 35, 40.
170. Cf. A. C. Thiselton, *The Two Horizons* (Carlisle: Paternoster Press, 1993), xix; 15–16; 439–445.
171. The phrase "first readers" is used to mean the same as "ancient Israelite readers".

God". The assumption made here is that ancient Israelite readers would have read the Pentateuch in the standardized Text/HB[172] for the first time,[173] beginning from Genesis (1:1), chapter by chapter and book by book, through to Deuteronomy (34:12) in the canonical Text.[174] An attempt will be made to discern how those "ancient Israelite readers" would have understood the motif of "seeing the face of YHWH/God", in light of the canonical context and in light of their understanding of the terms, phrases and concepts in the (canonically) earlier texts. These ancient Israelite readers of the text may be located in the period beginning with the fourth century BC, and would have been among the literate elements of the population in Yehud/Judea.[175]

In light of this assumption, the selected extant texts will be studied exegetically in their immediate canonical context and in the wider context of the "self-revelations" within the Pentateuch, in the hope that a canonical focus helps to have an awareness of the sequence of texts in which the

---

172. It is the stabilized HB at the end of the first century AD. The majority of scholars seem to agree that stabilization of the consonantal Text took place mid or late first century AD. For a discussion on chronological aspects, see Childs, *Introduction*, 96–100; Würthwein, *The Text*, 13–14; E. R. Brotzman, *Old Testament Textual Criticism* (Eerdmans: Grand Rapids, 1996), 25–46; Al Wolters, "The Text of the Old Testament", in *The Face of Old Testament Studies: A Survey of Contemporary Approaches*. Ed. D. W. Baker and B. T. Arnold (Baker Books: Grand Rapids, 1999), 19–37; I. Young, "The Stabilization of the Biblical Text in the Light of Qumran and Masada: A Challenge for Conventional Qumran and Chronology"? *DSD* 9 (2002), 364–390.

173. This does not mean that those literate readers had no prior knowledge of the Pentateuch (which perhaps gained recognition around the fifth century BC) at all. This dissertation presupposes that the readers in the fourth century BC and onwards read the Pentateuch in its more or less finalized form, depending on availability of texts.

174. For different aspects of the religio-historical process behind the HB, see F. M. Cross, "The Contributions of the Qumran Discoveries to the Study of the Biblical Text," *Israel Exploration Quarterly* 16 (1966), 81–95; B. J. Roberts, "The Old Testament: Manuscripts, Text, and Versions", in *The Cambridge History of the Bible*. Vol. 2. Ed. G. W. H. Lampe (Cambridge: Cambridge University Press, 1969), 1–26; E. Tov, *Textual Criticism*, 22–79; cf. 190; Tov, "History and Significance of a Standard Text", in *Hebrew Bible/Old Testament: The History of Its Interpretation*. Vol. 1. Ed. M. Sæbø (Göttingen: Vandenhoeck & Ruperecht, 1996), 49–66.

175. See P. R. Davies, "The Hebrew Canon and the Origins of Judaism", in *The Historian and the Bible*. Ed. P. R. Davies and D. V. Edelman (T. & T. Clark: London, 2010), 194–200. Davies suggests that the population of Judah in the third and early second centuries BCE was around 150,000 and that the literate elite among them were mostly confined to Jerusalem and they numbered in hundreds. It was these literate Jewish people, who would be able to read the written Hebrew text.

expression is utilized. This is not without challenge as there is a danger/temptation to take an ancient text out of context and to interpret it so as to suit one's opinions rather than letting the biblical text speak for itself. K. L. Sparks is right in saying that "it is quite possible for 'true facts' to be falsely and even harmfully understood".[176] As P. R. Ackroyd stresses, "ideally the meaning of any word in a given passage should be established in order that the exegesis of the whole passage can be set out without prejudice".[177] While exegeting the texts, the textual and grammatical difficulties in the Hebrew text will be discussed; special attention will be given to different aspects in the text which have close association with the theme of "seeing the face of YHWH/God. J. M. Soskice cites McClintock's statement, "Good research requires a disposition to hear what the material has to say".[178] Therefore, this study will take care to engage in interpreting by hearing what the text has to say on the theme of "seeing the face of God" within the given context.

The Masoretic Hebrew Pentateuch is used in this work.[179] The biblical references are to the Hebrew Bible. Unless and otherwise mentioned the translations of the Hebrew text are the researcher's own. Biblical books are abbreviated according to the *JBL's* "Instructions for Contributors".

---

176. K. L. Sparks, *God's Word in Human Words* (Grand Rapids: Baker Academic, 2008), 359.

177. P. R. Ackroyd and B. Lindars, "Meaning and Exegesis", in *Words and Meanings* (Cambridge: Cambridge University Press, 1968), 1.

178. J. M. Soskice, "The Ends of Man and the Future of God", in G. Ward, ed. *Postmodern Theology* (Oxford: Blackwell, 2001), 76, citing E. F. Keller, *A Feeling for the Organism: The Life and Work of Barbara McClintock* (San Francisco: W. H. Freeman, 1983), 199.

179. It is the Hebrew Pentateuch as found in BHS. For a discussion on this, see Childs, *Introduction*, 97–100; Clines, *Theme*, 13–14.

1.9 Specific Method in this Study and the Chapter Outline

This exegetical study will not be strictly inter-textual in that while exegeting a particular text, it will refer only to (canonically) earlier texts.[180] This means that while exegeting the selected extant texts only (canonically) earlier texts are referred to[181] with an assumption that the (canonically) earlier/previous texts would shed light in understanding the (canonically) later texts. An assumption is also made that the readers would have understood the meaning of the terms, phrases and concepts in the earlier texts, and that they would interpret the (canonically) later texts in light of their understanding of those terms, phrases and concepts in the earlier or previous texts studied.[182] This is to say that this study will not refer to the later texts for understanding the earlier texts (only backward referencing). For example, while reading a text in Exodus, this study will only refer to the texts in Genesis; and while studying the texts within Genesis traditions,[183] it will refer to previous traditions in that while studying Genesis 12, it will not refer to Genesis 17 rather it will refer to Genesis 3, and the same procedure will be followed throughout this study.[184]

---

180. Whenever "earlier" is mentioned in this work, it means canonically earlier, as placed in the HB.

181. This means referring back to the canonically earlier texts, as they appear in the (extant) HB. Whether the texts, for example, Genesis 17, were circulated as oral traditions, or even if they were circulated as written texts, how long they existed as independent written texts before they found their place in the stabilized canonical text (HB) is not the concern of this study; rather, the purpose in this work is to study every selected extant text within its immediate canonical context.

182. In some sense, it is the way Fishbane (*Biblical Interpretation in Israel* [Oxford: Clarendon Press, 1985]) reads the texts, but only in that the (canonically) previous texts are referred to in order to understand the (canonically) later texts. However, this study will not follow Fishbane's inner biblical exegetical approach in any other way. While Fishbane disagrees with the tradition-history in the way it distinguishes the *traditum* from the *traditio* and argues that there is no criterion to determine the origins of the traditions, he himself realized the tensions in distinguishing *traditum* from *tradition* when explicit statements such as "as it is written" are not mentioned (12–15).

183. The usage of "tradition" in this work has no connection with the tradition history.

184. This work supposes that the ancient readers would have read the Pentateuch (beginning from Genesis1:1) chapter by chapter and book by book.

Any parallel texts which appear beyond the Pentateuch will not be discussed in this work, the reason being that the major purpose in this study is to discern the possible origins/background of the motif "seeing the face of YHWH/God" within the Pentateuch; and to discern the significance it had played in ancient Israel. So, key texts from different parts of the Pentateuch are selected for the purpose of studying the motif of "face of YHWH/God". This study comprises seven chapters in three sections. The texts from Genesis will be studied in section one; the texts from Exodus in section two; and the texts from Numbers in section three.

Chapters 2 and 4 will study a variety of selected texts from the book of Genesis and Exodus respectively with the purpose of understanding how the divine self-revelations were perceived operative in Genesis and Exodus traditions. In other words, these texts may not have a specific mention of "'seeing the 'face' of YHWH/God" but will contain different aspects of the self-revelation of YHWH/God. Chapter 2 will study Genesis 3:8–10; 12:1–4, 7; 15:1–16; 16:7–14; 17:1–22; 18:1–2, 9–33; and chapter 4 will study Exodus 3:1–8 and 24:1–18. Although the texts in Chapters 2 and 4 will be exegetically studied, these two chapters will be somewhat different from chapters 3, 5 and 6 in terms of the structure and focus of the study. While the focus in chapters 2 and 4 will be on the self-revelations of YHWH/God" which may or may not involve the aspect of "'seeing the divine face", the focus in chapters 3, 5 and 6 will be on "'seeing the face' of YHWH/God". The study in chapters 2 and 4, it is hoped, will help in understanding the motif "'seeing the face' of YHWH/God" in chapters 3, 5 and 6, which are major chapters.

Chapters 3, 5 and 6 will exegetically study the selected texts which have specific usage of the noun פנים "face" or פנים אל־פנים "face-to-face" or pronominal suffixes (פני or פניו); and with the verb ראה (to see) in association YHWH/God. Chapter 3 will study Genesis 32:23–31, entitled, "I 'Saw' God 'Face-to-Face' and My Life is Rescued". The reason for this selection is that it records an explicit confession of Jacob that he saw God "face-to-face"; chapter 5will study Exodus 33:12–23, entitled, "You 'Cannot See My Face'; No One Can See Me, and Live". The reason for this selection is because the noun פנים is associated with the verbs ראה ("to see") and הלך

("to walk") and it also has (seemingly) conflicting statements pertaining the "seeing" aspect (vv. 14–15, 20, 23).

Chapter 6 will study Numbers 6:22–27, entitled, "Shining and Lifting of YHWH's Face". The reason for this selection is that the expression "face of YHWH" (פניו) is used in the context of worship at the Tabernacle. Chapter 7 will be the conclusions.

To summarize, the major purpose of this study is to understand the association of the verb ראה "to see" with פנים "face" of YHWH/God as portrayed in the selected texts in the Pentateuch; to discern how ancient Israel perceived the self-revelations operative, and how they understood the physicality of YHWH/God, in terms of the "human form" in which YHWH/God seemed to appear to different people; to detect if the background/origins of the motif "seeing the face of YHWH/God" had its background in the context of the divine self-revelations. In order to understand these aspects, this work now will turn to the study of the selected texts.

Section I

Chapters 2–3

Texts from Genesis

CHAPTER 2

The Self-Revelations of YHWH/God in Genesis

2.1 Introduction

This chapter studies the motif of the self-revelations of YHWH/God in Genesis with the objective of understanding how anthropomorphic appearances were perceived operative in Genesis traditions. The selected texts, Genesis 3:8–10; 12:1–8; 15:1–7; 16:7–14; 17:1–5; 18:1–8, 16–22; 28:12–22, will be studied within their immediate context and in light of the previous traditions, with an attempt to discern the aspects of divine communication, the mode of divine revelation and the function it played in ancient Israel. In some of these texts the verb ראה "to see" is directly associated with פנים "face" of YHWH/God and in others it is implied. An attempt will be made to discern what scope these texts give to associate פנים "face" with the anthropomorphic (bodily) person of YHWH/God. There will be a brief conclusion at the end of every text and closing remarks at the end of the chapter.

2.2 Genesis 3:8–10: God Walks

2.2.1 Canonical Context
According to the writer of Genesis, after having created the heavens and the earth and all that is in it (1:1–25), God fashioned man from the dust

and breathed into his nostrils "the breath of life" (נשמת חיים) and then man became a living being (2:7); God created humankind (אדם) in his image (בצלם אלהים), as male and female (1:26–27).[1] Having placed the man in the Garden of Eden, God commanded (צוה) him to eat freely from all the trees, but not to eat from the tree of the knowledge of good and evil lest they die (2:15–17). However, they disobeyed God's command, realized their nakedness and made a cover for themselves with fig-leaves (3:1–7). This was the situation Adam and Eve were in when God walked towards them.

2.2.2 Divine Self-Revelation and Communication

Genesis 3:8–10 relates that when Adam and his wife heard the voice (את־קול) of YHWH God (יהוה אלהים) as he walked in the garden in the cool of the day (לרוח היום), they hid themselves in the midst of the trees from facing (מפני) God. When YHWH God asked Adam where he was, the later replied that he heard the former's voice (את־קולך) in the garden, and that he was afraid, because he was naked, and he hid himself.

The phrase לרוח היום (lit. wind of the day)[2] is normally translated as "cool of the day" or "afternoon". J. J. Niehaus, however, discarding this translation "cool of the day" as an "interpretive guess", imagines a sinaitic characteristic of storm theophany here[3] and conjectures the Hebrew יום ("day") as "storm" and לרוח היום as "the wind of the storm";[4] accordingly,

---

1. For a discussion on the aspect of male and female (זכר ונקבה) in the "image of God", see A. Schüle, "Made in the 'Image of God': The Concepts of Divine Images in Gen 1–3", *ZAW* 117 (2005), 6–9.

2. The preposition ל in לרוח היום may suggest temporal sense (when fresh breeze blows). B. Bandstra, *Genesis 1–11. A Handbook on the Hebrew Text* (Waco: Baylor University Press, 2008), 185. See C. Westermann, *Genesis 1–11* (London: SPCK, 1984), 254. LXX reads τὸ δειλινόν, "towards the evening"; the Vulgate reads *ad auram post meridiem* "in the afternoon breeze". Several Eng.verses such as NKJ and RSV read "in the cool of the day" (NRSV reads "evening"). לרוח היום may be an indication that it was the cool of the day, as it is normal in the Middle East that the day is hot and gets cool towards the evening because of the breeze (Gen 18:1; 24:63).

3. J. J. Niehaus, *God at Sinai* (Grand Rapids: Zondervan, 1995), 155–157; also Niehaus, "In the Wind of the Storm: Another Look at Genesis iii: 8", *VT* 44 (1994), 263–267.

4. Referring to the Akkadian word *ūmu*, Niehaus argues that *ūmu* in Akkadian also means "storm" and it corresponds to a second cognate of Hebrew יום "storm". See *HELOT*, 398; *HALOT* 3, 384.

in Genesis 3:8 the storm wind was the advancing presence of YHWH who advances to judge "his guilty people".[5] However, יום here seems to indicate daytime (cf. 1:5, 16)[6] and the context here gives no clue to translate it as "storm" since there are no features of the storm described in the text.

The noun קול "voice" here seems to signify the sound that comes out of the vocal chords;[7] and the קול seems to refer to God's voice, given that the next verses (3:9–10) describe YHWH God calling (ויקרא) Adam, who in his reply said that he heard God's voice (את־קולך).[8] Whether קול should be translated as "the sound of" footsteps[9] or walking, the writer seems to insist that God was present in the garden; and the realism of the action that he was walking seems to indicate his physical presence. The hithpael verb מתהלך (walking to and fro) also seems to suggest "iterative and habitual aspects",[10] and מתהלך associated with YHWH God[11] probably connotes a relationship between God and the people.[12]

Both Niehaus' interpretation of קול as "theophanic thunder"[13] and Sailhamer's assumption that this text (Gen 3:8) resembles the theophany at Sinai (Exod 20:18–21)[14] seem improbable for the same reason that the text gives no clue to assume Sinai-like thunder in the garden. Rather, the casual way the writer describes YHWH God walking in the garden perhaps

---

5. Approaching this text from the perspective of "history of religions", Niehaus (*God at Sinai*, 18, 155–157) assumes a storm theophany here, because Akkadian *ūmu* is found in association with divine epithets (cf. Ninurta and Aššur) in the Akkadian literature; he compares it with YHWH's coming.

6. U. Cassuto (*A Commentary on the Book of Genesis* [Jerusalem: Magnes, 1961], 152) argues that the noun רוח as a cognate to Ugaritic root *rḥ* also gives the idea of activity (breeze!) in the afternoon.

7. L. J. Coppes, "קול", *TWOT* 2, 792.

8. LXX reads τὴν φωνὴν κυρίου τοῦ θεοῦ ' περιπατοῦντος "'voice' of the Lord God walking".

9. C. F. Keil, and F. Delitzsch, *The Pentateuch* 1 (Grand Rapids: Eerdmans, 1949), 97; Westermann, *Genesis 1–11*, 254; S.R. Driver, *The Book of Genesis* (London: Methuen & Co., 1904), 46; J. Skinner, *Genesis* (Edinburgh: T. & T. Clark, 1930), 76–77. NKJ and NRS read את־קול as the "sound" of YHWH "walking"; Cf. Wenham, *Genesis 16–50*, 76.

10. E. A. Speiser, "The Durative Hithpaʿel: A tan-Form", *JAOS* 75 (1955), 118–121.

11. Cf. Bandstra, *Genesis 1–11*, 185.

12. Cf. Lev 26:12; Deut 23:15.

13. Niehaus, *God at Sinai*, 155–157. He translates Gen 3:8 as: "... heard the thunder (קול) of YHWH God going back and forth (מתהלך) ... in the wind of the storm".

14. Sailhamer, *Pentateuch*, 105; see also chapter 1, 36–37.

indicates that it was the regular practice for God to visit Adam and Eve;[15] presumably, the couple are in the habit of meeting God, who created them, fearlessly prior to this incident. It is significant to note that at the end of the previous chapter (2:25), the writer says that Adam and Eve were naked, but they were not ashamed (nor was there any fear); but now, he seems to convey that their disobedience to the divine command brought them to a realization of their nakedness, and that when they heard the divine voice, fear gripped them.

In Adam's reply, the reason why they hide themselves (ויתחבא) is that they heard his voice (את־קולך) and were afraid of facing God; and this shows that God is understood to be physically present in the garden and that he is visible to the human eye. The writer uses the verb ויתחבא (hithpael of חבא) in verse 3:8 to inform his readers that Adam hid himself, and when Adam responded to God's call, he uses the verb אחבא (niphal of חבא) in verse 10; since both the verbs have a reflexive sense, the variation may be for a literary variety.[16] When it is said that Adam and his wife hid themselves מפני יהוה אלהים "from the face/presence of YHWH God" (3:8), the phrase מפני ("from the face of") is used in association with YHWH God, and this means that they hid from YHWH God himself. In this text, פנים "face" in the phrase מפני ("from the face of") retains its nominal sense, in that it points to YHWH God from whom/whose presence the separation took place (i.e.[[INSERT TEXT]]).[17] Since YHWH God is understood walking in the garden and calling Adam (v. 9), since Adam is said to have heard God's "voice" and hid himself from him, God is believed to be physically present there in the vicinity in a literal sense. Arguably, this seems an indication that there were direct meetings between God and the couple, which involved the aspect of "seeing", but now they hid themselves from fear. This means that their "fear" and "hiding" in a way have a state of cause and effect in that they disobeyed. Obviously, they are in fear of being seen by God (3:10).

---

15. Skinner, *Genesis*, 77.
16. J. S. Baden, "Hithpael and Niphal in Biblical Hebrew: Semantic and Morphological Overlap", *VT* 60 (2010), 36–37.
17. See chapter 1, 32.

The "fear" (ירא) in Adam is associated with his disobedience to God's command, and death is associated not with the action of seeing God, but with disobedience to his command (2:17). Because they disobeyed and hid themselves from YHWH/God, the divine-human relationship was disrupted. Furthermore, the writer's intention in placing this text here implies that his readers[18] would understand Genesis 3:8–10 in light of the previous chapters where God the creator was described in an anthropomorphic language, in that he brought animals to be named by Adam, brought woman and gave her to him as a wife (2:20–24) which means that God was in contact with the humans; as Fretheim thinks, Genesis 2 shows that God was in human form".[19]

These activities in Eden seem so dramatic that one might suggest that Adam and Eve saw the appearance or the "form" of YHWH/God in a literal sense as they spoke to each other from close vicinity in the garden. Since readers were acquainted with these vivid anthropomorphic descriptions, it would not be difficult for them to visualise YHWH/God walking in the garden. Furthermore, the text describes the couple hiding themselves from facing (the face of) God and suggests that God's physical appearance in that vicinity is in some sense "real". The writer seems to insist that YHWH/God was physically visible to the first couple, and by describing how they hid themselves from facing God, he shows that God was present in the garden, and presumably God was believed to be in anthropomorphized form, and it is possible that Adam and Eve saw the divine person literally (v. 21; cf. 2:19; 2:22), and that God communicated with Adam directly.

Eichrodt suggests that one should not lay much weight on the communion between God and humans in the garden, where God is described as walking, because they were expelled.[20] Although the death foretold (2:17) did not take place in a physical sense, it can be seen in the loss of privilege in that the couple could no longer live close to God.[21] However, God did

---

18. I.e. readers in ancient Israel.
19. T. E. Fretheim, *God and World in the Old Testament* (Nashville: Abingdon Press, 2005), 39.
20. Eichrodt, *OTT* 2, 20.
21. For a metaphorical understanding of death in Gen 3, see Moberly, "Did the Serpent Get it Right?", *JTS* 39 (1988), 17; Wenham (*Genesis 1–15*, 83) sees death as the distance

not cease to reveal himself even after their expulsion, as the latter chapters in Genesis show.

2.2.3 The Mode of Self-Revelation, Human Recognition and Response

The vivid anthropomorphic language used for God that he walks and calls seems to signify that he was in human disguise (3:8–10); that Adam recognizes God's voice seems to indicate that YHWH God was at the same level with the humans in terms of the communication, in that God spoke and humans recognized him. In order to discern how this communication between God and the couple was made possible, one may reflect on humans in association with the "image of God", as there seems some kind of inexplicable association between YHWH God and "image of God" (*imago Dei*) in humans.

Various scholarly arguments and theories have been put forward over time with regard to the "image of God" in humans in terms of (צלם and דמות) human "corporeal appearance" (Gen 1:26–27).[22] The foundational and most significant factor seems that נשמת חיים the "breath of life" breathed into humankind was something that came from God himself (Gen 2:7), and by doing so, one may assume that God imparted something of himself to Adam (humankind);[23] it was this God-given life (נשמת חיים) in humans that facilitated the scope for the communication with God, and it was this which helped humankind to recognize their creator.[24] As Fretheim puts it, "something of the divine self comes to reside in the human";[25] and

---

from God because of expulsion from Eden.

22. Due to the space limit in this dissertation, different theories and scholarly arguments on the aspect of צלם "image" (דמות) and "likeness" (Gen 1:26–27) will not be discussed here. For helpful discussion, see D. J. A. Clines, "The Image of God in Man", *TB* 19 (1968), 53–103; J. R. Middleton, *The Liberating Image: The Imago Dei in Genesis 1* (Grand Rapids: Brazos Press, 2005), 15–90; J. M. Miller, "In the 'Image' and 'Likeness' of God", *JBL* 91 (1972), 289–304; Schüle, "Image of God", 1–20; Fretheim, *God and World*, 1–67. S. J. Grenz, *Social God and the Relational Self* (Westminster: John Knox Press, 2001), 200–201; von Rad, *Genesis*, 59–60.

23. Gen 1:26; 2:5; cf. Isa 57:16: ונשמות אני עשיתי (and I have created breath/souls).

24. Given that Adam and Eve continue to be conscious of God, even after their disobedience (4:1–5).

25. Fretheim, *God and World*, 39.

as K. Barth understands, it is "the special feature of human existence in virtue of which man is capable of action in relation to God";[26] it is the God-given capacity to hear and respond to God.[27] A. Schüle maintains that "the rhetoric of the image" focuses on the particular relation between Adam and God himself.[28] All these scholars rightly focus on the aspect of the relationship between the creator and humankind.

Delitzsch articulates that God gave humans a bodily shape when he created them in his own image, and that he also revealed himself in a manner suited to human bodily senses, so that they might have a living communion with him, but bodily shape in an anthropomorphic appearance of God does not imply an essential characteristic of God.[29] Although bodily shape need not be an essential characteristic of God, as Delitzsch understands, it seems, however, as though a temporary disguise into a "bodily form" is essential for God in order to communicate with humans, and the anthropomorphic language signifies a relationship as though God and human beings were on the same level.[30]

There is evidence in the text to believe that God in the garden was in a bodily form, given that vivid anthropomorphic language is used to describe him that he was walking and talking. As Nötscher understands, Adam and his wife knew that God was coming in human *Gestalt* "form",[31] but the text does not give any details in terms of physical features of God, nor does it say from where God came into the garden, or where he went after he sent off the humans from Eden. But one thing is clear that in Eden, God took the initiative to communicate to the first couple.

2.2.3 The Function/Significance of Divine Revelation

This text perhaps functioned to show that YHWH God appeared in human form to the first couple, in that he walked in the garden and talked

---

26. K. Barth, *The Doctrine of Creation* (Edinburgh: T. & T. Clark, 1958), 199.
27. See Barth, 194–197.
28. Schüle, "Image of God", 4.
29. Keil and Delitzsch, *Pentateuch* 1, 97; Miller, "In the 'Image'", 291–292; Barr, "Theophany", 1–38.
30. Cf. Westermann, *Genesis 1–11*, 252.
31. Nötscher, *Angesicht*, 20–21.

to them, and was involved in the situation when they disobeyed. It would have helped the readers to understand that the disobedience of the first couple to God's command[32] generated fear (they were afraid) in the couple to an extent that they hid themselves from "seeing" and "being seen" by God. In brief, this tradition could have played a significant role to help in understanding that God took disobedience to his command (2:17) seriously and that their communion with their creator was disturbed;[33] and that "intimacy was replaced by fear and alienation".[34]

2.2.4 Conclusion

This brief study of Genesis 3:8–10 has shown that YHWH, who was believed to be the creator, walked in the garden and talked to the first couple whom he had created in his image. It was because of the "image of God" in humans that there existed a relationship with, and communication between, the creator and the created. YHWH God is featured in human-like form in the garden and spoke in a language that was understood by the first couple. One may presume the appearance of God was believed (in ancient Israel) to be in human bodily form, and that YHWH was physically present when he spoke with the first couple. Therefore, one may assume that the first couple had seen the face of God, but as a consequence of disobedience to the divine command, they lost their freedom to meet with God, and "hid" themselves out of the "fear" of seeing and being seen by him.

A glance beyond the present text shows that God did not cease to reveal himself to the humans, and continued his relationship with humankind.

---

32. Thus far the Hebrew term חטא "sin" is not used in Genesis (cf. Gen 4:7) but the first couple's "turning away" from obedience amounts to חטא. See G.H. Livingston, "חטא", *TWOT* 1, 277–279.
33. Cf. Rowley, *Faith of Israel*, 81.
34. W. P. Brown, *The Ethos of the Cosmos: The Genesis of Moral Imagination in the Bible* (Grand Rapids: Eerdmans, 1999), 57.

2.3 Genesis 12:1–8: YHWH Calls

2.3.1 Canonical Context
The writer's genealogical account of Terah, the father of Abram in 11:27–32, forms the background to his description of the divine revelation to Abram. YHWH/God presumably spoke to Abram first while the latter was still in Ur.[35]

2.3.2 Divine Self-Revelation and Communication
Genesis 12:1–4 portrays how YHWH told Abram to leave his country, people and his father's household and go to the land he would show, and made the promises that he would bless him so that all the families of the earth should be blessed through him. Verses 7–8 portray how YHWH appeared to Abram and promised him the Land; and that Abram built an altar there to YHWH, who appeared to him, and as he moved towards Bethel, there also he built an altar to YHWH and called on his name.

The writer simply introduces YHWH's revelation to Abram with the indirect statement, "YHWH said to Abram" (12:1), but one may assume that there was still some kind of divine manifestation,[36] given that in several instances in the previous traditions/texts, the phrase "YHWH/God said to" is used in association with the divine manifestations.[37] It is worth noting that earlier in Genesis, when God blessed (יברך) the first couple, he was understood to be physically present with them,[38] and even here in the present context, when YHWH promises his blessings (ברך occurs five times here in 12:2–3) to Abram, one may assume that while pronouncing his blessings, YHWH was physically present with Abram. Furthermore, the text insists that YHWH himself ordered Abram ([39]לך־לך: v. 1) to go

---

35. Gen 11:31c; 15:7.

36. Contra Westermann, *Genesis 12–36: A Commentary* (Minneapolis: Augsburg Publishing House, 1985), 147.

37. E.g. Gen 4:6–14; 7:1, 16; 11:5, 6.

38. E.g. Gen 1:28; cf. 9:1: God said to them, "Be fruitful and multiply"; ברך here has a wider connotation. Interestingly, the blessings to Abram in 12:2–3 also have a wider context.

39. ל with reflexive suffix perhaps puts emphasis on the subject. See Clines, ed., *The Dictionary of Classical Hebrew* (Sheffield Academic Press: Sheffield, 1998), 483.

from his father's house, which implies a direct communication of YHWH to Abram, whose understanding of what YHWH said to him caused him to leave Haran and go to the Land of Canaan (Land). Whether the verb נברכו[40] should be taken as passive (shall be blessed) or reflexive (shall bless themselves), the important feature here is that all the families of the earth shall be blessed through him in future, and people would either receive the divine blessings offered through Abram or reject them (12:3).[41]

Later on, the writer explicitly says that YHWH appeared to Abram (v. 7). The verb וירא (niphal of ראה) in association with YHWH signifies that he let himself be seen.[42] Since the niphal verb here has reflexive sense,[43] God becomes the subject and the agent of revelation. This may well mean that YHWH revealed himself to Abram so that he could be seen by the latter.[44] When the writer states, "YHWH appeared to Abram" (וירא: v. 7), he seems to understand YHWH as physically present (2–3) with Abram. Presumably then, Abram had a chance to see God in a physical sense, and during that appearance YHWH promised the Land to his descendants.[45]

The writer also insists that Abram built an altar to YHWH, "who appeared to him" (v. 7b) and this seems to confirm that YHWH's appearance to Abram was believed to be real. It seems that the building of the altar has a close association with the self-revelation of YHWH (v. 7). Since it is not explicit whether YHWH appeared to Abram again (v. 8), one may assume that it was with the consciousness of his earlier appearances to him that he built another altar at Bethel and called on the name of YHWH (v. 8).[46]

---

40. The preposition ב (בך) can be taken as "in" or "by". Interestingly, נברכו the niphal of ברך that occurs only three times in the Hebrew traditions is used in Gen 12:3; 18:18 and 28:14.

41. If נברכו is treated as passive and ב as "by/through" (instrumental sense), it makes better sense because Abram was called "amidst the multitude of existing nations" (von Rad, *Genesis*, 154) which were scattered all over the earth (cf. 11:8).

42. Cf. 17:1; 18:1; 26:2, 24.

43. Cf. Baden, "Hithpael and Niphal", 36.

44. The niphal of ראה does not exclude the visibility of YHWH, and it can well be translated as "YHWH showed himself".

45. Cf. Gen 13:15, 17; 15:18; 17:8; 26:3; 28:13, etc,.

46. Cf. Gen 4:26; 8:20 where "calling on the name of YHWH" was first mentioned.

2.3.3 The Mode of Self-Revelation, Human Recognition and Response

The divine revelation to Abram appears to include his appearance and the spoken word. The verb ראה ("to see"), used in association with YHWH in verse 7, seems to signify that the mode of YHWH's manifestation is understood to be in human form, and that YHWH was present with Abram, when he spoke to him. Since the text describes that YHWH ordered Abram to go to the Land of his choosing, it seems to indicate a direct divine encounter with Abram, and the divine appearance is understood to be in human form and was seen by Abram; but there is no description given in terms of physical features of the divine person.

Since Abram moved toward Canaan in obedience to the divine message, it implies that YHWH spoke in a language which Abram understood, and Abram seems to have recognized that it was God who spoke to him. The initiative to appear to Abram seems to have come from YHWH himself. In response to the divine revelation, Abram does not express any fear, but rather, altars were built as signs of worship; the building of an altar (מזבח) at Shechem was associated with the divine revelation (v. 7) and perhaps signifies the reality of YHWH's appearance. But the text gives no clue from where YHWH came, when he appeared and spoke to Abram, nor does it say where he went after he communicated with Abram.

2.3.4 The Function/Significance of Divine Revelation

This tradition of revelation perhaps played a significant role in ancient Israel to convey that the promise of the Land and descendants was closely associated with the self-revelations of YHWH to Abram; that Abram was blessed to be a blessing to all humankind, and that YHWH planned to bestow his blessings upon the whole humankind through Abram.[47] It may even be that the readers would have connected Abram's obedience to God's command (לך־לך in 12:1) and the divine blessings offered through Abraham as a replacement of the curse (Gen 3:17) that came upon humankind, because of the disobedience of the first couple; and they may have associated the divine promises with the divine revelation to Abram (12:1–3),

---

47. Cf. Acts 3:25; Gal 3:8.

and that Abram would play an important role in re-uniting an estranged humanity with God.[48]

2.3.5 Conclusion

Although it is not explicit in 12:1, it is clear in verse 7 that YHWH appeared to Abram, and the communication was direct and real. The divine promises are associated with the divine revelations to Abram, and the divine message was clearly understood and obeyed. The verb וירא (niphal of ראה) in association with YHWH seems to signify that YHWH lets himself be seen. The building of altars seemed to have a close association with the divine self-revelation. YHWH's communication with Abram seems direct and the writer seems to insist that the mode of YHWH's appearance was in human form and real; however, there is no description of this form, but only the divine message is given in detail.

2.4 Genesis 15:1–21: YHWH Appears in a Vision

2.4.1 Canonical Context

Readers would have been aware that YHWH had reiterated his promises to Abram regarding the Land and descendants (13:15–17), and that afterwards, Abram moved to Hebron and built an altar there to YHWH (v. 18).

2.4.2 Divine Self-Revelation and Communication

Genesis 15:1–21 relates that "the word of YHWH" came to Abram in a vision, saying, "Fear not (אל־תירא), Abram. I am your shield, your reward will be great" (15:1b); and in response to Abram's complaint that YHWH God (אדני יהוה) did not give him a child (2–3), "the word of YHWH" came to him and assured him that his own child would be his heir; then YHWH took Abram outside, showed him the sky and assured him that his

---

48. Cf. T. D. Alexander, *From Paradise to the Promised Land* (Carlisle: Paternoster Press, 1995), 48.

descendants would be innumerable like stars, and Abram believed (וְהֶאֱמִן) in YHWH and YHWH considered it to him as righteousness (צְדָקָה: 4–6).[49]

The reason why YHWH tells Abram "fear not" may not be because Abram is afraid of the appearance of YHWH, as some scholars think,[50] given that he was not afraid of YHWH's appearance when he appeared to him previously. The writer reported earlier that Sarai was barren and had no child (11:30) and now Abram expresses his despair over not having his own child despite YHWH's earlier promises (2–3, 8).[51] Perhaps, Abram is anxious about his childless state and so "fear not" is used to reassure Abram of God's promise for the offspring (13:15).[52]

Hamilton argues that there is no visual image here, but only a word from God.[53] However, the expression דבר־יהוה "the word of YHWH" need not exclude YHWH's appearance in the vision.[54] After YHWH made the self-assertion אני יהוה "I am YHWH",[55] Abram addresses this "word of YHWH" as אדני יהוה "YHWH Lord", and this suggests that "the word of YHWH" meant YHWH himself in that vision. While Driver thinks that it was simply prophetic intuition,[56] the writer is clear that it was in a vision (מחזה + ב) that God spoke to Abram. Furthermore, the writer describes how YHWH took him outside, showed him the stars and confirmed his promise (v. 5), and this seems to signify the revelation of YHWH within that vision. Given that the writer specifically mentions "on 'that day'

---

49. YHWH confirmed that it was he who brought Abram out of Ur, to give him the Land to possess, and as a confirmation of his promise, YHWH made a covenant with Abram "that day" (7–21).
50. For example, V. P. Hamilton, *The Book of Genesis* (Grand Rapids: Eerdmans, 1995), 417.
51. While the expression "I will be your shield" may include YHWH's protection from the enemy (Gen 14:1–20; cf. 21:17; 26:24.), "fear not" may be associated with Abram's childless condition.
52. Cf. Keil and Delitzsch, *Pentateuch* 1, 211; Westermann, *Genesis*, 147. The combination of יהוה with אדני used only twice in Genesis occurs here (vv. 2, 8) which may be for emphasis that Abram did believe in the divine lordship despite his complaint that YHWH did not give him a child.
53. Hamilton, *Genesis*, 418.
54. The Hebrew terms "appeared" (ראה); "revealed" (גלה) by his word (בדבר יהוה) seem to give the same idea of divine revelation (cf. 1 Sam 3:21).
55. This is one of the two occurrences in Genesis.
56. Driver, *Genesis*, 174.

YHWH made a (ברית) covenant with Abram" (v. 18), this signifies the reality of that vision, and the fulfillment of YHWH's promises. All these factors make this vision "real", since there is a visualization of YHWH, and the divine appearance in this vision does not lack directness.[57] By stating specifically that Abram believed in YHWH and that YHWH considered it to him as righteousness (v. 6), the writer seems to confirm that the divine encounter in that vision was no less significant, in terms of the divine message given to Abram. Readers are now exposed to YHWH speaking to Abram in a vision.

2.4.3 The Mode of Self-Revelation, Human Recognition, and Response

The description of the divine activity within Abram's vision, such as bringing Abram outside and showing him the stars (v. 5), making the covenant, and reiterating the promises, indicate that YHWH/God acted in human form and was visible within that vision. A divine-human dialogue takes place, and the language used by the divine figure is understood by Abram. All these factors seem to confirm that the revelation of YHWH was in human form. Here, since the divine self-revelation is in a vision, the question of where YHWH came from and where he went after speaking with Abram does not arise. How Abram recognized the one who appeared in his vision could be linked to his earlier acquaintance with YHWH in his previous encounters. The initial response to divine revelation is that of doubt (vv. 2, 8), but the response after divine assurance is that of faith in the one who spoke to him (v. 6). The initiative to reveal himself to Abram came from YHWH himself, and he also initiated the making of a covenant with Abram.

2.4.4 The Function/Significance of Divine Revelation

This vision tradition would have helped to understand that divine revelation in a vision was no less significant, in terms of the communication and the visualization of the appearance of the divine person, than the direct revelations described in the previous texts. It would have helped readers to understand how YHWH involved himself in Abram's life, and how the

---

57. See Barr, "Theophany", 33.

divine assurance in this vision helped Abram to trust in YHWH's words, and to maintain a righteous relationship with God.⁵⁸

2.4.5 Conclusion

Genesis 15:1–21 discusses divine self-revelation in vision, and explicates various significant aspects of divine revelation pertinent to a vision. The "word of YHWH" that came in Abram's vision is addressed as אדני יהוה "YHWH Lord" signifying that YHWH himself appeared in a vision. The divine appearance in this vision neither lacked directness and visualization nor communication. The divine activities which took place within that vision such as, bringing Abram outside and showing the stars (v. 5), or making a covenant with Abram (vv. 9–17) indicate the reality of the vision, and that within that vision, the anthropomorphic figure of YHWH was present. It is presumed that the language used by YHWH/God was human language, and that Abram understood what was spoken to him. All these factors seemed to indicate that YHWH, in his human form, was visible in the vision.

2.5 Genesis 16:7–14: YHWH Sees

2.5.1 Canonical Context

Abram and Sarai remained childless despite the divine promise of an heir (15:4). Thinking that YHWH prevented her from bearing children, Sarai brought Hagar into the scene, in order that Abram would obtain a child by her. However, when Hagar conceived and despised Sarai, the latter troubled the former, and Hagar fled from there (16:1–6).

2.5.2 Divine Self-Revelation and Communication

Genesis 16:7–14 relates that Hagar was travelling in the desert, when מלאך יהוה "the angel of YHWH" found (מצא) her by the spring of water, and initiated a conversation as if he was a co-traveller in the desert (vv. 7–8). After hearing Hagar's confession that she was fleeing from Sarai, "the

---

58. Cf. von Rad, *Genesis*, 180.

angel of YHWH" ordered her to go back and submit to Sarai, promised her a countless number of descendants; advised that she would name her son Ishmael because YHWH heard her trouble; and predicted the kind of man Ishmael would be (vv. 9–12). Hagar called on the name of YHWH who spoke to her, אתה אל ראי "You are the God who sees me", for she said, הגם הלם ראיתי אחרי ראי "Have I also seen him who sees me"? Therefore she called the well, [59]באר לחי ראי "the well of the living one who sees me" (vv. 13–14).

The text suggests that it is after the divine encounter wherein YHWH spoke to her that Hagar exclaims, "I have here also seen him",[60] and she also acknowledges God as the one "who sees" (ראי). Hagar seems to have seen God, in human disguise, and conversed with him. This implies that her experience of seeing God at the well was understood to be "real," and that God revealed himself to Hagar in a human bodily form. The "angel of YHWH" occurs for the first time here in Genesis. Some critical scholars[61] explain that it was due to embarrassment to think of a God coming down to earth in human form that at a later period YHWH/God was substituted by מלאך "a messenger" of God. However, YHWH and "angel of YHWH" in the text are used to identify the same person, and so the question of the embarrassment does not arise.[62]

The statement in verse 14 that the well was called באר לחי ראי (Beer Lahai Roi) "the well of the living one who sees me" may be intended to show that the well was named after Hagar's experience with God. However, one gets a sense that Hagar recognized her dialogue partner as God/YHWH just as he turned back to leave that place. Driver suggests that Hagar saw

---

59. The use of ראי and חי (in לחי) has been debated because if ראי is taken as participle with 1st person suffix, it should be ראֵנִי or רֹאַנִי (as in Isa 29:15 and 47:10). However, elsewhere in the HB, ראי is treated as first person suffix. Then, associating חי (in the phrase בְּאֵר לַחַי רֹאִי) with the divine person, בְּאֵר לַחַי רֹאִי is translated "well of the living one, who sees me" which is a possibility. ראי might also mean "my seer/God of my seeing". See Westermann, *Genesis* 12–36, 246.

60. LXX reads: γὰρ ἐνώπιον εἶδον ὀφθέντα μοι; chapter 1, fn. 8, 2.

61. For example, H. Gunkel, *Genesis: A Commentary* (Macon: Mercer University Press, 1997), 16. Westermann, *Genesis* 1–11, 243.

62. In 7–10, it was "angel of YHWH" who spoke to Hagar. But in v. 11 "angel of YHWH" told her that YHWH heard her trouble. Later in v. 13 it says that she called the name of YHWH who spoke to her. Cf. Gen 21:17; 22:11, 14, 15, 16 for a similar pattern.

only "after" (אחרי) God, as he left her, and then only she perceived that God had been present there.⁶³

In light of ambiguity in the Hebrew text (vv. 13–14) in terms of the association of ראי with חי (in לחי), some scholars⁶⁴ have associated חי with Hagar and, referring to Exodus 33:20,⁶⁵ argued that Hagar was afraid of death for seeing God and so expressed surprise that she still remained alive. However, the text gives no clue that Hagar was afraid. Furthermore, the surprise in her statement sounds a positive note that she met God.

Westermann assumes that there is neither a revelation nor a vision here and it is simply an encounter between two people, but he accepts that Hagar saw the one who met her.⁶⁶ However, the writer insists that Hagar recognized him as God himself, and that she was happy that YHWH saw her and that she too saw him. When God finds Hagar and initiates a conversation, she does not seem to think that he is any different from a co-traveller at first (Gen 16:7–8); but at the end of the encounter she exclaims, "You are the God who sees me" . . . "Have I also seen him who sees me"? This indicates that when God found Hagar in the wilderness (v. 7), the mode of his appearance was evidently in human form (v. 13). Since the name given to the well as *Beer Lahai Roi* is associated with her experience of seeing (ראה) God (v. 14), God was understood physically present with her in a real sense; and in line with the divine instruction, the name Ishmael was given to her son (v. 15).⁶⁷

2.5.3 The Mode of Self-Revelation, Human Recognition and Response

Although the writer discloses at the end that it was YHWH himself, he introduces him as the "angel of YHWH", and at the beginning Hagar did not know that it was God himself. It may be presumed that the "angel of

---

63. Driver, *Genesis*, 183.
64. For example, Keil and Delitzsch. *Pentateuch* 1, 221–222. Cf. RSV and NRSV.
65. Exod 33:20 has a very different context. See chapter 5, 154–166.
66. Westermann, *Genesis 12–36*, 242.
67. It seems as though Abram understood that God met Hagar and spoke to her, thus gave the child the very name Ishmael.

YHWH" looked like a human being, given that Hagar responds to his questions freely as though she was speaking to a co-traveller.

It appears that God (in disguise) revealed something of himself at that particular juncture perhaps just before he left that place, and this helped Hagar recognize her co-traveller as God. It is only because God let himself be seen by Hagar that she could claim that she saw God.[68] Perhaps, the writer intends to tell his readers that God revealed himself not at once, but at first he appeared like a normal person, initiating the conversation. Evidently, God appeared in human form.

Since Hagar understood the divine message and that she went back and gave the name "Ishmael" to her son (v. 15), this seems to show that the communication was in human language. These factors confirm that God appeared in human form and Hagar saw him. There is no information given in the text where YHWH came from, and where he went after turning away from Hagar. Here again, there is no description of the physical features of the anthropomorphized God.

2.5.4 The Function/Significance of Divine Revelation

This text could have helped in understanding God's involvement in the troubled and uncertain situation Hagar the Egyptian maid was caught in. Perhaps readers were not surprised by this divine revelation to Hagar, rather understood that by virtue of God being the creator of humankind (cf. Hebrew creation traditions in Gen 2–3) he had the freedom to reveal himself and speak to any one, just as he spoke to the first couple and Abram; although in a way Eve and Sarai witnessed the divine revelations, readers would have realized that this was the first instance of God revealing himself to a woman in a direct way.

2.5.5 Conclusion

The angel of YHWH found Hagar by the spring of waters in the desert (vv. 7–8); initiated the conversation and instructed her to go back to Sarai; to give the name Ishmael to her son (vv. 9–12).

---

68. Cf. von Rad, *Genesis*, 189; Driver, *Genesis*, 183; L. A. Turner, *Genesis* (Sheffield: Sheffield Academic Press, 2000), 79. Cf. Gen 32:31; Judg 13:20–22.

Although the writer introduced the divine person as the angel of YHWH, at the end of the passage Hagar expresses that it was God who spoke to her. It seems as though God revealed something of himself to Hagar just as he turned back to leave that place, in such a way that she recognized him as God. After the realization that it was God whom she saw, Hagar acknowledged that "she saw the God who saw her" (v. 13) and named the place where she had the divine encounter Beer Lahai Roi "the well of him (the living one) who sees me" (v. 14). Hagar did not express any fear of death for seeing God; rather her words reflect awe and joyous surprise at the fact that she saw the one who saw her.

2.6 Genesis 17:1–5: YHWH Appears

2.6.1 Canonical Context

As seen in the previous chapter (Gen 16), instead of waiting for the fulfillment of YHWH's promises for a child through Sarai, Abram fathered Ishmael through Hagar. At the end of the previous chapter the writer mentioned that Abram was eighty-six years old when Ishmael was born (16:16), and the present text (17:1) begins with mention of his age.

2.6.2 Divine Self-Revelation and Communication

Genesis 17:1–5 relates that when Abram was ninety-nine years old, YHWH appeared to Abram and said, "I am God Almighty (אני־אל שדי); walk before me (התהלך לפני) and be blameless (or upright); I will make my covenant between me and you, and will multiply you exceedingly". When Abram fell on his face, God continued to speak to him, saying that Abram would be a father of many nations; and then changed the name Abram to Abraham and that he would be father of many nations (17:1–5).[69]

The repetition of the age of Abraham and Sarah (cf. 16:16) seems intentional as though to convey that thirteen years have gone by since Ishmael's birth; that the divine promise of an offspring to Abram and Sarai is not

---

69. Some other significant aspects surrounding this text are establishment of the everlasting covenant with Abram (7–11); circumcision introduced and its importance explained (10–14).

yet fulfilled; and that it is in this complex situation that YHWH appears to Abram with an assertion אני־אל שדי"I am God Almighty". This name אל שדי "God Almighty", as K. Koch observes, is mostly associated with the blessing and increase of offspring;[70] the use of the verb ברך in association with אל שדי emphasizes the blessing of offspring. The reason why YHWH identifies himself as אל שדי "the Almighty" is perhaps to reassure Abram that "all powerful and Almighty"[71] God is able to give him a child through Sarai despite their old age.[72]

It is significant that the writer brings in YHWH's command to Abram before the confirmation of the covenant: התהלך לפני והיה תמים "walk before me, and be blameless". To be תמים (adjective) is to be "perfect/blameless"[73] and "upright".[74] Readers would be aware that Noah was described as just and perfect (צדיק תמים) in his generation and that he walked (התהלך) with God (6:9). Both literary and conceptual similarity is seen between these two texts. While תמים may not mean moral perfection, when used with people, it seems to involve one's relationship with God.[75] The second imperative והיה תמים may include a consequence that follows from the first imperative התהלך. The text stresses that Abram is ordered to live a blameless life in the consciousness of being לפני יהוה "in the presence of YHWH" continually,[76] in contrast to the hiding of the first couple who hid themselves "from before YHWH" (מפני יהוה: 3:8–10), in order to maintain a relationship with God; and Nötscher observes that seeing פני־יהוה "face of YHWH" is associated with an upright walk (17:1).[77]

---

70. K. Koch, "Saddaj . . .", *VT* 26 (1976), 309–316. Cf. Gen 28:3; 35:11; 43:14; 48:3.
71. LXX identifies שדי with παντοκράτωρ (Job 22:25) that has the idea of God's power and ability, hence Almighty.
72. W. Brueggemann, "Genesis 17:1–22". *Int* 45 (1991), 55.
73. LXX translates תמים Abraham's תמים here with ἄμεμπτος "blameless". Noah's תמים with τέλειος (Gen 6:9) "perfection".
74. Cf. K. Koch, "תמם", *TLOT*, 1428.
75. Von Rad, *Genesis*, 192; also J. E. Hartley, *Genesis* (Peabody: Hendrickson, 2000), 169–170; O. P. Robertson. *The Christ of the Covenants* (Grand Rapids: Baker Book House, 1980), 127.
76. The verb התהלך (hithpael) emphasizes the continuity of action. Cf. BDB, 236.
77. Nötscher, *Angesicht*, 116–119.

The Self-Revelations of YHWH/God in Genesis

Interestingly, in this text, where לפני "before/in front of" is employed, it is stated that "YHWH appeared to Abram" (ירא יהוה) and said . . . לפני התהלך "walk 'before me' (לְפָנַי) continually", והיה תמים "and be blameless". Does לפני "before me" with the verb הלך "to walk" connote a literal sense? The repeated use of the personal assertions and the personal/possessive pronouns used in the text involving YHWH,[78] and the direct speech indicate that YHWH was present with Abram (ירא יהוה); and that Abram fell על־פניו "on his face"[79] (v. 3) signifies that the anthropomorphic person of YHWH was present with him. The specific mention made in the text, that after he finished talking with Abraham, YHWH "went up" (ויעל אלהים)[80] from him (17:22), confirms that YHWH was present with Abraham earlier in a literal sense. In light of this, when YHWH tells Abram "walk לפני 'before me'", one can assume that YHWH was believed to be physically present with Abraham at that point, and that the phrase לפני exhibits a literal sense and the noun פנים "face" retains its nominal sense.

However, the sense in which לפני is used with the verb התהלך (walk continually)[81] and the adjective תמים (uprightly) is not straightforward, and one cannot assume that YHWH would continue to be with Abram on the earth, given that the writer made it clear that YHWH went up from Abraham (v. 22); nor can one think that the verb התהלך involves a literal walk (with two feet). Does this imperative "walk upright before me continually" mean "in the view/estimation of" YHWH in a non-literal sense? In order to discern how the Israelite readers would have understood the imperative "walk before me continually", one may refer to (canonically) earlier texts for the clues.

---

78. There are nine occurrences in these few verses: "I am God Almighty"; "walk before me"; "I will make"; "my covenant"; "between me and you"; "I will multiply you"; "as for me"; "my covenant is with you"; "I have made you".

79. The phrase על־פניו normally involves the persons/object before whom one falls. For example, Joseph's brothers יפלו לפניו ארצה "fell before him on the ground" (Gen 44:14; cf. 17:17; Josh 5:14).

80. See Gen 11:5 where it is said that YHWH "came down to see (ירד יהוה לראת) the city (cf. v. 7).

81. The verb התהלך (hithpael) emphasizes the continuity of action. See BDB, 236.

Earlier in Genesis, it is said that YHWH saw (וירא יהוה)[82] that the wickedness of humankind was great on the earth and that their thoughts were evil continually (6:5); later on, the writer brings in the aspect of YHWH/God as the creator, in that he was grieved that he made humankind (כי־עשה את־האדם) on the earth (v. 6); he would destroy humankind whom he created (lit. אשר־בראתי: v. 7). The writer understands that Noah walked before God (את־האלהים התהלך)[83] תמים "blameless" (vv. 8–9); he also informs his readers that God said (יאמר אלהים) to Noah, "I have seen (ראיתי) that you are (צדיק)[84] righteous (לְפָנַי) 'before me'" (7:1); it seems that God watched Noah's life and decided to save him. The verb הלך is not always used in terms of walking in a normal sense, and it also has an association with keeping God's ways;[85] since the verb התהלך emphasizes the continuity of an action, one may assume that הלך here means obedience to God's commands continuously.

These abovementioned texts convey that God sees (ראה) what happens on the earth—both evil and righteousness are לפני האלהים "before God" (6:11), and accordingly, he decides to judge or save (7:4, 12–24). Readers would also recall that they read earlier that YHWH came down to see (וירד יהוה לראת) the tower built by men, assessed the situation scattered the people abroad from the tower they built (11:5–8). It seems that God is understood as the one, who involves himself in the affairs of the humankind in a real sense, in that God comes to speak to Noah; sees the city and the tower, which the sons of men built (6:13; 7:1; 8:15; 11:5). Since the Israelite traditions believed their God to be the creator of the heaven and earth, it would not be difficult for them to believe that the whole earth is before him.[86]

These texts also give evidence for an understanding that God sees what happens on the earth and that the phrase לפני יהוה/אלהים (before YHWH/

---

82. It appears that he saw from heaven.
83. Earlier in Genesis (5:22, 24), Enoch is said to have walked (התהלך) before/with God (את־אלהים), and one can assume that Enoch walked in the consciousness of God.
84. The adjectives צדיק and תמים are often used to mean the same (e.g. Gen 6:9; cf. Prov 11:5).
85. Cf. 1 Kgs 3:14a (תלך בדרכי); Ps 119:1 (אשרי תמימי־דרך ההלכים בתורת יהוה).
86. Gen 1:1; 14:19, 22; 2 Kgs 19:15; 2 Chr 2:11; Pss 115:15; 124:8; 134:3; Acts 4:24; Rev 14:7.

God) also has the connotation that YHWH estimates/assesses the life and actions of the persons on the earth, and that he acts accordingly. One may assume that the Israelite readers would understand the command to Abraham in a similar fashion, in that he is expected to live uprightly לפני יהוה "before YHWH" continually (17:1) in the sense that he should live in the consciousness of being seen/watched by God from heaven;[87] since Abraham's upright walk involves his actions and their consequences,[88] they should be pleasing[89] to YHWH.

It seems, then, that the writer's use of לפני here is not meant to be a pure preposition, rather to convey to his readers that Abraham was expected to walk upright in the view of YHWH/God. If one thinks that לפני "before me" here means "in the sight of YHWH" in a non-literal/abstract sense, it does not seem to make sense in this context, in that when YHWH said to Abraham התהלך לפני "walk before me (continually)", he was present there with Abram; and also that the earlier traditions insist that YHWH/God sees the activities of humankind on earth. Therefore, one may argue that while לפני with התהלך may not mean walking with feet in a literal sense, it cannot be treated as metaphorical either, since God would be watching Abraham's life on earth, and in that sense Abraham's walk was still לפני יהוה "before YHWH"[90] (17:1) and Abraham's walk, in terms of his life and actions on the earth, would still be watched by YHWH; and this shows that while לפני ("before me") has prepositional sense, פנים in the phrase לפני retains its literal/ nominal sense.

The use of the verb [91]נתן with ברית as the object instead of the more usual כרת may be because it gives the idea of setting in operation the

---

87. Cf. Gen 22:11, 15: the angel of YHWH called Abraham from heaven; Prov 5:21; 15:3: the eyes of YHWH (עיני יהוה) watch the evil and the good.
88. See Koch, "תמם", 1427.
89. LXX reads εὐηρέστησεν (pleasing) where the MT has התהלך.
90. See Gen 24:40, where Abraham reflects later in his life: יהוה אשר־התהלכתי לפניו "YHWH, before whom I walked continually; this perhaps includes his obedience to the divine command which was watched by God from heaven (cf. 22:15–18).
91. נתן is used only here in Genesis (cf. Num 25:12).

promises in the covenant.⁹² The usage of בריתי "my covenant" seems central⁹³ since it signifies YHWH as the initiator of a (covenantal) relationship with Abram; and it was also "everlasting" and expresses God's promise of the Land to Abram and to his descendants through him.⁹⁴ God himself changes the name of Abram to Abraham in accordance with the role Abraham (אברהם "father of a multitude") would play in future as father of many nations (המון גוים),⁹⁵ and the change of name seems to have a functional significance here. The writer's use of the particle את with שמך may be to emphasize⁹⁶ the negation that "his name will no longer be called Abram" (לא־יקרא עוד את־שמך אברם), and later שמך is used without את when it is used with the new name Abraham (v. 5); this may signify the functional significance attached to the new name Abraham, given that the name Abram is no more used in the (canonically) later Hebrew traditions.⁹⁷

2.6.3 The Mode of Self-Revelation, Human Recognition and Response

The verb here in 17:1 is (cf. 12:7) niphal of ראה (וירא) and signifies that YHWH lets himself be seen by Abram.⁹⁸

In response to the divine revelation, Abram does not respond verbally (15:2) but "falls on his face" (נפל used with על־פניו)⁹⁹ before the anthropo-

---

92. Keil and Delitzsch, *Pentateuch* 1, 223.

93. "My covenant" occurs in vv. 2, 4, 7, 9, 10, 13, 14, 19, 21 and "everlasting" in vv. 7, 13, 19.

94. For a study of comparison between the covenant in Gen 15 and 17, see Alexander, *Paradise*, 48–52; P. R. Williamson, *Abraham, Israel and the Nations* (Sheffield: Sheffield Academic Press, 2000), 78–120. Cf. D. L. Peterson, ed., *Genesis* (Nashville: Abingdon Press, 1994), 458.

95. For the universal purpose of the covenant, see P. R. Williamson, *Sealed with an Oath* (Nottingham: Intervarsity Press, 2007), 44–52.

96. Normally, the particle את emphasizes the word attached to it.

97. The only two other occasions in which the name Abram appears (1 Chr 1:27; Neh 9:7) is only as a reference to the change of the name Abram to Abraham. However, in Gen 32:29 only שמך is used without the particle את and the name Jacob was still in use as a proper noun. See chapter 3, fn. 29, 79.

98. The verb ראה in niphal has the reflexive sense, and God is the subject and the agent of revelation. Cf. 18:1; 26:2, 24; 35:9.

99. The LXX here has ἔπεσεν "fell".

morphic person of YHWH in reverence.[100] The fact that the writer mentions clearly that "God went up"[101] (17:22) from Abraham implies that YHWH was present with Abraham and that Abraham had seen YHWH visually. The appearance of the divine person was very likely in human form, and the language spoken was understood by Abram. God took the initiative to reveal himself and to communicate his purposes. Abram does not express any fear (of death) on seeing YHWH (אל שדי); rather he expresses reverence by bowing before him.

2.6.4 The Function/Significance of Divine Revelation
This text on God's revelation could have played a significant role in ancient Israel in communicating the importance of the covenant made between YHWH and Abram and that Abram was called to be a blessing to the nations of the earth;[102] that the gesture of "falling on (one's) face" indicated that when God becomes real in one's experience, it leads to worship in a humble attitude; that the covenant was to be maintained by one's relationship with God, which includes living an upright life in the consciousness of God's presence; and that the covenant had the provision for everyone to enter into a relationship with God.

2.6.5 Conclusion
The study of Genesis 17:1–4 shows that YHWH appeared to Abram with an assertion "I am God Almighty" and Abram was commanded to live uprightly in God-consciousness. When YHWH appeared to Abram and says, "I am God Almighty . . ." (17:1), the speech was direct and might even be "face-to-face"; here too God was believed to be physically present in human form.

---

100. See S. E. Loewenstamm, "Prostration from Afar in Ugaritic, Accadian and Hebrew", *BASOR* 188 (1967), 41; Westermann, *Genesis 12–36*, 267; Driver, *Genesis*, 185; J.H. Hertz, ed. *The Pentateuch and Haftorahs* (London: Soncino Press, 1937), 18.

101. Hebrew traditions seemed to have perceived God as transcendent and also immanent.

102. Not only to the Israelites and Ishmaelites but to all the peoples, as listed in Gen 25:2–4. Cf. Driver, *Genesis*, 186. Hertz, *Pentateuch*, 18. See also Gen 12:2, 3; 15:5, 17–20; 17:7–8, 21.

God's covenant was made with Abraham for the sake of many nations. The fulfillment of the divine promise of an offspring to Abraham was reiterated and an everlasting covenant was established between God and Abraham and his descendants (v. 7). The changing of names of Abram to Abraham and Sarai to Sarah and the act of circumcision are other features surrounding the divine self-revelations in this text. Here again the divine revelation seemed to take place in human form, and the language spoken was human. That Abram fell upon his face (עַל־פָּנָיו), which is normally done in front of a visible person, and that God continued to speak to him, confirms that YHWH was understood as being present with Abram in human form, and possibly Abraham saw YHWH (v. 3) literally. It is not clear where YHWH came from, but the text says that YHWH/God "went up" (עלה: v. 22) after he spoke to Abraham, confirming that he was understood physically present with Abraham. In addition to this, the specific mention made in the text that "God went up" implies that YHWH transcends his human form while going up.

2.7 Genesis 18:1–8; 16–22: God Eats Food

2.7.1 Canonical Context
The previous text has portrayed that YHWH appeared to Abram and confirmed that he would establish his covenant with Isaac (17:21). Once again, YHWH appears to Abraham, who was still childless.

2.7.2 Divine Self-Revelation and Communication
Genesis 18:1–8; 16–22 relates that when Abraham sat at the oaks of Mamre, at the entrance of the tent door during the day, he saw three men standing nearby (who were supposed to be travellers), bowed himself (וישתחו) to the ground (before him), and set before them (לפניהם) food which they ate (18:1–8).[103] When Abraham walked with them to see them on their way, YHWH revealed that Sodom and Gomorrah's sin was great and that

---

103. Giving hospitality to strangers is practiced in several eastern cultures (e.g. India) even now.

he would go down to see; while the other two men went toward Sodom, Abraham "stood 'before YHWH'" (16–22).

The text here has a very vivid anthropomorphic description of YHWH, and the divine appearance in this text is somewhat different from the previous traditions in terms of divine appearance and activity. It is significant that the writer in his introductory sentence says that YHWH appeared to Abraham (v. 1), but the description given is that it was three men who stood by; and Abraham bows himself to the ground (וישתחו), which is normally done in front of visible persons.[104]

In light of the textual evidence, one may assume that when YHWH appeared to Abraham, along with two other persons,[105] Abraham set food לפניהם "before them". This indicates that YHWH and the other two were physically present with Abraham, and that לפני with the pronominal suffix (לפניהם) is used in a literal sense; later on, when it is said that Abraham עמד לפני יהוה "stood before YHWH" (18:22), the phrase לפני with the verb עמד is also used in a literal sense, as Abraham was understood standing before the person of YHWH,[106] who appeared to him in a human form; and to indicate where Abraham stood previously with YHWH, את־פני יהוה is used (19:27), signifying the nearness of YHWH. The phrase לפני "before" in these texts can only be interpreted literally,[107] and the noun פנים "face" (in לפני and לפניהם) has not lost its nominal sense.

This is the first instance in Genesis where the anthropomorphic person of YHWH is said to have eaten food. Although the writer informs his readers in the very beginning that YHWH appeared to Abraham, he has no hesitation in telling them that YHWH ate food just like any normal

---

104. It is generally observed that the act of "bowing before" someone is done out of respect in front of a visible person in Eastern cultures.

105. Although the text here does not clearly portray, one can assume that YHWH was one of the three persons who appeared to Abraham. See 18:1–2, 10, 13–14, 17–22, 33.

106. According to Tiqqune sopherim, originally Gen 18:22 read: "but YHWH remained standing before Abraham"; but since the idiom "to stand before someone" can mean "to stand in service before someone" (e.g. Gen 41:46), it was considered inappropriate and was changed to the present form. See E. Tov, *Textual Criticism of the Hebrew Bible* (Minneapolis: Fortress Press, 1992), 66; E. Würthwein, *The Text and the Old Testament* (Eerdmans: Grand Rapids, 1995), 17–18.

107. Cf. It is only here in Gen 18:16–22 that Nötscher (*Angesicht*, 87) locates לפני־יהוה in a theophany.

human.¹⁰⁸ Westermann insists that this event where YHWH ate human food should not be treated as an appearance of God,¹⁰⁹ but this is a key text to help understand the realism of the anthropomorphic appearance of YHWH and how differently self-revelations of YHWH/God were understood to be operative in ancient Israel. Interestingly, as human as he appeared, YHWH revealed Sarah's inner thoughts, and assured her that she would surely have a son (vv. 10–15).

The statement that YHWH knew Abraham (ידעתיו in v. 19) seems to refer to the close relationship established between YHWH and Abraham during the earlier revelations. YHWH declares that the outcry against Sodom and Gomorrah is great and that their sin is very great (וחטאתם כי כבדה מאד).¹¹⁰ Ironically however, the reason why YHWH communicates to Abraham his purpose of destroying Sodom and Gomorrah is that all the nations would be blessed by him (v. 18). These two aspects, namely, the divine assertion to make Abraham a blessing to the nations and the destruction of Sodom seem contradictory.¹¹¹ Nevertheless, one may understand that the divine blessing offered to the nations through Abraham is not associated with wickedness and sin but with a righteous (cf. 15:4–6) and blameless (cf. 17:1) life.

2.7.3 The Mode of Self-Revelation, Human Recognition, and Response

A feature of this revelation is that three figures appear at the same time, and disguised as though they were on their journey.¹¹²

Undoubtedly, this incident shows that Abraham's guests appeared in human bodily form, given that Abraham regarded them as the ordinary travellers who needed food and rest, and this implies that even YHWH/God appeared in a body which is normal to human beings; the Hebrew

---

108. Cf. von Rad, *Genesis*, 202.
109. Westermann, *Genesis*, 275.
110. Similar judgement was already pronounced on the wickedness of the people that led to the flood. The reason for the destruction of Sodom was explained (18:16–22).
111. Cf. J. Stephen, *Theophany: Close encounters with the Son of God* (Surrey: Day One Publications, 1998), 82.
112. On the appearance of three persons together, see von Rad, *Genesis*, 201.

tradition understands that they all ate normal (human) food, though there is no way of explaining this phenomenon on a naturalistic level.[113] One wonders if the writer had any polemical purpose in describing so vividly how YHWH ate food that he wanted to remove any negative connotations associated with human body.[114]

Contrary to the idea of audience, the writer insists that it was YHWH who appeared to Abraham, and that it was Abraham who took the initiative to invite them, as though they were the travellers who needed some rest. It is not clear at what point Abraham recognized one of his guests was YHWH but it may be when YHWH initiated the conversation with Sarah and assured her of the fulfillment of his promise for a son.[115] Although the expression "face-to-face" פנים אל פנים is not used in this theophany, in effect it is possible that YHWH spoke with Abraham "face-to-face",[116] given that Abraham waited upon his divine guests during the meal, walked with them (הלך עמם: v. 16) and stood before YHWH (עמד לפני יהוה: v. 22). One can see that עמד לפני "standing before YHWH" does not refer to having an *Audienz* before the king, as Nötscher insists;[117] rather, it refers here to standing before the anthropomorphized person of YHWH. Abraham does not express any fear of death for seeing YHWH even after the direct contact with him, but rather his conversation with YHWH has a friendly tone. Although the text does not say where he came from, it mentions that YHWH went away (v. 33: וילך יהוה). It seems that the Hebrew traditions understood YHWH/God both as transcendent and immanent.[118]

---

113. Cf. H. M. Morris, *The Genesis Record* (Grand Rapids: Baker Book House, 1976), 339.

114. It is generally observed that the body is treated unimportant in certain eastern religions (e.g. in some traditions in Hinduism); in one Islamic group, people beat their bodies to an extent of bleeding. One wonders if this kind of notion was there in the ANE, and that this incident, where YHWH was supposed to have eaten food may have meant to show that the body was not sinful.

115. Cf. Driver, *Genesis*, 191; see also vv. 10, 13, 17–22; 21.

116. Cf. I. M. Duguid. *Living in the Gap Between Promise and Reality* (New Jersey: P&R Publishing Company, 1999), 86.

117. See chapter 1, 6; Nötscher, *Angesicht*, 53–57, 87.

118. Given that Gen 19:24 tells that YHWH rained fire and sulphur on Sodom and Gomorrah from heaven, and at the same time 18:1–22 understood that YHWH appeared in a human body and ate food.

2.7.4 The Function/Significance of Divine Revelation

This tradition may have played a very significant role in helping ancient Israel understand that God, who they believed is the creator of humankind, who walked and talked in the garden, also appeared to Abraham in human guise and could disguise himself to the extent that he even ate food. That YHWH assured Sarah that she would surely have a son (vv. 10–15) would have helped them to understand the faithfulness of God, in terms of fulfilling his promise to Abraham and Sarah.

2.7.5 Conclusion

Genesis 18:1–22 has shown how YHWH appeared to Abraham along with two other (divine) persons near the tent of Abraham during the day in human disguise; they were understood as ordinary travellers, who needed food and rest (vv. 1–7), and when Abraham offered food to them, they ate it (v. 8). YHWH was ascribed more human characteristic features in this text than in the previous texts studied, in that he (and other divine persons) ate the human food offered to him by Abraham and Sarah (vv. 5–8). It is not clear, however, if ancient Israel understood YHWH as having flesh and blood in his bodily appearance;[119] but he is explicitly depicted as a human being. When Abraham gave them food, walked with them (v. 16) and stood "before YHWH" (v. 22), it is very likely that YHWH was present in human form and undoubtedly, Abraham saw him (even "face-to-face").

The practical aspects associated with this divine revelation, such as the reassurance to Sarah of her offspring and the prediction of the destruction of Sodom and Gomorrah seem to indicate the reality of the appearance of the anthropomorphic person in this text. The text clearly states that it was YHWH who appeared (v. 1); it was YHWH who came down because of the sin of Sodom (18:20); finally, having finished speaking with Abraham (vv. 20–32), YHWH went (וילך יהוה) away (cf. v. 33). All these factors confirm the possibility that when YHWH appeared to Abraham in a human body, he saw YHWH literally (may even be "face-to-face").

---

119. See below,

2.8 Genesis 28:12–22: God/YHWH Stands and Speaks

2.8.1 Canonical Context

According to Genesis 25:12–22, YHWH told Rebekah that the elder son would serve the younger one. Later in life, whether it was by deceit and supplanting[120] or in accordance with YHWH's precedence of Jacob over Esau, Jacob managed to get Esau's birthright of the first son (25:29–34) and receive the blessing from his father (27:4–36).[121] As a consequence, Jacob had to leave Canaan to go to Paddan-Aram to escape from Esau (27:41); when he was on his journey, he stayed in a certain place all night, and he took a stone, put it under his head and slept. It was that night that Jacob had a dream (28:10–12a).

2.8.2 Divine Self-Revelation and Communication

According to the text, in the night dream (vision) Jacob saw (הנה) a ladder (סלם) set between the earth and heaven, and the angels of God were ascending and descending on it (v. 12b); and YHWH stood above it and said, "I am YHWH the God of Abraham your father and the God of Isaac" (v. 13). YHWH reiterated his promises to Jacob that he would give him the Land and descendants, and that in his descendants all the families of the earth would be blessed (v. 14). YHWH also promised Jacob that he would be with him (אנכי עמך) wherever he went and would bring him back to Canaan (v. 15). Jacob woke up expressing his amazement over that place (vv. 16–17), and he took the stone (אבן) that was put under his head, set it up as a pillar (מצבה) and poured oil on top of it and called that place בית־אל "Bethel/ the house of God" (vv. 19–22).

The ladder in Jacob's dream is seen connecting earth and heaven, and God is standing on it and is visible. Whatever the significance of the ladder

---

120. It is said that Jacob went to Isaac with deceit (27:35: במרמה) and supplanted Esau twice (27:36: ויעקבני); and Jacob also questions Laban, "Why have you deceived me? (29:25: ולמה רמיתני).

121. Isaac's blessings to Jacob were in line with YHWH's blessings to Abraham (Gen 12:2–3; 27:29).

in its cultural context may be,[122] the canonical context reveals that YHWH/God appeared to Jacob in a peculiar vision that night and reminded him of the promises he made earlier to Abraham. The readers, who were aware that the promise of descendants and the Land was made earlier to Abraham,[123] would now realize that Jacob was one of the descendants of Abraham who would inherit that promise. By giving the details of YHWH's speech in that dream, the writer seems to stress that the dream-vision is no less important than the non-dream encounters and that it has the same significance, particularly in terms of communicating the message.

2.8.3 The Mode of Self-Revelation, Human Recognition and Response

Since YHWH/God introduces himself directly while addressing Jacob in the phrase "I am YHWH" and that YHWH is described standing, these two factors seem to indicate that even in that dream-vision YHWH's appearance was in human form. Since the ladder in this "dream revelation" is set between the earth and heaven, it probably signified the communication between the transcendent God from heaven and Jacob on earth. The language spoken by YHWH was understood by Jacob and the communication seemed to be at human level. The divine appearance was in human form but it is not clear if the description, YHWH "stood above" the ladder, meant that he spoke from (near) heaven (12b).

In terms of Jacob's response to his vision, it is noteworthy that the text tells that Jacob woke up from his sleep recognizing the presence of God in that place (v. 16); that Jacob was afraid (ויירא) and exclaimed that it was an awesome place (מה־נורא) and called that place "the house of God" (בית אלהים) and the gate of heaven (שער השמים: v. 17). Nötscher argues that Jacob only heard YHWH/God speaking to him and that Jacob did

---

122. See M. Oblath, "'To Sleep, Perchance to Dream': What Jacob Saw at Bethel (Genesis 28:10–22)", *JSOT* 95 (2001), 117–126. Assuming that the ladder is in keeping with ANE mythology, Oblath proposes סלם as an enclosed chamber or tunnel.

123. These include the promise of the land, descendants, and the future blessings to all the families of the earth (28:13–14; cf. vv. 1–4). Cf. Gen 12:1–4; 7–8; 15:1–21; 16:7–14; 17:1–4; 18:1–2, 9–33.

not see him,¹²⁴ but it is possible to have a clear vision even in the dreams, as Barr suggests.¹²⁵

It may be argued that Jacob saw YHWH speaking to him even in that dream vision, and so when he woke up he felt amazed and was afraid. However, it did not seem that Jacob was afraid of death after seeing God. Both qal (ויירא) and niphal (נורא) forms of the verb ירא express his amazement over the vision¹²⁶ and perhaps suggest that it was his first experience of a divine revelation. Jacob's response probably involved, as R. Otto suggests, a kind of "fear" (ירא) produced by the presence of the numinous, which becomes an attraction, leading to comfort.¹²⁷ This seems the case with Jacob, as he desired the divine presence in his future (v. 20).

When Jacob woke up in the morning he took the stone that was placed under his head and set it up as a pillar and poured oil on it and named that place בית־אל "the house of God" (vv. 17–19). Sommer argues for the possibility of this stone being endowed with life after Jacob anointed it with oil.¹²⁸ However, the text insists that by making אבן (simple stone) as a מצבה (pillar) and calling the place as בית אלהים, Jacob meant it to be a memorable sign of seeing God in his dream vision in the night, and this indicates the significance given even to a dream vision in ancient Israel.

2.8.4 The Function/Significance of Divine Revelation

The description that YHWH/God stood in the dream vision and repetition of the promises of the Land and descendants (13–14) would have helped readers to understand that the significance attached to the dream

---

124. Nötscher, *Angesicht*, 25–31.

125. See Barr, "Theophany", 33, for his arguments on the possibility of having clear visions in dreams.

126. The verb ירא in most of the divine confrontations seem to express reverence, amazement and surprise in a positive sense. See P. Satyavani, *Israelite Understanding of ירא in the Hebrew Bible and its Implications for Worship*. M.Th. diss. (Senate of Serampore, 1999).

127. R. Otto, *The Idea of the Holy* (London: Oxford University Press, 1925), 26–55. Using the terms "*mysterium tremendum et fascinans*", Otto explains how fear of the Holy God can lead to fascination.

128. Sommer, *Bodies*, 49–50. His argument is based on ANE religious literature. Putting a stone-pillar in a place of divine confrontation for a memory is also found in India even now.

vision was similar to the "divine-manifestations" (i.e. outside the visions) in terms of the visibility and divine communication; and the identification of YHWH as "the God of Abraham and the God of Isaac" would have helped them to understand the continuity in terms of the divine revelations to the fathers (13–14).[129]

2.8.5 Conclusion

When Jacob was on his way to Paddan-Aram, YHWH/God revealed himself to him from heaven by means of the ladder. The features in the divine manifestation in this dream vision are similar to the regular (non-dream) manifestations in terms of directness and verbal communication. The self-identification of YHWH as "the God of Abraham and the God of Isaac", repetition of the promises of the Land and descendants given to Abraham; and the promise for his continued presence in future (13–15) seem to be an indication that the "divine revelation" even in this dream vision signified authenticity.[130] Both visual and audible aspects of the anthropomorphic figure in this vision occurred simultaneously; it is presumed that Jacob saw YHWH speaking to him in the dream vision, given that Jacob was taken by fear (ויירא) after his vision. In memory of his vision in the dream, Jacob set up a stone-pillar and called the place בית־אל "the house of God".

2.9 Concluding Remarks

In light of the study of the seven selected texts in Genesis, a few overall comments may be made. The Hebrew texts/traditions give an understanding of how ancient Israel perceived their God to be the creator of humankind; he created them in his image so that there could be a relationship with humans. Ancient Israel believed that YHWH/God revealed himself to different people such as Adam (Eve), Abraham (Sarah), Hagar and Jacob. They believed that their creator walked in the garden, conversed with the first humans; appeared in human form, and initiated an everlasting covenant of relationship

---

129. Cf. Clines, *Themes*, 35, 111–112; Peterson, *Genesis*, 566.
130. Cf. von Rad, *Genesis*, 180–181.

with Abraham in order to bless him and his descendants. In return, a life of uprightness and blamelessness is expected from the people. The Hebrew writer describes how God/YHWH revealed himself in different modes: directly, in dreams and in visions. He revealed himself to Hagar, first as a man, and then revealed something of himself so that she identified God as God.

Contrary to Baudissin's assumption that theophanies and visions should be associated with the places of rituals,[131] the texts indicate that the divine revelations are seen as not restricted to a particular sacred or ritual place but took place during travels (Abraham, Hagar and Jacob), and by either day or night (Adam and Jacob). It is always God who took initiative and chose the place and time to reveal himself, and always with a purpose. There is no fear of death expressed in these texts; and Adam and Eve are shown having hidden themselves in fear (3:8), because of the consciousness of being disobedient to God's command. Although there is no uniformity in the divine manifestations, ancient Israel never seemed to have doubted the variety of divine manifestations, nor did the writers cease to describe YHWH in anthropomorphic terms; they seemed to have given a permanent value to the messages communicated during these divine revelations so that the subsequent generations also believed in a revealing God.

The study of these traditions/texts in Genesis has shown that ancient Israel perceived that the appearance of YHWH/God was in human bodily form, and that God was physically present when he spoke with different people. The possibility of seeing the "face" of YHWH/God during the encounters is established. These texts have shown that ancient Israel understood God both as the transcendent (cf. Gen 11:5; 21:17; 22:11; 24:7) and the immanent. It seems that it was only through these self-revelations that God the creator was made real to people. In all these texts, YHWH/God is described as coming down to meet with and communicate to the people (in human bodily form). One begins to sense that the motif "the face of YHWH/God" came to be used in the context of these divine "self-revelations".

It is against this background that the motif "seeing the face of God" will be studied in Genesis 32:23–31 in the next chapter.

---

131. See chapter 1, 4; Baudissin, "Gott schauen", 198–203.

CHAPTER 3

"I Saw God 'Face-to-Face' and My Life is Rescued": Genesis 32:25–32

3.1 Introduction

The purpose of this chapter is to study Genesis 32:25–32, where the verb ראה "to see" occurs in association with פנים "face" and אלהים "God". The expression פנים אל־פנים "face-to-face" occurs for the first time here in the context of the divine self-revelations in the Pentateuch. The text under study says that a "man" came and wrestled with Jacob when he was alone, and there was a conflict between them. However, Jacob claims: ראיתי אלהים פנים אל־פנים ותנצל נפשי "I saw God 'face-to-face', and my life is saved". Jacob's affirmation that his "life was saved" seems to have a close link with his claim that he saw God "face-to-face".

In light of the "divine revelations" which took place in "human form" in the Genesis traditions, as studied in the previous chapter, one could argue that the "man" who wrestled with Jacob is God himself in the disguise of "man"; and that Jacob's claim to have seen God implies physicality/corporeality. However, some scholars, such as Terrien, for example, argue that this expression פנים אל־פנים "face-to-face" is only an idiom and that "it should not be construed as referring literally to visual perception";[1] other scholars also interpret Jacob's claim of "seeing God" as a dream or an

---

1. Terrien, *Elusive Presence*, 90.

allegory.² Gunkel, interpreting the text from a form-critical perspective, concludes that the "man" was a demon³ and reconstructs this Hebrew tradition accordingly.

The main purpose of this chapter, then, is to identify the "man" in question and to explore whether the expression פנים אל־פנים "face-to-face" in Jacob's statement is an idiom, or if it involves the physicality/corporeality of God and a literal "seeing"; and to find in what sense Jacob is rescued. In order to understand these aspects, this text (Gen 32:25–32) will be studied within the context of the "self-revelations of YHWH/God".⁴ An attempt will be made to discern how the readers in ancient Israel would have understood this motif in light of their understanding of previous traditions. The text will be studied in two main sections: 3.3.1 Conflict and Conversation between the Man and Jacob: vv. 25–27; 3.3.2 Jacob Sees God 'Face-to-Face' and His Life is Saved: vv. 31–32.

3.2 Canonical Context

The study of Genesis 28:12–22 in the previous chapter has shown that when Jacob was journeying from Canaan towards Paddan-Aram, YHWH/God has appeared in a dream and assured him of his presence (28:12–22), and that after twenty years of his stay at Paddan-Aram (31:38, 41), YHWH guided Jacob to return to Canaan and assured him of his presence (31:3, 11–13, 24, 29). There is no textual evidence that God appeared to Jacob during his return journey from Paddan-Aram to Canaan; although the angels of God met him on his way, there was no verbal communication (32:2–3). Readers would remember that it was the fear of Esau that drove Jacob to Paddan-Aram (27:41; 28:5), and even now on his return journey,

---

2. For example, J. Skinner, *Genesis* (Edinburgh: T. & T. Clark, 1956), 410.
3. Gunkel, *Genesis*, 349–352.
4. As stated in chapter 1, in terms of the inter-textuality, only those texts which are prior to Genesis 32:23–31 will be referred to. For a comparative study of Gen 32:23–31 with parallel texts, Exod 4:24–26; Judg 6:11–22; 13:6–22 and Hosea 12:4–5, 13, see Satyavani, *Face of God*, 24, 30–39.

he feared that Esau would attack him and his family, as his prayer indicates (32:12).

One can assume that Jacob at the river Jabbok (יבק) is in a fearful situation, when the incident that is described in Genesis 32:25–32 takes place. The placement of the text here seems to fit well, as it helps to understand Jacob's struggle with the fear of Esau even during his re-entry into Canaan. Scholars are divided on the question of literary and thematic unity,[5] but the text does seem to exhibit a definite thematic affinity with the previous traditions; the term פנים that was used earlier (32:4, 6, 9, 14, 21) is also employed here (32:31: פנים אל־פנים) and the fear of Esau (27:41) comes back (32:12).

3.3 Exegetical Study of Genesis 32:25–32

3.3.1 Conflict and Conversation between the Man and Jacob: vv. 25–27

According to the text, having made his family cross the river Jabbok, Jacob stayed back alone that night; when he was alone, a "man" wrestled with him until dawn, and when the man saw that he could not overcome Jacob, he touched him by his hip, and Jacob's hip was benumbed. After Jacob's hip was benumbed, the man said, "Let me go, since the dawn is rising".[6] But Jacob answered, "I shall not let you go unless you bless me".

3.3.1.1 Jacob stays alone (v. 25)

For some reason, the writer wants his readers to know that Jacob stayed alone (לבדו)[7] that night when the man came to him. Is it possible to as-

---

5. Due to space limit in this work, scholarly arguments will not be discussed in detail. Gunkel (*Genesis*, 347–353) finds disunity in the text; those who find unity in the text are: A. Dillmann, *Genesis*. Vol. 1 (Edinburgh: T. & T. Clark, 1897), 277–279; Driver, *Genesis*, xx–xxii; J.L. McKenzie, "Jacob at Peniel: Gen 32, 24–32", CBQ 25 (1963), 71; von Rad, *Genesis*, 314–21; R. Barthes, *Structural Analysis and Biblical Exegesis* (Pittsburgh: Pickwick Press, 1974), 27–39; S. Frolov, "The Other Side of the Jabbok: Genesis 32 as a Fiasco of Patriarchy", *JSOT* 91 (2000), 47.

6. Perhaps dawn here denotes the time just before the sunrise.

7. בד which appears always with ל, expresses the idea of being "by oneself/alone". Cf. BDB, 94.

sume that Jacob is anticipating a revelation from God at this juncture? In the past, it was when Jacob was alone in the night that God spoke to him in a dream vision and assured him of his presence (28:12–16). One might assume that because of his desperate situation, Jacob stays alone that night in anticipation of another revelation of YHWH/God.

3.3.1.2 A man touches Jacob's hip (v. 26)

In the night a man (איש) comes to Jacob and wrestles with him. Presumably readers are aware that in Genesis traditions divine revelations took place at night in dreams (28:11–22),[8] but now they read that a direct (non-dream) confrontation takes place in the night between a man and Jacob. The verb אבק (to wrestle)[9] may not suggest a vigorous fight, but that there is some kind of conflict/clash between Jacob and the man in a physical sense. The reason given why the man touched Jacob's hip is that he could not overcome (יכל) Jacob. The verb יכל (v. 26a) is used earlier in the sense of overcoming a situation and achieving something in a conflicted situation.[10] One senses here that Jacob is aggressive towards the man, perhaps mistakenly suspecting him to be an enemy,[11] and presumably it is to take control of the situation (overcome) that the man touches (נגע) Jacob by his hip. By that touch Jacob's hip is "benumbed" (v. 26b).[12]

In light of his form-critical assumptions, Gunkel suggests that the man in view is a river demon, and that the man here cannot be YHWH.[13] However, Gunkel's view has no support in the text, which makes it explicit that the man was God himself in human form (v. 31); and if it was a demon, Jacob would not have asked for any blessing from him. Westermann's

---

8. Cf. 20:3; 31:24.

9. The verb אבק occurs in the sense of a fight only here (אבק occurs in Deut 28:24 and Nah 1:3 in the sense of "dust"). NKJ and NRS read the verb as "wrestled".

10. The verb יכל may give the sense of gaining control over the other. See P. R. Gilchrist, "יכל", *TWOT* 1, 377. Cf. Gen 30:8 where Rachel says that she is able (יכלתי) in the sense of winning over her sister.

11. Since Jacob feared an attack from Esau, it is possible that he was taken by fright at the appearance of the man at that hour and attacked the man.

12. The verb נגע with preposition ב gives the idea of negative effect (Gen 3:3; Num 4:15), and in some sense the man's touch brought a negative effect (as Jacob limped).

13. Gunkel, *What Remains of the Old Testament* (London: Unwin Brothers, 1928), 165; also *The Folktale in the Old Testament* (Sheffield: Sheffield Academic Press, 1987), 85–86.

suggestion that Jacob has received a lethal blow[14] is unlikely, given that the text makes it clear that Jacob carried on walking though limping (v. 32); Gunkel's assumption that Jacob has dislocated the man's hip is also unlikely,[15] given that it is Jacob whose hip is dislocated.[16] Since the writer insists that the man touched Jacob and that Jacob's hip was benumbed, this is an indication that the man was physically present with Jacob in a literal sense.

3.3.1.3 Conversation between the man and Jacob (v. 27)

Once the conflict is over the conversation begins. The imperative שלחני "let me go" also gives the idea "send me away". This expression "let me go" was used earlier in Genesis (30:25) when Jacob asked Laban to let him leave that place.[17] The reason given why the man says "let me go" is עלה השחר that the dawn was "rising" (v. 27a). Gunkel's assumption that the man was a river demon, and that he was held in Jacob's hands and needed a release has no support in the text.[18] This expression "let me go" may have been used to let Jacob know that the man will not be there for a long time. Here the imperative שלחני also indicates that the presence of the man was real and the conversation between the man and Jacob was direct and face-to-face. The text gives no scope to associate the Hebrew noun שחר "dawn" with the Canaanite deity Dawn.[19] Earlier in Genesis (19:15) השחר with the verb עלה ("to ascend/go up") was used in the sense of dawning of the

---

14. Westermann, *Genesis 12–36*, 321.

15. See Gunkel, *Genesis*, 349; *Folktale*, 83–84.

16. Despite the subject-object confusion in the Hebrew text (v. 26), one can identify subject and object of the verbs (vv. 26b, 28–29, 31–32); and איש fits better as the subject of אבק.

17. שלחני (piel impv. of שלח) "let me go" may be taken as an eastern (literary) style of taking leave which is like saying, "I am leaving/send me away", a kind of habitual/customary departing word before leaving from a place of visit/stay. This literary style of taking leave is common in India.

18. Gunkel finds a parallel in *Odyssey* IV, where Menelaus held the old man of the sea, Proteus, until he received his knowledge. See Gunkel, *Genesis*, 347–353; also *What Remains*, 165.

19. Since in Ras Shamra texts šḥr is referred to as the name of a deity Dawn, some scholars see a parallel here. For an argument on this, see J. Mackay, "Helel and the Dawn-Goddess", *VT* 20 (1970), 451–464; L. Ruppert, "שחר", *TDOT* 14, 570–582.

morning. Even here השחר with עלה seems to simply indicate the time before sunrise (cf. השמש in v. 32 indicates morning).

Why did the man associate his departure with the dawning of the day (השחר with עלה)?[20] Some scholars, who identify the man with God, have suggested that the man wanted to withdraw before dawn for Jacob's protection lest he dies seeing him.[21] However, it may not be a dark night, given that the text gives the impression that both the man and Jacob were visible to each other. Furthermore, the writer has previously conveyed that YHWH/God appeared to Adam, Abraham and Hagar during the day, and supposedly they saw God in his anthropomorphic appearance.[22] The noun השחר with the verb עלה seems to function to express the intention of the man to leave that place soon.

After the man touches Jacob's hip, one would expect Jacob to be angry with him, but instead, in response to the man's asking "let me go", Jacob says, לא אשלחך "I will not let you go" and puts a condition כי אם־ברכתני "unless you bless me" (27b).[23] Intriguingly, Jacob asks for the blessing only after having been touched by the man. What makes Jacob think that the man has the ability to bless him? Could it be that Jacob perceived something divine in the man during that touch, and suspected him to be God himself and asked for the blessing?

Jacob was aware of the divine blessings to Abraham and Isaac, and in fact the blessings he received from his father Isaac were the repetition of the divine blessings given to Abraham (27:29; 28:3). Those blessings were given earlier to Abraham in the context of self-revelation (12:1–4); and Jacob himself was assured by YHWH/ God of the fulfillment of the promises in his dream-vision (28:14). Furthermore, within the immediate context of

---

20. Targums viewed that the man was an angel of God's praise who had to go before the morning in order to join the heavenly choir before God's throne. See J. W. Etheridge, *The Targums on the Pentateuch* (London: William Nichols, 1862), 272–273; P. I. Hershon, *Genesis with a Talmudical Commentary* (London: Bagster & Sons, 1883), 396. For form critical comments, see Gunkel, *Genesis*, 347–353; *Folktale*, 86; cf. Skinner, *Genesis*, 409.

21. For example, Hamilton, *Genesis*, 332; D. Kidner, *Genesis* (Illinois: Intervarsity Press, 1982), 170.

22. Gen 16:7–14; 18:1–33.

23. Some scholars compare Jacob with Kirtu in the Ugaritic legend in terms of seeking blessings, although the context and concepts are different. J. C. De Moor, *The Rise of Yahwism* (Leuven: Leuven University Press, 1997), 364.

this text, the writer told his readers that Jacob prayed, addressing God as God of Abraham and Isaac, and had reminded God of his faithfulness to him in the past and prayed for God's protection in the present (32:9–11). Readers would also remember that even when God appeared to them during the day, Hagar and Abraham did not identify God in (human) disguise at first, but only at a later stage did they realize their interlocutor to be YHWH/God (Gen 16:7–14; 18:1–33). Presumably, then, the writer wanted his readers to know that Jacob perceived something of the divine in the man[24] during that touch, suspected him to be God himself, and asked for the blessing. It may be assumed that by insisting that Jacob's hip is benumbed by the man's touch and that Jacob asked for the blessings from the man, the writer wanted to convey that the man and Jacob were in a face-to-face conversation.

3.3.1.4 The name Jacob is changed to Israel (vv. 28–30)

According to the text, the man inquired into Jacob's name, and when Jacob told his name, the man said to Jacob, "Your name shall no longer be called Jacob, but Israel, for you have contended with God and with men and have overcome". Again Jacob requested the man, "Tell your name I pray", and the (man) asked, "Why is it you ask my name", and blessed him there (28–30).

Significantly, the man asks for Jacob's name (מה־שמך) and after Jacob tells his name, the man gives Jacob a new name: that he would no longer be Jacob (יעקב) but Israel (ישראל). What significance does the change of name have at this particular juncture in Jacob's life? While it is often said that in ancient Hebrew culture the name had close connection with the character of the one who bore it,[25] such theories about etymologies[26] may

---

24. Von Rad, *Genesis*, 321.
25. Von Rad, *Genesis*, 321; T. N. D. Mettinger, *In Search of God* (Philadelphia: Fortress Press, 1987), 7.
26. Since this work has no scope for a detailed discussion, some scholarly suggestions in brief are that יעקב (Jacob) means, "may God rule" (von Rad, *Genesis*, 322); "let El rule" (D. G. Barnhouse, *Genesis: chapters 23–50* [Grand Rapids: Zondervan, 1971], 125); "the righteous one of El" (E. Jacob, *OTT*, 203); "God heals" (W. F. Albright, "The Names Israel and 'Judah' with an Excursus on the Etymology of Tôdâh and Tôrâh", *JBL* 46 [1927], 154–168) ; "may God protect" (R. de Vaux, *The Early History of Israel* [London: Darton, Longman and Todd, 1978], 199).

have their limitations, as Barr notes.²⁷ However, in so far as the Hebrew tradition is concerned, the name Jacob (יעקב) is evidently (Gen 27:36)²⁸ associated with the nature of "supplanting/deceiving" and it may well indicate the characteristic of deceitfulness.²⁹

Jacob would have known that God appeared to Abram and changed his name to Abraham;³⁰ and now that his own name is changed to Israel there is a possibility that he begins suspecting the man to be an anthropomorphized divine person. Since the readers would be aware that earlier in Genesis YHWH/God changed the name of Abraham in the context of the divine-revelation to Abram (17:1–11), they would now identify the man as God in human disguise. If one is persuaded that the changing of name signifies God's authority (cf. 17:5),³¹ then, by changing Jacob's name, the man has declared his authority over Jacob. The reason given for this change of name is that Jacob has contended with God and with men (אלהים and אנשים)³² and has overcome (28–29). One may realize that although it is God's choice for him, Jacob struggled in his life over acquiring the blessings and competed with Esau first and then with Laban,³³ and prevailed (ותוכל) in the sense of being successful in all that he competed for.³⁴ The changing of his name from Jacob to Israel may have a functional significance,³⁵ since "Israel" functioned later as a collective name.³⁶

---

27. J. Barr, *The Semantics of Biblical Language* (Oxford: Oxford University Press, 1961), 107–160.
28. This can be seen in Esau's statement: "Is he not rightly named יעקב? For he has supplanted me (יעקבני) these two times" (Gen 27:36).
29. Cf. Mettinger, *In Search of God*, 7. However, the change of Jacob's name did not erase the proper name עקב (Jacob), as God was still known as the God of Jacob (e.g. Gen 49:24).
30. It is possible that either the oral traditions were in circulation or the written record was available.
31. W. C. Kaiser, "שׁם", *TWOT* 2, 934; Hartley, *Genesis*, 284.
32. Cf. the usage of אנשים and מלאכים in Gen 18:2–22; 19:1–15.
33. Gen 25:23; 27:41; 29:25–31.
34. It is possible, then, that the writer chose this word אבק as a word play (rhyme/assonance) on יבק (v. 23), אבק and יעקב (v. 25).
35. For a comment on functional significance, see chapter 2, 71.
36. Cf. E. Jacob, *OTT*, 204. The change of Jacobs's name in association with the divine revelation at Jabbok makes better sense than to think that the names Jacob and Israel belong to two different traditions, as G. A. Danell (*The name Israel in the Old Testament* [Uppsala: n.p., 1946], 37) suggests.

After the man has pronounced his new name, Jacob requests that the man state his own name (v. 30a).[37] Why does Jacob ask the man's name at this point? Westermann thinks[38] that Jacob's question here is a proof that the man is not God. But it may be, as noted earlier, that Jacob has already sensed some mystery about the man (after being touched) and asks for the blessing. It may be presumed that since Jacob has already prayed for God's protection (32:9–11), and that he is alone anticipating God's intervention; since the man does not introduce himself (cf. 28:13), Jacob is now keen to clarify if the man is God himself. Although the man responds to Jacob's query of his name (v. 30a) with a counter question "why is it you ask my name" (v. 30b), he blesses Jacob. In line with his identification of the man with the demon, Gunkel assumes that it is the demon that blessed Jacob;[39] likewise, Westermann takes the demon as the subject of ברך and suggests that the demon transferred its superhuman power to Jacob; but, Westermann also believes that Jacob experienced that God was with him[40]—one may ask here, if it was a demon that met Jacob, "how could Westermann think that Jacob experienced that God was with him"?

3.3.2 Jacob Sees God "Face-to-Face", and His Life is Saved: vv. 31–32.

3.3.2.1 Jacob calls the place Peniel (v. 31a)

According to the text, Jacob called the name of the place Peniel saying, "I have seen God face-to-face, and my life is saved". And the sun rose on him as he passed Penuel limping on his hip (31–32).

After having said that the man blessed Jacob in that place (30b), the writer now relates that Jacob called the name of the place (where he was blessed) Peniel and exclaimed ראיתי אלהים פנים אל־פנים ותנצל נפשי "I have seen God 'face-to-face' and my life is saved" (31). The conversation that

---

37. הגידה, hiphil imperative of נגד is not followed by indirect object לי in the text (cf. Gen 24:23).

38. Westermann, *Genesis*, 519.

39. Gunkel, *Genesis*, 350, 351.

40. Westermann, *Genesis*, 518, 521. His suggestion that a derivative of the verb ברך means "transfer" may be possible, but does not fit into this context.

began between Jacob and the man comes to a conclusion with Jacob's naming of that place פניאל "the face of God".[41] Calling the name Peniel need not be etiological, as form critics seem to assume.[42] As G. W. Savran observes, Jacob gave the name Peniel out of his experience of seeing God's face[43] and this is possible since ancient Israel believed that their God revealed himself and appeared to different people. Readers would remember that Hagar named the well באר לחי ראי (Beer Lahai Roi) after her experience with God, who revealed himself to her at the well (16:7–14). Jacob himself gave the name בת־אל (Bethel) "the house of God" to the place where the divine self-revelation took place and where he heard and saw God in a dream vision.[44] So, even here in the present text (v. 31), the writer seems to insist that Jacob called the place where he saw God (face-to-face) פניאל "face of God". One wonders how the readers would have understood Jacob's statement that he saw God "face-to-face", since they were told first that it was a man who came and wrestled with Jacob. This aspect will be discussed below.

3.3.2.2 *Jacob saw God face-to-face (v. 31b)*

While Jacob's confession is a clear indication that he saw God "face-to-face", it is not clear how he could make such an explicit statement. While it is possible that Jacob saw the man face-to-face when he was in conflict with Jacob that night, the latter did not know that he was God at that stage. However, intriguingly, Jacob is emphatic in his later statement that

---

41. Some versions such as Symmachus have פנואל where MT has פניאל. A. Salvesen, *Symmachus in the Pentateuch* (Manchester: University of Manchester, 1991), 50. The noun פְּנִיאֵל may be an alternative form of פְּנוּאֵל (32) reflecting the old nominative case ending. The vowel ו may be taken as the survival of the old nominative ending as it also occurs in the middle of (only) old proper nouns. Other examples are בתו in בְּתוּאֵל (Gen 22:22; cf. 1 Sam 1:20: שמו in שְׁמוּאֵל). See *GKC* § 90k.

42. Form critics think that it was the name of a Phoenician hill by name θεοῦ προσωπόν "face of God", and that this text was adopted into Israelite tradition only because of etiological features. See Gunkel, *What Remains*, 150–167; also Gunkel, *The Legends of Genesis* (New York: Schocken Books, 1964), 88–105. Cf. Terrien, *Elusive Presence*, 90–91; Reindl, *Angesicht*, 70–73.

43. G. W. Savran, *Encountering the Divine* (London: T. & T. Clark International, 2005), 184.

44. 28:12–19; cf. 32:3: Mahanaim; 33:20: El-Elohe-Israel.

he saw God face-to-face.⁴⁵ Why was the divine appearance mistaken first for a "man" and only afterwards was Jacob able to identify him as God? For some reason, the Hebrew writer maintained ambiguity over the identification of the man as God at the beginning of the text. R. Barthes argues that the writer wanted to create a paradoxical situation wherein the man becomes an opponent who wrestles with Jacob in order to prevent him from crossing the river.⁴⁶ But the extant text gives no clue to assume an association with the prevention of Jacob from crossing the river. One may realize that the readers were already exposed to this kind of ambiguity in an earlier tradition, in that Hagar did not know in the beginning that the man who spoke to her at the well (Gen 16:13–14)⁴⁷ was God himself, and recognized him as God only at the end of the encounter. Perhaps, here too the writer wanted his readers to know that Jacob recognized "the man" as "God" only at the end. Was it the writer who kept the identity of "the man" ambiguous till the end as some literary ploy? Or was this ambiguity in the tradition itself, and the writer simply conveyed that God did not let himself be seen all at once, but step-by-step? The second option seems more likely.

What makes Jacob identify the man as God? It appears that some kind of mysterious aspect of revelation is associated with the divine "departure". The man does not tell Jacob his name as he did in his dream-vision (28:13). As discussed earlier in this chapter, Jacob already suspected the man to be God and asked for his blessing and inquired into his name. Having said that the man blessed Jacob there, the writer tells his readers that Jacob recognized the man as God. Is it possible, then, that at a particular moment just before or while departing, God (who looked like a man until then) revealed himself in a specific way to Jacob so that he recognized the man as God and undeniably claimed: "I have seen God face-to-face". It is possible that the man revealed something of himself just before he left the scene, and Jacob identified "the man" as God at that particular juncture

---

45. LXX reads Εἶδος (an outward appearance) θεοῦ εἶδον γὰρ θεὸν πρόσωπον πρὸς πρόσωπον.

46. R. Barthes, *Image-Music-Text* (Oxford: Oxford University Press, 1982), 132–140. Also see V. Cunningham, "Roland Barthes (1915–1980): Introduction. Barthes Text: Wrestling with the Angel: Textual Analysis of Genesis 32:23–32", in *The Postmodern God* (Oxford: Blackwell Publishing, 2005).

47. See chapter 2, 64.

and categorically stated that he saw (ראיתי) God. It seems unavoidable to think that there was a kind of process in the divine revelation; that God appeared to Jacob in human form first and then, revealed some mysterious aspect of himself so that Jacob could perceive him as God.

One wonders if the expression [48]פנים אל־פנים "face-to-face" has special significance from the writer's point of view. A brief reflection of different divine manifestations associated with the Jacob cycle may help discern the significance of the expression "face-to-face" here. As discussed in the previous chapter, Jacob's dream vision in which YHWH was seen as standing comprised a directness and visibility (Gen 28:12–13).[49] While Jacob was still in Paddan-Aram, YHWH is said to have spoken to him in a dream directing him to return to his own land (Gen 31:3, 10–14). Although Jacob did not seem to explicitly confess that he saw God in those instances (possible that he saw God in his dream), his prayer claimed that YHWH told him to return to Canaan (יהוה האמר אלי), and Jacob received that message as authentic and acted accordingly and reached the border of Canaan (32:10). In addition to this, Jacob also saw (qal form of ראה) the angels of God who met him not very long before the Peniel incident (32:2–3). Now coming back to the expression פנים אל־פנים "face-to-face", this expression is used for the first time in the context of the divine revelations. Presumably, the readers would have realized that the expression "face-to-face" signified a different experience of Jacob with God.

Did Jacob see God's face in a physical sense? Scholars in general seem to have reservations in associating a literal "seeing" to the expression "face-to-face". As discussed in the introductory chapter,[50] Johnson maintains that the expression "face-to-face" here in Genesis 32:31 is only an idiom of seeing a person, and Terrien suggests that פנים אל־פנים "face-to-face" refers to the direct "person-to-person" encounter and it should not be taken

---

48. Of the five occurrences of פנים אל־פנים "face-to-face" in the HB, three of them occur within the Pentateuch in the context of self-revelations (Gen 32:32; Exod 33:11; Deut 34:10). Similar Hebrew expressions which Eng. verses translate as "face-to-face" are פה אל־פה (Num 12:8); עין בעין (Num 14:14); פנים בפנים (Deut 5:4).

49. See chapter 2, 80–81.

50. See chapter 1, 7.

literally as visual perception.⁵¹ However, the Hebrew tradition in Genesis 32:23–32 seems quite strong in believing Jacob saw God face-to-face, with the writer insisting that a literal "seeing" was involved. As discussed earlier,⁵² if Johnson admits that "to see my face" is an emphatic way of saying "to see me", this could well mean that Jacob saw God (in human-form) in a literal sense; contrary to Johnson's assumption that this expression פנים אל־פנים "face-to-face" (in 32:23–31) is used with a "perceptible weakening of its literal meaning", this text supports a literal interpretation of Jacob's claim that he saw God face-to-face; and if this expression פנים אל־פנים "face-to-face" denotes "the enjoyment of personal contact with someone", as Johnson admits, then Jacob's claim that he saw God face-to-face reflects the enjoyment of his personal contact with God that night. If the expression "face-to-face" refers to a person-to-person encounter, as Terrien opines, then, it is very likely that the writer has employed this expression פנים אל־פנים "face-to-face" to signify that Jacob had a direct encounter with God. Terrien assumes that Jacob's claim that he saw God face-to-face is only the narrator's insistence upon the concreteness, and that physical seeing is not possible because of the darkness of the surroundings.⁵³ However, it is worth noting that the text does not say that it is a dark night;⁵⁴ rather the Hebrew writer insists on the concreteness of the man in disguise that the man touched Jacob's hip, which was benumbed in a physical sense. The visibility of God seems dominant in Genesis 32:23–32.

Eichrodt assumes that the idea of seeing God is "difficult to integrate into the Israelite experience of God" and that these expressions on seeing the face of God should be treated as metaphorical.⁵⁵ However, Eichrodt himself realizes that the tradition in 32:25–32 (also 18:1–8) is "marked

---

51. Terrien, *Elusive Presence*, 91. For similar views on idiomatic expressions see J. M. Babut, *Idiomatic Expressions of the Hebrew Bible* (Texas: Bibal Press, 1999), 28, 56). See also D. H. Aaron, תניי *Biblical Ambiguities: Metaphor, Semantics and Divine Imagery* (Leiden: Brill, 2001).

52. Chapter 1, 8.

53. Terrien, *Elusive Presence*, 90–91; Hartley, *Genesis* 285.

54. Nomadic peoples in the East do travel during the (moonlit) nights, and all nights need not be dark nights.

55. Eichrodt, *OTT* 2, 20. But he does not explain how one can arrive at such a conclusion like this except referring to Exod 33:20.

by a descriptive realism" and also acknowledges that God temporarily incarnated himself in human form.[56] While Nötscher accepts that Jacob saw God at Peniel, he feels that the seeing aspect is not important,[57] but the seeing aspect also seems important to authenticate the message given; as seen above in this chapter, when Jacob saw angels at Mahanaim, it helped him to acknowledge that God was present there, but nothing is said about any message given to him.

Westermann argues that Jacob's claim that he saw God face-to-face provides no sufficient ground for understanding that there was an encounter between God and Jacob.[58] However, as discussed previously in this chapter, the evidence in the text from the beginning to the end seems to indicate that "the man" is no ordinary man, but was God in his anthropomorphic form; and there is nothing in the text which would have allowed the readers to assume that it was not an encounter between God and Jacob. Furthermore, this encounter is in line with the previous traditions where God and human encounters took place in a variety of ways. It would not be difficult for the readers to identify the "man" as God because they already knew that Abraham's divine guests looked like travelling men (Gen 18:2–4) but later, one of them turned out to be YHWH and the other two are said to be angels (18:22; 19:1).

In light of Hebrew traditions that God could appear in human form, Gunkel's assumption that the Tetragrammaton is not mentioned in this text and that it has no relevance for the Yahwistic religion[59] is questionable given that יהוה (YHWH) and אלהים (God) are often used alternately for the Israelite God[60] even within the context of divine revelations (cf. 28:13–14; 32:10). There seems no reason why this text has to be treated as a dream

---

56. Ibid., 20, 27.
57. Nötscher, *Angesicht*, 25–31.
58. Westermann, *Genesis*, 519.
59. Gunkel, *Folktale*, 85–87. However, one can be certain that the man whom Jacob identified as אלהים can also be identified as יהוה given that in the earlier theophanies, for example, in Gen 28:13–20, יהוה, יהוה אלהי אברהם, and אלהים are used for the same divine person.
60. Cf. R. W. L Moberly, *Genesis 12–50* (England: Sheffield Academic Press, 1992), 31.

or an allegory symbolizing the inward travail, as Skinner does,[61] since the text is very explicit in depicting a physical encounter between Jacob and the anthropomorphized person of God; and the specific mention made that Jacob left limping (v. 32) indicates the realism of the physical encounter.

Literally speaking, the usage of verb ראה "to see" is significant as it is used as the object of פנים "face" of אלהים "God",[62] and thematically it is significant as it represents the physicality of God, and involves Jacob with the "seeing" of God. Although it is God who revealed himself to Jacob, the fact that Jacob is the subject of ראה (qal form)[63] signifies that Jacob saw God. Furthermore, Jacob's confession of seeing God face-to-face also signifies that God was physically present with Jacob in a literal sense. By using the expression "face-to-face", which connotes "the intimate association that exists between participants"[64] and "the immediate proximity",[65] the writer seems to convey that Jacob was very near to God and saw his face in a physical sense. Although Korpel maintains that the expressions involving "seeing the face of God" are to be treated as metaphorical, she admits the possibility of Jacob seeing God פנים אל־פנים "face-to-face".[66]

As D. Shepherd comments, "there is something qualitatively different" about Jacob's experience at Peniel, which is perhaps "the physicality" of God.[67] This is not to say that the aspect of physicality was not present in the earlier traditions; and as seen in the previous chapter (Gen 3:8; 16:13–14; 18:1–15), and even in the dreams and visions, the idea of physicality was not absent (15:4–21; 28:13). The Hebrew writer employs this expression "face-to-face" for the first time to convey that Jacob had seen God face-to-face, and one may also sense that there is some difference between the

---

61. Skinner, *Genesis*, 410; J. H. Hertz, ed. *The Pentateuch and Haftorahs* (London: Soncino Press, 1937), 123.

62. For the use of plural nouns as singular, see N. Walker, "Do Plural Nouns of Majesty Exist in Hebrew?", *VT* 7 (1957), 208.

63. This is contrary to the arguments that the MT points to niphal form of ראה to avoid the seeing aspect. See chapter 1, 6; fn. 42, 10; fn. 87, 20.

64. Yofre, "פנים", 597.

65. L. Koehler and W. Baumgartner, eds., *HALOT* 3, 941.

66. Korpel, *Rift in the Clouds*, 103.

67. This comment was made on 16 Feb 2009 in one of the research discussions this researcher had during 2007–2009 with D. Shepherd (Principal, Bible College, Belfast).

previous texts and here and that difference may be in terms of the "expression" in "the 'face' of God". This aspect will be discussed below.

3.3.2.3 Jacob's life is saved (v. 31c)

Having exclaimed that he has seen God's face (ראיתי אלהים פנים אל־פנים), Jacob also declares: ותנצל נפשי "and my life is saved" (v. 31c). What is it in God's face that caused Jacob to be so moved that he exclaims that his life was saved? One may note that it is in conjunction with seeing God's face that Jacob says that his life has been saved.

As mentioned above, God seems to have revealed something of himself to Jacob because of which he claims that he saw God face-to-face. Although there is no description of how the anthropomorphized divine person God looked in terms of his facial features, in some sense one may assume that Jacob was allowed to see the divine face in terms of his facial features. Could it be, then, that Jacob had observed some favorable expression in the face of God which would have helped him realize that his life was safe? One may get some insights in terms of "facial expression" from an earlier tradition. Readers would remember that when Jacob saw (ירא) the פנים "face"[68] of (את־פני) Laban, he noticed that Laban was not as favorable towards him as before (Gen 31:2, 5), meaning that the expression in Laban's face (facial expression) was evident to Jacob; it also meant that Jacob saw the face of Laban (in a literal sense). It may be, then, that by using a similar expression where פנים acts as an object of the verb ראה the writer wanted his readers to know that Jacob saw the face of God in an anatomical and literal sense. However, in contrast to the expression in Laban's face, Jacob seems to notice a favorable expression in the face of God, which would have helped him say that his life was saved. The question, then, is in what way the favorable expression in the "face" of God is connected to

---

68. The term פנים "face" is used here in the anatomical sense. See Yofre, "פנים", 593.

his safety, so that he stated, ותנצל נפשי "'and'[69] my life is saved".[70] Earlier in the text, the writer has related how Jacob prayed that God would save him (הצילני) from Esau, whom he feared would attack him and his family (32:10–12) and now he relates that Jacob was assured that God saved him from his fearful situation.[71] As Yofre says, Jacob's statement that his life is saved, "underlines God's presence as the agent of Jacob's deliverance".[72]

The verb ראה "to see" used in association with פנים "face" of אלהים "God" clearly signifies the reality of the divine presence, and implies that Jacob has noticed a favorable expression in God's face in a literal sense. It is this realization that God has revealed himself to him that seems to help Jacob even before he faces Esau. At the end, verse 32 with its information that Jacob limps on his hip gives additional support for believing in a physical encounter between Jacob and God. One can expect that when readers would read what Jacob said to Esau, "I see your face is like seeing the face of God (ראיתי פניך כראת פני אלהים) and you are favorable to me" in 33:10 (just ten sentences away from 32:31), they would refer back to what Jacob claimed earlier that he saw God face-to-face. Jacob's comparison between God and Esau would make sense only if it refers back to 32:31, given that the object of the verb ראה "to see" is the "face" of both God and Esau; and it reflects Jacob's claim that he saw God face-to-face at Peniel, which supports the assumption that Jacob saw God's face in a literal sense. As J. McKeown observes, Jacob sees acceptance rather than vengeance in Esau's facial expression.[73] Since Jacob has noticed the favorable expression in Esau's face in a physical sense, it seems to support the assumption that

---

69. The waw consecutive (ו) in this work is translated as "and". The use of niphal form of the verb נצל here is significant, as it gives the idea of being saved by someone else. Some Eng. verses (KJV, NKJ) read ו in ותנצל as "and" and others read as "yet" (NIV and NRS). If ו in ותנצל is taken as conjunction (and), it means that because Jacob had seen God "face-to-face" he was assured of safety from God; if ו is taken as a contrast (yet), it reflects negative fear of death for seeing God's face. But, nowhere in the earlier texts was death associated with "seeing" God's face.

70. The noun נפש with נצל is also used in the sense of saving a person's life from death, deliverance from enemies, troubles, and even from "transgressions". See *TWOT* 2, 587–591.

71. K. Elliger, "Das Jakobskampf am Jabbok", *ZTK* 48 (1951), 29.

72. Yofre, "פנים", 597.

73. J. McKeown, *Genesis: Two Horizons Old Testament Commentary* (Grand Rapids: Eerdmans, 2008); cf. Hamilton, *Genesis*, 346.

Jacob has noticed a favorable expression in the face of God in a literal and anatomical sense.

3.4 Mode of Self-Revelation, Human Recognition, and Response

In this text human characteristic features are described vividly. God is described as a "man" who touched Jacob's hip; Jacob has explicitly stated that he has seen God "face-to-face" in a physical sense; this encounter involved directness and visibility. All this meant that the mode of God's appearance was in human bodily form with a human face in an anatomical sense. Presumably, God in disguise revealed something of himself in his face because of which Jacob recognized the man as God. It is not clear if the divine figure Jacob saw was similar to the divine figure in his earlier vision at Bethel. Since Jacob understood what was spoken to him, it seems that God in disguise spoke in human language with human voice. The initiative to reveal himself to Jacob is seen as coming from God himself. Nothing is said from where he came to meet Jacob and how he went away from there. Once his identity was revealed to Jacob in some way, he seemed to have gone, and it may be assumed that the embodied God transcended the human body which he assumed. Jacob's response to his experience of seeing God "face-to-face" was expressed in his safety, security and in his joyful exclamation that he saw God face-to-face.

3.5 The Function/Significance of Divine Revelation

This tradition of Jacob's Peniel experience would have played a significant role in providing the understanding of the variety of ways the divine revelations took place. Since the earlier established traditions had already described the self-revelations of YHWH/God, ancient Israelite readers would have understood without hesitation that their creator God once again took human form and revealed himself to Jacob. The Peniel incident signified God's faithfulness to his promise to Jacob that he would be with him and bring him back to the land (28:13–15); and how Jacob became fearless after that divine encounter (27:41; 32:12). This tradition would have helped ancient readers to desire God's presence.

3.6 Conclusion

In this chapter, Genesis 32:25–32 has been studied within the context of the "self-revelations of YHWH/God" with the purpose of understanding whether the expression פנים אל־פנים "face-to-face" has been used idiomatically or should be understood as involving the corporeality/physicality of God. In light of the previous anthropomorphic traditions, the man who has encountered Jacob is identified as God himself in human disguise, and Jacob's claim to have seen God is understood to imply physicality. Unlike in other anthropomorphic traditions, Jacob explicitly states here that he saw God "face-to-face" which signifies a direct and close involvement of both God (touches Jacob's hip) and Jacob (sees God).

This study helps to understand the writer's insistence that Jacob named the place where he has an encounter, Peniel, because of his experience of seeing the face of God, who appeared in human disguise. It is discerned that when Jacob saw God, he noticed a favorable expression in the face of God, which brought assurance that his life was saved. The possibility that the anthropomorphized divine person specifically revealed something of himself to Jacob is established by Jacob's claim that he saw God's face and was saved. Jacob's comparison of the face of Esau (33:10) with seeing the face of God (32:31) provided additional support for believing that God appeared in human bodily form to Jacob and that he saw a favorable expression in God's face.

The description in the text and the writer's insistence that Jacob saw God face-to-face in a literal sense shows that this text cannot easily be interpreted in any other way than as a real encounter. The arguments that this expression פנים אל־פנים "face-to-face" is only idiomatic or metaphorical have no support in the biblical text. Since the writer has described the encounter as involving the physicality of God, it should not be treated as a dream or an allegory. Gunkel's form-critical assumption that the "man" was a demon is found contradictory to the strong tradition of the self-revelations of YHWH/God.

There is a no reason why one cannot believe in the straightforwardness of the Hebrew text, that God revealed himself to Jacob in a human body. The Hebrew readers would not have had any difficulty in accepting the physical manifestation of God, since their traditions held that God is the creator of humankind and that he maintained a contact and a relationship by means of self-revelations. God was believed to have assumed a human body with a human face and revealed himself to Jacob, and Jacob saw God's face directly. This leads to the question of the possible origin or the background to the expression of "seeing the face of YHWH/God" as described in the context of the self-revelations of YHWH/God.

3.7 The Question of Background of the Motif פני־יהוה/אלהים "Face of YHWH/God"

As seen in the introductory chapter, situating the expression "face of God" in the ANE religious context, Baudissin and Nötscher concluded that the expression "seeing the face of YHWH" meant seeing the cult statue of YHWH ("die Kultstätte 'Jahwes besuchen'").[74] As discussed earlier, one can see the complication here as Nötscher himself understands. Since he could not accept the view that there was YHWH's statue in the temple, he associates this expression "seeing the face of God" with a general idea of "visiting the Temple" and then to a more secular idea of visiting the king for an *Audienz*.[75] Likewise, Hartenstein believes that the background of the expression "face of YHWH" was the idea of royal and cultic *Audienz*[76] in the analogy of YHWH as king. Although he accepts the idea of anthropomorphic form, since the king has a face, he too (like Nötscher) does not believe that there was a cult statue in the temple. Therefore he argues that the reference to the divine "face" was only a devotee's imagination. However,

---

74. See chapter 1, 4–6.
75. See chapter 1, 6–7. Cf. Nötscher, *Angesicht*, 53–54; 73–75; 87.
76. Hartenstein, *Angesicht*, 230–233.

when the motif of "seeing the face of YHWH/God" is placed in the context of self-revelations within the Pentateuch, the canonical texts show that the expression "face of YHWH/God" has strong roots in the context of the divine self-revelations; and the background to/origin of the motif "'seeing the face' of YHWH/God" is that he revealed himself anthropomorphically with a human body; when he revealed himself to different people either in dreams/ visions or directly, they saw his anthropomorphic "face."

The study of Genesis traditions in chapters 2 and 3 shows that there is no textual support to equate "'seeing' the face of God" (פני־יהוה) with seeing the king for *Audienz*, because the Hebrew traditions associate the expressions "seeing the face of God" and "seeing God face-to-face" with the divine revelations, in which YHWH/God took the initiative and came to different people in human form. It was God himself who assumed a human body and came to communicate with people, rather than the people seeking after him for an audience. With regard to the corporeal aspect/physicality of the anthropomorphized divine person, one cannot avoid asking if God took a human body when he appeared. The answer here is in the affirmative.[77] Although it is not clear whether the divine bodily form was fully human at that point or in a kind of replica of human being, it is clear that strong human personality/traits are associated with the anthropomorphized divine person.

Any assumption that divine manifestation in human form was felt to be an embarrassment, or was seen as offensive,[78] is not relevant for the Hebrew traditions, and if the Hebrew writers felt it offensive, they would not have associated "face" with YHWH/God and described him in a human form. One can discern that ancient Israel valued those divine manifestations as foundational for their faith and practice; and whenever God revealed himself to people in human form, he let himself be seen by them. Indeed the concept of "seeing the face of YHWH/God" is deeply rooted in the Hebrew traditions of the self-revelations of YHWH/God.

---

77. See B. Sommer, *Bodies*, 2–6; 40.
78. Korpel, *Rift in the Clouds*, 103–104. For counter arguments, see Sommer, *Bodies*, 1–108.

3.8 Beyond the Present Text

After meeting with Esau, when Jacob reaches Shechem, he builds an altar and calls it אל אלהי ישראל "El Elohe Israel" (33:18–20) which seems to signify his Peniel experience. It seems that ancient Israel greatly valued those divine revelations and made the places of worship memorable; it was because of these divine self-revelations that divine-human contact was made, and a divine message was conveyed; it was the recognition of the revealed presence of God that evoked the response of worship in them, and communion with God.[79] Later on Jacob tells Joseph that God appeared to him in the land of Canaan, and blessed him (Gen 48:3).

As the experiences of the fathers were passed on to their children, the promise of the Land continued to be the focus among the descendants of Abraham and Isaac. It is with this background that this work will now turn to the next section where the texts from Exodus will be studied.

---

79. Cf. Rooy, "פנים", *NIDOTTE*, 639.

Section II

Chapters 4–5

Texts from Exodus

CHAPTER 4

The Self-Revelations of YHWH/God in Exodus

4.1 Introduction

In line with chapter 2, this chapter further studies the motif of the self-revelations of YHWH/God in Exodus, with the objective of understanding how anthropomorphic appearances were perceived as operative in Exodus traditions. The selected texts, Exodus 3:1–12 and 24:1–18, will be studied within their immediate context and in light of the previous traditions with an attempt to discern the aspects of divine communication, the mode of divine revelation and the function it played in ancient Israel. While in Exodus 24:1–18, the verb ראה "to see" occurs in association with פנים "face" of "YHWH/God", in 3:1–12, the idea of "seeing the face of God" is implied. An attempt will be made to discern what scope these texts give to associate פנים "face" with the anthropomorphic (bodily) person of YHWH/God. These two texts will be studied in two separate sections and there will be a conclusion at the end of each section and closing remarks at the end of the chapter.

4.2 Exodus 3:1–12: YHWH/God Appears in the Midst of Fire

4.2.1 Canonical Context

The book of Exodus gives the information that Israelites settled in Goshen in Egypt and increased abundantly in their numbers;[1] Joseph and all that generation died (Exod 1:6–7; cf. Gen 50:26); a new king who did not know Joseph had afflicted the Israelites with hard labor (Exod 1:8–22); when "the children of Israel"[2] groaned under the oppression of Egypt, their cry for help went up (עלה) to God, who heard (ישמע) their groaning and remembered (יזכר) his covenant with Abraham, Isaac and Jacob; and God was aware (cf. וירא and וידע) of their suffering (2:23–25). It is in this context that Exodus portrays how YHWH/God appears to Moses and reveals his plan to rescue Israel from Egyptian oppression.

4.2.2 Divine Self-Revelation and Communication

Exodus 3:1–12 relates that when Moses came to Horeb (the mountain of God) to pasture his sheep, the "angel of YHWH" (מלך יהוה) appeared (וירא) to him in a flame of fire in the midst of a bush. When Moses saw that the bush was burning with fire but was not consumed, he turned to see that great sight, why the bush was not consumed; when YHWH (יהוה) saw that Moses turned towards the bush, he (אלהים) called him from the bush by his name, "Moses, Moses!",[3] and Moses replied, "Here am I" (vv. 1–3). As described in the text, God instructed Moses to take his sandals off his feet because the ground was holy, and said that he was the God of his father, "the God of Abraham, Isaac, and Jacob"; and Moses hid his face for he was afraid (ירא) to look at God. YHWH told Moses that he saw (ראה) the affliction of his people (lit., עמי "my people") in Egypt, heard their cry, knew their sorrow and came down (ארד) to rescue them (3:4–9) and that he would send Moses to Pharaoh in order that he would bring his people out

---

1. Gen 41:40; 42:1–6; 45:3; 47:1–7, 27; 49:33.
2. The expression בני־ישראל ("the children of Israel") is perhaps used to represent the new generations of Abraham's/Jacob's descendants in contrast to the fathers.
3. Cf. God calls Abraham by name in Gen 22:11.

of Egypt (v. 10);[4] and when Moses expressed his inability in carrying out the task, YHWH assured him saying, "I will be with you", and also gave a sign that when the people came out of Egypt, they would serve (עבד) God on that mountain (vv. 11–12).

Although Horeb was said to be "the mountain of God",[5] Moses is portrayed as not seeming to know of an association of God with this mountain,[6] nor does he seem to anticipate any divine revelation there. While the writer first tells that the מלאך יהוה "angel of YHWH" appeared to Moses in a flame of fire (v. 2a), it was יהוה (YHWH) who saw Moses (v. 4a); and again it was אלהים (God) who called Moses (v. 4b). Earlier in Genesis, different names were used for the Israelite God within a single text, and the readers presumably knew that these names belonged to the same God (cf. 16:10–13). Since Moses is asked to remove his sandals, one may assume that he is near the bush, and the reason God (from the fiery flame) tells him to remove his sandals is because the place is holy;[7] the place is said to be holy perhaps because of God's presence there, rather than because it was already regarded as holy.[8] As Houtman suggests, the removal of sandals may be "best regarded as an act of expressing one's reverence and the subjection to the one whom one wants to meet".[9] A brief reflection on the nature of the fire in the bush may help to understand the concept of holiness here. The odd situation Moses observes in the bush is that it is burning

---

4. Noth (*Pentateuchal Traditions*, 30, 36) understood Exod 3:1–12 as a fusion of theophany and call narrative from J and E. However, the text is clear that God appeared both to reveal himself to Moses and send him to Egypt. Cf. Gen 12 where the task to Abram was given during the revelation.

5. This reference to הר האלהים "the mountain of God" made it possible to presuppose that Horeb was treated as "the mountain of God" even before God appeared there to Moses. See S. R. Driver, *The Book of Exodus* (Cambridge: Cambridge University Press, 1953), 18–19.

6. It is possible that, because God revealed himself to Moses at this mountain, it came to be known as the "mountain of God" and this reference to the mountain seems to be a later editorial comment. Cf. W. Moberly, *The Old Testament of the Old Testament* (Minneapolis: Fortress Press, 1992), 8–9.

7. Cf. Josh 5:13–15.

8. T. E. Fretheim, *Exodus* (Louisville: John Knox Press, 1991), 56; cf. Eichrodt, *OTT* 1, 272; Deut 33:16, which alludes to God's appearance in the bush.

9. C. Houtman, *Exodus* 1 (Kampen: Kok Publishing House, 1993), 352.

without being consumed.[10] Since Moses is told that it is a holy place, one may assume that fire in the bush is not an ordinary fire, but something that emanated from the divine person himself (3:5). Given that God is said to have appeared in the flame of fire, and that the place is said to be holy, God is understood to be holy.

God's identification of himself as the God of "Moses' father" is interesting in this context. Hyatt opines that "your father" (v. 6) did not necessarily mean Moses' own father.[11] However, the usage "God of your father" was earlier employed in Genesis traditions where "your father" meant Abraham and also one's own father.[12] Here in the present context, it may well refer to Moses' (earthly) father who was a Levite (2:1), and one may assume that it was through his Levite father that Moses learned about YHWH and Hebrew worship. The first personal pronoun אנכי "I am" was used earlier in Genesis in identifying YHWH as the God of "the fathers"[13] in the context of the divine revelations to Isaac and Jacob (Gen 26:24; 28:13). One can discern that the theme of divine revelation in Exodus is a continuation from Genesis traditions. However, the readers would note that the divine revelation here in Exodus is accompanied by fire.

The writer informs his readers that when the person in the flame of fire reveals his identity as the God of the fathers, Moses hides his face (ויסתר משה פניו), and the reason given is that he is afraid to look at (כי ירא מהביט) God (Exod 3:6). The phrase פניו "his face" (3:6) signifies Moses' face in a literal sense; since Moses hid his face from looking at God, the noun פנים "face" seems to retain its literal sense in the phrase פניו "his face"; and this also shows that God was understood to be physically present in an anthropomorphic form, was visible to Moses and spoke to him.

When Moses heard the person calling him, and when he went closer to the bush and removed the sandals and listened to him, it is possible that he

---

10. While it is common to find fire in the desert areas, the writer seems to point to the fact that the fire in the bush, as described in the text, is strange and raised Moses' curiosity to go near the bush.
11. J. P. Hyatt, "Yahweh as 'The God of my Father'", *VT* 5 (1955): 133–136.
12. Gen 26:24; 28:13; 31:29; 43:23; 46:3; 50:17.
13. See A. Alt. "The God of the Fathers", in *Essays on Old Testament History and Religion* (Oxford: Blackwell, 1966), 10–15; 54–61.

saw God[14] and was not afraid. But, now the text gives the impression that the moment Moses hears that it is the God of his fathers who is speaking to him, he fears to look at him and hides his face. Why does Moses hide his face after hearing that the person in front of him is the God of his fathers? Previously, in Genesis traditions, it was assumed that God revealed something of himself at a particular moment to Hagar and to Jacob, so that they recognized him as God and exclaimed that they saw him (face-to-face).[15] Is it possible even here in Moses' case also that God revealed something of himself to Moses at that particular moment? It seems possible, since the writer insists that it is after YHWH identified himself as the God of the fathers that Moses hid his face.

Since the text clearly portrays that YHWH/God appeared in the flaming bush, possibly while identifying himself as God of the fathers verbally, God revealed something of his bright appearance to authenticate that he is God (in disguise); and Moses saw something of God because of which he was afraid. Fretheim thinks that Moses knew seeing God might mean death;[16] but the text gives no clue to assume that Moses feared death from his encounter, nor did Genesis traditions associate death with the divine revelations. L. Köhler understands that "the Hebrew is alarmed by the unexpected" (Exod 3:1-3),[17] and perhaps it is this unexpected exposure to God's bright (fiery) appearance/face, and the realization that it is God who spoke to him, that made Moses afraid/fear (ירא).

Some scholars, for instance M. Buber, are not convinced that Moses had corporeally perceived anything in any form.[18] However, the fact that Moses was afraid of (feared) looking at God may indicate that the divine person was physically present and real. As M. Noth has observed, God seems to have appeared in some visible way, and it was in fear of "the sight of God"

---

14. Fretheim, *Exodus*, 55.
15. Chapters 2, 62; 3, 96.
16. Fretheim, *Exodus*, 56.
17. L. Köhler, *Hebrew Man* (London: SCM Press, 1953), 134.
18. Kuntz, *Self-Revelation*, 142, citing M. Buber, *Moses: The Revelation and the Covenant* (n.p: Harper & Brothers, 1958), 41 (regret that Buber's book is not available for the use in this work).

that Moses hid his face.[19] Furthermore, presumably, the readers were conditioned by what they had read in the previous anthropomorphic traditions that when God appeared to people, he required a physical (human) form to communicate with people, but now they would realize that God revealed himself even in the flame of fire in (seemingly) human form.

After revealing his identity to Moses, YHWH also reveals his plan to Moses that he came down (ירד) to earth to rescue/save (נצל)[20] the Israelites from Egypt (vv. 4–10) because he saw (ראה)[21] the oppression of "his people" and knew (ידע) their sufferings and heard (שמע) their cry. Earlier in Genesis, the writer had used these terms and concepts in association with YHWH's self-revelations, that is, he came down (ירד יהוה) to see (לראת) and confuse people's language (Gen 11:5, 7); YHWH went down (ירד) to see (ראה), to know (ידע), and to detect the sinfulness of Sodom and Gomorrah (Gen 18:21). In all these texts, YHWH is the subject of the verbs ראה "to see", ידע "to know", ירד "to go down", נצל "to rescue". YHWH is described not as a static figure, but as an active person who involves himself in the lives of people on earth; both the aspects of transcendence and the immanence of God are seen in that while he is above (in heaven), he hears the cry of the people on earth and comes down to act on their behalf.

Now, coming back to the Exodus text, the variety of these verbs ראה "to see", שמע "to hear" and ידע "to know" (3:7; cf. 2:24–25), as Houtman suggests, "serves to bring out that God is in every way familiar with Israel's plight and that no aspect of it has escaped his attention".[22] YHWH comes down because he knows the sufferings of his people.[23] The use of the verb ידע "to know" here seems significant as it has the sense of knowing someone personally;[24] YHWH's claim that the children of Israel are (את־עמי "my

---

19. Noth, *Exodus*, 38.
20. Hiphil infinitive of להצילו (3:8; 6:6; cf. Gen 32:31) gives the idea of snatching someone from danger.
21. Exod 3:7, 9, 16.
22. Houtman, *Exodus* 1, 354.
23. On the subject of God in his relation to the suffering of people, see T. E. Fretheim, *The Suffering of God* (Philadelphia: Fortress Press, 1984), 56–66; 127–137.
24. See G. J. Botterweck, "ידע", *TDOT* 5, 448–481. This verb ידע occurs about 35 times in Exodus and most of them occur with YHWH as subject or object of the verb (e.g. Exod 3:19; 4:14; 5:2).

people") his people (vv. 7, 10) signifies a relationship between YHWH and the Israelites, a relationship that is formed by virtue of his covenant with Abraham. To this effect, the writer had earlier mentioned that the Israelites were groaning, and God remembered his covenant with Abraham, Isaac, and Jacob (2:24–25). The writer's intentional repetition that YHWH/God came down to rescue the people from Egyptian oppression (3:7–8)[25] may be to tell his readers that there was a direct (physical) presence and physical appearance of YHWH/God with Moses. The textual evidence gives more scope to interpret the divine person in the bush in terms of corporeality/ physicality than in any other way.

Having explained his purpose to rescue the suffering Israelites in Egypt, YHWH then reveals his plan to send Moses to Pharaoh that he might bring them out of Egypt (v. 10).[26] When Moses expresses his insignificance in carrying out the task,[27] YHWH promises that he will be with Moses (כי־אהיה עמד), which may even signify that he will continue to reveal himself to Moses even in the future.[28] And the sign given is that when Moses brings the people out of Egypt, they will worship/ serve (עבד)[29] God on that very mountain (Horeb), possibly signifying that God will continue to reveal himself to the community of Israel.

4.2.3 The Mode of Self-Revelation, Human Recognition, and Response

Since the flame of fire in the bush is visible to Moses and the person in the bush calls Moses by name, this seems to indicate that the person in

---

25. Exod 2:24–25; 3:15, 16; 4:5.

26. M. Noth (*Pentateuchal Traditions*, 30, 36) understood Exod 3:1–12 as a fusion of theophany and call narrative from J and E. However, the text is clear that God appeared both to reveal himself to Moses and send him to Egypt. Cf. Gen 12 where the task to Abram was given during the divine revelation.

27. Perhaps, Moses had not forgotten the trouble with Pharaoh because of his affinity with Hebrews, and it was because of the fear of Pharaoh, he fled from Egypt to the land of Midian (Exod 2:11–15), and now again it is for their sake that he was told to go back to Egypt to face Pharaoh.

28. For a study on different aspects of Moses' meeting with Pharaoh in Egypt and YHWH's intervention, see W. A. Ford, *God, Pharaoh and Moses* (Bletchley: Paternoster, 2006), 30–102, for a reference to the presence of YHWH in Egypt.

29. The Hebrew words עבד and שחה are used in the context of "worship".

the bush is present, and is in human form. Although the writer tells that YHWH/God appeared in a flame of fire in the bush, and gives the impression that the bush is on fire, there is no other odd situation (like smoke) surrounding the divine appearance; and Moses is not afraid of going near the bush. The fire seems to have an association with the divine person, perhaps, it is the divine radiance that emitted from the person of YHWH/God which looks like fire to the human eye, and yet the divine person seems to be in the disguise of a human form. Since Moses is told to remove sandals as he goes close to God, presumably he is close enough to see the person there in human form. Presumably also, the presence of the person in the burning bush is real to Moses. The language used for God is anthropomorphic in that he hears the cry of his people, comes down to rescue, and to call Moses; and Moses understood what God spoke to him. These factors also seem to indicate that the divine person is understood to have been in human form, speaking in a human language.

Moses is at a close distance to God, standing in a face-to-face position, when God in his bodily (human) appearance spoke to Moses.[30] Since it is assumed that God revealed something of his radiance to Moses following which he could perceive him as God, and since Moses hid his face from seeing God at that point, this seems to signify that the appearance of the divine person in the bush was corporeal,[31] and that Moses had envisaged the divine figure in a literal/physical sense, and that YHWH/God is understood as physically present with Moses. However, Moses did not seem to express any fear of death as such.

As in other places, the initiative is taken by YHWH/God to appear to Moses with a definite purpose of rescuing Israel from Egypt. Kuntz thinks that in the HB "never once did human effort cause him to appear",[32] but however, it may be discerned right here in this text that the reason why YHWH came down was because the people's cry prompted YHWH to take the initiative[33] (3:7–8), although ultimately the initiative is God's. It

---

30. Cf. Fretheim, *Exodus*, 56.
31. Ibid., 55.
32. Cf. Kuntz, *Self-revelation*, 33.
33. Cf. W. Brueggemann, *Old Testament Theology* (Nashville: Abingdon Press, 2008), 25.

is said that God came down (ירד) to bring Israel out of Egypt (3:4–9), but it is not said where he came from, but possibly he came from heaven.[34] God's rescue (deliverance) of Israel from Egypt was to be reciprocated in "worship/service" to God; and this seems to indicate that future worship of Israel and the revealed presence of YHWH/God are closely linked.

4.2.4 The Function/Significance of Divine Revelation

The motif must have played a significant role in conveying that YHWH/God, moved by the prayers of his suffering people, came down to earth in human form and delivered Israel through Moses from their difficult life situation in Egypt. This tradition would have helped the new generations of ancient Israel to understand a historical continuity, in that the God of their fathers also intervened in the sufferings of the younger generations of Israelites. This text would have also helped the Israelite readers to realize that when Moses expressed his inadequacy to carry out the God-given task of bringing the Israelites out of Egypt, God promised his very presence with Moses (vv. 11–12).

4.2.5 Conclusion

The writer is emphatic that YHWH/God appeared to Moses in a flame of fire at Horeb. The text makes it explicit that the reason why YHWH chose to reveal himself to Moses at that juncture in history was to send Moses to Egypt to rescue the suffering Israelites from Egyptian oppression (3:4–9; cf. 2:24–25). This study has shown that the evidence in the text is directed towards the possibility of YHWH/God being physically present in the midst of the radiant fire; and the anthropomorphic language used to describe the activity of the divine person is an indication that the writer wanted to impress upon his readers that YHWH/God appeared to Moses in a literal sense. In previous readings, this study has understood that YHWH/God revealed something of himself (as in the case of Hagar and Jacob) to Moses (apart from his physical appearance) because of which Moses was afraid to look at God and hid his face, but yet no fear of death is expressed. The text gave some scope to interpret the divine appearance in physical terms.

---

34. Gen 21:17; 22:11 (calls from heaven); cf. 2 Chr 7:14 (hears prayer form heaven).

Moses was called to be the mediator between God and Pharaoh in Egypt. The future aspect of worship at Horeb was associated with the divine presence.[35] In closing, a word about the name by which YHWH should be represented in Egypt, that is, the name אהיה אשר אהיה (lit., "I am who I am") which seems to mean the "ever-existing one"[36] perhaps implying God as the creator. Perhaps this name functioned as a "legitimating password"[37] for Moses to encourage the Israelites in Egypt that God the creator was also their deliverer from Egypt.

4.3 Exodus 24:1–18: YHWH/God Appears in the Cloud and Fire

4.3.1 Canonical Context

The writer informs his readers that the Israelites are now camped in front of Mount Sinai (19:1–2). In accordance with the sign YHWH gave Moses (3:11–12), they are under an obligation to worship/serve him at the mountain, and a new era of worship begins in the Israelite religious life at the mountain. With regard to the divine revelations, unlike in the Genesis traditions and in Exodus 3, here at Sinai YHWH/God explains to Moses the mode of his revelation in advance: that he would come to Moses in a thick cloud (אנכי בא אליך בעב הענן). YHWH continues to reveal himself on the mountain (chs. 19–23).

The significant feature of the divine revelations at Sinai is that the concept of holiness/sanctification is introduced; the priests and the people alike are to sanctify themselves (יתקדשו) in order to approach God, and death is associated with approaching a holy God in unholiness (19:9–15; 21–24). In the writer's description, the mountain is covered with smoke,

---

35. Even Pharaoh was to be told: "YHWH the God of the Hebrews met with us . . . let us go . . . that we may sacrifice to YHWH our God" (3:18).
36. For an etymological study of this construction, see E. Schild, "On Exodus 3:14–'I am that I am'", *VT* 4 (1954), 296–297. Schild's translation, "I am the one who is" also seems closer to the idea of YHWH as the creator. Cf. B. Albrektson, "On the Syntax of אהיה אשר אהיה", in *Words and Meanings*, 15–28. M. P. O'Connor, "יהוה", *TDOT* 5, 500–521.
37. Mettinger, *In Search of God*, 23.

and it trembled violently because YHWH descended on it in fire. Moses speaks to God even in that fearful situation, and God replies to him in a voice (והאלהים יעננו בקול) from the midst of that fire (19:18–20; cf. 3:1–7). The people stand at a distance and ask Moses: "You speak to us, and we will hear; but let not God speak to us, lest we die" (20:18–19). The "death" here is not associated with seeing God, but hearing God speaking. Moses' assurance to them is: אל־תיראו "fear not (cf. Gen 15:1), for God has come to test you that his fear (יראתו)[38] may be before you, so that you may not sin" (20:19–20). Later on, a series of divine instructions was given to keep them from sinning (20:21–23:33).

This is the context in which Exodus 24:1–18 has to be interpreted. This text forms part of a larger narrative that began in chapter 19 and concludes here,[39] and the extant text reflects a thematic consistency with the previous chapters, particularly in terms of the divine revelations/theophanies and the divine Law.[40]

4.3.2 Divine Self-Revelation and Communication

Exodus 24:1–18 relates how YHWH told Moses to go up along with Aaron, Nadab, Abihu and seventy elders of Israel, but only Moses went near YHWH, while the others worshipped at a distance (24:1–2). Moses conveyed to the people all the words YHWH spoke on the mountain and they answered with one voice (קול אחד) that they would obey God's words, and Moses wrote down all the words YHWH spoke (vv. 3–4). When Moses built the altar at the foot of the mountain, he sent "young men of the people of Israel"[41] (את־נערי בני ישראל) to offer burnt offerings and peace offerings to God. Moses took half of the blood from those sacrifices, and sprinkled it on the altar; he put the other half of the blood in basins

---

38. The verb ירא "to fear" is used as a protecting measure to keep people from sinning.
39. Cf. E. W. Nicholson, "The Interpretation of Exodus xxiv 9–11", *VT* 24 (1974), 77–97.
40. See B. S. Childs, *The Book of Exodus. A Critical, Theological Commentary* (Louisville: John Knox Press, 2004), 499–502. For the source critical analysis of these chapters, see M. Noth, *Exodus* (London: SCM Press, 1962), 194–201, 243.
41. The specific mention of "young men" in this context of offering sacrifices for YHWH seems significant as they represented the new generations of Israel.

till such time that he read from the "book of the covenant"[42] before the people. After the people responded, saying, "All that YHWH has said we will do and obey" (נעשׂה ונשמע), Moses took the other half of the blood and sprinkled it on the people (vv. 5–8).

When Moses, Nadab, and Abihu, and seventy of the elders of Israel went up, they saw the God of Israel; there was a paved work of sapphire stone under his feet and it was like the sky in its clarity; but God did not raise his hand against the children of Israel, and they saw God and ate and drank (9–11). After that, YHWH tells Moses to go further up so that he could give him the tablets of stone with the law and commands he had written for their instruction. The glory of YHWH rested on Mount Sinai, and to the Israelites the appearance of the glory of YHWH looked like a consuming fire on top of the mountain (12–17). Moses went up into the midst of the cloud, and was on the mountain forty days and forty nights (v. 18).

The act of sprinkling the blood, first on the altar and then on the people (24:6–8) is significant as the two parties, namely YHWH and the new generations of Israel (בני ישראל), are brought into a bond of relationship. This sprinkled blood is normally termed as "the blood of the covenant"[43] which perhaps signifies the sealing of the covenant (24:8).[44] Since the writer already told his readers that YHWH took an interest in rescuing Israel from Egypt because they were (already) "his people",[45] the covenant now established at Sinai seems to be the continuation of the covenantal relationship which was initiated with Abraham much earlier (Gen 15:8–21).

In contrast to the individual covenant made with Abraham, the one at Sinai is made with the whole community of Israel, and the community

---

42. See Exod 20:22–23:19. For literary arguments on the book of the Covenant as a coherent literary unit, see J. M. Sprinkle, *Literary Approach to the Book of the Covenant.* JSOTS, 174 (Sheffield: JSOT Press, 1994). For source critical arguments, see J. W. Marshall, *Israel and the Book of the Covenant.* SBLDS, 140 (Atlanta, Georgia: Scholars Press, 1992), 14, 19–59.

43. See E. W. Nicholson, "The Covenant Ritual in Exodus 24: 3–8," *VT* 33 (1982), 74–86.

44. Alexander, *Paradise*, 91; Childs, *Exodus*, 502; Keil and Delitzsch, *The Pentateuch 2 & 3* (Grand Rapids: Eerdmans, 1959), 156.

45. את־עמי: Exod 3:7, 10; 5:1; 7:4; 16; 8:1, 20–23; 9:1, 13, 17, 10:3–4. Cf. Fretheim, *Exodus*, 256.

as a whole is under obligation to live up to the divine words (המשפטים and דברים) and expectations of the covenantal partner, who is YHWH himself.[46] The repetition of the law to the people is obviously to convey the importance of obeying the law (24:3, 7; cf. 19:8). As K. Koch stresses, the Hebrew דברים (spoken words)[47] "are forceful words, capable of bringing about events"; and that the commandments not only convey a moral appeal, but also the word itself provides the ability to accomplish what is asked for.[48] Significantly, Moses wrote all the words of YHWH to make it a record, that is, "the book of the covenant" (ספר הברית), for permanent use (vv. 4, 7).

After the covenant making was over and when Moses, Aaron, Nadab, Abihu and the seventy elders of Israel went up to the mountain (higher level),[49] the writer explicitly states that they saw the God of Israel. It appears that while the process of making the covenant of blood[50] is going on at on the lower levels of the mountain, God is present on the top of the mountain. This seems to indicate that the presence of YHWH on the mountain was understood to be real and may indicate that the appearance was in human bodily form, given that feet are described.

Scholars differ in the aspect of the physicality and visibility of the divine person on the mountain. For example, J. I. Durham suggests that what Moses and the others saw was not the appearance of God but the appearance of what lay at his feet, and that it implies "a description of God original to this passage has been respectfully deleted".[51] However, nowhere in the texts studied in the previous chapters did the writer(s) give a (physical) description of God, although they used anthropomorphic terms to

---

46. This covenant is in line with what was discussed earlier in the Abrahamic covenant (Gen 17:1–4).
47. E.g. Exod 20:1; cf. 34:1, 28; Deut 5:22.
48. K. Koch, *The Growth of the Biblical Tradition: The Form-Critical Method* (London: Adam & Charles Black, 1969), 9–10.
49. Since the word עלה "ascend" (once בא) is used in seven different contexts of Moses' going up or coming down the mountain it seems to indicate different elevation sites and gradual ascent which climaxes in Moses alone reaching the top (24:1, 3, 9, 12, 13, 15, 18). Cf. Childs, *Exodus*, 504.
50. For a similar rite: see 29:19–21, 32–33, 35–37; cf. Lev. 8:22–31, 34.
51. J. I. Durham, *Exodus* (Waco: Word Books, 1987), 344.

describe his activity; and if the Hebrew writer was aware of any deletions, he would not have made the clear assertion that they saw God (vv. 10 and 11). Durham also assumes that what they actually saw was not the 'vision' of the person of God.[52] But, the Hebrew writer insists that what they saw was the actual vision of God.

Reflecting on this text, Eichrodt says that it can "hardly be disputed that the original narrative is concerned with an actual vision of God".[53] Whether or not there was any original version that was different from the extant text, the appearance of God on the mountain is understood as real appearance.

Delitzsch suggests that one must not go beyond the limits drawn in Exodus 33:20–23 in understanding what constituted the sight (חזה in v. 11) of God. However, he also suggests that one must regard it as a vision of God in some form of manifestation "discernible to the human eye". One can see that Delitzsch's attempt to interpret 24:10–11 in light of Exodus 33:20–23 (that no one can see God)[54] does not let him accept the physicality of the anthropomorphic appearance of God on the mountain, but at the same time, he realizes that the Hebrew writer's assertion that "they saw God" requires some form that was discernible to the human eye. Childs observes that some commentators followed the LXX[55] in avoiding the directness of the statement that "they saw God", and cites one such comment that "the verbs ראה and חזה must be understood as "intellectual perception, but in no way as a real perceiving with the eye".[56] Fretheim, however,

---

52. Ibid.
53. Eichrodt, *OTT* 2, 19.
54. Keil and Delitzsch, *Pentateuch 2&3*, 159; Also J. P. Hyatt, *Exodus* (Grand Rapids: Eerdmans, 1971), 256. It may be noted that while the context of 24:10–11 was that of covenant making and obedience to God's words, the context of Exod 33:18–20 was the covenant breaking and the sin of disobedience to God's commands (23:20–33; 32:30).
55. LXX reads the phrase in 24:10 ויראו את אלהי ישראל as τὸν τόπον οὗ εἱστήκει ἐκεῖ ὁ θεὸς τοῦ Ισραηλ "they saw the place where the God of Israel stood" and 24:11 as: ὤφθησαν ἐν τῷ τόπῳ τοῦ θεοῦ "they appeared in the place of God". For variant readings of "seeing the face of God" in LXX, see A. Hanson, "The Treatment in the LXX of the Theme of Seeing God", *LXX*. Eds. G.J. Brooke & B. Lindars (Atlanta: Scholars Press, 1992), 557–565.
56. Childs, *Exodus*, 506, citing Maimonides (Guide I. 4). For a discussion on the literal usage of these two verbs ראה and חזה, see chapter 1, 4–5.

acknowledges that the seeing of God is an actual seeing and not an inner perception.[57]

The description in the text seems to point towards the reality of the divine appearance. The Hebrew writer insists that Moses, Aaron, Nadab, Abihu and the seventy elders of Israel saw the God of Israel. The fact that the writer describes what lies underneath the feet of God indicates that the "God of Israel" revealed himself in an anthropomorphic (human) form even when the divine revelation is associated with fire and cloud.[58] Although the cloud played a role in accompanying YHWH/God, he was present in the cloud and the cloud in itself seems to have no capacity or significance except that it functioned as a cover.[59] Furthermore, God was described walking in the garden of Eden, and readers would presumably realize that God was believed to be in a human form who needed feet to walk on the earth; they would also remember that the verb (והשתחויתם) "to prostrate/bow before" (v. 1) was also used in the case of Abraham when he (וישתחו) "bowed" before the persons who were physically present before him (Gen 18:2, 22); and they would have no difficulty in visualizing that people bowed before God who was present and that God was in human form. The writer is emphatic that it is "the God of Israel" (אלהי ישראל), and all those who were with Moses "saw God" in a real and physical sense.

The writer describes something like a fashioned work of sapphire[60] under his feet (ותחת רגליו: v. 10b) only after he has made his explicit assertion that "they saw the God of Israel" (ויראו את אלהי ישראל: v. 10a). By using the qal forms of the Hebrew verbs ראה "saw" (v. 10: ויראו) and חזה "beheld" (v. 11: ויחזו), he perhaps wishes to emphasize that God manifested himself in (human) form. Above all, the Hebrew tradition makes it clear

---

57. Fretheim, *Exodus*, 260.

58. There is some assumption that the function of מלאך יהוה (angel of YHWH) and ענן (cloud) have similar manifestations in the context of the divine revelations. However, while מלאך represents the (divine) person, the cloud is an impersonal entity. See G. E. Mendenhall, *The Tenth Generation* (Baltimore: Johns Hopkins University Press, 1973), 58–59.

59. For a discussion on the function of cloud, see T.W. Mann, *Divine Presence and Guidance in Israelite Traditions: The Typology of Exaltation* (Baltimore: John Hopkins University Press, 1977), 256–257.

60. The sapphire stone (cf. 28:18; Isa 54:11) is generally compared with the opaque blue *lapis lazuli* (of Mesopotamia).

that the people on the mountain not only saw God but also ate and drank (v. 11), and the readers would recall that, earlier in Genesis traditions, covenant making and partaking in a meal together signified a binding between two parties (Gen 31:44–54: ויאכלו לחם).[61] Although the text is not explicit (v. 11) if God also partook in the meal,[62] the meal they ate was presumably real, since it was associated with a covenant;[63] and seems to signify their binding to God to obey the Law forever.[64] One can presume that YHWH/God is understood to be physically present there in a literal sense and it was his direct presence that had authenticated the covenant process and God's relationship with new generations of Israelites.

While they had a covenant meal together in the same vicinity where God was said to be present, neither Moses nor the Israelite elders seem to express any fear of death for seeing God. The Hebrew writer seems emphatic in saying that God did not raise his hand (לא שלח ידו) against the Israelites when they saw him (24:10–11). The fact that the writer specifically and explicitly states that God did not raise his hand against the leaders of Israel, consequent to the act of seeing, confirms and supports the assumption that they literally saw God. If the physical aspect was not involved in this seeing, there is no reason why the writer would state that God did not raise his hand against them. However, it is surprising that the writer states specifically that God did not raise his hand against them. Does this statement imply that there was a fear of death associated with seeing YHWH/God? A brief reflection on similar literary usage and the concepts in the previous traditions may help in understanding what the writer is trying to convey by using this expression "raising hand". שלח with יד (to raise the hand) was used in Exodus 3:20 in the context of striking Egypt. Apart from this, the readers must have been aware that when God saw that the wickedness of humankind was great on the earth, he destroyed all the people except Noah (Gen 5:6–7); when he saw that the sin of Sodom

---

61. Gen 26:26–31; Exod 18:12.
62. Even if the readers understood that God took part in the meal, it would not have surprised them given that the traditions where God appeared in human form and ate human food (Gen 18:5–8; 19:3).
63. So Childs, *Exodus*, 507, Hyatt, *Exodus*, 257–58.
64. Von Rad, *OTT* 1, 254.

and Gomorrah was great, he destroyed it (Gen 18:20–19:24).⁶⁵ It may be reasonable, then, to think that since the incidents such as the flood and the destruction of Sodom were associated with the self-revelations of YHWH/God, there could have been some kind of fear existing over the appearances of God in ancient Israel, but it does not necessarily imply that seeing God in itself results in death.

Presumably, by stating that God did not raise his hand against the children of Israel, the Hebrew writer wishes to remove that inhibition from the minds of his readers. In any case, no one is said to have died simply for seeing the face of YHWH/God. The writer's intention seems to be that he wanted his readers to know that God revealed himself to be seen by people and to maintain the covenantal relationship with the new generations of Israel. By telling that God called them up, the writer also conveys the significance of the divine revelation that God took the initiative to let himself be seen on the mountain by the chosen people.⁶⁶ The fact that the object of the verbs used for seeing is God and the subject of seeing are the people also signifies that "seeing the face of God" meant seeing the God of Israel in a literal sense; and what is more, the question of seeking audience with the king does not arise. On the contrary, it was God, who called them up, rather than they seeking audience with God.⁶⁷

Although it is not obvious that the theophany around the meal is associated with cloud or fire, later on it is. When God calls Moses still further up on the mountain (v. 12) to receive the tablets of stone and Moses goes up, the cloud covers the mountain, and YHWH's glory (כבוד) that is settled on the mountain looked like a consuming fire and people down below could see it (vv. 15–17). The text reveals that Moses was with God for forty days and nights, and YHWH/God spoke to him (25:1). The aspect of holiness (קדש) seems dominant in these chapters which describe how the Law is

---

65. See J. M. Roberts, "The Hand of Yahweh", *VT* 21 (1971), 244–251. In light of an Amarna letter from Cyprus and an Ugaritic letter, Roberts sees some association of death with the hand of the god(s).

66. Even in these Sinai theophanies (similar to the anthropomorphisms in Genesis) human characteristic features are attributed to the divine person.

67. Fretheim, *Exodus*, 259. NIV reads it as בקש את־פני (lit. seeking the face of) as seeking "audience" (cf. 1 Kgs 10:24; 2 Chr 9:23); the NRS, NAS read it as: "seeking the presence of" in an abstract sense.

to be maintained (25:2–31:18) and it is for this reason perhaps that the Law at Sinai becomes most significant. As Sommer reflects, it is the divine presence that endows the Law "in the narrowest and the broadest senses of the term, with holiness".[68] The Hebrew traditions seem to have believed in the active role YHWH himself played in giving the Law to Moses and it is specifically mentioned that YHWH wrote on the two tablets by his finger (אצבע אלהים: 31:18). By using such vivid anthropomorphic language, the writer seems to insist that YHWH/God on the mountain, in the midst of the fiery cloud, was in human form, and it also, as in the context of the meal covenant, involved a literal seeing of God, and one can convincingly affirm that the embodied divine person was present with Moses on the mountain.

4.3.3 The Mode of Self-Revelation, Human Recognition, and Response

The mode of divine revelation in this text is very different from those studied in the Genesis traditions; here the appearance of YHWH/God is associated with (dense) cloud, thunder and lightning, fire and smoke, and violent trembling. Earlier in the narrative, it is said that YHWH came down (ירד) to the mountain (19:20) and called Moses to go up, but there is no other reference to his coming down before this theophany here in chapter 24. The initiative to call Moses and others came from God himself. That those who were on the mountain are believed to have seen God, and that God was present with the people during the covenant meal (24:10), one can assume that he was in human bodily form.

There is no clue to think that Moses or others are afraid of death for seeing God. Rather, in response to seeing God, those who saw him prostrated themselves and worshipped him. The readers are introduced to a new mode of revelation of YHWH which is in association with his "glory" (כבוד־יהוה); when YHWH called Moses from the midst of the cloud, Moses went into/behind the cloud where he stayed forty days and nights with God (24:15–18). However, the language used in describing the divine

---

68. B. D. Sommer, "Revelation at Sinai in the Hebrew Bible and in Jewish Theology", *JR* (1999), 451.

appearance is still vividly anthropomorphic, with "feet" (24:10) and "finger" (31:18) ascribed to the divine person. It seems that even in the midst of his glory (כבוד), YHWH/God appeared in human bodily form and spoke to Moses at human level (25:1). In light of this textual evidence, one can assume the possibility of Moses seeing "the face of God" (even face-to-face) on the mountain.

4.3.4 The Function/Significance of Divine Revelation

This tradition could have played an important role in helping to understand God's character of faithfulness to his covenant to Abraham, in that he delivered Israel from the slavery of Egypt. The Law and commandments given at the mountain and the establishment of the covenant of blood would have signified God's continued relationship with the new generations of the Israelites; that the sanctification of people was closely associated with the worship of the holy God, that people were under obligation to obey the spoken words of YHWH, and that the worship was concerned with a larger group (vv. 24:9–11).

4.3.5 Conclusion

The text gave the impression that YHWH/God was present in human (bodily) form even in the theophanies which are associated with fire and cloud. On Mount Sinai, on the one hand, YHWH/God was accompanied by fearful elements, and on the other hand, he met with and spoke to Moses and others. It is understood that the covenant of blood was significant because it signified the continuation of God's relationship with the new generations of the Israelites. It was God's direct presence that authenticated the covenant process and God's relationship with the new generations of Israelites. Moses was understood to be with God for forty days and nights in the midst of the fiery cloud. In light of the description in the texts, it is understood that ancient Israel perceived that God on the mountain, both in the context of the meal covenant and in the midst of the fiery cloud, was physically present in human (bodily) form. In light of the textual evidence, one can convincingly affirm that the embodied divine person was present on the mountain.

4.4 Concluding Remarks

Since chapters 2 and 4 in this work have been focused on understanding the motif/theme of "the self-revelations of YHWH/God" in Genesis and Exodus traditions, a few overall observations are made here. The divine titles אלהים, יהוה, מלאך־יהוה are used in Genesis and Exodus texts in a similar fashion. While YHWH/God appeared to individuals (at time to couples) and worship was associated with individuals in the Genesis texts, he appeared both to individuals and to a larger group in the Exodus texts. In Genesis, the self-revelations are unexpected, mostly to individuals, casual and in the guise of a human form. The encounters are more informal and involved everyday life situations. Identity is revealed at some point, and the purpose of the revelation is communicated. It is very likely that when YHWH/God appeared, he appeared in human (bodily form) and is actively involved in conversation and communication.

Exodus 3 seems to represent both the Genesis pattern (in that it is to an individual and unexpected), and also the Exodus pattern (the divine person appearing in the midst of fire). The divine revelations in Exodus 24 are expected and are made more obvious; they are more formal, accompanied by cloud, fire and glory; and apparently the divine person is described appearing in human bodily form and letting himself be seen by those to whom he appeared; and no one died for seeing (the face of) God. Worship of the revealed person of God involves bodily posture and service both in Genesis and Exodus, although different Hebrew terms are used for worship.[69]

In closing, it may be reiterated that all the selected texts studied in Genesis and Exodus have shown that "the self-revelations" of YHWH/God were very real to the ancient Israelites, and that there is evidence to think that when YHWH/God revealed himself to different people, he let himself be seen by them, a seeing which evidently involved "seeing the face of YHWH/God". In light of this, one can also affirm that the background of "seeing God" was in the contexts of the self-revelations of YHWH/God, who came to meet with the people, and the question of seeking an

---

69. נפל + על־פנים "to fall on the face" (Gen 17:3); עבד "to serve" (Exod 3:12) and שחה "to bow" (24:1).

audience with the king does not arise. The term פנים "face" in the expression פני־יהוה/אלהים "face of YHWH/God represents the "face of the anthropomorphized person of "YHWH/God" in the context of his self-revelations.

While "seeing the face of YHWH/God" is not associated with a fear of death as such in the Genesis and Exodus texts studied in chapters 2–4 in this work, Exodus 33:20 records that YHWH said, "No one can see me and live". In order to understand this paradox, this work will now turn in chapter 5 to study Exodus 33:12–23.

CHAPTER 5

"You Cannot See My Face; No One Can See Me, and Live": Exodus 33:12–23

5.1 Introduction

The purpose of this chapter is to identify the tensions pertaining to the "seeing" aspect that surrounds the expression פני־יהוה "the face of YHWH"[1] and to study those tensions in light of the previously studied traditions in this work. The text selected for the study in this chapter is Exodus 33:12–23. The reason for selecting this particular text is that it contains significant statements on the theme of "'seeing' (and not seeing) the face of YHWH". In Exod 33:14, YHWH's promise to Moses was: פני ילכו "my 'face' shall go". However, in 33:20, it is stated that YHWH told Moses: לא תוכל לראת את־פני כי לא־יראני האדם וחי "you will not be able to see 'my face'; for no one shall see me, and live".

Literally speaking, these two statements are not without tension. Does the latter one mean that even Moses was not allowed to see the divine face? This has been a greatly debated issue in scholarly circles. Furthermore, 33:20 is said to stand in conflict with the statement in 33:11: וִדבר יהוה אל־משה פנים אל־פנים "YHWH used to speak with Moses 'face-to-face'". And yet in 34:29 it is stated: קרן עור פניו בדברו אתו "the skin of his (Moses') face shone when he spoke with him (YHWH)".

---

1. Where פנים "face" is associated with the verbs הלך and ראה (vv. 14–15, 20, 23).

In order to understand this tension, this study will refer back to the canonically earlier texts/traditions in so far as they help understand the tensions in the text under examination. This expression "'seeing' the face of YHWH/God" was earlier used in Genesis, and the readers would remember that Jacob, as his explicit statement demonstrated, had seen God פנים אל־פנים "face-to-face" (Gen 32:31); Moses, Aaron, Nadab and Abihu, and the seventy elders of Israel went up and saw God on the Sinai Mountain where Moses alone stayed with YHWH for 40 days and nights in glory while receiving the tablets of the law (24:9–11; cf. 3:1–12);[2] and YHWH spoke to him "face-to-face" (33:11). But here in this text, the readers are informed that YHWH told Moses: "You will 'not be able to see my face'" (33:20).

In light of the previous traditions, one may wonder how the readers of that day would have understood the negation, at least supposed, in 33:20. Had they taken it at its face value and thought that no one, including Moses, could see YHWH and live, in a literal sense? If this query is to be answered in the positive, the question, then, would be why the writer had retained the statement: "YHWH spoke to Moses 'face-to-face'" (33:11) just a few sentences before this verse. Furthermore, in the very next chapter,[3] it is stated that Moses' face shone because he spoke (בדברו) with YHWH, which seems to indicate the positive aspect of seeing (34:29).

Does the "face-to-face" speech (33:11) between YHWH and Moses affirm the possibility of Moses seeing the divine face? Does the "shining of Moses' face" necessarily confirm the potentially positive aspect that Moses saw the divine face, following which his face shone? If so, the tension still is how can one interpret the negation in terms of "seeing the divine face" in 33:20 and 23? Is the tension in these conflicting statements at a literary or theological level? Could it be that this tension in the statement in 33:20, which was supposedly made by YHWH, arose because of the contextual factors such as the sin of carving and worshiping the calf?

---

2. During which time, one may presume that he had seen some aspects of the divine face.

3. This statement placed in the very next chapter after the text 12–23 seems significant, as it might help interpret the negation in 33:20.

It is this tension that will be explored in this chapter with a view to understanding the expression "'seeing' the face of YHWH" and to discerning the function it had in ancient Israel. In order to understand if the negation in the statement in 33:20 ("you will not be able to see my face . . .") was made in contradiction to the positive idea of "the face of YHWH/God" in 33:14, or something else was being underlined, this text needs to be studied within the Sinai pericope.

The text seems to be an integral part of the section that consists of chapters 32–34, and gives information as to what happened and the order in which it happened.[4] The specific usage of פנים "face" in association with the divine person in 33:12–23[5] seems significant to understanding the theme of "seeing the divine face". Reading this section as a whole,[6] one gets an impression that the challenge of YHWH's continued presence with Israel (ch. 33) may have originated from the worship of the golden calf (ch. 32), which led to the renewal of the covenant later (ch. 34). Moses' intercession begins in chapter 32, continues in chapter 33, where the theme is the presence of God, and reaches its climax in chapter 34, where the assurance of forgiveness was granted by means of a specific divine revelation.[7] In chapter 34, verses 1–10 and 28–35 seem significant, as they describe a specific divine revelation on the mountain where Moses had a direct exposure to the divine glory.

Therefore, it seems important to interpret 33:12–23 in the context of the section 32–34 as a whole in order to understand the overall context in which the statement 33:20 is made. The exegetical study in this chapter will be limited to 33:12–23, but 34:1–10, 28–35 will also be given due importance with a view to understanding whether the shining of Moses'

---

4. A. Motyer, *The Message of Exodus* (London: Intervarsity Press, 2005), 298.
5. E.g. Exod 33:11 (פנים אל־פנים); 14 (פני ילכו); 15 (אם־אין פניך הלכים); 20 (את־פני); 23 (ופני); cf. 34:29 (ופניו); 30 (פניו); 33 (על־פניו); 35 (את־פני). It is noteworthy that the specific term פנים "face" is used more frequently in this section (chs. 32–34) than in other parts of the Pentateuch. Cf. F. Hartenstein, "Das 'Angesicht Gottes' in Exodus 32–34", in *Gottes Volk am Sinai*. Eds. M. Köckert and E. Blum (Gütersloh: Verlagshaus, 2001), 158.
6. Scholars who have studied Exod 32–34 as a whole include R. W. L. Moberly, *At the Mountain of God: Story and Theology in Exodus 32–34* (Sheffield: JSOT Press, 1983). Hartenstein, "Angesicht Gottes", 157–183; also *Angesicht*, 263–283.
7. See Childs, *Exodus*, 557–558.

face was the consequence of his seeing "the face of YHWH" or not. In addition to this, there will be some discussion of the theophany as described in verses 7–11, with an intention to understand whether the text gives a clue to Moses' seeing the face of YHWH during the פנים אל־פנים "face-to-face" speech between him and YHWH.

In light of the above discussion of important aspects surrounding the theme of "'seeing' the face of YHWH/God", this text will be studied under four main sections: 5.3.1 The Divine Task Given and Moses' Needs Expressed: vv. 12–13; 5.3.2 Moses' Requests Accepted and YHWH's Presence Promised: vv. 14–17; 5.3.3 Moses' Continued Requests and YHWH's Responses: vv. 18–20; 5.3.4 The Divine Revelation Promised and Moses' Desire Fulfilled: 33:21–34:1–10, 28–35.

5.2 Canonical Context

It was in accordance with his covenant with Abraham that YHWH brought the Israelites out of the slavery in Egypt into the freedom of worship at the mountain,[8] where they were on their way to reach the Promised Land (Land). The covenant made by YHWH with Abraham, as "a means of establishing a relationship",[9] was continued with the Israelites, who became a special people to YHWH (19:5, 6). The Israelites were told not to make any "image" (פסל) as an object of worship.[10] However, while their deliverance from Egypt was closely associated with worship at the mountain, by the time Moses carried the tablets of the divine Law, with the instructions related to the worship (Exod 24:12–31:18), the people had carved the image of a calf and worshiped it as their god (32:1–6; 15–19), who would go before them (לפנינו: 32:23).

---

8. Exod 2:24; 3:6, 8, 12, 15–16; 19:1–24:11.
9. W. S. Lasor and et al, eds. *Old Testament Survey* (Grand Rapids: Eerdmans, 1996), 73.
10. They should not carve any image in the likeness of anything that is in the created world nor should they bow before them for he is a jealous God (Exod 20:1–5).

That act of making a calf as an object of worship was treated as "great sin" (חטאה גדלה: 32:21, 30–31),[11] since it implied the people's unfaithfulness to the covenant, rejection of YHWH and broken relationship with him (32:9–10).[12] Even as YHWH was angry and wanted to destroy the people for their sin (32:10), Moses, acting as a mediator, prayed[13] for their forgiveness on the basis of YHWH's covenant with Abraham (32:11–13; cf. 31–32), after which YHWH relented and did not destroy the people as he said that he would (32:14).[14] Moses also saw the need for the people's consecration and atonement for their sin (32:29–30).

Regardless of the source analysis or the secondary accretion theory,[15] this whole chapter is formed around the theme of the divine presence, and, for that matter, the theme of theophany, which, as pointed out by F. Polak, "dominates the entire book of Exodus . . . and permeates all traditions, sources and redaction layers".[16] As J. Muilenburg has observed, "the major themes and keywords have also been so carefully woven into the literary fabric that it is difficult to believe that it represents anything less than a unified and coherent composition",[17] and that unity is also found in terms of Moses' conversation between YHWH and Moses.

Literary historical critics have associated chapter 33 with different sources,[18] but the writer's use of the literary variants seems to indicate dif-

---

11. Of the three Hebrew terms used for "sin", חטאה (other two being פשע and עון) seems most important and has the sense of "missing the way or to fall short of the standard"; and the object of the verb חטא (in qal) is often either God or his laws (e.g. Gen 4:7; 18:20; 31:36; Exod 20:20; 23:33; 29:14, 36; 32:21; 34:7–9).
12. They disobeyed despite their earlier agreement to maintain the covenant (19:8; 24:3–7).
13. Considering LXX's ἐδεήθη (aorist passive of δέομαι "to pray") in 32:11.
14. However, several people were killed for their sin (32:25–28; 33–35).
15. M. Noth, *History of Pentateuchal Traditions* (Englewood Cliffs: Prentice-Hall, 1972), fn. 114, 31.
16. F. Polak, "Theophany and Mediator", in M. Vervenne, ed., *Studies in the Book of Exodus* (Leuven: Leuven University Press, 1996), 113.
17. J. Muilenburg, "The Intercession of the Covenant Mediator (Ex. 33:1a, 12–17)", in *Words and Meanings*, 164–175. Although Muilenburg's comment is based on the composition of Exod 33: 1a, 12–17, the same coherence may be seen in the whole of ch. 33.
18. It is argued that in 33:1–3, an angel would go before them, but 3b gives the idea of judgment; in 32:10, YHWH was seen as angry but later in 33:19; 34:6, he is seen as merciful; 33:7–11 is out of place in this section of 32:1–34:9; and that 33:12–17 has a

ferent aspects in/of the divine revelation. Verses 7–11 are obviously an integral part of the larger section 32–34, in which פנים plays a significant role. The terms פנים "face" and דבר "to speak" (chs. 32–34) are significant in the context of the divine revelations;[19] and the noun פנים which is associated with the verb ראה and with הלך reflects the literary uniformity in the whole section.[20] Israel was given the divine Law which includes the Ten Commandments within the covenant tradition;[21] by virtue of his being their rescuer/redeemer, YHWH commanded them that they should have no other gods before him (20:1–2), but the people sinned against him by disobeying that very commandment (32:10; cf. Gen 3:16–24) because of which the covenant renewal came about. All this reflects a definite literary and thematic unity within the section, and it fits better as part of the Sinai pericope.

Chapter 33:1–3 is the continuation of 32:34a, where Moses was told to lead the people to the place of promise; and the theme of judgement connects these two chapters. Chapter 32 describes the breaking of the covenant, 33 shows Moses as the mediator, and 34 sees the restoration of the covenantal relationship between YHWH and the people. Any tension reflected within these chapters 32–34, then, seems to lie in the tradition itself: that there was a problem because of the people's sin, but that YHWH relented because of his mercy and forgave them. Coming to the immediate context within chapter 33, it may be significant that the writer now (after the calf episode) informs his readers that it is YHWH who repeats his

---

direct link with 32:34a rather than with 33:7–11; diverse abstract terms, כבד and טוב, are used in parallel with פנים to signify the divine presence; v. 20 says that no one can see YHWH's פנים but v. 14 says, "my פנים will go". For a detailed discussion, see Childs, *Exodus*, 584–597; Hyatt, *Exodus*, 305, 312–313. Hartenstein ("Angesicht Gottes", 157–158) treats Exod 32 as late pre-exilic, 33:7–11 as the post P and 34 as post exilic.

19. The term דבר (either as a noun or a verb) is mostly associated with YHWH himself. For example, Exod 32:7, 14, 34; 33:1, 11, 17 (twice); 34: 27 (twice), 31, 32 and 34 (twice). For a discussion on the verb form (piel form of דבר etc.), see B. Waltke and M. O'Connor, *Introduction to Biblical Hebrew Syntax* (Winona Lake: Eisenbrauns, 1990), 358.

20. פנים with הלך, in 32:1, 23; 33:14; ראה in 33:20, 23; 34:20, 23, 24, 25, 35; as a direct object with יהוה (32:11; 34:23, 24), and Moses (34:35). Cf. 32:12, 20; 33:16 (פנים as the face of the earth).

21. On the covenant making in ancient times in the ANE, see Mendenhall, *Tenth Generation*, 10, 21.

promise made with Abraham,[22] and tells Moses to lead the people towards the Land (33:1; cf. 32:34), even though this is unexpected after their sin with the golden calf.[23] However, YHWH said that he would send only "his angel" before (לפניך) them (32:34a; 33:2) but he himself would not go among/with them (בקרבך) lest he destroyed them for their (potential) stubbornness (33:3).[24] For some reason, the writer informs his readers that these divine words were evil tidings (את־הדבר הרע) which distressed the people and led them to strip off their ornaments (33:4–6), a sign of repentance or mourning.[25]

It is significant that immediately after informing his readers about stripping off the ornaments, the writer brings in a different theme in the subsequent passage (33:7–11) that portrays YHWH's appearance at the tent of meeting, and insists that the intimacy between YHWH and Moses was such that YHWH used to speak to Moses פנים אל־פנים ("face-to-face") in the tent as a friend would. It is important to give attention to this theophanic text, as it seems to have a direct bearing on the select text under study. Some scholars argue that verses 7–11 interrupt the narrative and do not fit into its present location;[26] that this passage may be accidental, or intended to show an indirect divine accompaniment.[27] However, as other scholars agree, this tent episode fits well within the larger section of the Israelites' sin

---

22. Interestingly, the Abrahamic covenant was mentioned by Moses earlier and now by YHWH. This repetition of the promise of the Land to Abraham was perhaps a reminder to the readers that it was the basis on which Israel was both called into being and was sustained (Exod 33:1–6).

23. W. J. Dumbrell, "The Prospect of Unconditionality in the Sinaitic Covenant", in A. Gileadi, ed., *Israel's Apostasy and Restoration. Essays in Honour of R. K. Harrison* (Grand Rapid: Baker Books, 1988), 150.

24. Literarily speaking, לפניך (2nd p. sg. suff.) would mean Moses alone (33:2), but it may be noted that in 33:3 the stiff-necked people (עם־קשה־ערף אתה) were the object of the verb "destroy" (אכלך has 2nd p. sg suff.). It seems that Moses was addressed in solidarity with the people.

25. In Exod 32:24 they gave their gold for carving the calf, but now they took off their ornaments as a sign of regret. In some sense here gold is associated with apostasy (20:23). Cf. Childs, *Exodus*, 589.

26. Durham, *Exodus*, 441; R. M. Billings, "The Problem of the Divine Presence: Source-critical Suggestions for the Analysis of Exodus 33:12–23", *VT* 54 (2004), 429.

27. Childs, *Exodus*, 591, 593.

of calf worship and Moses' mediation for their forgiveness (32:1–34:35).[28] The placement of this theophanic text seems intentional,[29] in order to inform the readers that the theophany was direct and that YHWH descended in the pillar of cloud and revealed himself to Moses at the tent.[30] Verses 7–11 lead well into the subsequent dialogue between YHWH and Moses that begins at verse 12.[31]

M. D. Wessner maintains that 7–11 is "marked by the exclusive use of" אהל (tent), מחנה (camp) and פתח (door) and that they occur neither before nor after the pericope,[32] but these terms occur prior to and also within this section.[33] Fretheim viewed the theophany in 7–11 as "a retrospective"[34] and Moberly argues that it functions aetiologically".[35] However, this tradition in 33:7–11 seems to describe the current theophany in the tent of meeting.[36] There is general agreement that the tent, pitched by Moses outside the camp, was a simple structure used as a place of "meeting" where YHWH appeared from time to time and communed with Moses.[37]

---

28. See Cassuto, *Exodus*, 407; Noth, *Exodus*, 241; Fretheim, *Exodus*, 279. The tent here may have functioned as the place where YHWH appeared despite Israelite's sin (vv. 7a–8).

29. This seems common in Eastern literature (particularly vernacular story/narrative writing in South Asia) that in order to explain a particular point, the writer may bring a different theme to enable the readers to understand the main theme better.

30. The verb יעד in niphal seems to give the sense: "to meet with", or to make an appointment with (33:7). So von Rad, *OTT* 1, 236.

31. Some assume that the construction of the ark from the ornaments between v. 6 and the description in vv. 7–11 was suppressed in order to make room for the P account (chs. 35–39), but this seems unlikely, as it could not have achieved any purpose. See J. P. Hyatt, *Exodus* (Grand Rapids: Eerdmans, 1971), 314.

32. M. D. Wessner, *Face to Face:* פנים אל־פנים in *Old Testament Literature*. MA. diss. (Regent College, 1998), 42.

33. For example, אהל מועד with פתח (Gen 18:1; Exod 29:4, 11, 32, 42), and מחנה (with/without a definite article) occur in Gen 32:3, 9; Exod 19:17; 32:19; 26; אל־אהל מועד in 30:26; 31:7.

34. Fretheim, *Exodus*, 295. This is owing to the imperfect verbal forms used in 33:7–11. However, the perfect verbal forms are also used here and v. 11 itself has both perfect and imperfect verbs.

35. Moberly, *At the Mountain*, 150.

36. It is possible however, that there was more than a single theophany at the tent (within the context of the calf episode), and that people used to go to the tent in order to hear YHWH's words through Moses (33:7).

37. See Noth, *Exodus*, 255–256.

In a technical sense, the tent does not reflect any features of a shrine (which was not yet constructed);[38] and so it is unlikely that it had any cultic significance,[39] and the idea of ancient "cultic liturgy" as proposed by Muilenburg[40] seems speculative.[41]

Now, in order to discern the visual aspect in this theophany, a brief reflection on the details surrounding it seems necessary. According to 33:9, whenever Moses went into the tent,[42] the pillar of cloud would descend and stand at the entrance of the tent (ירד עמוד הענן ועמד פתח האהל), and YHWH would speak with Moses in the tent פנים לא־פנים—this seems to indicate that it was a direct talk, possibly involving a visual aspect. T. D. Alexander suggests that the tent curtain shielded Moses, who was inside (33:9), from YHWH who was outside; and while acknowledging that YHWH and Moses were in close proximity to one another, he suggests that even Moses was not allowed to look directly upon God.[43] However, elsewhere in Genesis, the use of פתח האהל (at the door of the tent) also meant inside the tent.[44] It may be that the pillar of cloud functioned as a cover to prevent the people from seeing YHWH, and stood at the door (ועמד פתח);[45] YHWH being on the other side of the cloud was inside the tent speaking with Moses directly. It is doubtful if this tent had any (fixed)

---

38. Cf. LXX reads σκηνήν, "temporary shelter". אהל מועד seems to be different from מקדש (25:8) and משכן (26:1) the complex structure described in Exod 35–40, and there is no mention of the Ark/Tablets of Law or priestly sacrifices or blessing. N. M. Sarna, *Exodus* (Philadelphia: The Jewish Publication Society, 1991), 211; Noth, *Exodus*, 255–256; von Rad, *OTT* 1, 235–236; J. L. Mackay, *Exodus* (Fearn: Christian Focus Publications, 2001), 553.
39. See Wessner, *Face to Face*, 39.
40. Muilenburg, "Intercession", 159–181; M.S. Smith, *The Pilgrimage Pattern in Exodus* (Sheffield: Sheffield Academic Press, 1997), 101–108.
41. Cf. Childs, *Exodus*, 585– 2004.
42. The directional ה (האהלה) indicates that Moses went towards, i.e. entered the tent (cf. 33:8).
43. Alexander, *Paradise*, 71–72.
44. In Gen 18:10, Sarah was said to be פתח האהל (at the tent), but it meant באהל (18:9) inside the tent.
45. Evidently, the appearance of the pillar of cloud was a sign for the people that YHWH was behind the cloud (33:10) since they stood and worshiped, and possibly they were aware that YHWH was speaking to him in the tent.

curtain,⁴⁶ as it was supposed to be not a permanent structure but only a place of meeting, where YHWH appeared from time to time.⁴⁷

Furthermore, by employing the phrase פנים אל־פנים "face-to-face" and the simile of friends, the writer seems to convey that the appearance of YHWH in the tent theophany was real, and that the conversation (with Moses) was direct. As T. W. Mann suggests, verse 11 "accentuates the closeness with which Moses associates with Yahweh, who *speaks* to him *face-to-face*".⁴⁸ Since this phrase was also used in Jacob's claim that he had seen God פנים אל־פנים "face-to-face", it seems sensible to think that Moses was able to see the anthropomorphized divine person during that face-to-face conversation inside the tent. Durham's suggestion that face-to-face here is "to be understood as an idiom of intimacy, not as a reference to theophany"⁴⁹ seems unacceptable. "Face-to-face" speech could not be simply a "picture of a spiritual communion", as J. C. Rylaarsdam suggests.⁵⁰ As Driver notes, it was "not from the distant heaven, or . . . a vision or a dream,"⁵¹ and these theophanies seemed to signify the reality of the divine revelations among the people from time to time. Although Puritans did not seem to think of a corporeal God, the idea of God's corporeality is found in their aesthetic thinking.⁵² The text seems to insist that YHWH was physically present with Moses in order to speak to him.⁵³

As discussed earlier in this work, although Eichrodt acknowledges that it was a "direct personal meeting", he holds that it is "speaking with the invisible God which is described as speaking 'face-to-face'" and that this is

---

46. Given that Moses used to carry a temporary structure which he called: ויקרא לו אהל מועד "tent of meeting" (33:7).

47. Noth, *Exodus*, 255–256.

48. Mann, *Divine Presence*, 145.

49. Durham, *Exodus*, 443; cf. Reindl, *Angesicht*, 200.

50. J. C. Rylaarsdam, *Exodus. IB,* 1073.

51. Driver, *Exodus*, 360.

52. See L. Haims, "The Face of God: Puritan Iconography in Early American Poetry, Sermons and Tombstone Carving", in *Early American Literature*. Vol. 1 (n.d., 1979), 1–41. While J. Calvin accepts the idea of God's care in human terms, he rejects the idea of a corporeal God. See *Institutes* I, 13, 1.

53. Cf. M. Burrows, *An Outline of Biblical Theology* (Philadelphia: Westminster, 1946), 28.

a "heightened metaphor (Exod 33:11)".⁵⁴ But, the metaphorical idea has no support in the text, since the Hebrew writer insists that YHWH came in the cloud and was present in the tent, and it is more likely that it was with the visible anthropomorphized person that Moses spoke face-to-face. Furthermore, previous traditions have given a clear understanding that God's appearances were normally in human (bodily) form.⁵⁵ Presumably the readers were acquainted with Jacob's claim that he saw God "face-to-face" (Gen 32:31), which seems clearly to have involved physicality.⁵⁶ In light of earlier instances wherein YHWH revealed himself to Moses and communicated his messages, the readers presumably understood that Moses was able to see YHWH face-to-face in a literal sense.

The face-to-face theophany in 33:7–11, with its description of lively relationship between YHWH and Moses probably indicates the role the divine self-revelations played within the Exodus traditions, and also leads well into the next section (vv. 12–23) where the term פנים "face" occurs frequently in association with YHWH. At this juncture, it may help to look at the context to see if there is a definite purpose why this tent theophany is placed where it is placed. It may be noted that the question of YHWH's accompanying presence did not arise till after Israel's iniquity. Moses' identification with the people was such that he pleaded for YHWH's forgiveness on behalf of the people at the cost of his own life (32:11–14; 31–32). Later on, the people who were in a crisis situation (for making the calf go before them) showed signs of repentance (33:4–6). So one can expect that Moses was troubled, when YHWH told him that his direct presence with the people meant their destruction (33:3; 32:34b, 35), and that news would have raised the question as to whether YHWH would reveal himself on their onward journey as he did in the past, particularly on the mountain. Perhaps Moses needed a definite confirmation of YHWH's continued presence with him/them at this point.

It was in this larger context that the writer tells his readers that YHWH spoke to Moses "face-to-face" (ודבר יהוה אל־משה פנים אל־פנים), as though

---

54. Chapter 1, 9.
55. As discussed in chapters 2–4.
56. See chapter 3, 95–98.

he wanted his readers know that it was because of Moses' "incredible relationship with God"[57] that he stood before YHWH on behalf of the people.[58] Verses 7–11 seem to have functioned as a prelude/prologue to verses 12–23 and set the stage for Moses' prayer to YHWH where פני־יהוה "face of YHWH" plays an important role, as it seems to signify the self-revelation of YHWH. Ironically, it is in this context of Moses' close relationship with YHWH that the statement לא תוכל לראת את־פני ("you will not be able to see my face") is made by YHWH himself later in his conversation with Moses. This seemingly contradicting statement will be explored in the exegetical study of the selected text 33:12–23 in light of its association with 34:1–10 and 28–35.

5.3 Exegetical Study of the Text

5.3.1 The Divine Task Given and Moses' Needs Expressed: vv. 12–13

According to the text, Moses said to YHWH: "Consider, you say to me, 'Lead these people';[59] but you have not let me know whom you will send with me; yet you have said, 'I know you by name and you have also found grace in my eyes/sight'[60] (v. 12). So now I pray, if I have found grace in your sight, let me know your ways, I pray, that I may know you so that I may find grace in your eyes; and consider that this nation is your people" (v. 13).[61]

---

57. P. R. House, *Old Testament Theology* (Downers Grove: Intervarsity Press, 1998), 122.
58. Interestingly, Moses, who hid his face in fear (Exod 3:1–6) when YHWH appeared to him first, now is in an intimate relationship with YHWH, which he perhaps developed during the divine revelations.
59. The verb העל hiphil impv. of עלה gives the sense "to lead". Cf. LXX has ἀνάγαγε (from ἀνάγω "to lead"); the verb אמר may refer to 32:34 where the verb is נחה "to lead" or to 33:1 where עלה is used.
60. Cf. Exod 3:21; 11:3; 12:36, where YHWH is said to have caused חן in the eyes of the Egyptians.
61. It is not clear if this meeting was one of the tent theophanies or elsewhere near the Mountain.

5.3.1.1 Moses' dialogue with YHWH over the accompaniment (12a)

The conversation between YHWH and Moses (vv. 12–17) is not "loosely joined to 32:34a", as Noth thinks,[62] rather it seems to reflect the continuity of the conversation from 33:1 on the matter of moving forward towards the Land. According to 32:34b–35 and 33:3, YHWH would not go with the people lest they be destroyed on the way. Since the people had shown signs of repentance (33:4–6), perhaps, Moses wanted to know if YHWH would relent (cf. 32:14) from his earlier decision not to go with them. Moses' argument here is that YHWH gave him the task of leading the people forward but did not let him know[63] whom he would send with him (12a). The readers would remember that YHWH did not hide the matter from Abraham, whom he treated as his friend (Gen 18:17), and perhaps, the same is expected here, as the simile of friendship was used earlier in verse 11; the intimacy between YHWH and Moses was already made evident in verses 7–11.

Surprisingly, Moses insists that he knows who YHWH would send with him, whereas when YHWH told Moses to lead (נחה) the people, he also told him, מלאכי ילך לפניך "'my angel' shall go before you" (32:34); ושלחתי לפניך מלאך "I will send 'an angel' before you" (33:2). Why then, did Moses complain that YHWH did not tell him whom he would send with him, when the angel of YHWH was also able to give victory over the enemies (33:2)? It does not seem that he wanted to know "which of the angels", as Driver suggests.[64] Was Moses' concern for something more than the accompaniment of the angel (of YHWH)? Perhaps he was anxious to know if YHWH would continue to reveal himself in future.

The usage of "angel" in this context has gained much scholarly attention, and a brief reflection on the promise of the angel seems necessary here. In 32:34 it is said that מלאכי "my angel" (i.e. "the angel of YHWH") would go; and in 33:2 simply מלאך "an angel" is mentioned. Because of this variant reading some scholars have assumed that "an angel" (מלאך) in

---

62. Noth, *Exodus*, 256–257.
63. The use of אתה with הודעתני (2nd p. sg. hiphil of ידע) may be for emphasis.
64. Driver, *Exodus*, 360. The plurality of angels, in terms of going before the Israelites, is nowhere mentioned in these theophanic traditions.

33:2 was a different person from "my angel" (מלאכי) in 32:34. The usage of "my angel" is more intimate than "an angel"; R. A. Cole assumes that unlike the promise in 23:23 to send "his angel" (מלאכי), the promise made here is only for "an angel" (מלאך) and it meant "virtual refusal of the direct presence of God";[65] Moberly thinks that because of sin and the breaking of the covenant, the angel will not mediate YHWH's presence in the same way as before.[66]

Had Moses understood, then, that the employment of מלאך "an angel" here was the refusal of YHWH's presence, and that the angel's presence was less satisfactory? What was the writer trying to convey? It may be noted that in 23:20–21, even before the calf episode, the promise was made for מלאך "an angel" (without any possessive pronoun) whom they were not to provoke as he would not pardon their transgression because YHWH's name was in him (23:21: שמי בקרבו). In 23:22 the angel's voice (בקלו) and YHWH's speech (אדבר) are used interchangeably. And yet, in 23:23 מלאכי "my angel" (כי־ילך מלאכי לפניך) was mentioned. Even after their sin with calf worship, the promise made in 32:34 was to send מלאכי (i.e. "angel of YHWH"). One can see that the terms מלאך "an angel" and מלאכי "my angel" are used in the same context, and both the terms (23:20–24) identify the same divine entity with the same function.[67] The function of מלאך "an angel" (promised before the calf worship) in 23:20–22 and the function of the מלאך in 33:2 were the same in that through them the people's protection and victory were guaranteed (23:20–23). In light of all this, the slight literary variation between מלאך ("an angel") and מלאכי ("my angel") seems to carry no special significance. It seems also that the angel, who acts as a representative of YHWH, is not distinguishable from YHWH, and "in his appearing and speaking, clothes himself with Yahweh's own appearance and speech", as Eichrodt observes,[68] and that the Hebrew writer uses the term מלאך "angel" to refer to YHWH/God himself. Readers would

---

65. R. A. Cole, *Exodus* (London: Intervarsity Press, 1973), 222.
66. Moberly, *At the Mountain*, 62–63.
67. LXX has τὸν ἄγγελόν μου "my angel" (so NKJ) where the MT has מלאך in 23:20 and 33:2.
68. Eichrodt, *OTT* 2, 24, 27. Cf. Gen 21:18, 22; 31:11, 13.

"You Cannot See My Face; No One Can See Me, and Live"

remember that in several of the Genesis and previous Exodus traditions, YHWH's presence was associated with an angel.[69]

It may also be noted that in Exodus 32–33, when the people say to Aaron, "make us god which shall go 'before us'" (לפנינו) and when Aaron builds an altar לפני "before" the calf (32:5), the phrase לפני "before" seems to give a literal sense, because the people wanted a concrete structure to go before them in the place of Moses (Exod 32:1; 32:23). Likewise, when YHWH tells Moses, "my Angel shall go 'before you'" (מלאכי ילכו לפניך: 32:34) and "I will send an angel 'before you'" (ושלחתי לפניך מלאך: 33:2), one may assume that לפני has a literal sense, because "the angel" is said to lead them on their way, by means of self-revelations.

Coming back to Moses' inquiry, what could be the writer's intention in informing his readers that Moses wanted to know whom YHWH would send with him (אשר־תשלח עמי: 12b)? Was he trying to convey that Moses' concern was something different? Moses' inquiry in 12b needs to be discussed within the given context, especially in light of what YHWH told him after having made the promise to send his angel in 33:3b. While "the angel of YHWH" and YHWH are alternatively used to mean the divine accompaniment, YHWH also said: "I will not go among/ with you" (לא אעלה בקרבך). Even though מלאך is put in a contrast with YHWH (23:20; 33:2), any idea that "angel" meant a subordinate being to YHWH is to be ruled out, as von Rad suggests.[70] In these anthropomorphic theophanies, the angel was YHWH/God himself. Sarna is of the opinion that the term "angel" was used "to avoid the gross anthropomorphism of localizing God".[71] However, the Hebrew writers frequently describe God in anthropomorphic terms without any hesitation or avoidance, as discussed throughout this work.

The important clue behind Moses' inquiry seems to lie in 33:3b. The reason YHWH gives as to why he himself would not go (direct presence) with them, as recorded in 33:3b, was: פן־אכלך בדרך ". . . lest I destroy you on the way". One may recall that after that statement in 33:3 was made,

---

69. Gen 16:9–13; 21:17; Exod 3:2, 6; 13:21–22; 14:19.
70. Von Rad, *OTT* 1, 287.
71. Sarna, *Exodus*, 14.

the people mourned (יתאבלו) as a sign of regret/repentance. It may be that Moses expected YHWH to relent of his decision not to go with them. Is it possible, then, that Moses wanted to know if YHWH would continue to reveal himself in terms of פנים "face" (self-revelations) during their future journey without destroying the people anymore on the way? One may incline to think affirmatively, but this question needs probing. Scholars have taken different views on the statement: לא אעלה בקרבך ("I will not go among/with you"). Mackay argues that it refers to YHWH's presence in the tabernacle (25:8; 29:46), and that YHWH would withdraw permission for the construction of the tabernacle.[72] But, there is little reason/evidence whatsoever in chapters 32–34 to link this statement with the tabernacle, rather it is concerned with the future journey.

The relative pronoun אשר in 33:12b (את אשר־תשלח עמי) has been generally translated as "whom" (you will send with me). But Moberly treats this translation as misleading, and has taken אשר as impersonal "what" (you will send with me), and suggested that it was the special presence of YHWH in his shrine "in the midst" (בקרב) of the people that is now denied in 33:3b–6, and it was this shrine which Moses now seeks to restore.[73] Moberly also states that the immediate presence of God (בקרב) was "a concrete realization of YHWH's presence, that is, a shrine".[74] However, while it is possible to render אשר as an impersonal "what", it seems irrelevant here because:

a) the writer uses עמי (personal suffix) with אשר־תשלח: "whom you will send with me".[75] This seems to signify an ongoing personal presence of YHWH rather than the impersonal shrine; and this preposition עם used earlier (in 3:12), when YHWH assures Moses of his presence (אהיה עמך: "I will be with you"), it signified YHWH's (personal) presence. The prepositional usage of לפני "before" (32:34; 33:2), used as the object of שלח "send" is another indication that Moses' inquiry was to know as to "who" would go before the people;[76]

---

72. Mackay, *Exodus*, 549.
73. Moberly, *At the Mountain*, 69; see also above, 126, 132.
74. Moberly, *At the Mountain*, 67.
75. Cf. עמנו in verse 6: personal suffix with בלכתך: by your (YHWH's) going with us.
76. Cf. 32:1: People's intention in making the calf-god was that it would go before them.

b) the tent was already operative, and it functioned as a place of revelation[77] and as a place of meeting (33:11), rather than as a permanent structure.

Even if one takes אשר as a reference to the tabernacle/shrine, the tabernacle carries no significance unless YHWH himself facilitated a situation for maintaining a relationship with the people by his revealed presence.[78] Was Moses, then, albeit indirectly, referring to YHWH's going in terms of his direct presence which would mean the divine self-revelations? It may be a possibility in light of Moses' earlier experiences. He had already become acquainted with YHWH's direct self-revelations, beginning at the burning bush, throughout his journeys to and from Egypt, and later, on the mountain, and Moses had the experience of seeing and conversing with YHWH directly (3:1–33:11).

Obviously, Moses now needed similar assurance to that which he had earlier in bringing the people from Egypt (כי־אהיה עמך: 3:12), because he has to carry on the divine task of leading the stiff-necked people forward (33:3, 5). Therefore, Moses' prayer to YHWH here seems to express his desire that the one, who accompanied him from the burning bush into Egypt and until now, would continue to reveal himself on their way to the Land. It may be assumed, then, that Moses' inquiry here (12a) was in response to YHWH's statement that he would not go[79] with him/them (33:3), lest they be destroyed.[80] Although some ambiguity prevails, it seems that Moses understood this statement as though they would be deprived of divine self-revelations. Just as he needed YHWH's assurance: אהיה עמך (cf. 3:12) in

---

77. C.R. Koester, *The Dwelling of God. The Tabernacle in the Old Testament, Intertestamental Jewish Literature, and the New Testament* (Washington: Catholic Biblical Association of America, 1989), 7.

78. The terms שכן, אהל־מועד (Exod 29:42), מקדש (25:8; 29:45) are translated alternatively as sanctuary/dwelling place/tabernacle. Whether it was משכן or מקדש, YHWH would dwell there in order to speak to Moses and the Israelites (25:8, 22; 29:42); his glory would dwell there (29:43). Even when the pillar of cloud played an important role in the context of divine revelations, it was still YHWH who spoke to Moses and through him to the people (13:21–22; 14:19; 19:9, 22; 24:16).

79. The verb used in 33:3 is עלה with first person (אעלה), rather than פנים with suffix (פני).

80. Moses had already expressed his solidarity with the people (32:32).

the context of bringing the people out of Egypt, even now he needed assurance that YHWH would go with him/them.

Hitherto, YHWH's presence, as revealed by means of his self-revelations, was very real to Moses. But now, perhaps, Moses was confused as to whether YHWH would appear and speak to him as he did in the past, and this was a serious matter for him, as it meant that he had to lead people forward without YHWH's direct involvement. Presumably, Moses' desire was to know if YHWH would reveal himself during their onward journey.[81] In all probability, it seems that what Moses asked for was YHWH's direct revelation, similar to that which he had experienced earlier[82] both in terms of פנים "face" and כבוד "glory" at the mountain. As Balentine explains, the people sinned in substituting a golden calf for a holy God and subsequently in despising God,[83] and their covenantal relationship now was at stake (Exod 32:10). Evidently, Moses understood that only God's presence with Israel would distinguish them from others (33:15–16), not the Law.[84] Having already sought YHWH's forgiveness for the people (32:11–14; 32), now Moses pleads on behalf of the people.[85]

5.3.1.2 Knowing by name, finding grace and knowing YHWH's ways, and knowing YHWH (12b–13)

Moses here argues his present case based on what YHWH had supposedly told him: i.e. that he knew him; perhaps the use of אמר may be an indication that he was told in an earlier revelation.[86] YHWH knew him indeed, and when called by name, Moses responded saying "here I am" (3:4). The verb ידע "to know", which occurs four times in these two verses, stresses

---

81. If he would not go with them (אם־אין פניך הלכים), he should not let them go from there (33:15).
82. This may include the theophanies starting from Exod 3:1–6 until 33:11.
83. S. E. Balentine, *Prayer in the Hebrew Bible* (Minneapolis: Fortress Press, 1993), 121.
84. Cf. G. D. Fee, *God's Empowering Presence* (Peabody: Hendrickson Publishers 1994), 7.
85. In Gen 18 when YHWH decided to judge the sin of Sodom and Gomorrah, Abraham intervened.
86. אמר "said" used with God may signify his self-revelation. See S. Wagner, "אמר", *TDOT* 1, 335. Since there are several instances where YHWH and Moses had conversations from the burning bush until the calf episode, Moses may be referring to any of those instances.

the importance of knowing,[87] which expresses an intimate acquaintance,[88] and its association with "name" (ידעתיך בשם) here may signify the intimate relationship between YHWH and Moses[89] which is evident in their conversation. Moses claims that YHWH told him, "You have also found grace in my eyes".[90] This phrase used three times in these two verses seems to stress the need to have the divine grace continually.[91] Previously, the expression "finding grace" in someone's eyes was used in the sense of being accepted;[92] in the present context, when Moses prayed for YHWH's "grace", he probably meant that YHWH should consider them as his people (13b), which also meant granting forgiveness (32:11–14).

Surprisingly, Moses expresses his desire, "I may know you", even though he was supposedly in an intimate "face-to-face" contact with YHWH, and also "was known in a personal and direct way," as Clements affirms.[93] It seems as though "finding grace in YHWH's sight" would lead to "knowing his ways" (דרכך)[94] and this would further lead to "knowing him"—these three ideas seem to be closely interlinked (13a). Importantly, knowing YHWH's ways (דרכך) is associated with knowing YHWH himself. What were the ways of YHWH which Moses was seeking to know, and how were those ways connected to "knowing YHWH"? Earlier in Genesis the verb ידע was used in the context of God knowing Abraham (ידעתיו), and the way of YHWH was associated with commanding (יצוה) the future generations

---

87. Out of about 40 occurrences in Exodus, the verb ידע appears six times here in vv. 12–23. The expression of "knowing" YHWH/God is found throughout the book of Exodus (YHWH knows people's sorrows also: Exod 3:7). Other important terms in this passage are: פנים (out of 5 occurrences 4 appear in association with YHWH), ראה (7), חן (6), שם (3) and רחם (2).

88. God knew Moses "face-to-face" (Exod 33:17; cf. Num 12:8; Deut 34:10).

89. Moberly, *At the Mountain*, 70. Moberly observes that this combination of "knowing" and "by name" are unique here, though calling by name is found elsewhere in the HB (Isa 43:1; 45:3, 49:1).

90. It is not clear when exactly he was told but possible that it refers to 33:11a.

91. Cf. NIV translation of 13a: "I may continue to find".

92. This expression of finding grace was used earlier in Genesis that Noah found grace in the sight of YHWH (Gen 6:8), Joseph found favor with the jailer (39:21) and the Israelites with the Egyptians (Gen 6:8; 18:3; 32:5; 33:10; Exod 3:21; 11:3; 12:36).

93. Clements, *Exodus*, 215; cf. Exod 3:4; 3:17.

94. The noun דרך may be pointed singular (*GKC*. §91 k), but the plural noun here makes better sense.

that they too would keep the way of YHWH (דרך יהוה).⁹⁵ Knowing YHWH may be equated in the present context to obedience to the Law, and perhaps Moses' desire was to know if "knowing YHWH's ways" included his concern for the Law (and whether it would be given again).

One may recall that Israelite deliverance from Egypt was associated with the worship of YHWH (3:12b) at the mountain, but now, that very worship was disturbed by the calf episode. Furthermore, Moses himself broke the tablets of the Testimony (העדת) which YHWH had given him when he appeared in his glory on the mountain (32:15–19). One may sense here that Moses desired to know if the tablets of the Law and the commandments would be given again so that Israelites and their future generations might be taught the divine knowledge and continue the worship of YHWH.⁹⁶ Knowing YHWH's "ways" may also include knowing his nature and character,⁹⁷ even as Moses was desperate to know if YHWH would now forgive the people and accompany them in future. Moses' insistence that Israel was YHWH's people (עמך הגוי הזה: 13b) seems to reflect his desire "to repair the Yahweh-Israel covenant" relationship, as House opines,⁹⁸ and this would be possible only if YHWH would forgive and accept the people again. Obviously, Moses was aware of the ill effects of their sin (32:15–31) as the "rejection of the covenant meant breach of the covenant";⁹⁹ and the criterion to seek YHWH's forgiveness of the people was based on the covenant with Abraham (32:13–14). One may also discern here that Abraham's descendants were not only to appropriate the promises given to Abraham, but they were also to walk with integrity (תמים) before (לפני) YHWH in

---

95. Previously, a similar expression was used in Gen 18:19: "I have known him, so that he would direct his children to keep the way of YHWH (דרך יהוה) to do righteousness and justice (צדקה ומשפט).

96. והתורה והמצוה אשר כתבתי להורתם (Exod 24:12); cf. Deut 4:9.

97. Driver, *Exodus*, 360; cf. Moberly, *At the Mountain*, 73. This could be discerned from the divine reply that he would be gracious and merciful (v. 19).

98. House, *OTT*, 122.

99. Westermann, *Genesis 12–36*, 267.

accordance with the divine dictum given to Abraham.[100] Yet, people did not show integrity in obeying the Words given on the mountain.[101]

The LXX's rendering here seems to enhance the understanding of "knowing YHWH" according to which Moses' request was: "reveal yourself to me, that I may evidently see you".[102] This rendering supports Moses' desire to know YHWH in terms of seeing him which could be made possible only if YHWH revealed himself (self-revelation), and makes better sense in light of Moses' earlier experiences of seeing YHWH in the context of divine revelations. One may infer that knowing here involves seeing, and that Moses was anxious to know if YHWH would continue to reveal himself to him in a manner similar to that which he experienced on the mountain, which was also witnessed by the people, even if from a distance.[103] The fact that Moses reminds YHWH that "the people" were "his people" is an indication that Moses included the people in his prayer for divine accompaniment.[104] Earlier, YHWH declared that his "going" meant the destruction of the people, but now, Moses' use of "your ways" probably means something like "will you forgive your people and accompany them without needing to destroy them"? Again, one can assume that Moses was in need of a special theophany similar to the one he had on the mountain when he received the Law the first time. This would in effect be a sign to assure Moses that YHWH had forgiven (accepted) the people and worship could be restarted. Could it be then that Moses' request was to know if YHWH would reveal himself in glory, perhaps similar to his earlier experience on the mountain (24:12–18) and give him the Law a second time?

---

100. Cf. Gen 17:1–4; Exod 19:3–6 where their status of being YHWH's possession and a holy nation was linked to their obedience to the covenant.

101. Cf. Exod 24:3, 7; 32:5–8.

102. Gk. has ἐμφάνισόν μοι σεαυτόν γνωστῶς ἴδω σε for הודעני נא את־דרכך ואדעך (13b; cf. 18).

103. Exod 24:1–2; 10–12; 16–17.

104. A word play may be noted between את־העם הזה and עמי (v. 12) and עמך הגוי הזה (v. 13).

5.3.2 Moses' Requests Heard and YHWH's Presence Promised: 33:14–17

According to the text,[105] YHWH said, "My 'face' shall go 'before you' and I will give you rest" (v. 14); then Moses said to YHWH, "If your 'face' does not go, do not lead us up from here (v. 15); and how will it be known that I have found grace in your eyes, I and your people? Is it not by your going with us that we may be 'distinguished',[106] I and your people, from all the people who are on the face of the earth"? (v. 16). And YHWH told Moses, "I will also do this thing that you have asked because you have found grace in my eyes and I know you by name" (v. 17).

5.3.2.1 YHWH promises to accompany Moses (v. 14)

In response to Moses' request discussed above, YHWH's reply is פני ילכו "my 'face' shall go 'before/with you',[107] and I will give you rest".[108] This verse need not be treated as a question,[109] as it has a "positive affirmation".[110] The LXX reads αὐτὸς προπορεύσομαί σου: "I myself will go before you". This response seems to suffice for different aspects raised in Moses' prayer in terms of the divine presence.

One gets the impression that the writer is unfolding what Moses was aiming at by his queries: "who would go with me", "show me your way", and "I may know you and find grace" (in vv. 12–13), that is, the continuity of YHWH's presence with Moses. In other words, YHWH's grace (in vv. 12–13) meant his direct presence, in terms of his self-revelation. The writer's use of the expression פני ילכו "my face shall go" when he could have

---

105. It is not necessary that these verses should follow 34:9 (where Moses associates YHWH's ongoing presence with his grace). For the arguments, see Driver, *Exodus*, 361; Rylaarsdam, *Exodus*, 1073.

106. Niphal stem of פלה has the idea of being separated. LXX here has ἐνδοξασθήσομαι "I shall be glorified".

107. The MT has no object but the LXX has the preposition; Sym. has *qdmy zl* = לְפָנֶי לָךְ and several Eng. verses have added "with you".

108. והנחתי is causative, God being the subject.

109. There is some tendency to treat this verse (ויאמר פני ילכו והנחתי לך) as a question because of the repetition in v. 15 and *GKC*, §150a is referred to support this view, but הֲ, the mark of a question, is not used here. See *GKC*, §153, 2. See Childs, *Exodus*, 584, 594; Noth, *Exodus*, 257.

110. Moberly, *At the Mountain*, 74.

used אנכי אלך "I will go" (to indicate YHWH's accompaniment) seems significant. In the earlier traditions studied, when the term פנים ("face") was used in association with YHWH and in the context of the divine-revelations, it was understood as signifying the appearance of the divine person;[111] and here also the usage of פנים with הלך in association with YHWH may signify his continued personal manifestations, even in future during their onward journeys; and this promise to Moses seems "of God himself", as Clements suggests.[112]

As discussed elsewhere in this work, Terrien's suggestion that the term פנים "face" means "presence" (in an abstract sense) here in verse 14 (and "face" in 23)[113] has neither lexical nor textual support, and this term פנים "face" in both these places seems to mean "face;" the literal sense cannot be excluded.[114] As Yofre articulates, "the semantically constitutive" aspects of פנים "face" that make it "appropriate for a discourse" about YHWH are "the same that apply to human beings: real personal presence, relationship and meting".[115] The technical terms connected with the "face" of God cannot be simply treated as "idiomatic expressions", as Reindl holds.[116]

When פ נים "face", which involves physicality, is used to signify presence, it calls attention to the aspect of the interpersonal, and even "face-to-face" relationship.

As discussed in previous chapters, when this extraordinarily expressive term פנים "face" is used in association with YHWH/God, it signifies the divine revelations wherein YHWH/God appeared in a human form. In light of this, it seems difficult to accept Terrien's view that פני־יהוה implies a mode of "psychological communion" here.[117] Although Terrien admits that God "appeared" meant literally "showed himself",[118] he thinks that the storytellers merely said that God appeared. But, there could be no

---

111. Gen 32:31; Exod 33:11; cf. Judg 6:22.
112. Clements, *Exodus*, 214.
113. Terrien, *Elusive Presence*, 65; chapter 1, 11.
114. In secular contexts פני "my face" is used in a literal sense (Gen 43:3, 5; Exod 10:28).
115. Yofre, "פנים", 607.
116. Reindl, *Angesicht*, 200. Contra Hartenstein, *Angesicht*, 6.
117. Terrien, *Elusive Presence*, 140.
118. Ibid., 65.

reason why any writer should have simply said God appeared unless they found it in their Hebrew traditions. If the verb "appeared" literally means "showed himself", as Terrien himself claims, arguably God did show himself to people during his self-revelations. Moberly argues that פנים "face" is "frequently used in connection with the cultic, so that a shrine, a place for the divine presence (cf. Exod 29:42–46), is probably being alluded to, and as discussed earlier in this work,[119] he suggests that because "the shrine is movable that it is possible to speak of Yahweh's פנים 'going'".[120] However, as discussed earlier, one can find in several of the Hebrew traditions the term פנים "face" associated with YHWH/God to represent his "human (bodily) form" in the context of divine self-revelations.[121]

Now, coming back to verse 14: "My 'face' shall go 'before you'" and I will give you rest", one can see that it was YHWH himself promising to go with them (not the people going to him for an audience). When YHWH says, פני ילכו "my face shall go" (33:14), פני "my face" takes the place of the pronoun "I myself". Since this expression "my face" is used analogously to the personal pronoun "I" (myself), it can well mean YHWH's very presence, the very person himself,[122] and as Motyer puts it, "stands for the essential reality of personal presence"[123] of YHWH/God. It appears that the expression פני ילכו "my face shall go" is not an ordinary expression; and this association of פנים "face" with YHWH seems to signify the divine presence in terms of his self-revelation. Von Rad, while acknowledging that this "almost hypostatising independence here given to the 'face' (פנים) as a special form of manifestation" is distinctive, still assumes the possibility that this text had served as "the aetiology of the cultic mask" and asks: "why is Yahweh present only in the *panim*"?[124] The biblical text gives no scope to assume any cultic mask, but gives ample of evidence to believe that YHWH/God revealed himself by means of פנים "face", meaning that he

---

119. Chapter 1, 30.
120. Moberly, *At the Mountain*, 74.
121. As discussed throughout chapters 1–4.
122. Cf. A. H. McNeile, *The Book of Exodus* (London: The Westminster Commentaries, 1908), 214.
123. Motyer, *Exodus*, 298.
124. Von Rad, *OTT* 1, 285.

revealed himself in human form.¹²⁵ Interestingly, although Eichrodt treats פנים אל־פנים "face-to-face" as a "heightened metaphor" (Exod 33:11),¹²⁶ referring to פני ילכו "my face shall go" (v. 14), he says that "it is almost impossible not to conclude that we have here *another form of self-manifestation of the transcendent God,* by means of which his presence is . . . guaranteed to them".¹²⁷

YHWH's going with them meant giving Moses rest (14b). Some scholars understand the noun נוח "rest" as the settlement in the Land,¹²⁸ but it seems better to assume that it refers to the rest given to Moses over his anxiety about the uncertainty of God's presence, and whether God's presence would help him carry on the task of leading the stiff-necked people in their onward journey, a sign to Moses of YHWH's grace.¹²⁹ Eichrodt, with some emendation, translates this verse as: "my face shall go before you, and thus will I lead you".¹³⁰ But disagreeing with Eichrodt, Moberly says that the divine leadership is not the issue here, and the addition of לפניך "before you" is not necessary.¹³¹ Whether one agrees with Eichrodt's amendment or not, YHWH's earlier promise was that his angel would go before (לפניך) them (33:2 and 32:34), and an addition of "before" to פני ילכו makes sense, and it can well mean "divine leadership",¹³² as YHWH would go before and defeat the enemies.¹³³

It is noteworthy that when YHWH was supposed to have told Moses earlier that an "angel" would go, there was a negation in terms of his direct presence (33:3), but here YHWH promises that he himself would go, and

---

125. This aspect has been discussed throughout the previous chapters.
126. See above, 99.
127. Eichrodt, *OTT* 2, 37, 38.
128. For example, Moberly, *At the Mountain*, 74. Cf. Deut 3:20; 12:10; 34:4.
129. Cf. Num 11:11: Moses felt burdened (by the people) because he did not find חן "grace" in YHWH's eyes.
130. Eichrodt, *OTT* 2, fn. 1, 38. He emends וַהֲנִחֹתִי to וְהִנְחֹתִי and suggests addition of פני ילכו לפניך.
131. Moberly, *At the Mountain*, 74.
132. So is C. R. Erdman, *The Pentateuch: An Exposition* (Grand Rapids: Baker Books, 1987), 246.
133. See Exod 23:22–23; 33:2 where the angel's function was to go before them and defeat their enemies, and now YHWH himself would carry on the same. Cf. Muilenburg, "Intercession", 172; Von Rad, *OTT* 1, 288.

the term "angel" (of 33:2) plays no more role in the rest of the chapter. YHWH's reply פני ילכו ("I shall go") seems to be a sign of his חן "grace" for Moses.

5.3.2.2 Moses' continued insistence for the presence of YHWH (vv. 15–16)

One would expect Moses to have been satisfied after YHWH said פני ילכו that he himself would go. But, Moses reiterates the same request (v. 15). Dumbrell suggests that Moses doubted if YHWH would go with them,[134] but this repetition probably "accounts for the passionate urgency", as Muilenburg suggests.[135] Obviously, Moses was not satisfied by the promise for "rest" which included only him (14b); his insistence may be for the confirmation that his grace was for the people as well. The use of a conditional clause in Moses' argument, "if 'your face does not go' (אם־אין פניך הלכים), do not lead 'us' up from here" (אל־תעלנו מזה)[136] may be to express his need to know if YHWH had forgiven the people and if he would accompany them in future.

When Moses says, אם־אין פניך הלכים "if your face does not go" (v. 15) פניך "your face" takes the place of the personal pronoun "you". Since the self-revelations of YHWH/God were understood to be in human form, and that פנים "face" is associated with the anthropomorphic person of YHWH/God; and also in verse 20, "my face" (את־פני) acts in apposition with "me" (יראני)—in all these texts, פנים "face" seems to retain its nominal/literal sense.

Moses' rhetoric was: "how will it be known (יודע)[137] . . . Is it not by your going with us that we may be "distinguished"? From this, one may discern here again that to have divine grace meant the divine presence in terms of the divine revelation. Noth opines that "the thought here is of the worship of Yahweh in the cult at the sanctuaries of Israel, to which men go to 'see'

---

134. Dumbrell, "Prospect", 151.
135. Muilenburg, "Intercession", 173.
136. NRS: "do not carry us up from here" (cf. Exod 19:4: bore you on eagles' wings and brought you).
137. The niphal of ידע gives the sense of making oneself known and hence "to reveal". See BDB, 394.

the divine 'face'",[138] but this seems unlikely given that the context here is that of YHWH's accompaniment on their onward journey.

In solidarity, Moses identifies with the people and seeks divine grace even for them, who were designated as "YHWH's people". This can be seen in the terminology used: "I and your people" (אני ועמך used twice here) and "with us" (עמנו; cf. עמך הגוי הזה in 13). Presumably, Moses saw that the evidence that YHWH would still be gracious to them was only by his going with them (16a); and significantly, the nations around them would recognize Israelites as YHWH's people only by his going/presence with them.[139] Moses was aware that it was because of the covenant made with Abraham that YHWH revealed himself to Moses and delivered them from Egypt (3:6); without YHWH's presence, their existence would be threatened and his absence would jeopardize their identity. If it was only YHWH's presence that could distinguish the Israelites from all other peoples, it would be deeply ironic if the covenant people were deprived of the presence of their divine covenant partner. For this reason, Moses earnestly intercedes on behalf of the repentant people (33:3–6).

5.3.2.3 Moses found grace in the eyes of YHWH (v. 17)
Once again, YHWH replies with a positive note: "I will also do this thing that you have asked because you have found grace in my eyes and I know you by name", which forms a kind of inclusio with verse 12. The divine response probably means that all the requests Moses made on behalf of the people, including the one in verses 15–16, that is, for YHWH's accompaniment in terms of his פנים "face", would be granted. In other words, YHWH promised that he would go with them on Moses' terms because he found grace in YHWH's eyes, and knew his name. YHWH's earlier statement that he would only send an angel does not seem to mean the

---

138. Noth, *Exodus*, 257; cf. 192.
139. Moses' reasoning was probably based on the past events in which YHWH's presence was made evident by his mighty acts performed in delivering them from Egypt; in future, YHWH's presence with them will be made evident by the defeat of their enemies; possibly, because of the pillar of cloud and fire the other nations realized that YHWH went before them (cf. Num 14:14).

"hiding of YHWH's face", as J. S. Exell thinks,[140] but that his accompaniment would mean the destruction of the people; and now that Moses has interceded on behalf of the repentant people, YHWH promises that he would accompany them (14–17). One may assume that it might also mean YHWH's accompaniment in terms of the self-revelations during their onward journey, without needing to destroy the people on the way (33:3).

5.3.3 Moses' Continued Requests and YHWH's Responses: vv. 18–20

The text relates that Moses said, "Cause me to/let me see your glory, I pray" (v. 18). But YHWH replied, "I will cause all my goodness to pass before you, and I will call out before you by "my"[141] name/title YHWH and I will be gracious to whom I will be gracious, and I will have mercy on whom I will have mercy (v. 19). And he said, "You will not be able to see my face; for no man shall see me, and live" (v. 20).

5.3.3.1 Moses' desire to see the glory of YHWH (v. 18)

When YHWH assures Moses that he would do what Moses asked him, it meant that he would accompany the people (v. 17), and one would expect Moses to be satisfied. However, he continues to request YHWH: ויאמר הראני נא את־כבדך[142] "cause me/let me see your glory" (v. 18). Perhaps, as von Rad assumes, Moses was afflicted by anxiety about the uncertain way that lies before him, and requests with boldness, "show me your glory".[143]

It is intriguing to note the sequence of YHWH-Moses conversation in these verses, especially from 13–19,[144] which seems to reflect his concern for the people. As an answer to Moses' inquiry as to who would go with him (vv. 12–13), YHWH's response is פני ילכו "my 'face'/I shall go" (v.

---

140. J. S. Exell, *Exodus: A Commentary* (Grand Rapids, Michigan: Baker Books, 1996), 514.
141. This possessive pronoun is not in the MT but the LXX has ἐπὶ τῷ ὀνόματί μου for Heb. בשם יהוה.
142. The particle את is perhaps to put emphasis on כבדך "your glory".
143. G. von Rad, *Moses* (London: Lutterworth Press, 1960), 25.
144. Because of the short divine answers, the literary structure is treated as a reflection of cultic and oracular formulation. See Muilenburg, "Intercession", 168–174.

"You Cannot See My Face; No One Can See Me, and Live"   153

14), which would perhaps signify the self-revelations of YHWH in terms of his פנים "face", that is, anthropomorphic appearance.[145] Moses includes the people while making his request in verses 13, 15, 16; hence, one can assume that YHWH's reply in verse 17 meant that he would accompany the people as a whole.[146] Despite those divine promises in verses 14 and 17, Moses asks yet again, using a different term כבוד "glory". Now, Moses' request is not in association with YHWH's פנים "face" (as in v. 15) but with his "glory" (את־כבדך).

Why did Moses specifically ask for YHWH's glory to be shown at that point? Was his perception of divine self-revelation, in terms of כבוד "glory", different from that of פנים "face"? Perhaps this query has to be answered in light of the Hebrew understanding of the term כבוד "glory" and Moses' earlier theophanic experience of "glory". The Hebrew word כבוד "glory",[147] when ascribed to God, seems to refer, as H. P. Smith puts it, "to some manifestation of him rather than to his *being* in itself";[148] hence the כבוד of God may be treated as some visible appearance made known by outward appearance which could be seen, even "in the proper sense".[149] This expression כבוד יהוה "glory of YHWH" associated with the divine revelation seems to signify a more direct, intense, magnificent aspect of the divine person, rather than, as Eichrodt thinks of it, as an indirect and weakened appearance distinct from the true essence of God's person.[150]

Previously, in Exodus tradition, when the "glory of YHWH" appeared in the cloud, it was visible to the people.[151] YHWH's glory, then, seems to

---

145. Cf. Gen 32:31; Exod 33:11 where this expression was associated with the divine self-revelations.

146. Cf. Childs, *Exodus*, 595.

147. The basic meaning of כבוד, when used for people, primarily suggests an outwardly visible aspect—whether it is of wealth or outward position of power/honor (e.g. Gen 13:2; 31:1; Exod 18:18; 40:34; 45:13). Previously, it was said that YHWH would be glorified/honored when the Egyptians were defeated Exod 14:17 (ואכבדה); 14:18 (בהכבדי).

148. For a discussion on the question of whether God's glory is the external manifestation of something within, that is, an intrinsic glory of God, see H. P. Smith, "The Scriptural Conception of the Glory of God", *OTS* 3 (1884), 325–329; Eichrodt, *OTT* 2, 29–35.

149. Smith, "Glory", 327–328.

150. Eichrodt, *OTT* 2, 23. For Eichrodt, "angel" and "face" also have the weakened appearance.

151. For example, Exod 16:10; 24:15–17; 40:34; cf. Num 14:10; Deut 5:22–24; Isa 6:3; Ezek 1:28, 3:23. Even though the divine person was made visible even in

include an aspect that relates to appearance and is visible to the eye. The כבוד "glory" of YHWH also seems to signify "the striking radiance" which proceeds from YHWH and can also be perceived by the people through revelation.¹⁵² It appears that on the one hand, the divine "glory" has a broader sense in that it is something that encircles/envelops the person of YHWH which would look like fire to the onlookers (24:16–17), and on the other hand, it has a narrower sense in that the radiance seems to emanate from the very person of YHWH (24:10–11; 3:2).

Presumably readers, who were aware of YHWH's face-to-face meeting with Moses (33:10–11) during his revelation in the tent,¹⁵³ would recall that the scene on the mountain was different when "YHWH's glory" appeared in magnificence.¹⁵⁴ Since the writer informs his readers now that what Moses wants to see was the divine glory, readers would connect it to the divine self-revelation in terms of כבוד "glory" and understand that it was different from the revelation in terms of פנים "face". It seems that just as the association of פנים with YHWH would signify his self-revelation, the association of כבוד "glory" also signifies the same. When Moses had gone into the realm of glory on the mountain, YHWH spoke to him and gave the Law.¹⁵⁵ One cannot miss noticing the vivid anthropomorphic language used in this context,¹⁵⁶ and one may assume that even as the glory is revealed, the divine person seems to appear in human form.

The LXX's rendering here: δεῖξόν μοι τὴν σεαυτοῦ δόξαν "reveal/manifest your glory to me"¹⁵⁷ helps to assume that Moses' desire was to "see" the divine glory, which would also mean the divine-revelation in terms of

---

anthropomorphic theophanies as seen in Gen 16:10–16; 18:1–33; 32:31; 33:11, theophanies in association with כבוד are more majestic.

152. Eichrodt, *OTT* 2, 30; cf. Noth, *Exodus*, 257.

153. Although the cloud accompanied YHWH, the divine glory did not seem to appear in the tent as it was only a temporary structure.

154. YHWH's glory dwelt on Mt. Sinai (וישכן כבוד־יהוה על־הר סיני ויכסהו הענן), and the appearance of the glory of YHWH was like a consuming fire (ומראה כבוד יהוה כאש אכלת).

155. Exod 24:16–18; also see chs. 25–31.

156. YHWH gave Moses the tablets of stone inscribed by the finger (Exod 31:18).

157. Where MT has הראני נא את־כבדך. Cf. v. 13: ἐμφάνισόν μοι σεαυτόν.

כבוד "glory"; and this would be "a pledge of the divine grace" (33:18)[158] for Moses. The reason why Moses desired to see YHWH's glory specifically at that point, in spite of the divine assurance to accompany them, may be linked with the worship and the Law on the mountain. As the people were deprived of YHWH's worship after the calf episode, and the Law was also broken, Moses was concerned for the renewal of the worship at the mountain. Could it be, then, that Moses desired to see the divine glory in a similar manner to what he had envisaged on the mountain, and to receive the Law from YHWH's hand again? If the answer is affirmative, the question now is what one can make of the divine assurance, פני ילכו, that is, the revelation in association with פנים. As mentioned above, YHWH appears even in glory in "human form". It seems as though YHWH's face and YHWH's glory are to be seen together in this context. In the previous traditions, YHWH/God appeared by means of "face" (Gen 18:1–33; 32:23–31) without an obvious association with glory, but, however, when he appears in terms of glory, anthropomorphic association is made with the divine person. As studied earlier, even in Sinai theophanies, divine-human meetings take place, the description of the revealed divine person is the same as in the other anthropomorphic appearances, in that he has feet and hand; the language used is anthropomorphic, and he calls and speaks.[159] One can assume that when Moses requested YHWH הראני נא את־כבדך "show me your glory", he did not nullify his earlier request in verse 15 אם־אין פניך הלכים "if your 'face' does not go". Rather, Moses' desire "to know YHWH" (in v. 13) was to seeing YHWH's face in his glory at that juncture.

5.3.3.2 YHWH gives details of his self-revelation (v. 19)

To Moses' request "show me 'your glory'" (את־כבדך), YHWH responds saying, "I will cause 'all my goodness' (כל־טובי) to pass 'before you'" (על־פניך); "I will call out the name YHWH לפניך 'before you'"[160]; the first part of this reply takes a different turn, in that it was not his glory but all his goodness that would be revealed. The LXX here has τῇ δόξῃ μου "my glory" (where

---

158. Eichrodt, *OTT* 2, 31.
159. See chapter 4, 124–127.
160. Some scholars think that the continuation of v. 18 is in vv. 22–23 (see Noth, *Exodus*, 256–257), but the canonical order in the text helps understand the tension better.

MT has כל־טובי) and "goodness" can well be paralleled with "glory".[161] It is possible that the noun טוב here has the aspect of intrinsic glory of YHWH/God in the sense of his character of benevolence.[162]

It seems that the abstract noun [163]כל־טובי is personified, and, as Clements describes, YHWH is "wholly good so that his *goodness* inevitably means his whole being",[164] hence טובי "my goodness" may even be equated with כבוד "glory", which means YHWH himself.[165] The verb עבר "to pass" is used in a positive sense probably for the first time here in the context of divine self-revelations.[166] All this means, as Sarna explains, that YHWH's goodness as a benevolent attribute would be manifested in his dealings with Moses and the people;[167] perhaps as a sign of his goodness, YHWH would reveal himself. Although כל־טובי "all my goodness" is (personified) abstract noun, since it is used in apposition with YHWH, and that later on, YHWH himself passed before Moses (34:6), פנים "face" retains its nominal sense in the phrase על־פניך ("before you").

The recurring theme of "the divine name" comes in again, in that YHWH would call his name before Moses (v. 19a). Significantly, this divine name that was used earlier in the context of redeeming people from Egypt[168] is now used in the context of leading them towards the Land. At the end, YHWH declares that he would be gracious to whom he would

---

161. But in 33:22: בעבר כבדי, the MT and the LXX have similar expressions, i.e. בעבר כבדי = μου ἡ δόξα "my glory" will pass by.

162. Cf. Gen 32:13 where the verbal form of טוב is used in this sense. Cf. Motyer, *Exodus*, 309; W. H. Propp, *Exodus 19–40*. AB. Vol. 2 (New York: Doubleday, 2006), 19–40, 607, 681.

163. This usage כל טובי is found only here in the context of divine-revelations.

164. Clements, *Exodus*, 216.

165. Cf. Ps 27:4 where בנעם־יהוה is treated as parallel to לראות בטוב־יהוה in v. 13. For a comparison of this parallel in terms of a kingly audience, see Hartenstein, *Angesicht*, 103–118.

166. עבר was used in the context of harm (Gen 31:52) and in the context of judgment (Exod 12:23). Cf. the verb פסח used in the context of passing over to protect Israel from the destroyer.

167. Sarna, *Exodus*, 214.

168. Cf. YHWH identifies himself as the God of Moses' fathers (יהוה אלהי אבתיכם), and mentions that this is his name forever and a memorial forever (3:15), and declares: אני יהוה (6:2–7); and brought Israel out of Egypt (20: 2: אנכי יהוה אלהיך). The assumption that this text reflects polemics between the anthropomorphisms (of J) and the Deuteronomic theology of the "divine name" is not necessary. On this subject, see Noth,

be gracious, and he would have mercy on whom he would have mercy (v. 19b).

J. R. Lundbom argues that this Semitic (*idem per idem*) expression serves as a closure device, and that here it is used to terminate their debate. He translates these verses: "I will proclaim . . . ; *but* I will be gracious . . . *Thus* he said, 'You cannot see my face . . .'".[169] He assumes that 19b and 20 meant to place a limit on the goodness promised in 19a, "thus Moses cannot see God's face . . . to this request God's grace is denied him".[170] However, this interpretation clashes with the overall context of the text. Nevertheless, Lundbom seems to realize that chapter 34 poses a challenge to his own assumption; therefore, he takes the dialogue beginning in 34:1 "to be from a later time".[171] Driver suggests that this (*idem per idem*) expression was employed "where the means or the desire to be more explicit does not exist".[172] If so, this statement means that YHWH's gracious dealing with Moses was ultimate/final and testifies to the divine freedom.[173] This statement seems to reflect more of a positive aspect, as though it meant: "I will be gracious so that humanly impossible things (v. 20) can be made possible (v. 19)".

Significantly, this freedom of bestowing grace and mercy is mentioned in the context of Moses' request for a revelation of the divine glory; and by telling Moses of his characteristic features (of mercy and grace), YHWH assured Moses that he would reveal himself to him. This may be a hint that he would be gracious not only to Moses but also to all the people (v. 17). In his dialogue, Moses repeatedly sought YHWH's grace and interceded in solidarity with the people in terms of YHWH's going with them (12–13, 15–16), and now YHWH assures Moses of his "grace" which (perhaps) meant the divine presence with the people (v. 17), forming an inclusio.

Exodus, 173–175; 253–258; M. Weinfeld, *Deuteronomy and the Deuteronomic School* (Oxford: Clarendon Press, 1972) 191–207.

169. J. R. Lundbom, "God's Uses of the *Idem per Idem* to Terminate Debate", *HTR* 71 (1978), 198; also 194–195, 199. This is because he takes ו in וחנתי in (19b) as "but" and the ו in ואמר (20a) as "thus".

170. Lundbom, "God's Uses", 199.

171. Ibid., 199.

172. Driver, *Exodus*, 362–363.

173. Childs, *Exodus*, 596.

In addition to calling his own name, YHWH would also reveal his characteristics, even as the name is understood to connote one's character.[174] The fact that the abstract nouns כבוד "glory", טוב "goodness", חן "grace" and רחם "mercy" are used in association with the concrete noun פנים of YHWH and his שם "name" is used in the same thread of thought and in the same context seems to be, as Clements expresses, "tantamount to God disclosing his true nature and identity to Moses".[175] Andx as a manifestation of his mercy and graciousness, YHWH would let his goodness pass by Moses.[176] However, a different scenario beckons in the next statement.

5.3.3.3 "You will not be able to see my face; for no man shall see me, and live" (v. 20)

Surprisingly, the second part of YHWH's reply to Moses' request (v. 18) was לא תוכל לראת את־פני לא־יראני האדם וחי "you will not be able to see 'my face'; for humankind shall not see 'me' and live" (v. 20); interestingly, "my face" and "me" (YHWH) are used in apposition.

Treating this statement as a contradiction with verse 14, where YHWH promised "my face shall go", A. F. Campbell argues that it has a "fragmentary character",[177] and Noth says that it is due to "a secondary accretion".[178] However, literally speaking, this verse has no contradiction with verse 14 since it does not refer to seeing YHWH's face. When YHWH answered: "my face shall go", the question of "seeing" or "not seeing" the divine face did not arise, but it meant a positive consent that YHWH would go with the people, in terms of his פנים "face" (v. 14).[179] In order to determine if the negation in verse 20 (you will not be able to see my face) was made in contradiction to 33:14 or something else was being underscored, this statement (v. 20) will be studied within the immediate context, especially in light of the face-to-face relationship Moses had with YHWH (v. 11)

---

174. Sarna, *Exodus*, 214; Eichrodt, *OTT* 2, 40.
175. Clements, *Exodus*, 216.
176. חן and רחם appear 7 times in vv. 12–17.
177. See A. F. Campbell and M. A. O'Brien, *Sources of the Pentateuch: Texts, Introductions, Annotations* (Minneapolis: Fortress Press, 1993), 263.
178. Noth, *Pentateuchal Traditions*, fn. 114, 31.
179. The aspect of כבוד "glory" is not associated here with YHWH.

which is placed only a few sentences before the present text (v. 20); and in the context of the theme of self-revelations of YHWH/God as discussed in the previous chapters.

In an attempt to reconcile the negation supposed in verse 20, in light of the פנים אל־פנים relationship (33:11), Wessner conjectures that "the original readers of the text realized that Moses . . . could not be the active agent (Qal) in seeing the Lord's *face*. The Lord would not let his face be the passive object of someone else's seeing (Niphal)". Wessner thinks that the idea of YHWH's "*actively* speaking (דבר) to Moses face-to-face and the Lord's face being passively seen (ראה) deal with different issues, they are not in contradiction" but clarify the nature of YHWH's "revealing of himself, both verbally and physically".[180] However, whether the verb ראה is used in qal stem (in active sense: e.g. A sees B) or in niphal stem (in passive sense: e.g. B is seen by A), the significant factor is that YHWH appeared in anthropomorphic form and was visible to the human eye. Furthermore, one can expect that the readers were aware of Jacob's claim ראיתי אלהים פנים אל־פנים (Gen 32:31) where the qal form of ראה was used and פנים was the object of ראה; in the context of Sinai theophany it was stated: ויראו את אלהי ישראל (Exod 24:10) and again the qal form of ראה was used and God becomes the object. Therefore, Wessner's view that YHWH "would not let his face be the object of someone else's seeing" is unacceptable. Wessner reads verse 11 in light of verse 20, instead of reading verse 20 in light of verse 11.

B. Jacob treats this expression פנים אל־פנים only at the level of speech,[181] since the verb used here is דבר and not ראה and that "seeing" God always refers to "an inner experience".[182] However, the text gives no scope to treat

---

180. Wessner, *Face to Face*, 49.
181. B. Jacob, *Exodus* (New Jersey: KTAV Publishing House, 1992), 975; cf. Wessner, *Face to Face*, 52. These two scholars refer to Num 12:8 ("mouth to mouth") to support their view of Exod 33:11, but the references to פה אל־פה and עין בעין (Num 12:8; 14:14) do not reduce the direct contact and visibility. Furthermore, several Eng. verses have translated פה אל־פה (also עין בעין in 14:14) as "face-to-face". Wessner (52) also argues that the LXX uses ἐνώπιος ἐνωπίῳ here instead of usual πρόσωπον πρὸς πρόσωπον. However, the LXXE translates ἐνώπιος ἐνωπίῳ as "face-to-face" and one manuscript of the LXX is said to have πρόσωπον πρὸς πρόσωπον here. The LXX is also consistent in its translation of פנים אל־פנים as πρόσωπον πρὸς πρόσωπον in all other places (e.g. Gen 32:31; Deut 34:10). Hanson, *LXX*, 56; A. Soffer, "The Treatment of Anthropomorphisms and Anthropopathisms in the Septuagint of Psalms", *HUCA* 28 (1957), 86–90.
182. Jacob, *Exodus*, 975.

'seeing' as an inner experience since it is clear that YHWH was present with Moses, and that YHWH spoke to Moses face-to-face. Although the verb ראה is not specifically used, it was because YHWH revealed himself to Moses that face-to-face speech was possible. For Eichrodt, 33:20 means "no one, not even such an elect man of God as Moses, can in any circumstances look upon the pānīm of God".[183] Korpel suggests that what Moses saw (cf. Num 14:14) was not the actual פנים "face" of YHWH but only a פנים "face" of clouds.[184] Since YHWH revealed himself to Moses in the burning bush, and he also saw God on the mountain, there is no reason to think that the "visibility" of the "face" was not involved during their conversations, given that the writer informed his readers that YHWH used to speak with Moses "face-to-face".

One has to realize that the context in which this statement (v. 20) is made is that of sin, in relation to "the accompanying presence" and the "appearance" of YHWH.[185] In spite of the assurance to go with him in verse 14, Moses requests to see YHWH's (face in) glory (v. 18); and only after Moses made that request (to let him see YHWH's glory) was YHWH's reply given in negation (v. 20). Now, the complication is with "seeing the face" that is negated. Was seeing the divine "glory", then, different from seeing the divine "face"? Was Moses included in the negation that even he could not see YHWH in glory? One may recall that, earlier, Pharaoh used a similar expression, כי ביום ראתך פני תמות "for in the day you see my face you shall die" (Exod 10:28) in the sense of a direct meeting in future, and the context in which Pharaoh made that statement was when he was angry with Moses. Likewise, YHWH was angry with the people when they sinned, and although he relented from his decision to annihilate them after Moses interceded (32:14), he was reluctant to accompany them in future lest they be destroyed if he goes with them directly (33:3).

It is important to remember here that Moses' prayer has been in solidarity with and for the people and he constantly referred to them in his

---

183. Eichrodt, *OTT* 2, 36.
184. Korpel, *Rift in the Clouds*, 103–104.
185. Cf. Barr, "Theophany", 36.

conversation with YHWH.[186] Earlier in the narrative, YHWH said to Moses, "'your people' (עַמְּךָ) whom you brought up out of Egypt" (32:7), but from then onwards, Moses refers to them as YHWH's people, and so "the people" were placed at the center of their conversation. Since Moses requests the divine grace, not for himself but for the people as a whole, it may be that his request to let him see the divine glory was also not only for his own sake, but also for the sake of all the people. In the first part of his reply in verse 19, YHWH mentions that his goodness would pass by and that he would be gracious and merciful on whom he would. After that, he continues his reply in verse 20: "You will not be able to see my 'face'". What Moses asked for was glory, but the divine reply was: "you will not be able to see my 'face'" (v. 20a).

However, YHWH's reply expresses no displeasure with Moses' request, "show me your 'glory'", but rather assures Moses of a theophany of "goodness" which was equated to "glory" (v. 22); nor did Moses' request to see the divine "glory" exclude his earlier request, "if your 'face' does not go" (v. 15). It seems, then, that Moses' desire to see YHWH in glory (in theophany) would include seeing his face (in glory).[187] The writer seems to have efficiently brought out the request for "glory" (v. 18) after YHWH's promise that his face would go (v. 14), as though to disclose the aspect of the divine appearance in the revealed glory. Onkelos reads here "Thou canst see the face of my Shekinah",[188] and this too seems to confirm that what Moses asked for was the manifestation of the divine glory, which meant the appearance of the anthropomorphized divine person in glory.

At this juncture, a reflection on the previous traditions might help to discern if the biblical writer meant that this statement had to be taken negatively—that no one can ever categorically see the face of God—and discern how the readers of that day would have understood it. As discussed in chapters 2–3, YHWH/God revealed himself in human form in the context

---

186. In 32:32: Moses seeks forgiveness for the "people"; 33:12: " to lead 'the people'"; 33:13: "your people"; 33:15: "let 'us' not go"; 33:16: "I and your people"; cf. 34:9: "go with 'us'; forgive 'our' wickedness and 'our' sin; and "take 'us' as your inheritance".
187. In construct with YHWH, כבוד may have adjectival sense, making YHWH's face "glorious".
188. J. W. Etheridge, *The Targums of Onkelos and Jonathan Ben Uzziel. Pentateuch* (London: Longman, 1862), 424.

of the divine-revelations. Obviously, there has been a definite continuity of the theme of "seeing (the face of) YHWH/God" from the (canonically) earlier traditions,[189] and the readers were told that, within the Sinai pericope, the seventy elders saw God, and that Moses was with YHWH in glory for forty days and nights, during which time the Law was said to have been written by YHWH's finger (31:18), there was a possibility that Moses saw YHWH's face. One can see that nowhere is it said in the previous traditions that people died on account of seeing the face of YHWH/God as such.[190] Even in the description of YHWH speaking with Moses face-to-face, tent theophany had no association with death. Since more texts testify that Moses and others saw the face of God, it may be assumed that the negation in the statement 33:20 was not made in a categorical sense.

However, it may be noted that the tension between "seeing" and "not seeing" was also present in the previous traditions within the Sinai pericope. There was a warning to people not to force themselves to see YHWH lest they perish (19:21); and even the priests were not permitted to go near YHWH without consecrating themselves (v. 22). There, death was associated with the priests in terms of their rites.[191] In the present context, the writer had earlier conveyed that YHWH's presence with them meant their destruction (32:10; 33:3, 5) not for seeing the divine face as such but because of their sin[192] of calf worship, which meant covenantal unfaithfulness.[193]

Readers would realize that Moses was requesting YHWH to go with them (in solidarity with the people). So, one may assume that when YHWH told Moses that "his face would go" (vv. 14, 17), he meant that he would go with all the people. Later, when Moses requested YHWH to show him

---

189. For a detailed study of Genesis traditions on self-revelations, see chapters 2–3, 37–68.

190. M. Haran, *Temples and Temple-Service in Ancient Israel: An Inquiry into the Character of Cult* (Oxford: Clarendon Press, 1978), 187; Propp, *Exodus*, 689.

191. Exod 28:35, 43; 30:20–21; cf. Lev 8:35; 10:6–7, 9; 16:2, 13; 22:9; Num 1:53; 4:15, 19–20; etc.

192. Out of 12 occurrences of "sin" in Exodus up to this point (9:27; 10:16–17; 20:20; 23:33), here in Exod 32–34 itself there are nine occurrences: חטאה: 32:21, 30, 31, 32; 34:7, 9; עון: 34:7, 9; פשע: 34:7.

193. Cf. Exod 4:24–26 where YHWH confronts Moses for his failure in circumcising his son.

the divine glory, one may assume that Moses meant that the people also would be given a chance to see YHWH's glory. If so, in YHWH's reply the statement of negation made in verse 20 was not for Moses, but for the sake of the people who were still kept at a distance from YHWH. YHWH has not denied his accompaniment with the people in terms of פנים "face" (14, 17), nor does it seem that YHWH meant that Moses would not be able to see the divine glory. Rather, it seems that YHWH would not let Moses see his "glory" in front of all the people, who were in the habit of watching the advent of YHWH in the cloud though from a distance (33:10).

It seems, then, that the use of פנים "face" in 33:14 and פנים "face" in 33:20 are not used in contradiction, but rather they seem to be signifying two different kinds of manifestation of YHWH. It is possible that while verse 14 indicates the divine revelation by means of פנים "face", verse 18 indicates the divine revelation by means of כבוד "glory" similar to the one that took place on the mountain. While "face" in verses 14 and 15 signifies YHWH's self-revelation in association with פנים "face", Moses' desire in verse 20 signifies YHWH's revelation in terms of his כבוד "glory". Having already portrayed that YHWH and Moses were in a face-to-face relationship, then recording the divine reply in verse 14, the biblical writer now carefully articulates that Moses' desire (in v. 18) was to see YHWH not simply by means of his (anthropomorphic) "face" but by means of his (glorious) "face" in כבוד "glory".

Did the writer convey then, that if YHWH were to appear in his glory (which includes physicality) in the sight of all the people, they would not be able (it would be fatal) to face God in his glory? This may be answered in affirmative. Even before their sin with the calf, the people were afraid of hearing God speaking to them directly, and requested Moses to relay the divine words to them (20:19). Although the statement תוכל לראת את־פני "you will not be able" was addressed to Moses, it seems that he would not be able to see YHWH's glory at that time, and as though YHWH understood the desire of Moses for the people (that they would see God's glory), he says that no man can see and live.

As Lundbom suggests, the "glory" in this context meant "God's bright, "beneficent face".[194] Likewise, Propp understands, את־פני "my face" in this context (in v. 20) to be the same as "glory."[195] Previously, within the Sinai pericope both these terms כבוד "glory" and פנים "face" have been used in association with the anthropomorphic person of YHWH/God when he appeared on the mountain. One may also recall that when YHWH/God appeared in his glory, he was also described in terms of human form; this is to say that the glory of YHWH settled on the mountain in a broader sense and looked like a consuming fire, but at the same time, he was said to have given to Moses the tablets of stones inscribed by his finger (24:9–10; 16–18; 31:18).

Since YHWH is described even within the glory as an individual entity, in human form, one gets a sense that "YHWH's glory" here meant glory as personified as a "single entity" by which he could pass by Moses. Arguably, Moses' desire was to see YHWH in his glory, which meant to see "the face of YHWH in glory" (glorious face). It may be that "my face" here is meant to be the anthropomorphic divine revelation within the glory similar to the divine appearance on the mountain. It was this radiant and glorious face that could not be envisaged by the people in general, but only by Moses because of divine mercy and grace. One can discern that Moses' desire was to have a similar experience of seeing YHWH in glory, but at the same time Moses was also mediating on behalf of the people. So the statement in 33:20 has to be seen in that context. Since Moses was interceding in solidarity with the people (12–13, 15–16), and given that YHWH had already responded favorably to Moses (in v. 17), the *idem per idem* statement in terms of grace and mercy seems to signify that YHWH would be gracious and merciful not only to Moses, but also to the people, although it is not yet clear as to how the people would experience his grace and mercy (perhaps, through Moses' mediation).

---

194. Lundbom, "*Idem per Idem*", 198.
195. Propp, *Exodus 19–40*, 689. Eichrodt (*OTT* 2, 38) suggests that כבוד "glory" and פנים "face" are never combined with one another since these two nouns derive from different roots. However, both these nouns are used in association with the same divine person.

The assumption that verse 20 was inserted by a later editor/redactor, who had reservations about reference to God's face on a theological basis,[196] seems speculative, given that the writer/editor would not insert something to contradict himself or (canonically) an earlier text. By placing verse 11 just a few verses before verse 20,[197] the writer affirms that YHWH and Moses were in a "face-to-face" relation, which arguably included a "seeing" aspect. It is in light of this that verse 20 will be interpreted. Sarna is of the opinion that "by virtue of their humanity, human beings (ha-adam), including Moses, cannot directly and closely observe God's Kabod";[198] and Jacob stresses that "no mortal could ever have claimed that he had seen his face, nor had Moses made such a request".[199] However, as Eichrodt affirms, "the best instance of the extremely concrete way in which this vision of the divine majesty was experienced is to be found in the description of the Sinai theophany";[200] and, as discussed earlier, several of the Hebrew traditions have portrayed YHWH/ God appearing in human form, and some people claimed that they had seen God and his face.[201]

Moses' request for the vision of glory (v. 18) at that juncture, as noted earlier, was because he was keen to experience the unmediated and direct manifestation of God similar to that which he had envisaged on the mountain where he saw him in his glory just before the calf episode. What the first part of verse 20 seems to portray is that if YHWH were to manifest himself in glory at that place (in the same way as he did earlier on the mountain), the people who were nearby would not be able to envisage God in glory. It seems, then, the revelation by means of פנים "face" is treated somewhat different from the revelations by means of כבוד "glory".

---

196. Noth, *Exodus*, 258; Billings, 439–442.

197. In fact, verse 11 may be the key to help in understanding the tension in verses 12–23.

198. Sarna, *Exodus*, 214; cf. E. W. Nicholson, *Exodus and Sinai in History and Tradition* (Oxford: Basil Blackwell, 1973), 79.

199. Jacob, *Exodus*, 975.

200. Eichrodt, *OTT* 2, 16. See Exod 19:18–25; 20:18–22.

201. E.g. Jacob (Gen 32:31) and Gideon (Judg 6:22).

A. Orlov,[202] comparing this biblical text with 2 Enoch 39:3–6, where "the 'face' is closely associated with the divine 'extend'",[203] assumes that "face" is to be treated "not simply as a part of the Lord's body (his face) but as a radiant *façade* of his anthropomorphic 'form'";[204] and argues that in 33:20 the "impossibility of seeing the Lord's face is understood not simply as the impossibility of seeing the particular part of the Lord but rather as the impossibility of seeing the complete range of his glorious 'body'".[205] Comparing some kind of "danger motif" in 2 Enoch 39:8 with 33:20, Orlov concludes that 2 Enoch "supports the idea that human beings can actually see the 'face of God' and that Moses could see the divine form".[206] However, Orlov's view is complicated by the fact that he understands "face" not as part of the body (i.e. in the anatomical sense) but as an endlessly grown "extend" or form, while the Hebrew text understands it anthropomorphically. His equation of כבוד "glory" with פנים "face" that is, "anthropomorphic extend",[207] seems strange to the biblical understanding since the Hebrew term פנים used for human beings and for the anthropomorphic divine figure is the same.[208]

As discussed above, even in the texts where כבוד "glory" is associated with the manifestation of the transcendent God, פנים "face" is implied because

---

202. A. Orlov, "Ex 33 on God's Face: A Lesson from the Enochic Tradition", *SBL Seminar Papers* 39 (2000), 130–147.
203. 2 Enoch 39:3–8 (the shorter recension): "I have gazed into the eyes of the Lord, like the rays of the shining sun and terrifying . . . I have seen the "extend" of the Lord, without measure and without analogy, who has no end" . . . who will be able to endure the infinite terror or of the great burning?". For a comprehensive study, see F. Andersen, "2 (Slavonic Apocalypse of) Enoch", in *The Old Testament Pseudepigrapha*. Vol. 1. Ed. J. H. Charlesworth (New York: Doubleday, 1985), 102–221. 1976), 107–110.
204. Orlov, "Ex 33", 135.
205. Ibid., 136. He seems to ascribe a kind of "glory" shaped "form" to YHWH's "face".
206. Ibid., 140. Contra Dyrness (*Themes in Old Testament Theology* [Carlisle: Paternoster Press, 1977], 35), who thinks that God allowed his form to be seen, but not his face.
207. This idea of "extend" (2 En 39:8) finds a parallel in an Aryan-Hindu tradition where the god Brahma (from a Sanskrit root: *brh* [identical with the Semitic root br' = ארב]), who extends beyond himself in size. http://en.wikipedia.org/wiki/Brahman.
208. Orlov's assumption (137, 142, 147) that Exod 33:18–23 and Slavonic Enoch 39:3–6 represent a single tradition seems questionable, as the traditions differ greatly. The role of Moses as the covenant mediator is in the heart of the biblical tradition, whereas Enoch asks, "Who would pray for me"? (2 En 7:3). 2 Enoch need not even be a Jewish book, as it exists mostly in Slavonic.

the divine person who appeared in glory is described in anthropomorphic terms which imply "face". Eichrodt thinks that this vision of glory (v. 18) has a deadly effect, and yet, believes that "by a special gift of God's grace that Moses is finally allowed to see the divine glory".[209] Motyer thinks that "to see the face of God was an impossibility", but he believes that Moses had a glimpse of the divine glory (vv. 20–23).[210] Since Moses himself had experienced the divine revelation in the (fiery red) glory (24:16–18), one may affirm that Moses was not included in the negation in verse 20.

As observed earlier, calf-worship had caused the crisis in terms of the covenantal obligation, and Moses too had broken up the Law of the Covenant. It is possible that Moses' concern at that juncture includes the worship, which was disturbed. Perhaps, Moses understood that God's presence and worship of God in obedience to the divine Law were interrelated. Previously, it was when YHWH revealed himself in glory that Moses received the tablets of Law. Moses' utmost concern was to know if YHWH would manifest himself in his glory as he did earlier and would give him the Law a second time. Perhaps, nothing less than receiving the Law would be a confirmation to Moses that YHWH would go before people without destroying them. In some sense it appears that Moses was expecting a special theophany similar to the one he had experienced on the mountain.

Now coming to the second part of the statement, לא־יראני האדם וחי "for no one shall see 'me' and live" (v. 20b): the writer uses the term [211]האדם "the man" (which could mean humankind) in the divine reply to Moses instead of עם "the people" which has been frequently used in this section. Readers would realize that now this statement was made in the context of the sin of "his people" and that some of them were already struck by the plague, and that God would not go with the rest of them lest he destroyed them on the way (32:34–35; 33:3). Previously in Genesis the term האדם "the man" was used in a generic (universal) sense in the context of sin

---

209. Eichrodt, *OTT* 2, 31. He thinks that the divine glory passed before Moses' veiled eyes and that he saw it from behind, but it seems that the theophany foretold in 22–23 took place in the way it is described in ch. 34. See next section.

210. Cf. Motyer, *Exodus*, 307.

211. This term אדם is normally used with the article ה in a generic sense. See F. Maass, "אדם", *TDOT* 1, 75–98.

and flood;[212] and in the present context also the term האדם is used in the context of sin and punishment. One may also recall that sanctification was required of the people in general, for approaching God's presence lest they die (19:9–15; 21–24).

In some sense, this statement means that there is no difference between the people under the covenant ("my people") and humankind (האדם) in general, and that no one can approach or face God's revealed presence (appearance) without sanctification. These verses 19–20 seem to insist that the people of the covenant who had sinned would not be able to see the "divine glory" as they did earlier when it appeared on the mountain (24:1–11), but the divine grace and mercy were bestowed upon Moses so that he could see. While the divine promise (in 14, 17) was to go with the people in terms of פנים, he could not reveal his "glory" directly because they would not be able to see, but perhaps, divine grace and mercy might be granted later.

If one takes 33:20 to mean literally and categorically that no one can see YHWH's face and live, then the evidence that some people had seen the divine face (face-to-face), as discussed in the previous chapters, needs accounting for. Moses did not fear to express his desire to see YHWH's glory, nor did he seem to think it was fatal. It is worth noting that "hearing" God's speech was also associated with death, in that people told Moses, "You speak with us and we will hear; but let not YHWH/God speak with us lest we die" (Exod 20:18–20).[213] If one takes the "seeing" aspect as absolute negation, then, one ought to take the death associated with the "hearing" also in an absolute sense, and as a consequence there could be no communication or connection between God, whom the Hebrew traditions portray as the creator and humankind.

---

212. Gen 6:5–6; 8:21: when the wickedness of man (האדם) was great, and the intention and thoughts of man את־האדם were evil continually, he was grieved for making man on the earth and destroyed them.
213. Cf. Deut 5:24: "We have seen this day that God speaks with man; yet he still lives".

5.3.4 The Divine Revelation Promised and Moses' Desire Fulfilled: 33:21–34:10, 28–35.

5.3.4.1 *The details of the proposed divine revelation (vv. 21–23)*

In addition to his earlier statement (in v. 20), YHWH told Moses, "There is a place by me, and you will stand upon the rock (21); when my glory passes by, I will put you in a cleft of the rock, and I will cover you with my hand until I have passed by (v. 22); then I will take away my hand, and you shall see my back; but my face shall not be seen" (v. 23).

Surprisingly, the divine "back" is mentioned here after a series of divine revelations where "face" or "face-to-face" have been used. Moses appears to be silent at this proposed theophany allowing him to see YHWH's glory from the back, and he seems dissatisfied with the prospect of seeing the divine back. How can one understand the aspect of the divine "back" in association with the divine glory? The Hebrew noun used for the "back" in the anatomical sense is not אחרי but גו,[214] but אחרי as an adverb was used earlier in Genesis in the context of seeing after/behind the anthropomorphic divine figure.[215] Although the contrast is made from פנים "face" to אחרי "back", the employment of "back" does not reduce the validity of the divine revelation in terms of the physicality nor does it nullify the divine appearance.[216]

Some scholars have commented on this proposed theophany as though it has taken place in the same way foretold here in verses 21–23. Clements thinks that "even Moses was not granted the "privilege of seeing God's face";[217] Hertz states that Moses could not see the full manifestation of the

---

214. See Korpel, *Rift in the Clouds*, 87–95. But it may be noted that the אחרי is used earlier in the narrative in a nominal sense to denote the backside of the tabernacle (Exod 26:12: אחרי המשכן).

215. See Gen 16:13. The phrase רָאִיתִי אַחֲרֵי רֹאִי used here is similar to וְרָאִיתָ אֶת־אֲחֹרָי (v. 23). It was when the divine person was about to turn away to go that Hagar recognized him.

216. Cf. *Targums,* Onkelos (424) reads "my aspect" (de-kadamai) for "my face" and Palestine (557) "the visage of my face".

217. Clements, *Exodus,* 216.

divine radiance, but only its afterglow.[218] Noth suggests that God would cover Moses protectively with his hand because of the danger involved.[219] However, there seems no reason why Moses was to be prevented from seeing YHWH's glory, since the readers were already informed that Moses was with YHWH in the realm of his glory for forty days and forty nights on the top of the mountain (24:15–18). Furthermore, there is no textual evidence to suggest this proposed theophany in verses 21–23 has taken place at the foot of the mountain,[220] and the theophany in 34:1–19 is different from what is foretold here. Because this theophany foretold in 33:18–23 is not available in the text, Mettinger supports the idea of "aetiology"[221] but acknowledges that "the presence of God is made manifest by God's own proclamation of his Name" in the theophany which took place only on the mountain.[222] As Rylaarsdam understands, 34:6–7 is the fulfillment of God's promise in 33:19.[223]

The negation in verse 23b, that is, "my face shall not be seen" is arguably for the people at the foot of the mountain. The emphasis was already made of the distance between the people and the tent of meeting (33:7) where YHWH used to come and speak with Moses face-to-face (v. 11). It seems, then, that the statement in both verses 20 and 23 was meant for the people, and Moses was not included (cf. v. 20). Whether this conversation took place in the tent of meeting (cf. 7–11) or elsewhere, the use of "rock"[224] and "cave/cleft" imply that it was somewhere at the foot of the mountain (in 21a; cf. 34:2) and possibly all the people were close by. It appears as though YHWH was not willing to reveal himself in his glory at that spot (the foot of the mountain) because it would have meant destruction for the people, who were in the habit of watching his coming to and meeting with Moses.

---

218. J. H. Hertz, ed. *The Pentateuch and Haphtarahs* (London: Soncino Press, 1937), 363; cf. Driver, Exodus, 362–363; Mackay, *Exodus*, 559.
219. Noth, *Exodus*, 258.
220. Jacob, *Exodus*, 981.
221. T. N. D. Mettinger, *The Dethronement of Sabaoth: Studies in the Shem and Kabod Theologies*, (CWK Gleerup: Malmö, 1982), 119.
222. Mettinger, *Dethronement*, 125.
223. Rylaarsdam, *Exodus*, 1075–1080.
224. For an association of rock in the theophanies, see I. Gruenwald, "God the 'Stone/Rock': Myth, Idolatry, and Cultic Fetishism in Ancient Israel", *JR* 76 (1996), 428–449.

In the previous sections, an assumption has been made that Moses' desire was to see the divine revelation in terms of glory similar to that of Sinai, and now that assumption is confirmed, as YHWH calls Moses to go up on to the mountain; and one may speculate here that Moses was upset that he was permitted to see only the divine back and not his glory, and that YHWH told him something like, "you cannot see my glory here in the visibility of the people but come up to the mountain where you can see my glory and also receive my Law (Words) again" (cf. 34:1–4). This leads to the next section where Moses goes to the Mountain again.

5.3.4.2 YHWH reveals himself to Moses on the Mountain (34:1–7)

The writer tells that YHWH told Moses to cut two stone tablets like the first ones, on which he would write the words that were on the first tablets which Moses broke; to go up in the morning,[225] and stand before him (ונצבת לי) on the Mountain.

As Moses goes up to Mt. Sinai with the two chiselled stone tablets, in fulfillment of his promises to Moses,[226] YHWH descends (ירד) in the cloud and stands[227] and passes by (ויעבר יהוה על־פניו) close to Moses' face[228] and proclaims[229] "YHWH, YHWH God, merciful and gracious, longsuffering (ארך אפים)[230] and abounding in goodness and truth (5–6); maintaining great kindness (רב־חסד) for thousands, lifting (נשא) iniquity (עון), transgression (פשע) and sin (חטאה) by no means clearing the guilty, visiting the iniquity of the fathers upon the children and the children's children to the third and the fourth generation" (v. 7).

---

225. Cf. Exod 9:13; 24:4 where Moses was to rise up in the morning to be on the divine task.
226. Exod 33:16, 17, 19, 21–23.
227. ויתיצב (hithpael of יצב) gives the idea of presenting oneself.
228. על־פני may be more distinct than לפני. See BDB, 818–819. Soffer, "Anthropomorphisms," 86.
229. Despite some confusion over the subject of the verb יקרא (יהוה יהוה ויעבר יהוה על־פניו ויקרא) the context confirms that YHWH is the subject (cf. v. 19).
230. The derivation of אפים seems uncertain but some Eng. verses (e.g. KJV and NKJ) read it as "long suffering" and the LXX has translated it as μακρόθυμος "longsuffering or patient."

The special mention made that YHWH "passed by" seems significant for two reasons. This theophany seems different from the previous mountain theophanies, in that the appearance of the glory was not made obvious, perhaps even to the people at the foot of the mountain (20:18; 24:17).[231] In this theophany, YHWH's appearance is described more as a single entity perhaps similar to the one Moses saw in the bush; rather than in a broader sense, and there were no signs of thunder or lightening.

Earlier in Exodus, the verb עבר was used when YHWH passed (יהוה עבר) through the land of Egypt in the context of judging the Egyptians;[232] and despite YHWH's anger (אף) to destroy the people for their sin (32:10),[233] his promise was to pass by in terms of his goodness/glory (בעבר כבדי) before Moses (33:19, 22). Interestingly, here it (ויעבר יהוה) is used in the context where both the mercy and justice are proclaimed together.[234] While YHWH's mercy is available to forgive wickedness, lawlessness and sin, his justice is also emphasized, in that the guilty, even of future generations, would not be left unpunished (34:6–7).[235]

This divine name plays an immensely significant role in the theophanies, in that YHWH himself proclaims his name [236] as an act of, or maintenance of, the covenant.[237] Significantly, in conjunction with this divine name the

---

231. In earlier theophanies, the people witnessed thunder, lightning, and smoke, on seeing which the people trembled (Exod 20:18); the appearance of "glory" on the Mountain was made obvious in that it looked like fire to the people who watched from the foot of the Mountain (Exod 24:17; cf.16: 10).

232. While the verb עבר is used in association with YHWH (עבר יהוה) in the context of the judgement in Exod 12:23a, ופסח יהוה is used (12:13, 23b) in protecting Israel from the destroyer; the LXX has σκεπάσω "shall cover" where MT has פסח in 12:13. For a discussion on this, see Hartenstein, *Angesicht*, 278.

233. It was when YHWH's wrath burned against the people for their sin (32:10) that Moses began interceding on behalf of the people (32:11–13), and YHWH relented (32:14).

234. Hartenstein suggests YHWH's "passing by" in 34:6 is to be treated as a dialectic between "seeing God" in the Psalms and God's "sparing" his people from his anger. See Hartenstein, *Angesicht*, 279–282.

235. This may be a hint that the covenant requirements are to be taken seriously.

236. Mettinger, *In Search of God*, 9; Eichrodt, *OTT* 1, 206. Cf. Exod 3:14; 6:3; 33:19; 34:6–10.

237. This name that was specifically mentioned by YHWH himself in the context of saving the people from Egypt (6:2–9) is used here (34:6–7) in the context of forgiving people, renewing the covenant and possessing the Land.

divine character is also revealed; and expanded into a list of qualities mostly associated with forgiveness.²³⁸ In contrast to his earlier decision to destroy the people, now YHWH will lift up/remove²³⁹ their sin. By using all the three important Hebrew terms for sin, עון (Gk. ἀνομίας "lawlessness"), פשע (Gk. ἀδικίας "unrighteousness") and חטאה (Gk. ἁμαρτίας "guilt") in the same sentence (v. 7) to indicate the variety of sins committed by the people, and by replacing them by the variety of the divine qualities: רחום "merciful", חנון "gracious", ארך אפים "slow to anger" and רב־חסד ואמת "abundant in goodness and truth", the writer displays the contrast vividly.

Child suggests that "the special divine revelation which Moses requested and God provided was "in terms of his attributes rather than his appearances".²⁴⁰ However, it is obvious that in accordance with his earlier promises, YHWH revealed himself on the mountain. Smith's suggestion seems plausible in that he proposes that the "glory of YHWH" revealed on the mountain was "moral glory, a manifestation of the moral attributes in the divine character," and "the manifestation of his love and his justice in his dealings with his creatures". At the same time, as Smith states, YHWH's glory is "something made known by outward appearance".²⁴¹ One may conclude that YHWH revealed himself to Moses in a human form and also proclaimed his character. Obviously, the theophany that took place on the mountain was a direct theophany, in some ways different from what was foretold, but it seems that the writer understood this theophany as the fulfillment of the one foretold in 33:33:19, 20–23. Since טוב "goodness" and כבוד "glory" are used in apposition to YHWH himself, it seems that both "goodness" and "glory" are inbuilt characteristics of YHWH, who also possesses some kind of "glory" which could be made visible at the same time; perhaps Moses saw something of that divine glory.²⁴²

As Fretheim understands, "there is a visible appearance of God in the center of the text that cannot be argued away", and the anthropomorphic

---

238. G. Ashby, *Exodus* (Grand Rapids: Eerdmans, 1998), 135.
239. English versions have translated נשא (lit. lift/take away) as "forgiving".
240. Childs, *Exodus*, 596.
241. Smith, "Glory of God", 327–328.
242. Cf. Mackay, *Exodus*, 548.

language for God is consistent with the human form of other theophanies.[243] It is possible that Moses had face-to-face interaction with YHWH in a literal sense since he had "an unparalleled exposure to the divine glory", as Niehaus affirms.[244] The writer's purpose in using the abstract noun "my glory" with the concrete term, "my face" and the abstract nouns, glory, goodness, grace and mercy used with the proper name YHWH, seems to signify a kind of intrinsic glory of YHWH in terms of his character (mercy, grace etc.) that was expressed by means of his outward glory. The writer also seems to insist that it was truly YHWH himself who "passed" before Moses in a literal sense, and also that by letting himself be seen by Moses showed his character of grace and mercy. These anthropomorphic features of YHWH are beautifully woven into his divine character of grace and forgiveness.

Finally, at the end of the to and fro conversation between YHWH and Moses, the covenant initiator revealed himself both in terms of פנים "face" and כבוד "glory" to the covenant mediator. Since YHWH revealed his glory to Moses on the mountain as an assurance of his continued presence on their onward journey, his name and character are significant for the future aspect of his relationship with the people. In all this activity, YHWH is understood as a "living God" because he himself descended in the cloud, stood with Moses there and proclaimed the name YHWH, also making a confession of his character (34:5–7) where his שׁ "name" and his חן "grace" are mentioned. As Lasor reflects, YHWH made his presence with the Israelites visually known and proved to be "a revealing God".[245] There is no reason to think that "an additional safeguard against literalism is provided by the sense of awe and mystery associated with religious experience";[246] rather the awe and mystery can only be an outcome of, or produced by, an experience of seeing YHWH/God, as in the case of Moses. Although YHWH had already manifested himself in his glory to Moses in

---

243. Fretheim, *Exodus*, 300.
244. Niehaus, *God at Sinai*, 213.
245. Lasor, *Survey*, 106.
246. I. Barbour, *Myths Models and Paradigms* (New York: Harper & Row, 1974), 50.

the past, he seems to have had a different experience here, in such a way that his face shone and a mystic element may be detected.

5.3.4.3 Moses bows before YHWH and worships (Exod 34:8–10)

The writer relates that after having heard YHWH's proclamation on the mountain top, Moses at once/immediately bowed towards the earth and prostrated/ worshiped (ויקד ארצה וישתחו);[247] then, he prayed: "If now I have found grace in your eyes, O Lord (אדני) let my Lord[248] (אדני), go with/ among us;[249] for the people are stiff-necked people; pardon our iniquity and our sin, and take us as your inheritance"; and then YHWH told that he would make a covenant and would do marvels among them in such a way that all the nations would see his work (vv. 8–10).

The reason for using both the verbs קדד and [250]וישתחו in a gesture of worship with similar meaning could be for emphasis. It seems very likely that YHWH appeared to Moses from close vicinity and that he bowed before that revealed divine person. Although לפני is not mentioned here, one may presume that YHWH's appearance on the mountain was visible to Moses in a human (bodily) form given that Moses prostrated himself before YHWH.[251] YHWH's promise that all his goodness (כל־טובי) would pass before Moses (לפניך: 33:19) is fulfilled now when YHWH appeared in his glory as a "single entity" and passed before Moses. And seeing the anthropomorphized person of YHWH, one can assume that Moses is satisfied

---

247. Some Eng. verses (e.g. NRS and NKJ) read "bowed 'his head'" but the noun ראש (head) is not in the MT; however, it is possible since קדד has the sense of "bowing down", which means that head is bent down towards the earth.

248. Cf. LXX has: ὁ κύριός μου.

249. LXX has μεθ' ἡμῶν i.e. "in company with us".

250. השתחו is commonly treated as hishtaphel of חוה. However, scholars still do not seem to be decisive about the etymology of this verb. Both שחה and חוה are considered as possible roots of השתחו, though שחה is preferred. See J. A. Emerton, "Etymology of *histahawah*", *OS* 20 (1977), 55. Cf. G. I. Davies, "A Note on the Etymology of *histahawah*", *VT* 29 (1979), 493–495; H. D. Preuss, "חוה *hwh*; הִשְׁתַּחֲוָה *histahawah*", *TDOT* 4, 249–257. In the HB, it is used to mean "bow" before someone as a mark of respect or "prostrate oneself" in worship.

251. Since "my face" and "me" are synonymously used for YHWH himself (33:24, 20), it is YHWH who appeared in his glory. Cf. Ezek 1:28: I saw the appearance of the likeness of the glory of YHWH, and fell on my face.

and prostrated before the one whose glory he wanted to see. It is possible that it is in that humble spirit of prostration before YHWH that Moses once again intercedes and raises his concerns on behalf of the people, and repeats his earlier prayer for the divine accompaniment[252] acknowledging YHWH's leadership over the people.[253] Moses not only acknowledges the people to be stiff-necked, but includes himself in seeking the divine forgiveness[254] (v. 9b: וסלחת לעוננו ולחטאתנו), and requests YHWH to inherit them (ונחלתנו), that is, to treat them as his possession.[255]

In reply to Moses' request for forgiveness, YHWH tells Moses that he was making a covenant with him, perhaps a renewal of it, as a sign of forgiveness.[256] This would have meant that the people would be forgiven. This divine revelation seems highly significant for the renewal of the covenant and the worship of YHWH, even as the divine Law was given a second time (vv. 11–28). It is worth noting here that YHWH promises his involvement in future, that he will do wonders (אעשה נפלאת), and that all the people will see it (v. 10); and arguably, this divine assurance is an indication that God will continue to reveal himself to the people even in the future (cf. 33:16). There is no reason to think, as Durham does, that 34:1–18 has been 'woven into' its present position to suggest the renewal of the covenant relationship,[257] and as Motyer has articulated, there is no difficulty in saying "the verses are where they are because that is the way things happened".[258] The purpose of this divine-revelation, as emphasised in verses 1–4 was to give the Law again so that the worship, halted because of the calf worship, could be restarted. In this anthropomorphism, one

---

252. 34:9a (אם־נא מצאתי חן בעיניך); cf. 33:12–13, 16.
253. The repetition of the divine title אדני "Lord" in v. 9a (אדני ילך־נא אדני בקרבנו) may indicate acknowledgement of the divine lordship in a greater measure. The term אדני is used to address secular masters. See Gen 18:3, 27, 31; 23:11; 15; 24:12; Exod 32:22.
254. W. Brueggemann, "The Travail of Pardon: Reflections on slh", in *A God So Near*. Eds. B. A. Strawn, and N. R. Brown (Winona Lake, Indiana: Eisenbrauns, 2003), 284–285.
255. Cf. Gen 31:14; the noun form of נחלה is used in the sense of inheritance.
256. Cf. Num 14:19–21: "Pardon the iniquity . . . according to your mercy . . .; YHWH said, I have pardoned, according to your word; but truly, all the earth shall be filled with the glory of YHWH".
257. Durham, *Exodus*, 458.
258. Motyer, *Exodus*, 299.

"You Cannot See My Face; No One Can See Me, and Live" 177

can also detect anthropopathism²⁵⁹ in that YHWH expresses his feeling of jealousy in terms of exclusiveness of worship (34:14).

Before moving to the next section on the shining of Moses' face (vv. 27–29), one may note that the verb ראה is used in verses 23–24 in association with פנים "face" of YHWH in the context of worship. The instruction in these verses is that people were to go to see "the face of YHWH" three times in a year in the future, during which time one would perhaps expect YHWH/God to reveal himself.²⁶⁰

5.3.4.4 *The shining in Moses' face (Exod 34:27–29)*

YHWH renewed his relationship with Israel under the covenant in accordance with the Law; while Moses was on the mountain with YHWH forty days and forty nights, he wrote on the tablets the words of the covenant, that is, the Ten Commandments; when Moses came down from the mountain with the two tablets of the covenant in his hand, he did not know that the skin of his face shone because Moses spoke with YHWH (v. 29).²⁶¹

The writer specifically informs his readers that the skin of Moses' face shone when YHWH spoke to him (כי קרן עור פניו בדברו אתו) but he did not know that his face shone (v. 29). The Hebrew term used here is the qal form of the verb ²⁶²קרן "to shine" which seems to signify that there was shining/radiance in Moses' face (עור פניו). But some old versions, taking this as the noun קרן ("horn") understood that the skin of Moses' face was "horned".²⁶³ However, scholars in general suggest that the verb קרן is to

---

259. On this subject, see Soffer, "Anthropomorphisms", 85–107.
260. Although MT renders the forms of ראה as niphal stem in vv. 23 (אלהי ישראל יראה את־פני יהוה) and 24 (לראות את־פני יהוה אלהיך), it is possible to (re) point as qal grammatically, as Smith (*Pilgrimage*, 101) suggests, and given that in vv. 23 and 24 את־פני are used as the direct objects of the verb ראה. One may also note that since these instructions are given in the context of the divine revelation on the Mountain, it may be an indication that even in future the divine revelations would take place in the context of worship.
261. The piel form of דבר used five times in vv. 29–35 seems to signify the direct contact between YHWH-Moses and Moses-Israel.
262. The qal stem of קרן occurs only here in vv. 29, 30, 35.
263. For example, Aquila and Vulgate base their translations on Ps 69:32 where מקרן (hiph. part. of קרן) is used (cf. Hab 3:4 and Amos 6:13 where the noun קרנים is used). Moberly too (*At the Mountain*, 107) thinks that Moses was accredited with horns reflecting the calf they worshiped (Exod 32:1–6).

be interpreted as "shining/rays" of light; which means that the shining in Moses' face signifies those rays of radiance streaming from Moses' face",[264] and "was only a reflection of God's glory"[265] after he met with God (v. 29); this interpretation seems "most conducive to the word used and the context".[266]

Noth is of the opinion that the skin of Moses' face shone because of his "unique meeting with God" and he had to cover up the glow on his face;[267] and one cannot fit קרן as a noun into this context (in 34:29) and say that the skin of the face is "horned"[268] as it does not make sense in the given context. Furthermore, the writer insists that the cause of radiance in Moses' face was that YHWH spoke with him.[269] The writer's description that "the skin of 'his face' (פניו) shone" seems significant, and at this juncture it might help to discern the possible reasons how and why Moses' face shone. The context in which Moses' face shone was a theophany on the mountain where YHWH revealed himself in glory and passed by Moses. Therefore, one can assume that the shining in Moses' face was a reflection of YHWH's glory;[270] that it was not the product of a subjective experience but a transformation that took place when Moses approached the sphere of YHWH's revealed glory.[271] It is very likely that it is the divine "glory" that was passed on to Moses on the mountain, when YHWH spoke to Moses directly.[272] Since it is Moses' face that shone, and that YHWH was the source of

---

264. Most of the English versions have translated it as "radiance/shining". Curiously, a Sanskrit word *Kiran* gives the idea of a "ray" of light/Sun.

265. Cassuto, *Exodus*, 448; Childs, *Exodus*, 619; M. Haran, "The Shining of Moses' Face", in *The Shelter of Elyon*. JSOTSS 31 (Sheffield: JSOT Press, 1984), 159–168; Jacob, *Exodus*, 1005–1006.

266. W. R. Baker, "Did the Glory of Moses' Face Fade? A Re-examination of καταργέω in 2 Corinthians 3:7–18", *BBR* 10 (2000), 6.

267. Noth, *Exodus*, 267.

268. Ibid. Even if the verb קרן was developed from the noun, it does not make sense here.

269. The subject and object of the verb דבר is not clear in the Hebrew text (i.e. בדברו אתו) as to who spoke with whom, but 34:10 gives the clue to think that YHWH is the subject of speaking.

270. Lasor, *Survey*, 79.

271. Motyer, *Exodus*, 300–301.

272. Cf. C. Meyers, *Exodus* (Cambridge: Cambridge University Press, 2005), 266.

shining, it is possible that the face of YHWH was also shining and perhaps the radiance was transmitted from YHWH to Moses.

Given that Moses was with YHWH for forty days and forty nights in his (glorious) presence, it is possible that the direct and "face-to-face" conversation between YHWH and Moses continued even in the realm of glory; and it was the divine glory/radiance that reflected in his face,[273] which in return witnesses to his relationship with YHWH. Since the glory that passed by was YHWH himself and the divine glory and the divine person seem inseparable, it may be assumed that during such time when Moses was in front of YHWH, the radiance that was something from YHWH's very self (glory) was passed on to Moses.

Readers would be aware that in the previous Sinai traditions YHWH appeared in a radiant fire. As M. Widmer argues, Moses' face reflects the divine radiance.[274] It is plausible to think that Moses' face shone because he had seen YHWH's face in glory, given that he was in the habit of face-to-face conversations in the tent (33:7–11). One can even argue the other way round that since Moses' face shone because of his direct exposure to YHWH's glory on the mountain, there is more reason to believe the possibility of Moses seeing YHWH's face in the tent.

Presumably, readers would have understood that something of the divine radiance was imparted to Moses' face. This may well mean that Moses was not included in the statement of negation in 33:20, "you shall not be able to see (לא תוכל לראת) my face"; and as Haran understands it, the negation rather expresses the incapacity of the people "to stand the exceeding brilliance radiating from the divine image",[275] particularly in light of the broken covenantal relationship by calf worship.

Eichrodt suggests that כבוד "glory" includes a visible appearance and "the extreme realism" which was attached to ideas connected with כבוד "glory" may be seen in its reflection on the face of Moses.[276] If Moses had seen the divine glory, then, he had also seen YHWH's face in glory.

---

273. Jacob, *Exodus*, 1006.
274. M. Widmer, *Moses, God, and the Dynamics of Intercessory Prayer* (Tübingen: Mohr Siebeck, 2004), 222.
275. Haran ("shining", 166) thinks that לא תוכל implies "you shall not be able".
276. Eichrodt, *OTT* 2, fn. 1, 31.

Evidently YHWH passed on his כבוד to Moses' face so that "the skin of his face was made glorious".²⁷⁷ From the connection between כבוד (33:18) טוב (33:19) and קרן "shining" in Moses' face, then, it seems that by his very appearance in glory, YHWH projected his goodness in terms of all the attributes mentioned in his proclamation, by means of his revelation.

If one generalizes that the negation in 33:20 is categorical and that no one could ever see the divine face, then, the burden of proof is to explain how Moses' face shone here, how Jacob could claim that he had seen God face-to-face (Gen 32:31), why Moses hid his face (Exod 3), and how the representatives of the people saw God on the mountain (Exod 24). The fact is that the writer makes it clear that Moses' face shone because YHWH spoke with him (34:29), and there seems no reason why one cannot believe that Moses' face shone because he saw the face of YHWH in his anthropomorphic form in his "glory" (glorious face) in a literal sense.

Significantly, despite the fact that Moses was in the realm of YHWH's glory, and that he got the tablets of the Law dictated by YHWH himself on the mountain (34:28; cf. 24:12–18), he was neither harmed, nor was the idea of death associated with seeing YHWH's glory. The readers would remember that God did not raise his hand against Moses and others when they saw God (24:10–11), and now would realize that 33:20 did not prove fatal for Moses, even after the divine glory shone upon him. In conformity with the assumption made earlier in this chapter, Moses was anxious over the broken tablets of the Law and the obstacle to worship, and now he receives the tablets on which YHWH/God's Words (of the covenant) were written a second time.

5.3.4.5 *Fear generated by the shining in Moses' face (Exod 34:30–32)*

When Aaron and all the Israelites saw that Moses' face was radiant, they were afraid to come near him, but when Moses called them, they all came near him and Moses spoke to them all that YHWH ordered them on the mountain (vv. 30–32).

---

277. Considering LXX's δεδόξασται (for the MT's קרן עור) from the verb δοξάζω "to glorify".

Surprisingly, although he was with Moses when he saw God earlier (24:10), Aaron, along with the others, was afraid of seeing Moses' face.[278] The reason why people were afraid (וייראו) of going near him may be because the shining in Moses' face looked extraordinary. It may be that the reflection of God's glory in Moses' face was similar to the divine glory, and perhaps the sudden appearance of Moses with his shining made them afraid and attempt to go away from Moses. One cannot avoid sensing a negative fear[279] in them, because they were still in a broken relation with YHWH and were not yet certain of the divine forgiveness. Since some of the people were already afflicted (32:28, 35), they might have developed a negative fear—even fear of death in that particular context of sin.

Propp's idea that Moses' face was disfigured because of the burning/blisters seems very unlikely,[280] given that Moses was not even aware that his face was shining. Orlov compares the shining in Moses' face with the radiant metamorphosis of Enoch, who resembled the divine and whom no human being could look at because it was dangerous.[281] But there is no danger motif associated with Moses' experience, nor does the text say that the people were affected (physically) for seeing YHWH's glory as reflected in Moses' face. Although they were taken by some kind of fear, when Moses called them, they came near him and listened to the commands which Moses received from YHWH on the mountain. They did not express any more fear for seeing the shining in Moses' face. While Moses saw the divine "glory" directly, all other people witnessed to the divine glory reflected in Moses' face. This means that by reflecting his glory in Moses' face (as a visible sign), YHWH had not only established his intimate relationship with Moses, but also perhaps confirmed that Moses was the mediator of

---

278. The reason could be because Aaron was also involved in the calf episode.

279. In some contexts, the verb ירא "to fear" is used in contrast to the reverential fear.

280. See W. H. Propp, "The Skin of Moses' Face: Transfigured or Disfigured"?, *CBQ* 49 (1987), 375–386. The idea here is that Moses' face was disfigured because of his overexposure to God.

281. 2 En 22:8–9 describes that when the archangel Michael anointed Enoch by oil and clothed him, he became like one of the glorious ones (radiant metamorphosis), and there was no observable difference. And after that divine encounter (2 En 37) the angel chilled Enoch's burning face, and without this chilling no human being could look at Enoch's face. See Orlov, "Ex 33", 141.

YHWH's word to his people.²⁸² The shining of the divine glory through Moses' face would have been a confirmation to the people that God would go with them without needing to destroy them on the way.

5.3.4.6 Moses puts a veil on his face (Exod 34:33–35)

Whenever Moses finished speaking with them, he put a kind of veil (מסוה)²⁸³ on his face, but whenever he went לפני יהוה "before YHWH" to speak with him, he removed the veil until he came out. And whenever he came out and told the Israelites what was commanded him, they saw Moses' face was radiant, and Moses put the veil again on his face until he went in to speak with YHWH (33–35).

H. Gressmann argues²⁸⁴ that the Hebrew word מסוה ("veil") indicates a mask, and these cultic masks²⁸⁵ are comparable with Hebrew תרפים *teraphim*.²⁸⁶ However, scholars in general seem to agree that מסוה should be translated as "veil" rather than "mask" because the object does not represent the deity, and ritual masks provide no insight in this context;²⁸⁷ and as M. Haran affirms, any identification of *teraphim* with a mask is mere conjecture,²⁸⁸ and the shining in Moses' face was understood as "the divine

---

282. D. Peterson, *Engaging with God* (Downers Grove: Intervarsity Press, 1992), 35; Lasor, *Survey*, 79.
283. The etymology of מסוה seems uncertain, but it may be something to cover the face.
284. H. Gressmann, *Mose und seine Zeit* (Göttingen: Vandenhoeck & Ruprecht, 1913), 246–51. Gressmann, approaching this biblical text from the viewpoint of comparative religion and source criticism, arrived at his conclusions; he assumed that vv. 29–33 and vv. 34–35 belong to two different sources, which is not necessary, as they seem to fit into the biblical context.
285. The mask is a portrait of the deity and has the cultic basis, and the one who wore it would be equated with the god/s. There seemed to be a practice in the ANE religious context whereby the priests used to cover their faces with the mask during the cultic ceremonies.
286. The term *teraphim* is associated with the household idols/gods (cf. Gen 31:19 31:30, 32; cf. Judg 17:5; 18:14). See K. van der Toorn, "Teraphim", *DDDB*, 844–850.
287. T. B. Dozeman, "Masking Moses and Mosaic Authority in Torah", *JBL* 119 (2000), 21–45; Cassuto, *Exodus*, 450; Haran, "Shining", 160–165.
288. Haran, "Shining", 165, 168–169. The parallel in the ANE to the shining of Moses' face may be the Mesopotamian mythological object *melammu*, a mask of light which radiates from the gods (around their heads). See S. L. Sanders, "Old Light on Moses' Shining Face", *VT* 52 (2002), 400.

radiance" and the "veil" was meant to be a cover for the shining in the face of Moses.

The writer insists that Moses went לפני יהוה "before YHWH"[289] and came out and spoke to the Israelites, which could mean that YHWH continued to appear to Moses on the mountain, and that Moses went to see him. Noth associates this tradition with the tent, comparable to 33:7.[290] However, it may be recalled that in a previous theophany (Exod 24:1–12) Moses also shuttled between YHWH, who was on the mountain, and the people, who were at its foot; it may even be that Moses went to speak before YHWH on the mountain. M. Haran understands that the formula לפני־יהוה "before YHWH" is an indication of "the existence of a temple at the site" and that it belongs to the temple's terminology".[291] However, the phrase לפני־יהוה "before YHWH" may signify a literal sense[292] and, presumably, Moses was before the revealed person of YHWH which involved seeing his face. When Moses puts (יתן) a veil על־פניו "on his face" (34:33, 35); when the Israelites see את־פני משה "the face of Moses" and find that עור פני "the skin of his face" shone (v. 30); later on, when the text says that whenever Moses goes לפני יהוה "before YHWH" to speak with him, he removes the veil until he comes out (v. 34)—in all these instances, one can discern that פנים "face" retains it literal sense.

Some scholars opine that Moses made a cultic use of the mask inside the tent and that it implies a cultic setting.[293] But the text is clear that whenever Moses went to speak "before YHWH" he removed the veil until he came out, and only after he spoke with the Israelites he put the veil again on his face. Furthermore, the text gives no clue that the place of theophany shifted from the mountain to the tent; and that Moses wore the veil inside any tent. Therefore, it is unlikely that the covering of Moses' face had any

---

289. Although the phrase לפני "before" acts as a preposition, here it seems to signify YHWH's presence in his revelation (cf. Gen 18:22).
290. For example, Noth, *Exodus*, 267.
291. Haran, *Temples*, 26.
292. Going before (לפני) someone may signify being with someone in a literal sense. There are several instances in Genesis and within Exodus where לפני "before" is employed to signify literal sense. For example, Gen 18:8, 22; 20:15; 41:46; 42:6; 43:15; 43:26; 43:33; 44:14; 47:2, 7; 10; Exod 4:21; 9:10, 13; 29:10; 34:3; 34:6; 34:23; 34:34.
293. Cf. Gressmann, *Mose*, 249–251; Dozeman, "Masking", 31.

cultic basis/significance. Moreover, as discussed earlier, this tent was "not a cultic institution",[294] but was "a venue of occasional theophany".[295] The writer seems to emphasize that when Moses spoke for YHWH, in his face people were brought into an awareness of God's revealed presence.[296]

The fact that Moses was not veiled while speaking with the people may be to show that the shining in his face functioned as a sign to let the people know that the radiance in his face was due to his exposure to YHWH's glory, and that they too were given a chance to witness to YHWH's glory, which probably worked as a "legitimation of Moses' credentials", as Baker puts it.[297] Obviously, the function of the מסוה "veil" was not to hide the shining of the divine glory in Moses' face from the people, but to let them see and be assured that YHWH met with Moses on the mountain as a sign of his grace to Moses and to them, which would have also meant that YHWH would accompany them.[298] As H. M. Wolf reflects, in Exodus 24, YHWH/God revealed his glory on the mountain "in an awe-inspiring display",[299] and here he displayed his glory through Moses to all the people.

It is worth noting that Moses never seemed to have feared death for seeing the face of YHWH/God, even in glory. Once the covenant was renewed (in some sense), none of the people seemed to have feared for seeing the divine radiance in Moses' face. Rather, when they saw the radiance in Moses' face, it would have served as a confirmation that Moses was given the divine Word.[300] All this must have proved to Moses (and to the people) that YHWH would go with them, which meant that divine revelations would continue to take place even in their future journey.

---

294. Haran, *Temples*, 266.
295. A. M. Cooper and B. R. Goldstein, "At the Entrance to the Tent: More Cultic Resonances in Biblical Narrative", *JBL* 116 (1997), 202.
296. Cf. Freitheim, *Exodus*, 311.
297. Baker, "Glory of Moses' Face", 7.
298. While there is some ambiguity as to why Moses covered his face when he was not communicating to the people, it may be to avoid from being seen by the people continually, or it could be that his shining would be fading away between his speaking with the people and his meeting with God.
299. H. M. Wolf, *An Introduction to the Old Testament Pentateuch* (Chicago: Moody Press, 1991), 151.
300. Haran, "Shining", 162.

5.4 Mode of Self-Revelation, Human Recognition, and Response

The writer described YHWH in the tent in anthropomorphic language, that he came down in the pillar of cloud and spoke with Moses "face-to-face" (Exod 33:11); even on the mountain (34:1–7) YHWH descended in the cloud and stood with Moses, passed before him and spoke to him. Presumably, in both these instances, even when YHWH appeared in cloud or in glory, he appeared in human form, and the divine speech was in human language, which Moses understood. The writer does not say where he came from and where he went away to after speaking to Moses (33:7–11; 34:5–28). Israelite readers would be aware that YHWH was understood as the God of heaven and the God of the earth (Gen 24:3; cf. 22:11), as transcendent and immanent God;[301] and that the transcendent God manifested himself in human form and was involved in the lives of his people.[302] However, it was YHWH who took the initiative to reveal himself to Moses in the tent and also on the mountain, and this confirms that the divine revelations took place only by the divine initiative.[303] But the divine appearance in this theophany was not abrupt or sudden, as it was in some earlier traditions (cf. Gen 32:25; Exod 3:2–4), and Moses is said to have waited in the tent and also on the mountain in anticipation of YHWH's coming (33:7–9; 34:1–4). One may realize here that, contrary to the audience concept, it is YHWH/God himself who took the initiative and came to meet Moses.

Consequent to Moses' exposure to the divine glory on the mountain, Moses' face shone and a face-to-face interaction could not be ruled out. It seems possible to affirm that in both these cases (33:7–11; 34:5–35) the anthropomorphic person of YHWH was in view, and Moses saw YHWH in a literal sense, which involved "seeing the face of YHWH/God". The writer tells that after having heard YHWH's proclamation on the mountaintop, Moses responded instantaneously by bowing his head (prostrating

---

301. R. E. Clements, *God and Temple* (Oxford: Basil Blackwell, 1965), 136.
302. P. D. Miller, "Prayer and Action", in *God in the Fray*. Eds., T. Linafelt and T. K. Beal (Minneapolis: Fortress Press, 1998), 212–213.
303. Rowley, *Faith of Israel*, 23.

himself) toward the earth (presumably, before YHWH), and this is another confirmation that God was present with Moses in a bodily/physical form. Although the physicality of the divine person is described in terms of activity (he spoke, gave, passed by, etc.), it is not said that he was in flesh and blood, nor is it described how the figure looked in terms of physical features. But, the "face-to-face" (פנים־אל־פנים) speech between YHWH and Moses and the bodily aspect (פני ילכו "my face will go") associated with the revealed divine person seem to signify that he was in bodily form though ambiguity persists as to whether it was in an anatomical sense[304] or was only in disguise. However, the bodily aspect in these divine revelations should neither be overestimated nor be underestimated.

5.5 The Function/Significance of the Motif

These traditions on the divine self-revelations (in 32–34) would evidently have helped the subsequent generations in ancient Israel to understand that YHWH/God continued to reveal himself to their fathers on their way to the Promised Land. Since their faith and practices were centered on the Sinai covenant, they would have realized that obedience and faithfulness were expected of the people with whom the divine covenant was made.

In light of the previous traditions, the readers in ancient Israel would have realized that the statement of negation in 33:20 was made because of the sin of the people (cf. calf worship) and that failure in covenantal obligations to God deprived them of his presence. These traditions would have functioned to help them understand that despite the people's unfaithfulness, YHWH's character of "grace" and "mercy" (Exod 33:19; 34:6–7) and the mediatory role of Moses had brought reconciliation between God and the people. These traditions could have functioned to establish the validity of the divine revelations particularly in the context of Israel's worship, within the framework of the divine covenant, divine Law, sin and God's

---

304. Cf. Gen 18:8; 19:3.

forgiveness;[305] and that God's presence was indispensable for their continued survival as God's people.[306]

The tradition that Moses prostrated himself in worship in the revealed presence of God would have signified the reality of God's presence in worship and an unbreakable association between the presence of God and human worship. Muilenburg has rightly observed that these traditions have the "content focused upon the motif that is central to all worship, namely, the presence of God, for worship is only possible when and where God is believed to be present".[307] This aspect of worship would have helped them realize that it was their creator God who revealed himself, and this realization must have produced reverential fear in them. As Otto reflects, "in the feeling of complete humility, in its experience of absolute dependence . . . the creature becomes conscious of itself as a creature, and experiences with full clearness what it means to be a 'creature' and 'created'".[308] Finally, these traditions would have helped them to perceive their creator God as the living One and to realize that they were under obligation to prostrate/bow before him in worship.

5.6 Conclusion

In this chapter, Exodus 33:12–23; 34:1–10 and 28–35 have been exegetically studied within the context of chapters 32–34 in the Sinai pericope, and in light of the canonically earlier texts/traditions, in order to understand the tensions surrounding the "seeing" aspect in the statement "you 'cannot see' my face; 'no one can see' me, and live". The conclusions arrived at are as follows.

---

305. Cf. B. S. Childs, *Introduction to the Old Testament as Scripture* (London: SCM, 1979), 165.
306. Cf. D. L. Peterson, ed. "Exodus". *NIB*. Vol. 1 (Nashville: Abingdon Press, 1994), 938; E. F. Davis, *Getting Involved with God* (Cambridge: Cowley Publications, 2001), 155–156.
307. Muilenburg, "Intercession", 176. See also Clements, *God and Temple*, especially, 63–78; 123–134.
308. R. Otto, *Naturalism and Religion* (London: Williams and Norgate, 1913), 373.

This passage fits well in its context of chapters 32–34 both literarily and thematically, and also has links with the theme of "seeing the face of God" (face-to-face) in the previous traditions studied in this work, from Genesis and within the Exodus traditions.[309] The divine revelations described in these texts (33:7–34:1–8; 29–35) are multifaceted and associated with "pillar of cloud", "face", "goodness" and "glory". However, in all these associations, פנים "face" seems most significant as it represented the anthropomorphic form/physicality of YHWH/God in the context of his self-revelations.

The findings of this study in terms of the tension surrounding the aspect of "seeing" have been that the statements made in 33:14 (פני ילכו "my 'face' shall go") and in 33:20 (לא תוכל לראת את־פני כי לא־יראני האדם וחי "you will not be able to see 'my face'; for no one shall see me, and live") are not necessarily in conflict; rather these two statements reflect two different aspects of the self-revelation of YHWH/God. The statement in 33:20 does not seem to stand in conflict in the narrative with the statement in 33:11 (וידבר יהוה אל־משה פנים אל־פנים "YHWH used to speak with Moses 'face-to-face'") but rather the "face-to-face" speech between YHWH and Moses (in 33:11) helps to clarify the tension in 33:20-23, and confirms the possibility of Moses' seeing the divine face. The concept of the presence of YHWH in this text (33:20) is not found to be antithetical to the theme of "face of YHWH" as found in the Psalms of worship, as Hartenstein had suggested.[310]

The theophany in 34:29 in which Moses spoke with YHWH and received the Law from him a second time confirms that the divine revelation on the mountain was understood to be a reality, and establishes the possibility that the shining of Moses' face was the consequence of "seeing" the face of YHWH. The possibility of Moses seeing the divine face when he spoke with YHWH "face-to-face" in the tent (33:11) and the shining of his face which was the possible consequence of his speaking to and seeing YHWH on the mountain, both mutually confirm the positive aspect of Moses' "seeing" the divine face. The possibility of Moses seeing "the face of

---

309. As studied in chapters 2–4.
310. Cf. Hartenstein, *Angesicht*, 279–282.

YHWH" is more dominant in this section than the negative assumption that he had not seen the divine face.

There is no textual evidence to establish that "'seeing' the divine face" resulted in the death of anyone. Rather, it was the sin of seeing "the calf" and its worship that caused death (32:35), because it meant unfaithfulness to, and rejection of, YHWH/God himself. Since Moses was interceding on behalf of the people who made and worshiped the golden calf, the Israelite readers had probably associated the negation in 33:20 with the sin and disobedience of the people; the reason why YHWH could not let even Moses see his glory at that place was for the sake of the people, lest they would perish if they were to witness his glory. The repentant people were given a chance later to see the divine glory that was passed on to and reflected in Moses' face. Mending the broken covenantal relationship meant its renewal, for which Moses had mediated and facilitated the situation for the divine forgiveness and divine accompaniment. This renewal of the covenant was made possible because of the divine character, which includes his mercy, grace, patience, loving kindness and truthfulness, combining all this with the divine justice in dealing with the guilty.

The scholarly arguments that the expressions related to "seeing the face of YHWH/God" were metaphorical and that face-to-face conversation occurred only at the speech level, seem contrary to the textual evidence that Moses' face shone when YHWH appeared to him in his glory; and the Hebrew writer seems to insist that the divine self-revelations took place in a real sense. Had it not been for YHWH's self-revelations in human form in a real/physical sense, the covenant made by YHWH, the Law given on the mountain and everything connected to worship would not have been significant for the faith and practice in ancient Israel. It seems more plausible to think that face-to-face conversation involved physicality and a visual aspect, and that the face-to-face conversation took place in a literal/real sense. It seems more credible to believe that Moses had seen the divine face both in the tent and on the mountain, than not to believe it.

In light of scholarly arguments that the expression "seeing the face of God" was borrowed from the ANE where the face of idols was a reality,[311]

---

311. See ch. 1, 5–7.

the textual evidence as discussed stands in contradiction to these arguments. Hebrew traditions could not have associated "seeing the face of God" with the face of any idols/images, bearing in mind the disastrous results calf worship had caused and the punishment the people incurred. And given that the term "face" was used in association with YHWH/God even in the context where calf-worship was treated as sin, one can confirm that the concept of "seeing the face of YHWH/God" had origins in the divine revelations.

Similarly, the improbability of scholarly arguments associating the motif "the face of YHWH/God" with the *Audienz* concept has been discerned in light of the textual evidence that it was YHWH/God himself who took the initiative to reveal himself and to meet and communicate with Moses. The vivid description of the divine appearances in anthropomorphic terms seems to be an indication that ancient Israel understood YHWH/God in human terms, and the Hebrew writer insists that God appeared in his human form; and ascription of the physicality does not seem to reduce God's transcendent nature.

In light of the textual evidence in this chapter and the previous traditions, it is convincing to establish that YHWH/God was understood to have appeared in a human (bodily) form in his "glory" on the mountain and made himself visible to Moses, and that Moses had seen "the face of YHWH/God" in a literal sense, and worshiped him in humble prostration. This study shows that the theme of "seeing the face of YHWH" played a significant function/role in ancient Israel, as it was associated with the divine revelations, and signifies that the divine presence and the human worship are inseparable.

5.7 The Question of Background of the Motif פני־יהוה "Face of YHWH/God"

Hartenstein approached Exodus 33:12–23 in light of his findings in Psalm 27 and understood that the motif "the face of YHWH" in this text is antithetical to the idea of audience and protection in Psalm 27. However, when this text is studied in its canonical context, and in light of the previous traditions (as studied in chapters 2–4), it did not exhibit any antithetical idea in contrast to the idea of protection in Psalm 27. Furthermore, in Psalm 27 itself (also in some other psalms) where the idea of protection is understood, "hiding of the face of YHWH/God" is also expressed;[312] and, as seen in this study, in Exodus 32–34 where the negative idea of "seeing the face of YHWH/God" is mentioned (33:20, 23), 34:5–35 portrays that YHWH/God revealed himself in his glory, and assured Moses of his continued presence as a sign of his forgiveness and protection from the enemies (34:11–12).

Hartenstein suggests that the expression "face of YHWH" had its background in the Jerusalem Temple in the analogy of the royal and cultic *Audienz*[313] in the analogy of YHWH as king. However, Israelite understanding of YHWH/God as the creator of humankind seemed to be the foundation to understand the motif "the face of YHWH/God"; however, when Exodus 32–34 is placed within the Hebrew traditions of the divine self-revelations, this present exegetical study of the text has shown the possibility that the motif "the face of YHWH/God" had its background in the self-revelations of YHWH/God. The expression "seeing the face of God" has a definite association with the revealed anthropomorphized divine person of YHWH, who was understood to have revealed himself and let himself be seen by the people. The idea of royal audience finds no textual support and on the contrary, it is YHWH who is seen to have taken the initiative to reveal himself to the selected people. Therefore, one can reasonably associate "seeing the face of YHHW/God" with the anthropomorphized figure of YHWH/God, who revealed himself to and let himself be seen by the people. Is it possible, then, to establish that the tradition of the expression "'seeing' the face of YHWH/God" had its origin in the context of the divine self-revelations? The present exegetical study of Exodus 32–34 points in that direction.

---

312. Pss 27:9: אל־תסתר פניך ממני (do not hide your face from me); 13:1: עד־אנה תסתיר את־פניך ממני (how long will you hide your face from me?); 44:25: למה־פניך תסתיר (why do you hide your face?); 143:7: אל־תסתר פניך ממני (do not hide your face from me).

313. Hartenstein, *Angesicht*, 230–233.

5.8 Beyond the Mountain

After the episode of shining in Moses' face, when the Israelites move away from the mountain towards the Land, the venue of the divine revelations shifts from the mountain and is confined to the tabernacle/tent. Exodus 40:33–35 describes that after the completion of the tabernacle, YHWH appeared in the tabernacle in his "glory". The divine revelations continue to take place in association with כבוד "glory", and the "shining" of פנים "face". In order to study how YHWH made his face shine upon his people, this work will now turn to Numbers 6:22–27.

Section III

Chapters 6

Text from Numbers

CHAPTER 6

YHWH Makes His Face Shine upon and Lifts His Face toward Israel: Numbers 6:22–27

6.1 Introduction

The purpose of this chapter is to study the expression פני־יהוה "face of YHWH" with particular reference to divine self-revelations in the context of worship. The text selected for the study is Numbers 6:22–27. Here the expression "face of YHWH" is used in the context of (organized) worship. This text describes a kind of modus operandi/pattern, which was to be used by Aaronic priests in blessing Israel (vv. 22–23). The significant feature in this text is that it has a specific usage of פנים "face" in terms of "shining" (יאר יהוה פניו: v. 25) and "lifting" associated with YHWH (ישׂא יהוה פניו: v. 26).

Some scholars treat the motif יאר יהוה פניו "may YHWH cause his face to shine" as a metaphorical expression "likening God to light";[1] and suggest that it has associations with the dawn shining at the start of a new day.[2] Hartenstein associates יאר with the idea of a courtly-cultic audience and sees a solar connection in terms of YHWH's kingship.[3] However,

---

1. G. Wenham, *Numbers* (Leicester: Intervarsity Press, 1981), 90; D. T. Olson, *Numbers* (Louisville: John Knox Press, 1989), 41–42.

2. W. Riggans, *Numbers* (Edinburgh: The Saint Andrew Press, 1983), 55–56; cf. 2 Sam 2:32.

3. Hartenstein, *Angesicht*, 8, 194, 290; cf. Prov 16:15.

other scholars understand the motif יאר יהוה פניו "may YHWH cause his face to shine" as an anthropomorphic expression;[4] as "unselfconscious anthropomorphism";[5] as having links with the theophany on the mountain where YHWH's glory was supposed to have caused Moses' face to shine (Exod 34:29).[6]

The significant features in this text are that the verbs אור "to shine" and נשא "to lift" in association with פנים "face" of YHWH (פניו) are used only here in the Pentateuch. In light of the previous traditions studied,[7] it seems significant that the Hebrew writer uses these verbs אור and נשא in association with פנים "face" of YHWH, particularly in the context of worship. It seems also significant that most of the Hebrew verbs and nouns in this text (Num 6:22–27) such as ברך "to bless", שמר "to keep", חנן "to be gracious", פנים "face", and שם "name" in association with YHWH have been previously used in the context of the divine revelations. Furthermore, divine revelations in Leviticus have been described in association with the tabernacle in which the glory of YHWH appeared (וירא כבוד־יהוה) to all the people (Lev 9:23); and YHWH appeared above the place of atonement in the tabernacle (16:2b). This gives the impression that the expressions, יאר יהוה פניו "may YHWH cause his face to shine" and ישא יהוה פניו "may YHWH lift his face" (Num 6:25, 26) could have been used in association with the divine revelations in the tabernacle.

One wonders how the readers would have understood the expression פני־יהוה "face of YHWH" in association with יאר and ישא in Numbers 6:25–26. Is it possible that they associated יאר יהוה פניו "may YHWH cause his face to shine" and ישא יהוה פניו "may YHWH lift his face" with the divine revelation in the tabernacle in terms of the "glory of YHWH"? Or did they treat it as metaphorical expression having some association with light or sun? What function could these motifs have played for religious life in ancient Israel? In order to understand if פני־יהוה "the face of YHWH" in these above expressions has an association with the divine

---

4. J. Milgrom, *Numbers* (Philadelphia: The Jewish Publication Society, 1990), 51.
5. M. Noth, *Numbers: A Commentary* (London: SCM Press, 1968), 59.
6. R. B. Allen, *Genesis-Numbers* (Grand Rapids: Zondervan, 1990), 754–755.
7. Chapters 2–5, 37–184.

revelations in the tabernacle, this chapter will exegetically study Numbers 6:22–27 within its canonical context and in light of the previous traditions in Genesis-Exodus. Since the book of Leviticus describes the divine self-revelations in terms of כבוד "glory",[8] some significant aspects of these revelations[9] will also be discussed in so far as they enhance the understanding of the text under study.

Considering the important aspects surrounding פני־יהוה "face of YHWH" in the context of worship, the chapter is structured broadly as follows. A. The Pronouncement of YHWH's Blessing to the Israelites: vv. 22–23 and B. Name of YHWH Leads to Future Blessings: v. 27.

6.2 Canonical Context

A brief reflection on how the divine revelations were associated with the "glory of YHWH" in the previous traditions may help to understand the (possible) association of Numbers 6:22–27 with the divine revelations in the tabernacle. Readers were informed earlier in Exodus that YHWH came down (ירד) to the mountain in the sight of all the people and dwelt/settled (וישכן) there, and called Moses from the midst of the cloud (19:11, 20; 24:16). Later, YHWH promised that he would "dwell" (שכנתי "I will dwell) in the sense that he would appear[10] in the sanctuary (מקדש) among them; would meet with and speak to them from above the mercy seat (Exod 25:8, 22; 29:42b). It seems that just as he appeared in glory on the mountain from time to time, now he would appear in the tabernacle also

---

8. This does not mean that the noun פנים "face" in association with YHWH/God is not given importance in Leviticus, but פנים "face" in Leviticus is associated with the appearances of YHWH/God, who is described as appearing in "glory".

9. No particular text is selected from Leviticus for the study (i.e. in a separate chapter) in this work because of the brevity of specific texts which describe the expression "face of YHWH/God" specifically with seeing, though פנים "face" with its pronominal suffix occurs a few times in association with YHWH in terms of setting his face against Israel (Lev 17:10; 20:3, 5, 6; 26:17).

10. Considering the LXX that has the verb ὀφθήσομαι (fut. pass. of ὁράω "to see") "will appear/be seen" in Exod 25:8 where MT has שכנתי. This may be an indication that YHWH appeared from time to time.

from time to time.¹¹ Exodus 40:33–35 describes that after the completion of the tabernacle, when YHWH appeared in the tabernacle in his "glory" (וכבוד יהוה מלא את־המשכן), even Moses was not able to enter the tent of meeting (את־אהל מועד) because YHWH's glory filled (וכבוד יהוה מלא) the tabernacle (את־המשכן). It seems that the appearance of "the glory of YHWH" in the tabernacle at that instance (in Exod 40:33–35) was as intense as it was on the mountain, which looked like consuming fire.¹² In a way, as Milgrom says, "the *kavod* at Sinai's summit has transferred itself to the Tabernacle";¹³ this may have been to show that the holy aspect of YHWH was the same, even when he appeared in the tabernacle.

Interestingly, however, while the book of Exodus ends with the information that even Moses was not able to enter the tent of meeting when YHWH appeared in his glory (40:34–35), Leviticus begins with the statement that YHWH called Moses from the tabernacle (מאהל מועד)¹⁴ and spoke to him (Lev 1:1; Num 1:1). At this juncture, a brief reflection as to how the divine appearances in the tabernacle are described in Leviticus might help understand the themes in Numbers 6:22–27. As part of their worship in the tabernacle, the priest would sprinkle blood לפני־יהוה "before YHWH" in front of the veil in the sanctuary (Lev 4:6, 17). Earlier in Exodus (25:22), the writer informed his readers that YHWH told Moses that he would appear above the place of atonement (מעל הכפרת) in the tabernacle; and now informs them that Moses knew in advance¹⁵ that "the glory of YHWH" (כבוד־יהוה) would appear,¹⁶ and that he instructed Aaron

---

11. The same verb שכן "to dwell" is used for YHWH's "dwelling" in the tabernacle (Exod 25:8) and for YHWH's "dwelling" (in the sense of temporary dwelling) on the Sinai Mountain in Exod 24:16. When YHWH was not present in the tabernacle, it would perhaps be reduced to a structure; Num 1:51; 4:5 describe that whenever Israelites moved, Aaron and his sons would dismantle and carry it.

12. See 24:17: ומראה כבוד יהוה כאש אכל; cf. Num 9:15: כמראה־אש. The terms (theophanic) cloud and "glory of YHWH" are synonymously used in the context of theophany.

13. Milgrom, *Numbers*, xxxviii.

14. It may be noted that both משכן and מאהל מועד are used in these texts to mean the same structure.

15. Cf. Exod 33:8–9 where Moses knew beforehand that YHWH would appear on the mountain.

16. The specific mention of that day היום (9:4) seems to indicate another new appearance of YHWH in the tabernacle; LXX has σήμερον "today, this very day".

to offer sacrifices לפני־יהוה "before YHWH" (9:4, 6), which may indicate לפני "before" the revealed presence of YHWH in the tabernacle.[17] The use of לפני־יהוה "before YHWH" seems significant, as it is used in association with the divine revelations and worship.[18]

In contradistinction to scholarly views that the phrase לפני־יהוה "before YHWH" was used in analogy of being "before" one's superior for gaining an audience,[19] the Hebrew writer describes how YHWH himself came to be present with the people. As discussed in the previous chapter, Haran's suggestion that the phrase לפני־יהוה "before YHWH" belongs to temple terminology[20] is not necessary, since לפני "before" can mean before someone in a literal sense, as it has been used in several instances in Genesis and Exodus traditions to signify a literal sense.[21] Presumably, by employing this phrase לפני־יהוה "before YHWH" the writer wanted to convey that sacrifices were offered "before" the revealed anthropomorphic person of YHWH. One may assume that Aaron sprinkled the blood before the veil when "the glory of YHWH" was present (dwelt) behind the veil in the tabernacle, given that earlier in Exodus, when Moses sprinkled the blood on the altar, YHWH was understood to be present (dwelt) on the mountain (Exod 24:1–10). When the sacrifices were offered (Lev 9:15–22), the glory of YHWH appeared (וירא) to (or was seen by) all the people. The events described in verses 22–24 show that it was after making all the offerings[22] that the glory of YHWH appeared to all the people (את־העם וירא כבוד־יהוה); this may be an indication that YHWH was already present inside the tabernacle, and that it was after the sin offerings were made that YHWH appeared to all the people.

---

17. Priests were to offer sacrifices of והעלה, החטאת and והשלמים (i.e. sin offering, burnt offering and peace offerings) "before YHWH" (Lev 9:22) and eat the remaining beside the altar (7:5–6; 10:12, 17).

18. The phrase לפני־יהוה occurs about 100 times in Leviticus-Numbers combined. Although לפני functions as a prepositional phrase, when it is specifically used in association with the divine person, one may assume that the anthropomorphized divine figure is in view. For a general discussion on לפני־יהוה, see Fowler, "*lipne* YHWH*", 384–390.

19. Chapter 1, 6–8.

20. Haran, *Temples*, 26.

21. See chapter 1, 29–31.

22. See fn. 17.

In Leviticus 9:24, when the writer resolutely states that אש "fire" came מלפני יהוה "from before/the presence of YHWH", either to consume the burnt offerings or to consume Nadab and Abihu (Lev 9:24; 10:1–2), in his understanding "fire" has a definite association with the person of YHWH.[23] However, it is not clear in the text as to in which sense fire comes out from the presence of YHWH.

Earlier in Genesis, it is said that fire was rained from YHWH (יהוה ואש מאת) out of heaven (Gen 19:24); in Exodus, fire was associated with YHWH, in that he appeared in the midst of the flame of fire in the bush (Exod 3:2); he descended upon Mt. Sinai in fire (Exod 19:18; 20:18); the sight of כבוד יהוה "the glory of YHWH" was כאש אכלת "like a consuming fire" (Exod 24:17). When the "fire" (אש) is associated with YHWH and the verb אכל (to consume), it is even named as אש־יהוה "the fire of YHWH", in that when YHWH's anger (אפו) arouses, אש יהוה "the fire of YHWH"[24] consumes some people in the camp (Num 11:1); fire comes out (יצא)[25] "from YHWH" (יצאה מאת יהוה) and consumes two hundred and fifty men (Num 16:35). Whether fire comes "from YHWH" (מאת יהוה) or "from before YHWH" (מלפני יהוה), it seems that YHWH is understood as the source of fire,[26] which also means that "fire" comes out (יצא) from YHWH himself.

Since כבוד יהוה "glory of YHWH" is said to have appeared to all the people, כבוד "glory" here seems to have a narrower sense[27] in that the fiery radiance emanates from the very person of YHWH, which is understood to have a power to burn/consume. Since it is said that "fire" came out מלפני יהוה "from before/presence of YHWH", one may assume that מלפני "from before/the presence of YHWH" means from YHWH's very self,

---

23. LXX has ἐξῆλθεν πῦρ παρα κυρίου "fire came forth from the Lord".
24. Cf. 1 Kgs 18:38 where אש־יהוה "the fire of YHWH" is said to have consumed the burnt sacrifice.
25. The verb יצא, used for Moses and Aaron coming out of the tent in a literal sense (Lev 9:23), is used for the "fire" coming out "from before YHWH".
26. Cf. Num 17:7–11 where קצף "wrath" is used similar to that of "fire" of YHWH, and the verb אכל "consume" is also associated with the wrath of YHWH.
27. Chapter 5, 162–164.

perhaps from his פנים "face" or פה "mouth",[28] given that פה "mouth" is a synonym with פנים "face".[29]

Theophany took a dramatic form as the fire came out מלפני יהוה ("from before/from the presence of YHWH") and consumed the burnt offerings.[30] As T. M. Willis describes, "the action now takes place at 'eye level', as the divine glory appears to the people".[31] Although it is not explicit whether the people had envisaged the divine person in his physicality, since the text says that fire came from before him, one may argue that YHWH was present there in his anthropomorphic form within the tabernacle, and people saw "him".[32] As B. W. Anderson comments, God "condescends" to the tabernacle in the midst of the worshipping people,[33] and when all the people saw[34] him (וירא כל־העם) they shouted for joy (וירנו)[35] and ויפלו על־פניהם "fell on their faces"[36] (Lev 9:23–24). This indicates perhaps "the awe-inspiring reality of God", as Wenham comments.[37] Since the writer stresses that the glory of YHWH appeared to all the people (וירא כבוד־יהוה אל־כל־העם) and also that people fell on their faces, one may assume that YHWH let himself be seen from within the Tabernacle; and the bodily posture, a

---

28. The noun פנים "face" is also treated as a synonym with פה "mouth". One of the possibilities suggested as the stem of פנים is פה "mouth". See Woude, "פנים", 998; Yofre, "פנים", 590. Eng. verses (e.g. NKJ and NRS) have translated פה אל־פה "mouth to mouth" (in Num 12:8) as "face-to-face".

29. It may be noted that in Hebrew thought, אש "fire" is also seen as coming from פה "the mouth" of YHWH/God: devouring fire goes from his mouth (ואש מפיו) and coals were kindled by it (2 Sam 22:9; Ps 18:9V); flames go out מפיו "from his mouth" (Job 41:11); cf. Rev 9:17: ἐκ τῶν στομάτων αὐτῶν ἐκπορεύεται πῦρ "out of their mouths fire came out".

30. The consumption of the offerings by the divine fire was seen as an approval of the offerings. Cf. Judg 13:15–22; 1 Kgs 18:38–39 where people fall face down to the ground.

31. T. M. Willis, *Leviticus* (Nashville: Abingdon Press, 2009), 89.

32. The object is not provided in the Hebrew text and several Eng. verses added "it"; but the object of seeing can well be YHWH himself since the glory of YHWH is associated with the person of YHWH.

33. B. W. Anderson, *Contours of Old Testament Theology* (Minneapolis: Fortress Press, 1999), 122.

34. The verb used here is qal imperfect of ראה.

35. The root רנן has the sense of cry with joy (cf. 42:5; 126:2; 132:16). See N.E. Wagner, "רנה in the Psalter", *VT* 10 (1960), 435–441.

36. The use of יפלו על־פניהם (cf. Gen 17:1) is similar to the verb שחה "to bow" (see Ch. 5, fn. 252).

37. Wenham, *Leviticus*, 150.

sign of worship, seems to indicate a literal sense and suggests that people bowed before the revealed anthropomorphic person of YHWH who was in their view.

It seems that when the writer mentions that "the glory of YHWH" appeared in the tabernacle, he does not mean in an abstract sense but in a concrete sense, given that he describes in a vivid anthropomorphic language that it was YHWH himself who would speak from the tabernacle. So one may well assume that when "the glory of YHWH" appeared in the tabernacle, YHWH was present within that glory in a human form to whom "face" could be ascribed. There seems a close association between the divine "face" and "glory" (cf. Exod 33:14–19; 34:5–8). Those who witnessed earlier at the mountain the visible signs of YHWH's appearance from afar[38] now seem to witness to the divine presence from close vicinity at the tabernacle.[39] These divine revelations may have functioned as evidence for YHWH's continued presence that was promised earlier to Moses (Exod 33:14–17).[40]

In the above-discussed theophany (Lev 9:6–7; 22–23) there is no evidence in the text that any one died or feared death for seeing/being in the revealed presence of YHWH (in glory); rather, they worshipped him joyfully. The text here has not associated death with the face of YHWH, even when it says that fire came "from before YHWH" (מלפני יהוה), rather fire seems to signify a positive affirmation of the divine presence in the context of worship. Paradoxically, however, the writer informs his readers later that Nadab and Abihu, the priests,[41] offered "strange" fire[42] "before YHWH" contrary to the divine command, and fire came out מלפני יהוה (from before/the "face of YHWH") and consumed them (Lev 10:1–2). The reason

---

38. Cf. Exod 19–24; 33:10.
39. Willis, *Leviticus*, 90.
40. Cf. A. P. Ross, *Leviticus: Holiness to the Lord* (Grand Rapids: Baker Academic, 2002), 225.
41. Nadab and Abihu (cf. Exod 24:1), the sons of Aaron were ordained as priests (Lev 8:30).
42. The fire for incense was supposed to be taken from the altar inside the tent (Lev 16:12; cf. Exod 30:9); but they took their own censures. The Hebrew word אש זרה probably signifies something from foreign or pagan practices, which caused the death of Nadab and Abihu (cf. Exod 32:35; associations with Molech would cause death [Lev 20:2, 3; 18:21]).

why Nadab and Abihu died is not for seeing the divine face as such, but for not regarding YHWH as holy; and the reason given for the death of Nadab and Abihu, in Moses' words, is that YHWH must be regarded as holy by those who go near him so that he would be "glorified" before (על־פני) all the people (10:3); and it is their disobedience to the divine command that was treated as sin.[43] Eichrodt disagrees with E. König's assumption that "the face of YHWH" must have been present even when only "the glory of God" was perceived.[44] However, König's assumption has textual support here that "the glory of YHWH" included the person of YHWH in his anthropomorphic (bodily) form. Since the text stresses that fire came from before the "face" of YHWH and consumed Nadab and Abihu when they were inside the tabernacle, one may assume that YHWH appeared in his "glory" inside the tabernacle and at the same time was described having a "face" from where the fire came.

Earlier in Leviticus the whole (worshiping) community of Israel were instructed that they should be holy because YHWH himself is holy (קדוש אני "I am holy");[45] the priests too are expected to make atonement for themselves and must keep themselves pure, so that they could make atonement for the people.[46] The theme of holiness is dominant in Leviticus. It is said that YHWH would appear in the cloud above the place of atonement (כי בענן אראה על־הכפרת) inside the veil (Lev 16:2b) in his glory; it was for this reason that the tabernacle,[47] where YHWH would appear, and also the priests who enter there, should be consecrated.[48]

---

43. S. E. Balentine, *Leviticus*. Interpretation (Louisville: John Knox Press, 2002), 126. Cf. Gen 3:11.

44. Eichrodt, *OTT* 2, 38, citing E. König, *Theologie des Alten Testamentum* (n.d), 127. Eichrodt (*OTT* 2, 38) did not think that כבוד has connection with פנים.

45. Lev 11:44–45: והתקדשתם והייתם קדשים; cf. 19:2: כל־עדת. When the people were brought into a covenantal relationship with YHWH, they were also given the Law through Moses which was to be obeyed (Exod 19:5–9; Lev 10:11; 22:31; 27:4, 34; Cf. Anderson, *Contours of Old Testament*, 122.

46. Lev 8:33–35; 9:6–21; cf. Exod 29.

47. See K. Koch, "אהל", *TDOT* 1, 127. Koch observes that much importance was attributed to the tent (also called משכן) which was used as the sanctuary during the wilderness wanderings.

48. The aspect of holiness at the tabernacle is similar to that of Sinai; and the outsider who comes near the tabernacle shall be put to death. See Exod 19:12–13; 29:43–44; Num 1:50–51; 3:10; 18:7.

Literarily speaking, the text in verses 24–26 is poetically framed[49] each line having two verbs;[50] the pronouns are addressed in the singular while the two verses 23, 27 in the frame are addressed in the plural,[51] which indicates that either every Israelite is addressed individually, or it is a "collective field of reference";[52] in any case, it seems the entire group, comprising of individuals, is addressed.[53] Fishbane observes that the action in the second clause in each line is the consequence of the state in the first, that is, the blessing results in protection.[54] Yet, it seems that the action in the second clause includes the people's responsibility in maintaining it, in that people need to respond in obedience to be in the state of divine protection; and grace is not without justice, and people are not to sin, lest he hides his face (cf. Lev 26:3–6; 15–17).

Some scholars have questioned the literary placement of the text and assumed that Numbers 24–26 is a reference to the priestly blessing in Leviticus 9:22 where Aaron had blessed the people;[55] that it was later woven into its present place.[56] However, there is no obvious reason why the writer (or even a later editor) would have shifted the text from Leviticus to its present place. After the laws on purity of the camp (Num 5:1–31) and Nazirite laws (6:1–21), Numbers 6:22–26 serves as an introduction to the

---

49. For a poetical analysis of this text, see M. C. A. Korpel, "The Poetic Structure of the Priestly Blessing", *JSOT* 45 (1989), 3–9. For a reflection on Hebrew poetry, see Lasor, *Survey*, 231–242.

50. The Hebrew text has three, five and seven words and fifteen, twenty and twenty-five consonants respectively and it is in a rising crescendo. See Milgrom, *Numbers*, 51.

51. Because of this singular and plural number variation, critical scholars ascribe pre-exilic status and to Josiah's reform. For example, G. B. Gray, *Numbers* (Edinburgh: T. & T. Clark, 1956), 72. However, as Noth (*Numbers*, 58) affirms, the pattern of blessings in the text does not make it post-exilic; using singular number for Israel in a collective sense is not uncommon in the HB (e.g. Exod 20:2–17).

52. Noth, *Numbers*, 58.

53. Cf. Allen, *Genesis-Numbers*, 754.

54. M. Fishbane, "Form and Reformulation of the Biblical Priestly Blessing", *JAOS* 103 (1983), 115–116. As Fishbane suggests, these three lines have not six actions but only three, and it is possible that ו in between the verbs in these three lines (24–26: וישמרך, וישם and ויחנך) is more than a mere conjunction. Cf. P. D. Miller, "The Blessing of God", *Int* 29 (1975), 243.

55. Fishbane, "Form", 116. Also see Milgrom, *Numbers*, 51; cf. Ross, *Leviticus*, 224. But there is no clue if similar words were said in Lev 9:22.

56. T. B. Dozeman, *The Book of Numbers* (Nashville: Abingdon Press), 1998, 65.

consecration of the tabernacle (Num 7:1–3).⁵⁷ The text as a whole has the blessing pattern (24–26), and its association with Aaron's priesthood fits well into the wilderness journeys towards the Land. Where Leviticus ends with a reference to the Law which YHWH gave to Moses on the mountain (Lev 27:34), Numbers begins stating that YHWH spoke to Moses in the tent of meeting (Num 1:1) and this indicates that the divine revelations continued to take place in the tabernacle and that YHWH spoke to Moses.⁵⁸ It is in this context of tabernacle theophanies that Numbers 6:22–27 will be studied.

6.3 Exegetical Study of Numbers 6:22–27

6.3.1 The Pronouncement of YHWH's Blessing to the Israelites: vv. 22–23

According to the introductory words in the text, YHWH spoke to Moses, saying (לאמר), "Speak to Aaron and his sons, saying (v. 22), 'This way (כה)⁵⁹ you shall bless the children of Israel' (את־בני ישראל); say (אמור)⁶⁰ to them'" (v. 23). The communication of this mode of blessing through Moses to Aaron and his sons may signify that Moses continued to be the mediator of the covenant.⁶¹ However, the source of the blessings (subject of ברך) is YHWH himself (cf. v. 27). The use of אמר with God as subject seems to signify direct revelation of YHWH/God.⁶² Milgrom interprets "thus" in

---

57. In a broad sense, it concludes a larger section of different instructions on worship and priestly legislation from Leviticus to Numbers 6.

58. Cf. Exod 33:7–11: Moses used to enter into the tent and YHWH would speak to him face-to-face.

59. As a demonstrative adverb of manner כה can mean "the way of saying". See Ringgern, "כה", *TDOT* 7, 123–127.

60. The infinitive absolute of אמר "to speak" is here used as an imperative. Similar function may be seen in other places in Hebrew. See B. A. Levine, *Numbers: 1–20* (New York: Doubleday, 1993), 227.

61. For this reason, this text which is generally coined as "Aaronic blessing" may even be named as "Mosaic blessing".

62. The adverb כה with אמר (e.g. Exod 4:22; 9:13; 11:4) seems to emphasize what is said. For the construction of ל+אמר, and for the theological significance of the usage of אמר with God as subject, see S. Wagner, "אמר", *TDOT* 1, 333–335.

verse 23 as "when you bless, use this formula, not one of your devising",[63] which affirms YHWH as the source of the blessing. According to Sailhamer the central task of the priests was to be a source of blessing; the blessing of the people depends on their "recognition of the divine sanction of the priesthood".[64] However, as Fishbane stresses, YHWH alone will perform these actions, the priests are merely the agents of the blessing;[65] this is further affirmed by the emphasis put on the name in association with blessing (in v. 27) that YHWH alone is the source of blessing and that the priests were only the mediators.[66]

6.3.1.1 YHWH blesses his people to keep/protect them (v. 24)

The first line (v. 24) in the poetic frame reads: "may YHWH bless you (יברכך) and keep/protect[67] you (וישמרך)". Although the Hebrew text here has imperfect verbs, one may sense in this verse a "desire/wish".[68] This line seems to have a definite association with the previous traditions in terms of the divine revelations.

The important aspect of the verb ברך "to bless"[69] seems that it is normally pronounced when both the person who pronounces and the receiver who receives the blessing are present in a direct and even in face-to-face contact in a physical sense. For example, in a secular context, Rebekah's brothers blessed her (Gen 24:60); Isaac blessed Jacob (Gen 27:4), and Jacob blessed Joseph (Gen 48:15). Even in the context of the divine pronouncement of the blessings, direct contact may be assumed. For example, when God the creator blessed the first couple, "Be fruitful" (Gen 1:28; cf. 9:1); when YHWH appeared (וירא) to Isaac and said, "I will be with you (כי־אתך אנכי) and bless you" (וברכתיך: Gen 26:24), met with Jacob and blessed him (32:30)—in all these incidents the blessings were uttered in

---

63. Milgrom, *Numbers*, 51.
64. Sailhamer, *Pentateuch as Narrative*, 379.
65. Fishbane, "Form", 115.
66. Cf. Noth, *Numbers*, 58.
67. LXX here has the verb φυλάσσω "to protect".
68. Imperfect verbs may also be treated as Jussive, and so v. 24 (also vv. 25–26) is translated here as "may YHWH bless . . ." See GKC §48, 4; §128, 315–316.
69. For different nuance of meaning of ברך, see M. L. Brown, "ברך", *NIDOTTE* 1, 757–767; J. Scharbert, "ברך", *TDOT*, 2, 279–300.

the context of divine revelations and the speech was direct, and in some cases, there was even face-to-face contact (Gen 32:31); blessing also meant accompaniment of the divine presence (Gen 26:24; 28:15). In light of this, one may assume that in some sense the priestly wish for the divine blessing (v. 24) may have been associated with the theophany in the tabernacle, given that the tabernacle was the place where YHWH appeared in his glory; a direct contact between YHWH and the people may be assumed, since YHWH appeared before all the people (Lev 9:22–24).

The verb [70]שמר "to keep" is also used in the context of divine revelation. For example, when YHWH spoke to Jacob (in his dream) and said, "I am with you (אנכי עמך) and will keep you" (ושמרתיך: 28:15), the divine presence was promised to protect Jacob. YHWH promised that he would send his angel to protect them on the way (לשמרך בדרך: Exod 23:20–23), which meant divine presence. This verb שמר "to keep" was also used in terms of keeping the covenant (Gen 17:9, 10; Exod 19:5–9) to keep the way of YHWH (ושמרו דרך יהוה), in terms of directing the future generations in righteousness (Gen 18:19); to be obedient to the commandments (ולשמרי מצותי: Exod 20:6); and in warning the people not to worship other gods (לא. . .תשמרו: Exod 23:13; cf. 34:14). It seems significant that in all these cases, the promise "to keep/protect" was used by YHWH/God himself in the context of divine revelations. While the divine (keeping) protection involves the "preserving power"[71] of God, it also seems to involve a human response to be obedient to YHWH.[72]

As one can see, these verbs ברך "to bless" שמר "to keep" have been associated with the divine presence even when they are not used in the same sentence.[73] Now, the question to ask is: was there any specific purpose why the writer combined these two verbs together in the same line (v. 24),[74] particularly as these two verbs have clear associations with the divine

---

70. For different nuances of the verb שמר, see G. López, "שמר", *TDOT* 15, 286; E. Carpenter, "שמר", *NIDOTTE* 4, 182–183.

71. Ashley, *Numbers*, 152.

72. A. Frisch, "The Priestly Blessing", Bar-Ilan University's Centre. *Parashat Naso* 5765 (2005): gottlii@mail.biu.ac.il. Cf. Lev 26:3–10.

73. This is what Korpel ("Poetic Structure", 5–7) coins as internal parallelism.

74. This may be the only place in the HB where both these verbs are used in the same sentence.

revelations? It seems a reasonable inference that the writer wanted to indicate that the two verbs ברך "to bless" and שמר "to keep" in the priestly wish has a definite association with the divine revelations. Earlier when Aaron blessed the people, it was in the context of worship, during which time "the glory of YHWH" appeared to all the people (Lev 9:22, 23). So, it seems appropriate to think that this priestly wish for YHWH's blessings also has significance for the worship that would take place in future, in that they would experience the revealed presence of YHWH.

This priestly blessing itself seems a prayer that YHWH/God would grant his gracious presence and watch over his people;[75] would protect the people from the enemy (Exod 23:20–23), from disobedience to the divine Law (Exod 20:6; Lev 18:26) and from the sin of worship of other gods (Exod 23:13; 32:30). It appears that this priestly "wish" was not meant for a verbal repetition, but in some sense by means of this "wish" priests were given the responsibility to facilitate an atmosphere of worship by offering sacrifices and sanctifying themselves and the people, so that YHWH would appear (Lev 9:4–6; 16:2), and people would witness to the divine revelation in their worship even in future—whether it would be in the tabernacle or in Jerusalem Temple.

6.3.1.2 YHWH shines his face upon his people out of his grace (v. 25)

The second line (v. 25) in the poetic frame reads: "may YHWH cause his face to shine upon you (יאר יהוה פניו) and be gracious (ויחנך) to you" (אליך).[76]

YHWH himself is the subject of יאר[77] and it is he who lets his face shine on people; the "shining of YHWH's face" may be the consequence of his grace. It seems significant that the verb אור with פנים "face" is used only

---

75. T. R. Ashley, *The Book of Numbers* (Grand Rapids: Eerdmans, 1993), 149.
76. See fn. 68 for a comment on translating the imperfect verbs as jussive.
77. This verb occurs mostly in hiphil (about 45 times in the HB) but rarely in qal and niphal. The cognate of the verb אור in Ugaritic is *'r*, "to illumine". For different aspects of אור, see S. Aalen, "אור", *TDOT* 1, 148–150; H. Wolf, "אור", *TWOT*, 25–27; M.J. Selman, "אור", *NIDOTTE* 1, 324–329.

here. However, as observed in the previous chapter,[78] Moses was personally exposed to YHWH's radiant face on the mountain, and the divine glory was reflected on his own face.[79] Aaron and other people were also exposed to that "radiance" through Moses (Exod 34:30). In light of this, one may assume that Moses and Aaron had associated the "shining of YHWH's face" with the appearance of YHWH's glory in the tabernacle. D. L. Stubbs observes that the connections between Moses' encounter with YHWH on the mountain and this verse (Num 6:25) are too many to ignore.[80] Others, such as Gray, argue that the effect of the glory of YHWH on Moses' face in 34:29 has no association with this expression.[81] However, as K. D. Sakenfeld reflects, shining of YHWH's face "calls to mind" YHWH's glory that shone in Moses' face.[82]

Some scholars understand the "'shining' of YHWH's face" metaphorically for divine benevolence and favor/grace;[83] Wenham treats it as a "vivid metaphor likening God to light",[84] and Riggans thinks that the shining of face arose from its association with the dawn shining at the start of the day.[85] However, earlier in Genesis, the Hebrew creation traditions show that God himself created the light and light does not exist independently of him (Gen 1:3–5, 15–18). So, it seems unlikely that אור "the light" of YHWH's face could be associated with any normal light or the dawn,[86]

---

78. See chapter 5, 190–195.
79. Cf. R. Brown, *The Message of Numbers* (Leicester: Intervarsity Press, 2002), 57–58; Allen, *Genesis-Numbers*, 755. Although the verb used for shining of Moses' face is קרן, it was God's glory that caused the shining in Moses' face (Exod 34:29–35).
80. D. L. Stubbs, *Numbers* (London: SCM Press, 2009), 75.
81. Gray, *Numbers*, 72–74. This is because he thinks that חנן never occurs in P source.
82. K. D. Sakenfeld, *Numbers: Journeying with God* (Grand Rapids: Eerdmans, 1995), 44.
83. For example, W. H. Bellinger, Jr, *Leviticus, Numbers* (Peabody: Hendrickson Publishers, 2001), 202; J. Sturdy, *Numbers* (Cambridge: Cambridge University Press, 1976), 55; Noth, *Numbers*, 59; S. Aalen, "אור", *TDOT* 1, 161; T. E. Fretheim, "*Numbers*" (Oxford: Oxford University Press, 2001), 116; Levine, *Numbers: 1–20*, 14.
84. Wenham, *Numbers*, 90. Wenham refers here to ancient Semitic idiom, "to make light shine upon", which meant "to set free"; he also refers to Pss 31:17; 67:2; 80:4, 8, 20.
85. Riggans, *Numbers*, 56. He refers to Pss 77:19; 97:4 and 2 Sam 2:32. Cf. Olson, *Numbers*, 42.
86. Although there was apostasy among Israel (2 Kgs 23:11) there is no evidence that the sun was equated to God either in the Pentateuch or later in the cult. Only twice God is compared with sun in the HB (in Ps 84:12; Mal 3:20), which perhaps had a polemical usage.

and this expression appears rather to involve a concrete divine manifestation of God himself. Although the verb אור is associated with the pillar of fire which shone in the night (בעמוד אש להאיר להם: Exod 13:21; 14:20), it is still YHWH who manifested his presence in the pillar of cloud and caused the night to be bright with light;[87] the flashes of lightning on the mountain were also associated with the manifestation of YHWH (Exod 19:16; 20:18).

Hartenstein, in light of his study of Psalm 27:1 where the verb אור is used in connection with the "face of YHWH",[88] suggests in his approach to Numbers 6:24–26 that "shining of face of YHWH" is to be linked with the gracious permission to enter into the courtly-cultic *Audienze*, and that solar references in connection with YHWH's kingship are implied.[89] Readers would be aware, however, that, contrary to the idea of divine status ascribed to the king, Genesis relates that it is Jacob who blessed Pharaoh (Gen 47:7, 10), and it is YHWH/God who took the initiative to be present with the people in the context of worship. Furthermore, since the Hebrew traditions associate the shining with כבוד (glory) of YHWH/God, it is difficult to assume any solar connections. Above all, it may be noted that "fire" is used in association with כבוד "glory" (in Exod 24:17; Lev 9:24), and even here in verse 25, it seems that "shining" of YHWH's face is associated with his "glory".

Presumably, the phrase יאר יהוה פניו "make his face shine" (Num 6:25) would have taken the readers back to the mountain where Moses was exposed to the divine glory (34:1–10), and to the bush at Horeb where Moses was exposed to the appearance of God in fire. As discussed earlier, in the previous chapters, when YHWH appeared in fire in the burning bush, he was described in anthropomorphic language and the divine person was in view even in that (holy) fire (Exod 3:3–6);[90] in the theophany on the mountain, he was envisaged by Moses and others (Exod 24:10) even when YHWH's glory was said to have looked like fire (כבוד יהוה כאש:

---

87. Cf. Selman, "אור", 324; Aalen, "אור", 164.
88. He also compares with Pss 31:17; 44:4; 67:1–2; 80:4, 8, 20 where "shining of face" is employed.
89. Hartenstein, *Angesicht*, 8, 194, 290 (Prov 16:15: באור־פני־מלך).
90. When Moses realized that he was seeing God of his fathers, he hid his face.

24:17). And so, the readers would have associated "YHWH's face" with his appearances in his glory in the tabernacle.

Earlier in Exodus, when YHWH's glory passed by Moses (Exod 33:22; 34:6), the anthropomorphic person of YHWH was evoked,[91] and even here in Numbers 6:25, one may assume that when "the glory of YHWH" (כבוד־יהוה) appeared in the tabernacle, it means that YHWH was present in his anthropomorphic form in his glory. It is YHWH himself who is present in the tabernacle, since "face of YHWH" signifies the person of YHWH himself.[92] Furthermore, readers would remember that YHWH promised Moses that he would reveal himself to meet and speak with him from above the mercy seat, from between the two cherubim which are on the ark of the testimony, and would give him his commandments for the children of Israel (cf. Exod 25:22). Then they were told that YHWH appeared in the cloud over the place of atonement (Lev 16:2) where the blood sacrifice was offered and from where he revealed himself to them.[93] It seems, then, that "shining of face" in the priestly prayer has strong links with the self-revelation of YHWH in the tabernacle, and one may convincingly associate the "face of YHWH" with the glory of YHWH (כבוד־יהוה) as it appeared in the tabernacle in his anthropomorphic form. In other words, it is YHWH's glory that would shine on the worshiping people through his face in glory.

Noth sees this phrase "YHWH cause his face shine" as an "unselfconscious anthropomorphism",[94] and the Hebrew writers seem unhesitant to describe the divine self-revelations and to associate פנים "face" with YHWH/God.

Readers would be aware that earlier in Exodus, YHWH's presence among the people was associated with his grace, and this association can be seen in Moses' repeated requests: "If I have found grace . . . go with us" (Exod 34:6, 9; cf. 33:16–17). It seems significant that even here in Numbers 6:25 ("shining of") YHWH's face is associated with divine grace

---

91. See chapter 5, 184–185.
92. Cf. W. Zimmerli, *Old Testament Theology in Outline* (Atlanta: John Knox Press, 1978), 73; R. K. Harrison, *Numbers* (Chicago: Moody Press, 1990), 133.
93. Ross, *Leviticus*, 317.
94. Noth, *Numbers*, 59.

(ויחנך); it may be that by this combination, the priestly blessing in verse 25 assures the worshipers that YHWH would continue to reveal himself to them in his glory because of his grace.

Since the assumption was already made that the expression "YHWH bless you and keep you" has definite association with the divine revelation, one may unhesitatingly associate the "shining of YHWH's face" also with the divine appearances in the tabernacle. It may be that the priestly wish here includes a desire for the people that they would see the face of YHWH when he appears in the tabernacle during their worship. It seems that by means of pronouncing this wish, priests were to facilitate an atmosphere of worship by offering sacrifices and consecrating themselves and the people; and on the part of people, they were to be faithful to maintain the covenantal relationship so that the divine revelations would take place and they would experience the divine presence in worship continually.[95] Readers might recall that Moses had interceded for the divine presence on behalf of the people, and now Aaron was to wish the divine presence for the people.

6.3.1.3 YHWH lifts his face toward his people to grant peace (v. 26)

The third line (v. 26) in the poetic frame reads: "may YHWH lift up his face unto you (ישא יהוה פניו אליך) and grant you peace" (וישם לך שלום).

The verb נשא[96] "to lift up" has been used both figuratively and literally in several phrases in the previous traditions. Figuratively, it has been used in the sense of "taking away" one's sin, iniquity and transgression both in a secular context[97] and in the context of seeking divine forgiveness.[98] Significantly, the verb נשא "to lift" was used earlier in describing the divine attribute of forgiveness to Moses, in that YHWH himself proclaims his

---

95. This wish may also include that just as the shining in Moses' face was visible to others, the shining on the people of Israel would also be made visible to the nations (blessed to bless: Gen 12:3).
96. For different nuances of this expression, see H. Ringgren, "נשא", *TDOT* 10, 24–40; see also M. I. Gruber, "The Many Faces of Hebrew נשא פנים 'lift up the face'", *ZAW* 95 (1983), 252–260.
97. In seeking forgiveness of Joseph by his brothers (שא נא פשע אחיך וחטאתם): Gen 50:17); cf. Pharaoh who seeks forgiveness of Israel (Exod 10:17).
98. Moses seeks forgiveness of YHWH on behalf of Israel (אם־תשא חטאתם: Exod 32:32).

character of forgiveness.[99] To this aspect of forgiveness, one may also add a figurative sense of "looking at" with favor toward others, as נשׂא with the preposition אל seems to indicate positive and desirable connotations,[100] and "turning away" one's anger.[101] The verb נשׂא "to lift" has been also used in a literal sense[102] and may be treated as a sign of appearance/presence, in contrast to hiding of his face.[103] "To lift up one's face" may mean turning towards someone, which involves action,[104] and it may also imply meeting someone in a friendly attitude.[105] Eichrodt suggests that the expression "lifting up of YHWH's face" (Num 6:25–26) in no way implies the idea of a visible form,[106] but the biblical context gives the reason to think that "to lift" YHWH's face can imply his visible form. Earlier in Genesis, נשׂא with פנים (ישׂא פני) is used when Jacob hopes his brother Esau will (lift his face) accept him in a literal sense as a sign of favor (32:21).[107]

Significantly, this verb נשׂא "to lift", with YHWH (ישׂא יהוה פניו) as its subject, is not found elsewhere, and the verb used here is in qal stem. One may ask why this expression ישׂא יהוה פניו אליך ("YHWH lift his face unto you") is employed in this particular priestly blessing associated with worship. Again, presumably, this expression was associated with YHWH's appearance in the tabernacle in terms of his glory. Readers may recall that earlier in Exodus it was described that YHWH would appear in a cloud

---

99. Exod 34:7: נשׂא עון ופשׁע וחטאה; cf. Num 14:18.
100. See Milgrom, *Numbers*, 52; D. W. Baker, *Idiomatic Expressions in Hebrew and Akkadian Relating to the Head*. M.Phil. diss., University of London (1976), 90–107; Gruber ("Many Faces", 95 254) translates this clause as, "may the Lord smile upon you", and compares the usage ישׂא פנים with Akkadian parallels (lift up PN's face) where it means "pleasure and affection"; for a similar usage of "lifting" of the divine face in Babylonian literature, see K. Seybold, *Der aaronitische Segen: Studien zu Numeri 6:22–27*(Neukirchen-Vluyn: Neukirchener Verlag, 1977), 32.
101. N. H. Snaith, *Leviticus and Numbers* (London: Thomas Nelson, 1967), 207.
102. Ringgren, "נשׂא", 37. "To lift up the eyes" is also used pleonastically in a physical sense (Gen 13:10, 14; 22:13; 33:1 43:29; Exod 14:10; cf. 2 Kgs. 25:27.
103. Sturdy, *Numbers*, 55; Exod 33:12–19; Deut 31:17–18. "Hiding of God's face" is seen as the result of Israelite's sin. For a study on this theme, see Balentine, *Hidden God*, 45–79; 115–176.
104. Gen 19:21; 32:21. Cf. A. Murtonen, "Lᵉbârek and bᵉråkåʰ in the Old Testament", *VT* 9 (1959), 162.
105. Cf. J. Marsh, *Numbers*, *IB* 2 (Nashville: Abingdon, 1952), 174; 2 Sam 2:22.
106. Eichrodt, *OTT 2*, 36–37.
107. Cf. Olson, *Numbers*, 42.

above the place of atonement (which perhaps meant an elevated place (Exod 25:8, 22; cf. Lev 16:2).[108] The text gives reason to think that the place of atonement was on a higher level, given that Aaron stepped down (וירד) from the altar area after offering the sacrifices (Lev 9:22), and since YHWH would appear above the atonement place, it would mean the place of his appearance would be still higher than the atonement place. The verb נשׂא "to lift" may refer to a physical movement of lifting or raising one's face,[109] and both the expressions ישׂא יהוה פניו (lifting of YHWH face) and יאר יהוה פניו ("shining of YHWH's face") have YHWH as the subject and are associated with the tabernacle.

The expressions ישׂא יהוה פניו "may YHWH cause his face shine" (v. 25), and יאר יהוה פניו "may YHWH lift up his face" (v. 26) are associated with the self-revelations of YHWH/God in the tabernacle (cf. Lev 9:23–24), and YHWH is the subject of the verbs "to shine" and "to lift". Therefore, one can assume that פניו "his face" (in vv. 25–26) signifies YHWH himself; and although the noun פנים "face" is used with the personal suffix (פניו "his face"), it appears that פנים "face" exhibits its literal sense, in that "his face" meant "the face of YHWH" (יהוה פניו) in a literal sense, as face is seen as the source of shining. One may also note that whenever נפל with על־פניו ("on his face": Gen 17:3) or with על־פניהם ("on their faces": Lev 9:24) is used, פנים "face" seems to retain its literal sense, in that people literally fall down on their faces as a sign of worship.

In light of the above discussion, one may assume that YHWH would be present in the tent above the elevated place in the tabernacle and turn his face (by himself) toward the people[110] and cause his face to shine so that all the people (presumably) standing outside the tabernacle would have a glimpse of YHWH's face in his glory in a literal sense. Lifting of YHWH's face towards the people includes the assurance of divine forgiveness of their

---

108. See Ringgren, "נשׂא", 27. In Niphal, "נשׂא" may give sense similar to the verbs רום and קום.

109. Cf. Deut 32:40: כי־אשׂא אל־שמים ידי.

110. One can sense a polemical use here in that YHWH himself lifts (qal stem) his face, unlike some non-Israelite religious customs where the priests lift the idols to a higher place to let the worshipers see the faces of the idols. See chapter 1, fn. 22; fn. 98, 22.

sins (cf. Exod 34:7) and acceptance of the people.[111] This divine act of forgiveness and acceptance would bring divine שלום "peace"[112] to the people in worship (26b). In a general sense, the noun שלום shalom has the sense of a situation where "all things function in harmony",[113] particularly in terms of friendly relation between people (e.g. Gen 26:31; 28:21; 34:21), hence, as Sturdy suggests, this may signify "a right relationship with God"[114] in terms of covenantal faithfulness. Earlier in Leviticus, this term שלום was used of YHWH granting Israelites "peace" in the Land and that they would be freed from the fear of enemies, YHWH protects, shows his grace and peace. But human responsibility in maintaining the situation of שלום "peace" by obedience to the divine Law is not excluded (Lev 26:3, 6).

In this priestly wish, one may sense again that the priests were to facilitate an atmosphere of worship by offering sacrifices, so that YHWH would appear in the tabernacle on the atonement place and the people could see his appearance and be assured of divine forgiveness and peace. It is worth noting that YHWH's "face" is specifically used in terms of "shining" and "lifting" in the context of worship, but fear[115] is not associated with (seeing) the "face of YHWH", rather peace seems the end product. As Zimmerli reflects, in the priestly blessings (vv. 24–26), YHWH promises his presence to the people, and it does not cost them their lives.[116]

---

111. In the sense of paying attention to his people. Cf. Levine, *Numbers*, 228; Gen 43:29.
112. For different nuances of this term, see R. E. Averbeck, "שׁלם", *NIDOTTE* 4, 131–132.
113. Murtonen, "L^ebârek", 162.
114. Sturdy, *Numbers*, 55.
115. In the sense of fear of death.
116. Zimmerli, *OTT*, 73.

6.3.2 Name of YHWH and Future Blessings: v. 27

The final line (v. 27) in the text reads: "So[117] they shall put my name upon the children of Israel and I[118] (the Lord)[119] will bless them" (אברכם).

6.3.2.1 *Putting the name (27a)*

In addition to the threefold repetition of the Tetragrammaton in 24–26, the emphasis here is to put the name "YHWH" on Israel, and this may signify the association of the people to this name.[120] The usage of בני ישראל (children of Israel) may well point to the future[121] generations of Israel who, by putting the name YHWH on themselves, would declare their acceptance of YHWH as the source of their blessing,[122] and that they belonged to him.[123] Putting YHWH's name[124] implies YHWH's "ownership of Israel",[125] that they belonged to YHWH,[126] which includes his constant care.[127]

The importance attached to the name YHWH, particularly in earlier Exodus traditions, goes without saying, and one may remember that the name YHWH carries the connotation of the "ever-existing/ever-living one".[128] W. Kaiser rightly stresses that שם "name" is "so inextricably bound up with the being of God, that it functions almost like an appearance of

---

117. Eng. verses read ו conjunction in ושמו as "so", but Levine, *Numbers* (14), reads "when".
118. אני("I") with אברכם ("I will bless them") here is emphatic to express the importance given to the subject. GKC: §32 b; §135 a. In this small verse 27, the Tetragrammaton is mentioned three times in the first person, that is, את־שמי "my name", אני "I", אברכם "'I' will bless"; the object of the blessing twice על־בני ישראל ("children of Israel"), אברכם (I will bless) "them".
119. LXX has ἐγὼ κύριος εὐλογήσω αὐτούς: "I the Lord will bless them" (in LXX v. 27 follows v. 22).
120. For details see F. V. Reiterer, "שם", *TDOT* 15, 128–174; W.C. Kaiser, "שם", *TWOT*, 934–935.
121. The imperfect verb of ברך may be an indication.
122. Cf. C. R. Erdman, *The Pentateuch: An Exposition* (Grand Rapids, Baker Book House, 1987), 411.
123. Cf. P. J. Budd, *Numbers* (Waco: Word Books, 1984), 76.
124. For an assumption that the priestly blessing was "worn on the body in the form of amulets", see Milgrom, *Numbers*, 52; Stubbs, *Numbers*, 72. Cf. Exod 28:9–10.
125. Stubbs, *Numbers*, 72; Millgrom, *Numbers*, 52.
126. Cf. Budd, *Numbers*, 26; Deut 28:10.
127. Cf. Brown, *Numbers*, 59.
128. See chapter 4, 119.

YHWH".¹²⁹ As von Rad suggests, one must not lose sight of the fact that this name YHWH was seen as the guarantee of the revelation of deliverance.¹³⁰ When Moses requested YHWH to show him the glory, the latter says that he would proclaim his name, YHWH (33:19); this signifies that the proclamation of name is equivalent to his self-revelation;¹³¹ and as discussed earlier, in YHWH's proclamation on the mountain, he made mention of his שׁם "name" along with a confession of his character of חן "grace" (Exod 34:5–7). Since "to keep" name and character are closely associated, the stress on the name may have a deeper significance than simply identifying YHWH as the source of the blessings. In line with ancient belief that the name represents one's "presence and character" (Exod 34:5–7),¹³² putting YHWH's name on them perhaps "implies that Israel is supposed to behave in a way that corresponds to the character and ways of God", as Stubbs states.¹³³ The divine name YHWH upon the Israelites seems to signify not only his presence with them, but also exhibits his character.

6.3.2.2 *The Name and the Blessing (27b)*

An earlier Exodus tradition describes what YHWH told Moses to convey to the children of Israel—that he speaks from heaven, and yet in every place where his name is remembered on earth he would come to them and bless them. The blessing is associated with offering of the sacrifices and the remembrance (אזכיר) of his name and with the self-revelation of YHWH (Exod 20:22–24).¹³⁴ The "name of God" and "glory of God" seem closely associated with the tabernacle where they believed that YHWH would reveal himself. Putting on the name, then, would signify that Israel belonged to YHWH and that they were supposed to worship YHWH alone; this

---

129. Kaiser, "שׁם", 935. It seems that שׁם "name" of YHWH is association with the ark/tabernacle is used not in an abstract sense or in a symbolic way, but rather, it is associated with the self-revelations of YHWH/God (Exod 20:24; 23:20–21; 33:19 34:5–7).

130. Von Rad, *Moses*, 24.

131. Reiterer, "שׁם", 155.

132. See R. Gane, *Leviticus, Numbers: The NIV Application Commentary* (Grand Rapids: Zondervan, 2004), 540; Deut 12:5, 11, 21.

133. Stubbs, *Numbers*, 72.

134. They should not profane YHWH's holy name: Exod 20:7; Lev 21:6; 22:32; 24:16; should not worship any other gods: Exod 20:3–7; 22–23.

may confirm the assumption made earlier in this chapter that priestly blessing is to be associated with YHWH's appearance in the tabernacle.

Interestingly, verse 27 refers to the entire group of Israel in contrast to verse 24–26 where the pronouns are in singular number; this seems to signify that Israelites are given importance both individually (vv. 24–26) and collectively (v. 27); while every individual Israelite takes part in worship, everyone is part of the larger group,[135] an "organic body".[136] The Israelites are treated as one large group because they are united under the name of YHWH, they are given the same Law, and their worship is organized around the same tabernacle. Although this pronouncement is made for the people as a whole, "its force is to be realized in the life of the individual", as Allan stresses,[137] and the blessing is to be appropriated by the individuals within the community of the Israelites. As Noth points out, it is not a question of "either-or"; this blessing is "intended for the whole of Israel as well as individuals".[138] Perhaps, the term "community" has to be treated not in an abstract sense but in a concrete sense, that it comprises the individuals called to live under the common covenantal Law and regulations; individual accountability to YHWH cannot be excluded.[139]

Finally, it may be reiterated that the priests were given the duty of facilitating a situation through consecration and sacrifices so that the children of Israel would be conscious that the name YHWH is central to their worship even in the future.

---

135. While the use of singular number for Israelites is common in Pentateuch (Exod 20: 2–17; Deut 5:6–18), the shift from singular number (in vv. 24–26) to plural number (in v. 27) seems significant.

136. J. H. Hertz, ed. *The Pentateuch and Haftorahs* (London: Soncino Press, 1937), 595.

137. Allan, *Genesis-Numbers*, 754.

138. Noth, Numbers, 58–59. See also B. L. Ross, *The Individual in the Community: Personal Identification in Israel*. Ph.D. diss. (Drew University, 1979); G. W. Anderson, "'Sicut cervus': Evidence in the Psalter of Private Devotion in Ancient Israel", *VT* 30 (1980), 388–397.

139. As seen in the context of the calf worship (Exod 32) and in the case of Nadab and Abihu (Lev 10:1–2).

6.4 Mode of Self-Revelation, Human Recognition, and Response

It is not clear how YHWH is understood to have appeared when he spoke to Moses (Num 6:22). It seems that he was already present in the tabernacle. Presumably, the pattern of the appearance of YHWH's glory is similar to the pattern found in Leviticus where the "the glory of YHWH" appeared to, or was seen by (i.e. וירא), all of the people (Lev 9:23–24), but YHWH was understood to have come down in the cloud in his glory; YHWH's appearance in the cloud seems to mean that YHWH was present above the place of atonement in a corporeal sense (Lev 16:2); and when Moses would go into the tent of meeting to speak with YHWH, YHWH would speak to him from between the two cherubim (cf. Num 7:89).[140] It seems that Moses had readily recognized the appeared person as YHWH/God and related himself to him without any fear. But, there is no clue given in the text on how YHWH's anthropomorphic person looked in terms of his physicality. It was on his own initiative that YHWH revealed himself in his glory.

6.5 Function and Significance

The motifs in Numbers 6:24–26 could have played a significant role in the context of worship in ancient Israel; this text perhaps functioned to remind the worshipers of the divine presence and the divine involvement in their lives in terms of God's blessings, protection and peace. Since the themes in the text have been associated with divine self-revelations, it may have helped the new generations of ancient Israel to believe that YHWH/God had revealed himself to their fathers so that they too could trust in a God who would reveal himself and be present even in their worship. Since the name YHWH is associated with his character, they would have realized

---

140. Since several terms and themes from this text in Numbers have been used in the psalms of worship later in the temple worship, one may assume that the divine manifestations continued to take place above the place of atonement in the temple and the priest would have either seen or heard him speak.

that those on whom the name YHWH is put are expected to live a life that represents his character.

Evidently, the blessing pattern in Numbers 6:24–26, which seems to be part of the organized worship at the tabernacle, was greatly used by the later generations of Israel in the psalms of their worship in the temple;[141] and several terms and themes are alluded to in their psalms.[142] There is also some evidence that this blessing pattern has been used widely in ancient Israel at different occasions; the Kuntillet ʿAjrud inscription and the discovery of the priestly blessing in Keteph Hinnom valley may be an indication of this.[143]

6.6 Conclusion

In this chapter, Numbers 6:22–27 has been exegetically studied within its canonical context, with a special focus on the motifs of יאר יהוה פניו "YHWH cause his face to shine" (v. 25) and ישׂא יהוה פניו "YHWH lift his face" (v. 26), in order to understand its associations with the self-revelations of YHWH in the tabernacle and worship. The text has been studied in light of relevant texts in Exodus-Leviticus where the divine revelations have been associated with the tabernacle in terms of "the glory of YHWH".

This study has shown that the verbs ברך "to bless", שמר "to protect", אור "to shine", חן/חנן "to be gracious", נשׂא "to lift"; the nouns פני־יהוה "face of YHWH" and שׁם "name" reflected a definite literary and thematic association with several (canonically) previous texts in Genesis-Leviticus where they were used in association with divine revelations. There are some unique features, both literarily and thematically in the text here, in that

---

141. See Pss 29:11; 31:17; 67:1; 80:4, 8, 20; 119:135; cf. Dan 9:17.
142. For example, the term ברך occurs in Pss 128:5–6; 134:3; שמר 6 times in Ps 121; חנן in 123:2–3; 130:2; and שלום occurs in 29:11 and 122:6–8.
143. See G. Barkay, "The Priestly Benediction on the Ketef Hinnom Plaques", *Cathedra* 52 (1989), 37–76; see A. Yardeni, "Remarks on the Priestly Blessing on Two Ancient Amulets from Jerusalem", *VT* 41 (1991), 176–185. G. Barkay and et al. "The Challenges of Ketef Hinnom", *NEA* 66 (2003), 161–171. The blessing amulets discovered in a burial cave lead to an assumption that the blessing was associated with life after death. Cf. Pss 25:20; 34:21; 86:2; 97:11 where שלום and שמר are used in the context of dead seeking peace and protection for the נפשׁ "soul".

the verbs ברך "to bless" and שמר "to keep" occur in the same sentence. The verbs אור "to shine" and נשא "to lift" with פנים "face" with YHWH (פני־יהוה) as subject are used only here, and signify that "shining" and "lifting" of YHWH's face were associated with the self-revelation of YHWH in the holy place within the tabernacle where he appeared in anthropomorphic form.

The use of פנים "face" of YHWH (פני־יהוה) as subject of the verbs אור "to shine" and נשא "to lift" signify the anthropomorphic form in the context of the self-revelation of YHWH, and this seems to support the assumption that the "shining" and "lifting" of YHWH's face may have been associated with worship, where YHWH would shine upon and lift his face toward the worshipping people. Given that previous texts described YHWH anthropomorphically, even when he appeared in the midst of fire and glory (3:2–6; 24:10, 17), it can be presumed that readers understood that this expression יאר יהוה פניו ("cause his face shine") involved "the appearance of YHWH" in his anthropomorphic person, and that it was the radiant face ("glory") of YHWH, which was associated with the shining on the people. YHWH/God appeared above the place of the atonement, which was supposed to be on a higher/elevated place in the tabernacle (Lev 9:6–22; 16:2; Exod 25:8, 22), and he was believed to be physically present inside the Tabernacle. In light of this, an assumption is made that these expressions יאר יהוה פניו and ישא יהוה פניו (6:24–27) have close association with the self-revelations of YHWH in terms of worship at the tabernacle, and YHWH/God let himself be seen by the people from inside the tabernacle in his glory (cf. Lev 9:23–24).[144]

With regard to scholarly opinions likening the verb "shining" with sun/sunlight, this study has not found textual evidence to associate the verb אור "to shine" (v. 25) with sun/sunlight; rather it has found that the expression "the face of YHWH" has strong links with the divine self-revelations in the tabernacle where YHWH appeared in his glory and where fire went from the face of YHWH (9:24), and on the mountain where Moses' face shone because he was exposed to the divine glory (Exod 34:5–35). Hartenstein's

---

[144]. For a discussion on the association of the person of YHWH with his glory, see chapter 5, 187–188.

suggestion that the motif "shining of YHWH's face" has associations with the courtly-cultic *Audienze* does not seem to fit with the given (canonical) context, where the text insists that it was YHWH/God who took initiative and came to meet people. It therefore seems appropriate to associate the expressions in verses 25–26 with the self-revelations of YHWH/God as described in the Hebrew traditions particularly in Exodus-Leviticus.

Furthermore, it has been discerned that the appearance of "the glory of YHWH" in the tabernacle was used in a corporeal sense, in that YHWH himself was present anthropomorphically; this association is strengthened by the previous traditions in Exodus, which showed that even when YHWH was said to have appeared in the midst of fire and glory, the divine anthropomorphized figure was present and spoke to Moses and others (e.g. 3:2–6; 24:10, 17); just as in the previous traditions, Moses bowed down to earth and worshiped (ויקד ארצה וישתחו) YHWH (Exod 34:5–35) and Abram fell on his face (על־פני) before YHWH/God, all the people fell on their faces as a sign of worship (ויפלו על־פניהם) when they saw YHWH, who appeared in his glory (Lev 9:23–24). It is assumed that the shining and lifting of YHWH's face can be associated with the worship context where YHWH revealed himself by means of glory and face.

The divine revelations were associated with the worship of the community, and yet the divine blessings were to be appropriated by individuals within the community (vv. 24–26; 23, 27), and this meant that YHWH would bless future generations of Israel both individually and as a community. On a practical level, the blessings included divine protection, divine forgiveness and the divine shalom "peace", but on a human level the people were to maintain the covenantal relationship in obedience to the divine Law/Words.

This study has suggested that the reason why the duty of pronouncing the blessing was given to the priests in the form of a "wish" was not for simple verbal repetition, but that by means of this blessing pattern (of wishing), the priests were instructed to facilitate an atmosphere of worship by offering sacrifices and consecrating themselves and the people, so that "the glory of YHWH" would appear in the tabernacle and the younger generations of Israel would be able to see the face of YHWH/God shining on them in grace and favor in their worship continually.

6.7 The Question of the Background of "Shining and Lifting YHWH's Face"

One may recall that Nötscher had associated the idea of "seeing the face of YHWH" with the cultic realm in the ANE; Hartenstein endorsed Nötscher's view and concluded that the background to "the face of YHWH" was in the second temple in Jerusalem. Although Hartenstein accepted the concrete idea in association with the "face of YHWH", he linked it with the "face" of the king in analogical terms. However, the study of different Hebrew texts in the previous chapters 2–5 gave an understanding that the background to "seeing the face of YHWH/God" was the "self-revelations" of YHWH/God, and, arguably, that the motif was rooted in the Israelite belief that God revealed himself in a human form in a corporeal sense, and consequently that different people saw "the face of YHWH/God" in a literal sense.

As argued earlier in this chapter, the sanctuary (מקדש) was treated as a dwelling place (in the sense of temporary dwelling) because YHWH/God would reveal himself (שכנתי) among the children of Israel from time to time, so that they would know him as their Lord/God (Exod 25:8; 29:45–46). Since the motifs יאר יהוה פניו and ישא יהוה פניו (shining and lifting of YHWH's face: Num 6:25–26) have strong links with the "appearance of YHWH" in the tabernacle, it seems appropriate to conclude that these expressions had their origin/background in the divine self-revelations in the tabernacle in the context of worship.

Some scholars, comparing the expression "shining of YHWH's face" with parallel texts in the psalms have suggested that this expression had roots in the pre-exilic temple.[145] However, when the text is placed within its canonical context, "the face of YHWH" (in Num 6:25–26) reflects its association with the self-revelations of YHWH/God in the tabernacle, specifically in the context of worship. The reason why the motif "face of YHWH/God" is found in the context of the temple worship could be because the later/subsequent generations in ancient Israel believed that YHWH/God revealed himself even in their organized worship in the temple. Clements'

---

145. For example, Budd, *Numbers*, 25. Cf. Pss 4:7; 31:17; 80:4, 8, 20.

arguments on the association of the self-revelations of YHWH/God with the temple's worship are helpful. He suggests that in temple worship, God "'came' to manifest his presence there", that YHWH's dwelling in the temple was "justified and explained on the basis of his appearing there in a theophany", and that the tendency to regard YHWH's presence in the temple as static "can only be regarded as a loss of the true significance of the temple". He rightly argues that YHWH's presence was always "an active coming to his people";[146] and it seems that YHWH/God continued to maintain his covenantal relation with his people through his self-revelations.[147]

In light of the canonical order, the temple worship seems a continuation from the worship that is described in the tabernacle in terms of the self-revelations of YHWH/God, hence, one can confidently affirm that the background of the motif "the face of YHWH/God" was the divine self-revelations.

6.8 Looking beyond Numbers 6:22–27

A glance beyond the text studied in this chapter shows that YHWH/God continued to reveal himself in terms of his glory at the tabernacle,[148] and continued to guide them by means of his presence in (the cloud of) "glory" (Num 9:15, 17–23). In light of Moses' earlier experience with YHWH, the statement that Moses had looked at (נבט) YHWH's תמונה "form" (Num 12:8b) can be confirmed; YHWH/God continued to go with/before the Israelites to an extent that even the other nations had heard that YHWH was among them and was seen עין בעין נראה "eye to eye" (Num 14:14b).

One significant feature may be that in the context of Korah's rebellion, when the glory of YHWH appeared to all the assembly (16:19–21) and where YHWH wanted to put an end to them, Moses and Aaron fall face down and cry saying, "O God, the God of the spirits of all flesh"

---

146. Clements, *God and Temple*, 64.
147. Cf. Kuntz, *Self-Revelation of God*, 114.
148. Num 12:1–9; 14:10–24; 16:19–50; 17:8, 15; 20:6.

(אל אלהי הרוחת לכל־בשׂר: 16:22).[149] The usage הרוחת here seems to point to God as the creator of all humankind.[150] Later on, the readers were informed that the divine revelations took a different turn as God seemed to have met with and spoken to Balaam the non-Israelite prophet (Num 22–24);[151] Balaam knew that God was speaking to him, and he also spoke to God (24:4, 16), and understood that it was God's will to bless Israel, and that God is not a man that he should lie (Num 23:19).[152] Even in the context of a non-Israelite, the mode of divine manifestations is the same (22:7–20);[153] it is God who initiated the conversation, it is God who made himself accessible even to the non-Israelite prophet anthropomorphically to communicate his purpose. YHWH/God spoke and controlled a non-Israelite prophet, who was working against his plans for his people, and fulfilled his purposes for them. As Wolterstorff stresses "there is nothing incoherent or impossible in the claim that God speaks—and as presented in the Bible—"God does indeed speak".[154] Going a step further one can also say that it is not impossible to think that the Hebrew writers believed that God revealed himself in human form[155] to communicate to his people, and also to communicate his message to non-Israelites.

In the book of Deuteronomy,[156] which is more of a recapitulation of the past, Moses, with whom YHWH used to speak פנים אל־פנים; whose face shone because he was with YHWH in glory on the mountain (Exod

---

149. For the same usage see Num 27:16 (יהוה אלהי הרוחת לכל־בשׂר), the only difference being that YHWH is used here instead of אל.

150. Perhaps, נשמת חיים (Gen 2:7) and רוח are taken as synonyms. Cf. Isa 42:5 where ורוח and נשמה occur together.

151. See M. Douglas, *In the Wilderness: The Doctrine of Defilement in the Book of Numbers* (Sheffield: Sheffield Academic Press, 1993), 216–234.

152. See R. W. L. Moberly, "God is not a human that he should repent", in *God in the Fray*. Eds. T. Linafelt and T. K. Beal (Minneapolis: Fortress Press, 1998), 119.

153. Milgrom (*Numbers*, 189) sees similarity with the dream theophanies to Abimelech (Gen 20:3) and Laban (Gen 31:24).

154. N. Wolterstorff, *Inquiring about God*. Ed. T. Cuneo (Cambridge: Cambridge University Press, 2010), 240.

155. It is said that nowhere in the rabbinic literature is a statement made that rejects the notion of divine corporeality. See D. H. Aaron, "Shedding Light on God's Body in Rabbinic Midrashim: Reflections on the Theory of a Luminous Adam", *HTR* 90 (1997), 299–314.

156. Unable to discuss more details due to space limit.

33:18; 34:29–35); with whom YHWH spoke "face-to-face" (פה אל־פה: Num 12:8), reminds the people of their past experiences with YHWH, and instructs them for the future. Moses reminds them that YHWH spoke to them "face-to-face" (פנים בפנים: Deut 5:4) on the mountain from the midst of the fire. In future, when they would go לראות את־פני יהוה "to see the face of YHWH"[157] in the place of his choosing, all the people (including women, children and strangers) should be gathered, so that they might learn to fear YHWH by following the words of the Law; and through them their children, the new generation of Israel, who have not known the law yet, might also hear the divine words and learn to fear God (Deut 31:10–13). After all, the Israelites needed to realize that YHWH blessed them to become instruments of blessing to the nations around them (Gen 12:3; 22:18; 28:14).

---

157. Although the MT points the infinitive of ראה as niphal, לראות with את־פני יהוה as the object gives the idea that YHWH is the object of "seeing".

CHAPTER 7

Conclusion

7.1 Conclusions in Summary

The "Face of YHWH/God" (פני־יהוה/אלהים) is an important expression in the Pentateuch, occurring mostly in the context of divine self-revelations; its association with the verb ראה "to see" signifies corporeality/physicality of YHWH/God. The term פנים "face" has a clear association with the "self-revelations of 'YHWH/God'" in the Pentateuch.

Throughout the Pentateuch, different people such as Hagar (16:13) and Jacob (Gen 32:31) claimed to have seen God's face (sometimes face-to-face); the elders of Israel were supposed to have seen God (Exod 24:10–11); YHWH is said to have spoken to Moses "face-to-face" like a friend (Exod 33:11). At the same time, Exodus 33:20, where YHWH is reported as saying to Moses, "You cannot see my face; for no man shall see me, and live", seems to stand in conflict with the above-mentioned texts. Deuteronomy 4:12, 15 relates that at the mountain when YHWH spoke out of the fire, the people heard only a voice and "saw no form". Because of this tension between different statements, previous scholars either argued against the corporeality of YHWH/God and treated it as metaphorical or compared it with the faces of gods and goddesses in the ANE religious context.

Approaching the subject of "seeing the face of YHWH/God" in the HB from the perspective of (old) literary and historical criticisms, particularly that of the *Religionsgeschichte* and *Traditionsgeschichte*, scholars such as Baudissin and Nötscher placed the Israelite concept of "'seeing the face of YHWH/God" in the ANE cultic context and compared it with "seeing the face of Ištar's *Kultstätte* in the temple, maintaining that the Israelites borrowed the usage of the "face" of YHWH from the cultic face of Ištar, and concluding that in Israel also the term implied visiting the temple or seeking *Audienz* before the king (ch. 1, 5–6). Some other scholars treated this expression "seeing the face of YHWH/God" as idiomatic or metaphorical (ch. 1, 7–8). Hartenstein (in line with Nötscher) took Psalms as a proof that "face of YHWH" had its background in the cultic context, especially in the Jerusalem Temple in the analogy of seeing the king for *Audienz*. Although Hartenstein accepted the idea of anthropomorphic form (since the king has a face), he argued that the reference to the divine "face" was only a devotee's imagination (ch. 1, 9–10).

However, these scholars did not give an adequate rationale as to why the Hebrew writers used the term פנים "face" in association with "YHWH/God" in the worship context in the temple, nor did they attempt to associate the motif the "face of YHWH/God" with the appearance of YHWH/God, who supposedly appeared to different people in human form. In order to understand the association of פנים "face" with יהוה/אלהים "YHWH/God" in the Pentateuch and to discern what function the motif played in ancient Israel, this work studied selected biblical texts within the canonical context and placed the motif in the context of the self-revelations of YHWH/God.

The approach taken in this study has been the exegetical study method. The selected biblical texts have been interpreted within their immediate and wider context within the Pentateuch. In terms of intertextual references, this work has referred to (canonically) earlier texts, with an assumption that earlier texts would help understand the (canonically) later texts.

Section I of this work comprises chapters 2 and 3. In chapter 2, Genesis 3:8–10; 12:1–8; 15:1–7; 16:7–14; 17:1–5; 18:1–8, 16–22; 28:12–19 were studied with the objective of understanding how ancient Israel perceived the expression "the face of YHWH/God" in association with the divine self-revelations. The study of these traditions/texts helped to elucidate the Israelite concept of God as the creator (Gen 1:1) and the "image of God" in humankind as a means of maintaining the divine-human relationship. The creator God walked in the garden and spoke to the first couple in a language that was understood by them—this aspect of the divine actions in

Genesis set the basis for understanding the anthropomorphic appearance of God.

The study of these biblical texts in Genesis led to the understanding that ancient Israel perceived that YHWH/God had revealed himself to different people such as Adam (Eve), Abraham, (Sarah), Hagar and Jacob both directly, and in dreams and visions; the divine revelations were not restricted to a particular (sacred) place but rather they took place during travels (Abraham, Hagar and Jacob), by day and by night (Adam and Jacob). Contrary to the idea of seeking an audience from the king, these texts show that YHWH/God himself came to meet with and communicate to the people in a human bodily form; the background to the motif אלהים/ פני־יהוה "the face of YHWH/God" has been shown to be the context of "self-revelations of YHWH/God". This study led to the understanding that ancient Israel perceived that the appearance of YHWH/God took place in human bodily form, and that YHWH/God was believed physically present when he encountered different people and spoke with them. The possibility of different people seeing the "face" of the anthropomorphic person of YHWH/God during those encounters is established.

The study of Genesis 32:25–32 in chapter 3 has shown that the statement made by Jacob ראיתי אלהים פנים אל־פנים ותנצל נפשי "I saw God 'face-to-face', and my life is saved" signified the direct and active involvement of both God (who touched Jacob's hip) and Jacob (who saw God). The text gives an impression that the anthropomorphic divine person has specifically revealed to Jacob something of himself by means of a favorable expression in his face, from which he was assured that his life was saved. The description in the text, the writer's insistence that Jacob named the place after his experience and the explicit claim supposedly made by Jacob that he saw God פנים אל־פנים "face-to-face" all seemed to imply that he saw the physical appearance of God in a real/literal sense. Jacob's comparison of the face of Esau with seeing the face of God (32:31 and 33:10) is additional support to believe that God appeared to Jacob in human bodily form.

Section II of this work comprises chapters 4 and 5. In chapter 4, Exodus 3:1–12 and 24:1–18 were studied with the objective of understanding how the "face of YHWH/God is associated with the anthropomorphic appearances in the Exodus traditions. Unlike in Genesis, where the self revelations were unexpected and informal, in Exodus 24, the divine revelations were expected, were more formal, and were accompanied by cloud, fire and glory. The study of these two selected texts helped in understanding that in the revelations in the fiery bush, and in the theophanies associated with fire and cloud on Mount Sinai, YHWH/God was understood to be physically present in human (bodily) form; the possibility of Moses' seeing YHWH/God at the fiery bush, and Moses, Aaron, Nadab, Abihu and seventy elders of Israel seeing God on the mountain was established. In light of this, it was further reiterated that the background of "seeing God" was the self-revelations of YHWH/God.

The study of Exodus 33:12–23; 34:1–10, 28–35 in chapter 5 explored the divine revelations described in these texts (includes 33:7–11), which are multifaceted and associated with "pillar of cloud", "face", "goodness" and "glory". The findings of this study in terms of the tension surrounding the aspect of "seeing" (and "not seeing") are that the statements made in 33:14 (פני ילכו "my 'face' shall go") and in 33:20 (לא תוכל לראת את־פני כי לא־יראני האדם וחי "you will not be able to see 'my face'; for no one shall see me, and live") are not in conflict, rather these two statements reflected two different aspects of the self-revelation of YHWH/God. The statement in 33:20 does not stand in conflict in the narrative with the statement in 33:11 (ודבר יהוה אל־משה פנים אל־פנים "YHWH used to speak with Moses face-to-face"), but rather the "face-to-face" speech between YHWH and Moses (in 33:11) helped to clarify the tension in 33:20–23, and confirmed the possibility of Moses' seeing the divine face.

The theophany in 34:29 in which Moses spoke with YHWH and received the Law a second time also confirmed that the divine revelation on the mountain was believed to be a physical reality, and established the possibility that the shining of Moses' face was the consequence of "seeing" the face of YHWH. The possibility of Moses seeing the divine face when he spoke with YHWH face-to-face in the tent (33:11) and the shining of his face the possible consequence of his speaking to and seeing YHWH on the mountain, both mutually confirmed the positive aspect of Moses' "seeing" the divine face. The possibility of Moses seeing "the face of YHWH" is more dominant in this section than the negative assumption that he has not seen the divine face.

There is no evidence in these texts to establish that death is associated with "seeing the divine face", rather, even the repentant people are given a chance later to see the divine glory that is passed on to, and reflected in, Moses' face. Since Moses is interceding on behalf of the people who worshiped the golden calf, the negation in 33:20 is connected with the sin and disobedience of the people; the reason why YHWH could not let even Moses see his glory at that place and in that particular instance was for the sake of the people, lest they would perish if they were to see him in his glory, since they were under the effect of sin.

The scholarly arguments that the expressions related to "seeing the face of YHWH/God" are metaphorical are contrary to the textual evidence discussed in this thesis, and the Hebrew writer insists that the divine self-revelations took place in a real sense. Had it not been for YHWH's self-revelations, the covenant made by YHWH and the Law given on the mountain would not have had the same significance for faith and practice in ancient Israel. With regard to Deuteronomy 4:12–15, the text does not necessarily indicate the non-corporeality of God, since the readers were told earlier that Moses was given the two tablets of the covenant inscribed by God's finger (Exod 31:18). It is suggested that Exodus 33:20 and Deuteronomy 5:24–26 do not deny the corporeality of YHWH/God or the possibility of "seeing the face of YHWH/God".

The textual evidence stands in contradiction to the scholarly arguments that the expression "seeing the face of God" was borrowed from the ANE where the face was associated with the idols. The Hebrew readers would not have associated "seeing the face of God" with the face of idols or images, bearing in mind the disastrous results of calf-worship. Since the Hebrew writers employed the term "face" in association with YHWH/God even in the context where calf-worship is treated as sin, it is argued that the concept of "seeing the face of YHWH/God" had its background in the divine self-revelations.

Chapter 6 opens section III of this work. In this chapter, the motifs of יאר יהוה פניו "may YHWH cause his face to shine" and ישׂא יהוה פניו "may YHWH lifts his face" in Numbers 6:22–27 have been studied in association with the tabernacle in terms of "the glory of YHWH" within the context of Exodus-Leviticus. It is understood that the association of the "face" of YHWH (פני־יהוה) as subject of the verbs אור "to shine" and נשא "to lift" signified an anthropomorphic form in the context of the self-revelation of YHWH/God. The appearance of "the glory of YHWH" in the tabernacle is understood as YHWH himself being present anthropomorphically, and this factor is supported by Exodus 3:2–6; 24:10, 17 where YHWH is said to have appeared in the midst of fire. In light of the previous texts which portray Moses bowing down before (ויקד ארצה וישתחו) YHWH (Exod 34:5–35) and all the people falling on their faces as a sign of worship (ויפלו על־פניהם) when they saw the glory of YHWH (Lev 9:23–24), it is understood that the shining and lifting of YHWH's face can be associated with the worship context where YHWH revealed himself by means of his face (himself) in glory. Since the motifs יאר יהוה פניו and ישא יהוה פניו and the Tetragrammaton (Num 6:25–26) have strong links with the "appearance of the glory of YHWH" in the tabernacle, this study placed these motifs in the "self-revelations" of YHWH in the context of worship, where the priests wished that YHWH would reveal himself to the worshipers.

The divine blessings, which included divine protection, divine forgiveness and the divine peace, were associated with the worship of the community (vv. 24–26; 23, 27). On a practical level, worshipers were to maintain the covenantal relationship in obedience to the divine Law/Words. The reason why the duty of pronouncing the blessing was given to the priests in the form of a "wish" was not simply to provide a pattern for verbal repetition, but that by means of this blessing pattern (of wishing), priests were instructed to facilitate an atmosphere of worship by offering relevant sacrifices and consecrating themselves and the people, in order that "the glory of YHWH/God" would continually appear within the worship context, even among the subsequent generations of Israel.

With regard to the question of the background of "seeing the face of YHWH/God", the Hebrew traditions associated this expression "seeing the face of God" with anthropomorphic revelations. The strong tradition/s in ancient Israel that YHWH/God appeared in "human form" shows that they valued these traditions as foundational for their faith and practice; and when God the creator revealed himself in human (bodily) form to different people, he let himself be seen by them, which evidently involved "seeing the face of YHWH/God". Indeed the motif of "seeing the face of YHWH/God" was rooted in the Hebrew tradition/s of the self-revelations of YHWH/God. Ancient readers would not have had any difficulty in accepting the physical manifestation of God, since their traditions perceived God as the creator of humankind, and held that he maintained a contact and a relationship by means of self-revelations.

This study suggests that the Hebrew writers employed the term פנים "face" in association with "seeing YHWH/God" (פני־יהוה/אלהים) in order to represent the "'face' of the anthropomorphic person of YHWH/God".

7.2 The Face of God and His Physicality

7.2.1 The Face of YHWH/God

This study has shown that when the noun פנים (in its construct form פני) is developed as the personal pronouns (with suffixes) and as the prepositional phrases לפני, מפני and מלפני, it does not necessarily lose its nominative character, nor do these phrases act as (pure) prepositions at the expense of the nominal value of פנים "face". The combination of לפני, מפני and מלפני with YHWH ("before/from before YHWH") has been used in the context of the self-revelations of YHWH/God, whether it is at random (at any place) or in localized places (on the mountain or in the tabernacle/tent). Contrary to Fowler's arguments that לפני יהוה "before YHWH" often has the nuance "in the estimation of YHWH" rather than "in the presence of YHWH", the textual evidence, as discussed in this work, has shown that לפני יהוה "before YHWH" is closely associated with the self-revealed direct presence of YHWH. And also, contrary to Johnson's argument that פני יהוה "face of YHWH" and לפני יהוה "before YHWH" are to be treated as idiomatic and as figures of speech, the textual evidence confirms that these expressions are associated with the anthropomorphic person of YHWH in the context of the divine self-revelations. The Hebrew writer(s)' choice of employing the noun פנים with suffixes (to signify personal pronouns) is significant, as they frequently choose a phrase like פני ילכו ("my face shall go"), where as a phrase like אני/אנכי אלך ("I shall go") could have been used instead, and

פנים "face" is mostly associated with the anthropomorphic divine person in the context of the self-revelations of YHWH/God. The adverbial or the temporal meaning of the phrase is not found in these texts studied. It therefore seems likely that the Hebrew writer(s), by using such vivid expressions involving פנים "face", wanted to convey that these expressions are not to be treated as merely prepositional.

7.2.2 The Physicality of YHWH/God and His Human Form

As observed throughout this study, the theme of "the face of YHWH/God" in the Pentateuch is situated in the context of the divine self-revelations: whenever YHWH/God reveals himself to different people in the Pentateuch, he is understood to be physically present in human form, and it is this aspect that will be recapitulated here.

7.2.2.1 The Appearance of YHWH/God in Human Form: Normal Life Situations

When YHWH God is said to be walking in the garden and calling to Adam, he is understood to be in human form (Gen 3:8–10). The reason why the first couple hide themselves is because they are afraid of seeing/being seen by YHWH God; this shows that God is understood to be physically present in the garden and that he is visible to the human eye.

When the writer states, "YHWH said to Abram" (12:1) or "YHWH appeared to Abram" (וירא: v. 7), he understands YHWH as physically present (2–3) with Abram; his insistence that YHWH speaks to Abram directly and orders him to go (לך־לך: v. 1) from his father's house implies that YHWH is understood to be in "human form"; and it is possible that Abram sees him during that meeting. The statement that Abram built an altar to YHWH, "who appeared to him" (v. 7b), confirms that YHWH's appearance to Abram was believed to be real.

When God finds Hagar and initiates a conversation, she does not seem to think that he is any different from a co-traveller at first (Gen 16:7–8); but at the end of the encounter she exclaims, "You are the God who sees me" . . . "Have I also seen him who sees me"? This indicates that when God found Hagar in the wilderness (v. 7), the mode of his appearance was evidently in human form (v. 13). Since the name given to the well as *Beer*

Lahai Roi is associated with her experience of seeing (ראה) God (v. 14), and God was understood physically present with her in a real sense.

When YHWH appears to Abram and says, "I am God Almighty . . ." (17:1), the speech is direct and may well be "face-to-face"; here too God is believed to be physically present in human form. That Abram falls upon his face (עַל־פָּנָיו), which is normally done in front of a visible person, and that God continues to speak to him, confirms that YHWH was understood as being present with Abram in human form, and that Abram saw him (v. 3). The mode of appearance is in human form, and the specific mention made in the text that "God went up" (עלה: v. 22) implies that YHWH transcends his human form while going up.

In Genesis 18, YHWH and the other two divine persons were understood as ordinary travellers, who needed food and rest (vv. 1–7), and when Abraham offered food to them, they ate it (v. 8). It is not clear, however, if ancient Israel understood YHWH as having flesh and blood in his bodily appearance; but they have explicitly depicted him as a man. When Abraham gave them food, walked with them (v. 16) and stood "before YHWH" (v. 22), it is very likely that YHWH was present in human form and undoubtedly, Abraham saw him (even "face-to-face").

In Genesis 32, YHWH/God is depicted as a "man" and came into conflict with Jacob in a physical sense (v. 25). Jacob's exclamation that he saw God "face-to-face" (פנים אל־פנים) is a clear indication that it was God whom Jacob saw (v. 31) and God looked first like a man (as in 16:7–8). Since the object of the verb ראה "to see" is God, it signifies that God was physically present with Jacob whom he saw "face-to-face". The man's touch of Jacob's hip, which caused his limp (v. 26, 32), confirms that he (God) was understood as physically present with Jacob, and the mode of God's appearance was obviously thought to be in human form.

When YHWH/God appears in a flame of fire in the bush, he calls Moses from there and speaks to him (Exod 3:2–4). The reason given why Moses hides his face is that he is afraid to look at God (v. 6), signifying that the appearance of YHWH/God is understood as physically present even in the fire and perceptibly in human form; presumably, Moses is afraid because the person in the bush identifies himself as God (v. 6), and Moses perceives him as God.

In Exodus 24:1–18, it is said that Moses, Aaron, Nadab, Abihu and the seventy elders of Israel saw "the God of Israel" on the mountain. Even when the mode of divine revelation on the mountain is associated with cloud and fire and "the glory of YHWH" is described as consuming fire (19:18), YHWH/God is believed to be physically present in human form. The repetition of the visual aspect that they "saw" (ויראו) and "beheld" (ויחזו) emphasizes that people saw God's physical form (10–11); the mention made to God's feet and hands (vv. 10–11) confirms that God was understood as present in human form; since YHWH calls Moses from within the cloud of glory (vv. 16–17), it also confirms that he was understood as present in human form; when Moses goes up into the midst of the cloud, where he stays with YHWH for forty days and nights (v. 18), YHWH speaks to him there (25:1) and writes the Law on the two tablets with his finger (31:18)—all this signifies that the Hebrew traditions believed that YHWH/God was present in human form, even in the midst of his fiery glory.

In Exodus 33, where the mode of appearance is associated with the pillar of cloud/glory (v. 11), the self-revelations of YHWH in the tent are also described in terms of anthropomorphic language and human form; YHWH's conversation with Moses is described as פנים אל־פנים "face-to-face" and is compared with that of a friend (v. 11), indicating that YHWH was understood to be physically present with Moses in human form and was in direct contact with Moses; evidently, Moses sees the face of YHWH in the tent.

The expression פני ילכו "my face shall go" signifies the self-revelation of YHWH in terms of his physical appearance (v. 14), as the term פנים "face" is normally associated with anthropomorphized person of YHWH/God. When Moses asks for YHWH's glory to be shown, he means divine self-revelation in association with כבוד "glory" and פנים "face" (v. 15, 18); when YHWH promises that he would pass by before Moses in terms of his glory, it is understood that YHWH himself would pass by (vv. 19, 22) in human form. It seems that even when YHWH descends in the cloud, he appears in human form, given that YHWH stands with Moses on the mountain and passes by before him (34:5–7), and is believed to be physically present in association with both פנים "face" and כבוד "glory". Since YHWH passes by Moses in his glory, and since Moses worships (ישתחו) and prays to YHWH (8–10), one may assume that YHWH was physically present with Moses. Since the reason given for the shining of Moses' face is that he spoke with YHWH (v. 29), and since Moses spends forty days and nights with YHWH in the cloud of glory, Moses is evidently exposed to the divine glory (33–35), and presumably, the divine glory is passed on from YHWH to Moses' face. When Moses is with YHWH in the midst of the radiant fiery cloud, YHWH says to him, "Write down these words" (27–29), the speech is direct and YHWH is understood as physically present in human form with Moses, and in all probability, Moses sees YHWH.

In Leviticus and Numbers, when "the glory of YHWH" appeared in the tent/tabernacle, it is understood in a concrete sense, in that YHWH is present within his glory and פנים "face" is also ascribed to him; "the glory of YHWH" in the tabernacle is understood both in a broader sense and at the same time, as a single entity; YHWH is believed to be present in human form within his glory in the tent, in that he calls Moses from the tent (מאהל) and speaks to him (Lev 1:1). Since it is said that blood is sprinkled (4:6, 17) and sacrifices are offered (9:4, 6) לפני יהוה "before YHWH", and that YHWH is believed to appear in the cloud above the place of atonement (16:2; Num 7:89), one may assume that YHWH is understood to be physically present in human form during the worship. Since it is believed that YHWH/God was physically present in his glory in the tent, when the fire comes out מלפני יהוה "from before YHWH" the fire is understood to have come "from before" him. That the people fall on their faces (ויפלו על־פניהם) suggests that they bow before the visible form of YHWH, who is present there within his glory (Lev 9:23–24), and a close association between the divine "face" and "glory" is discerned.

The pronouncement of the priestly blessing (Num 6:22–27) is associated with the tabernacle, where YHWH's self-revelations would take place. Since it is said that "YHWH spoke to Moses, saying . . . " (22–23), it signifies that YHWH was believed to be physically present with Moses in human form and spoke to Moses. Given that the blessing is normally pronounced in a direct, and even in a face-to-face contact; and since YHWH is the subject of "blessing", "shining" and "lifting" of his face, the priestly wish, that is associated with YHWH, who is believed to be present in the tabernacle, perhaps anticipates similar divine revelations even in future.

7.2.2.2 Appearance of YHWH/God in Human Form: Visions and Dreams

7.2.2.2.1 Visions

Genesis 15 describes that "the word of YHWH" came in a vision to Abram (v. 1); however, "the word of YHWH" is identified as YHWH himself, and even in that vision, the physical aspect YHWH is not absent. Given that YHWH said to Abram, "I am your shield"; Abram addresses "the word of YHWH" as אדני יהוה "YHWH Lord", it signifies that YHWH is understood to be in a human form, even in that vision. The description of the divine activity within the vision, such as bringing Abram outside and showing him the stars (v. 5), making the covenant and reiterating the promises (9–18), indicate that YHWH is understood to be in human form (having the attributes of a human) and is visible within that vision; and the divine appearance in the vision does not lack directness, and possibly, Abram sees YHWH in that vision. The writer's comment: "on 'that day' YHWH made a covenant with Abram" (v. 18), signifies that the covenant made within that vision is understood to be as significant as the covenant made in normal life situations. The Hebrew traditions seemed to understand that the divine revelations in those visions, in terms of the visibility/physicality of YHWH/God and the messages given in those visions, were as authentic as the direct revelations described in real life situations.

7.2.2.2.2 Dreams

Even in Jacob's night dream (28:12–22), YHWH is described in human terminology that he stood on a ladder. The self-assertion made, "I am YHWH the God of Abraham . . . ", indicates that YHWH is understood to be physically present within that dream, and it is possible that Jacob saw the appearance of God in that dream, given that the text describes YHWH as addressing Jacob in a direct speech (13–16). Even in this dream, YHWH is supposed to be in human form, given that the features in the divine appearance are similar to the non-dream revelations, in terms of physicality, directness of vision, verbal communication and the promises made (v. 15, 20). Since the promises made earlier to Abraham in a real life situation are repeated here in this dream, one can discern that there is a close connection (and continuity) between the revelations in the non-dream situations and the revelation in this dream (v. 14; cf. 17:2–7; 26:4); there is also some connection between the vision to Abram and this dream to Jacob, in terms of the descendants and the Land (15:5, 18; 28:13).

Jacob's post-dream expression, "surely YHWH is in this place", seems to indicate that the divine appearance is visible to Jacob within that dream, and Nötscher rightly argues that YHWH was seen in a bodily presence even in this dream; arguably, Jacob sees YHWH in human form within that dream. And Jacob's action of setting up a pillar (מצבה) and pouring oil, which is a sign of worship (vv. 16–22), is similar to Abram's act of building the altar after YHWH appeared to him in a real life situation (cf. 12:7–8).

Later in his life, while Jacob was still in Paddan-Aram, YHWH is said to have spoken to him in a dream directing him to return to his own land (Gen 31:3, 11–13), and Jacob received that message as authentic and accordingly left Paddan-Aram, as Jacob's prayer indicates (32:10). All this signifies that YHWH/God's physical appearances even within those dreams are understood as genuine, and the message received in those dreams is no less significant than the appearances in non-dream or real life situation.

7.2.2.3 Human Form and the Bodily Aspect in the Appearance of YHWH/God

7.2.2.3.1 Human Form

As seen above, the biblical texts give ample evidence that the ancient Israelites believed that YHWH/God appeared to different people by means of "human form"; and whether he appeared in a cloud/fire or in glory, on the mountain or in the tabernacle, in real life situations or in visions and dreams, he was understood as physically present in human form. Even those texts, which describe YHWH/God being present in "glory", have implicitly ascribed human form to him (e.g. Exod 3:1–8; 24:1–18). It seems that in ancient Israel, one could not think of a mode of the divine appearance in any other form than in human form; and whenever YHWH/God appeared in the form of human being, he was understood as having a body. This leads to the question of whether the human bodily form in which

YHWH/God appeared was only assumed, or was, in any way, associated with his inherent being, and this aspect will be discussed below.

7.2.2.3.2 Human Body

The textual study in this dissertation shows that the Hebrew traditions in the Pentateuch believe that YHWH/God appeared in "human bodily form". Contrary to Brueggemann's idea that the concept of an embodied God is absent from the Hebrew Bible, this study finds that almost every time the Hebrew traditions describe YHWH/God, they describe him in association with human (bodily) form. However, one may ask if the Israelite writers understood "human bodily form" of YHWH/God as inherent to his being, or only assumed temporarily in his appearances.

Although strong human traits are associated with the anthropomorphized divine person, it is not clear whether YHWH/God took a fully human (biological) body in any of his appearances or only a kind of disguise of a human being. In some instances, it appears as though he is thought of having a fully human body with flesh and blood. For example, YHWH/God takes a rib out of Adam and makes a woman out of it (Gen 2:21–22) and touches the hip of Jacob that is benumbed (32:25–26), but these actions in themselves do not give scope to think that YHWH's bodily form has (human) flesh and blood. However, YHWH is also understood to have a bodily form which approximates to that of a fully human being, in that YHWH is described as having eaten human food (Gen 18:8). One might tend to think that YHWH took a human body (in a biological sense) with flesh and blood, at least for a short while. But the text gives no scope to think that YHWH was bound by flesh and blood like any other human being (despite the supposition that he ate human food), given that after speaking to Abraham (v. 33), YHWH is believed to have transcended his human body, in which he appeared, and went to heaven (19:24); from this, one may infer that from time to time, YHWH/God appeared in a human body on this earth for a short time, and later he transcended his embodied human form.

In light of the prohibition of making of idols (Deut 4:15–16), some scholars assume that the HB emphasizes on the incorporeality of God. However, in the texts studied in this work, the "form" and "face" are associated not with any idol, but with YHWH/God, who is understood as a living person, who could manifest himself in a concrete "bodily form" and relate himself to humankind. It is difficult to imagine an incorporeal God in the HB; and in light of their creation traditions (Gen 1:1–2:25), it would not be difficult for the ancient Israelite readers to believe that the creator of humankind was capable of assuming a "human body", in order to relate himself to and commune with the people; and the humankind that is created in the "image of God" is capable of recognizing God, when he appears in human form.

However, "image of God" in humankind (Gen 1:26–27) does not seem to mean that it consists of a physical resemblance between creature and creator, as some scholars think. For example, Gunkel assumes that the "image of God" would presuppose that God too has a physical body and that God is like a man. Von Rad suggests that the whole man is created in God's image; he thinks that "Israel conceived even Jahweh himself as having human form"; and that "it cannot be said that Israel regarded God anthropomorphically, but the reverse that she considered man as theomorphic".

However, from Genesis traditions, it is obvious that God did not create man from his own "being" but out of the earth, although נשמת חיים "the breath of life" God breathed into humankind was something that came from himself (Gen 2:7).

Hebrew creation accounts do not seem to give the scope to assume that physical body was intrinsic to God. In light of the texts, which describe the divine appearances of YHWH/God, one can understand that he appeared in a normal human bodily form; and there was never an incident where God is described appearing as a giant or oversized person, as Hendel seems to suggest. While the body in which YHWH/God appears does not seem to be an essential characteristic, it seems that God appears temporarily in a human bodily form in order to communicate with the humankind. This human body seems to be more of a temporary disguise, given that God disappears in a manner unlike human beings.

The Hebrew traditions neither portray YHWH/God as impersonal spirit nor do they explain if a bodily form is inherent to him; but they understand YHWH/God both as transcendent and immanent, in that he "comes down/descends" (ירד: Gen 11:5; Exod 19:20) and "goes up/ascends" (עלה:

17:22); when the Israelites' cry for help goes up (עלה) to him, he comes down (ירד) and rescues them (Exod 2:23–25).

YHWH/God is also seen as describing himself in human language, in that he sees the oppression of "his people" and hears their cry—as though ears (to hear) and eyes (to see) are inherent to his being (Exod 3:4–10). However, one lacks the textual evidence to show whether the "human (bodily) form", which YHWH/God assumed in his appearances, had some association with his inherent being, or whether it was completely separate from his inherent existence. In terms of the true nature of the bodily appearance of YHHW/God, perhaps one has to admit that the secret things belong to YHWH God, but those things which are revealed (והנגלת) belong to the people on this earth, so that they may obey the Law (Deut 29:28).

At the end, it may be said that in ancient Israel, when YHWH/God appeared to different people, even in a flame of fire or glory, he was understood to be physically present in human form (e.g. Exod 3:1–8; 24:1–18). The vivid anthropomorphic language used in depicting YHWH/God is such that one could only envisage him in human-form, whether in real life situations or in dreams and visions. The mode of appearance in the texts, however, is not uniform. The transcendent God becomes immanent by means of self-revelations, and incarnates himself temporarily in human bodily form in order to commune with the people. The Israelite understanding seems to be that whenever YHWH/God appeared to humankind, he was required to assume a human body.

Appendices

APPENDIX I

Contribution of Canonical Context and the Interpretative Results of the Texts Studied

The findings in this dissertation are very different from that of the findings of previous scholars. Previous scholars approached the theme of "seeing the face of YHWH/God" from the perspective of (old) literary and historical criticisms, particularly that of *Religionsgeschichte* and *Traditionsgeschichte*, and located the motif in the ANE religious and secular context. Several of them, primarily on the basis of Exodus 33:20 and Deuteronomy 4:12 and 15, have suggested that the references to "seeing the face of YHWH/God" in the Israelite traditions should be treated as metaphorical/idiomatic or in an abstract sense of "presence", rather than literal ("face") and argued against the corporeality of YHWH/God.

Several of them have equated "seeing the face of YHWH/God" with visiting the temple; and that the expressions פני־יהוה "face of YHWH/God" and לפני יהוה meant having an *Audienz* before the king. As the review of the previous scholarship shows, Baudissin and Nötscher were followed by the subsequent scholars—Johnson, Eichrodt, Reindl, Fowler, Terrien and Hartenstein—both in terms of their approach to the subject and in accepting most of their conclusions. None of these scholars, however, has attempted to discern the reason why the Hebrew writers have described/depicted יהוה/אלהים "YHWH/God" in an association with the noun פנים "face" and with the verb ראה "to see".

However, the approach in this dissertation has yielded different interpretative results in understanding the purpose for which this motif, "seeing the face of YHWH/God", existed and the significance it played in ancient Israel. When the selected texts in the Pentateuch are interpreted within their immediate canonical context and in reference to the previous texts,[1] the findings in this dissertation have been different from the findings of the previous approaches and these findings are briefly discussed below in the same order of the books as studied in chapters 2–6.

I.1 In the Texts in Genesis

Approaching this text from the perspective of "history of religions", Niehaus associates sinaitic characteristics to the divine appearance in Genesis 3:8–10, and accordingly, interprets the "storm wind" לרוח היום as advancing presence of YHWH and קול as "theophanic thunder". Sailhamer, who claims that a close study of the final form sheds light, also interprets Genesis 3:8 in the context of Sinai tradition (Exod 20:18–21) and concludes that the "wind" in Genesis 3:8 resembles the "powerful wind" similar to that of Sinai. However, when this text is interpreted exegetically, within its immediate context, both these above interpretations are challenged, as the text gives no clue for assuming Sinai-like thunder in the garden; and the earlier (backward) traditions/texts helped to understand that YHWH God, being the creator of the humankind (Gen 1:1–2:25), continued his contact with the humankind (2:20–24), and את־קול "voice" is understood as voice of YHWH God, who is believed to be physically present in the garden (3:9–10); and the possibility of Adam and Eve seeing God in a literal sense is assumed.[2]

Since Genesis 12:1–8 begins with an indirect statement "YHWH said to Abram" (12:1), Westermann thinks that there is no divine manifestation, but when studied in its immediate context and in light of the earlier

---

1. Immense care has been taken throughout this dissertation not to make reader response critical statements, rather to interpret the theme "seeing the face of YHWH/God" within the given canonical context of the texts; and it is also assumed that the ancient Israelite readers would have interpreted the texts within the canonical context of the received Text, and not followed their own existing context.
2. Chapter 2, 38–43.

texts, the text shows that the statement "YHWH/God said to" was previously used in association with the divine manifestation (Gen 4:6–14; 7:1, 16; 11:5, 6); and that "YHWH appeared to Abram" (v. 7) signifies that YHWH is believed to be present with Abram and lets himself be seen by him.³

Hamilton argues that there is no visual image in the vision in Genesis 15:1–21, because the text says that it was the "word of YHWH" that came to Abram and Driver thinks that it was simply prophetic intuition. However, this study has shown that there is a clear visualization of YHWH within that vision, in that YHWH introduces himself as אני יהוה "I am YHWH"; Abram addresses him as אדני יהוה "YHWH Lord"; YHWH takes him outside, shows him the stars, confirms his promise (v. 5), and makes the covenant with Abram (v. 18)— all this clarify that "word of YHWH" is YHWH himself and he is understood present with Abram within that vision.⁴

Contrary to Westermann's assumption that there is neither a revelation nor a vision in Genesis 16:7–14, the text insists that Hagar claimed that she saw God, who encountered her at the well. Referring to Exodus 33:20 that has a very different canonical setting, rather than referring to the immediate context, Delitzsch associates ראי with חי (in לחי), חי with Hagar and argues that Hagar was afraid of death for seeing God. However, the immediate context of Genesis text does not give any clue that Hagar expressed any fear of death, nor is there any clue in the earlier texts to associate fear of death with seeing God as such.⁵

Among others, Eichrodt and Fowler treat the expression (standing) "before YHWH" לפני יהוה (עמד) metaphorically or in analogy of gaining an audience with one's superior. However, this study has shown that לפני is used in a literal sense. When YHWH says to Abram, "walk 'before me'" (לְפָנַי) in Genesis 17:1–5, he is believed to be literally present with Abram (cf. v. 22); and in Genesis 18, when Abraham is said to have eaten normal food (vv. 1–8), when he is said to be "standing before YHWH"

---

3. Ibid., 45–47.
4. Ibid., 49–51.
5. Ibid., 53–55.

(vv. 16–22), YHWH is understood to be with Abraham in the guise of a human person in a literal sense.[6]

From the perspective of form-critical approach, Gunkel and Westermann assume that "the man" in Genesis 32:25–32 was a demon; however, the canonical context of the text proves Gunkel's assumption to be groundless; and the earlier texts showed that the encounters between God and humans took place in a variety of ways in which YHWH/God appeared in human form (e.g. 16:7–14; 18:2–8, 22; cf. Exod 4:24). The man in Genesis 32:25–32 is understood as God himself in human disguise. Contrary to Johnson's view that the expression פנים אל־פנים "face to face" is used with a weakening of its literal meaning"[7] and Terrien's suggestion that it should not be taken referring literally to visual perception,[8] the Hebrew tradition/text insist that the literal meaning in the expression "face to face" is not weakened, rather Jacob's hip was touched and benumbed by God literally, because of which Jacob walked limping. Jacob's claim that he saw God פנים אל־פנים "face to face" (v. 31 cf. 33:10) involves visual perception. Finally, from the literary perspective, Wessner claims that his "careful reading" of Genesis 32:25–32 shows that איש (the man) is only a man sent to Jacob on behalf of God, but the text echoes Jacob's voice that the man he saw that night was God himself.[9]

I.2 In the Texts in Exodus

Scholars such as Buber do not believe that YHWH/God was physically present in the fiery bush (Exod 3:1–12). However, in this study, the textual evidence, supported by earlier texts, helped to interpret the divine person in the bush in terms of corporeality. Since YHWH is said to have come down (v. 8) and spoke with Moses, he is believed to be present in the bush; and Moses sees him.[10]

---

6. Ibid., 57–60; 61–63.
7. Chapters 1, 8 and 3, 85.
8. Chapter 1, 11.
9. Chapter 3, 75–91.
10. Chapter 4, 100–103.

Contribution of Canonical Context and the Interpretative Results   249

Interpreting Exodus 24:10–11 in light of 33:20–23 (canonically later text), Durham comments that in Exodus 24:1–18 what Moses and others actually saw was not the appearance of God;[11] Delitzsch argues that it was only a "vision" (because of חזה in v. 11) of God on the mountain;[12] However, this study shows that the explicit statement, that they saw God (vv. 10–11), implies that God was physically present on the mountain and that the people saw him in a literal sense;[13] the verb חזה is used in the same sense as that of ראה;[14] and the terms such as "feet" (24:10) and hand (v. 11) suggest that it was not a vision, but God was understood physically present on the mountain in human form.

In Exodus 33:12–23, several scholars assume a contradiction between verses 14: "my 'face' shall go" (פני ילכו) and 20: "you will not be able to see 'my face'; for no one shall see me, and live" (לא תוכל לראת את־פני כי לא־יראני האדם וחי); assuming that verse 20 negates verse 14, they argue for the non-corporeality of YHWH/God.[15] However, when this text is interpreted within the immediate context of 33:11 and in light of chapters 32–34, and placed it in the context of the divine self-revelations, it shows that the verb ראה with the פנים "face" of YHWH signifies the physicality of YHWH/God; פנים "face" in verse 14 and פנים "face" in verse 20 do not convey contradiction, but rather they reflect two different aspects of the self-revelation of YHWH. YHWH's revelation in verse 18 is by means of פנים "face" and in verse 20 by means of כבוד "glory"; when YHWH tells Moses that "his face would go" (vv. 14, 15, 17), he means that he would go with all the people; but when Moses requests YHWH to let his glory be seen (18, 20), it is assumed that he means that all the people should be given a chance to see YHWH's glory, given that Moses constantly refers to the people in solidarity with and for them (32:32; 33:12, 13, 15, 16; 34:9). If YHWH were to make his glory manifest at that place to Moses, the people would not be able to see his glory directly, because of their sin. It is found that the negation in verse 20

---

11. Ibid., 109–110.
12. Ibid., 110.
13. Ibid., 111–115.
14. See chapter 1, 4–5.
15. Chapter 5, 131–196.

לא תוכל לראת את־פני כי לא־יראני האדם וחי cannot be treated categorical, because the aspect of seeing the "face of YHWH/God" (even "face to face") was dominant in several earlier texts, which understood that YHWH/God appeared to different people (including to Moses), who were believed to have seen YHWH/God and even stayed with him for several days.[16] In addition to these, later on, YHWH reveals himself in glory to Moses on the mountain (34:5–34), where Moses' face shone as a consequence of his direct exposure to the glory of YHWH on the mountain (34:29); and YHWH's glory is seen by all the people as reflected in Moses' face (vv. 30–32).

Contrary to scholarly arguments that YHWH's פנים אל־פנים "face to face" speech with Moses in the tent (v. 11) should be treated as metaphorical or as an idiom of intimacy, this study discerned that YHWH was physically present with Moses in the tent; and it is found that verse 11 is not in conflict with 33:20, rather it clarifies the tension in 33:20–23.[17] Since YHWH is believed physically present with Moses both in the tent and on the mountain, it is discerned that Exodus 33:20 does not contradict verse 14 and that YHWH revealed himself to Moses on the mountain by means of his פנים "face" and כבוד "glory" in "human form" (33:7–34:1–8; 29–35). In light of this, scholarly arguments that Deuteronomy 4:12, 15 disapproves the corporeality of YHWH/God are found inappropriate, and Deuteronomy 5:4 reiterates that YHWH spoke with the people "face to face" (פנים בפנים) from the midst of the fire on the mountain (Exod 20:19–21; 24:12–17) where YHWH/God was believed to be physically present,[18] and, Exodus 33:20 does not disapprove the corporeality of God either. There is no textual evidence to establish that "'seeing' the divine face" resulted in the death of anyone in Exodus 32–34.

---

16. Gen 16:1–6; 32:25–32; Exod 24:1–18.
17. Chapter 5, 188–189.
18. Chapter 1, 21–26.

I.3 In the Text in Numbers 6:22–27

Wenham, Olson and Riggans treat the expression "may YHWH cause his face to shine" (Num 6:25) as a metaphorical expression of likening God to light or to the dawn; for Eichrodt "shining/lifting up" of YHWH' face (vv. 25–26) are only metaphorical expressions and imply no visible form; and Hartenstein sees a solar connection in terms of YHWH's kingship.[19] However, when this text is studied in light of the earlier texts and placed it in the context of the self-revelations of YHWH/God in the tabernacle, it is found that פנים "face" in יאר יהוה פניו and ישא יהוה פניו (vv. 25–26) is to be associated with YHWH/God, who is understood to be physically present in his כבוד "glory" in the tabernacle and visible to the people in the context of worship.

It is observed that because YHWH is believed to be present inside the tabernacle/tent, offering of sacrifices and sprinkling of blood take place לפני יהוה "before YHWH" (Lev 1:5, 11; 4:17–18; 9:2, 15–22) in a literal sense; and this understanding is supported by an earlier tradition in Exodus which understood YHWH to be present (dwelt) on the mountain when Moses sprinkled the blood on the altar (Exod 24:1–10).[20] And when it is said that the fire came, either to consume the sacrifices or to consume the disobedient Nadab and Abihu, it is understood that "fire" came (מלפני יהוה) from YHWH himself, since he is believed to be present (dwelt) inside the tabernacle in an anthropomorphic form.

It is observed that by introducing Numbers 6:22–27: "YHWH spoke to Moses, saying, 'Speak to Aaron and his sons' . . ." (22–23), the writer associates this text with the direct revelation of YHWH/God. Since the verbs אור "to shine" and נשא "to lift" in association with פנים "face" of YHWH (פניו) are used only here in (vv. 25–26) the Pentateuch, and that YHWH himself is projected as the subject of יאר, YHWH is believed to be present above the place of the atonement, which is described as an elevated place in the tabernacle (Lev 9:6–22; 16:2; cf. Exod 25:8, 22). In light of this, an assumption is made that these expressions in verses 25 (יאר יהוה פניו) and

---

19. Chapter 6, 194, 221.
20. Ibid., 198–199.

26 (ישא יהוה פניו) are to be associated with the self-revelations of YHWH in the tabernacle/tent from where YHWH would shine upon and lift up/turn his face toward the worshiping people.

Contrary to the scholarly arguments that the expressions in verses 25–26 are metaphorical, this study has shown that "shining and lifting" of YHWH's face involve concrete ideas; and solar connections or kingship ideas are not detected in this text, rather, these expressions are directly associated with the revealed anthropomorphic person of YHWH, who came to meet with the people at the tabernacle. There is no textual evidence that anyone dies or fears death for seeing the face of YHWH/God in glory, rather, when they see him in his glory, they joyfully worship him (Lev 9:23–24).

APPENDIX II

Relevance, Usefulness and Future Scope of this Dissertation

II.1 Relevance and Usefulness for Other Fields of Research

1. With regards to the question of relevance of the biblical texts/themes to the present day readers of the Pentateuch,[1] it is often said that the ancient readers of the texts and the modern readers of the Bible are "separated by an enormous cultural gap".[2] However, even within ancient Israel, there were several (subsequent) generations of people who believed God as the creator and that he revealed himself to their fathers. If one believes that the HB contained the revealed teachings of God (of their fathers), it may continue to be the book of authoritative teachings, as M. Fishbane suggests.[3]

2. It will hopefully help those (teachers/interpreters) who wish to present the biblical theme of "seeing the face of YHWH/God" to the present generation of readers. Clines expresses that in a postmodern world interpretations of the biblical text are far more problematic activities than a few decades ago.[4] Those who have been engaged in interpreting the canonical

---

1. For the importance of making the biblical text relevant to present day readers, see D. Stuart, *Old Testament Exegesis* (Louisville: Westminster John Knox Press, 2001), 1.
2. See J. H. Hayes and C. R. Holladay, *Biblical Exegesis* (London: SCM Press, 1999), 15.
3. See M. Fishbane, *Judaism: Revelation and Traditions* (New York: Harper San Francisco, 1987), 26.
4. Clines, *Theme*, 131–133.

text of the ancient past to the present day readers or listeners would realize that this task has not been easy. However, if one takes the creation traditions of the HB seriously and communicates to the readers that this creator reveals himself to the humankind,[5] this theme might become relevant for all generations of humankind. The understanding of God as the creator and redeemer, and the sin that brought a separation between the creator and the created may stand above the generation gap.[6]

3. It is anticipated that this study will contribute to discussions:

   a) of self-revelation of God in the NT, where "face" (Matt 17:2) and "glory" (2 Cor 4:6) are used in association with Christ.
   b) of Old Testament theology specifically and biblical theology generally by providing a textually grounded reference point for discussions of the theological significance of the motif of "seeing the face of God", which may function as a connecting theme between the HB and the NT.
   c) at a more practical level, this study will enhance the understanding of the self-revelations of God in Christian worship.
   d) and allow for comparisons with other religious traditions, which would form dialogue on the "divine presence" in a pluralistic religious context,[7] acknowledging that the humankind that has been created in the image of God has a capacity of having some truth in their thinking of God, and based upon that thinking, bridges of communication may be built.[8]

---

5. Cf. R. Rendtorff, "Creation and Redemption in the Torah", 311–320. In L. G. Perdue, *The Blackwell Companion to the Hebrew Bible*. (Oxford: Blackwell, 2001), 316.

6. Cf. S. J. Grenz, *Theology for the Community of God* (Grand Rapids: Eerdmans, 2000), 99, 98–212; S. J. Grenz, and R. E. Olson, *20th Century Theology: God and the World in a Transitional Age.* (Downers Grove: Intervarsity Press, 1992), 310.

7. Cf. J. Runzo, "Religious Pluralism". In P. Copan, and C. Meister, eds. *Philosophy of Religion* (Oxford: Blackwell, 2008), 52.

8. For a cross-cultural understanding of worship in association with "faces" see D. Eck, *Darshan, Seeing the Divine Image in India* (Chambersberg: Anima Books, 1985); Propp, *Exodus*, 297. See also C. D. Stanley, *The Hebrew Bible: A Comparative Approach* (Minneapolis: Fortress Press, 2010), for a comparative approach within the contemporary religious beliefs.

II.2 Scope for Future Research

This study will provide a reference point for an exploration of the association of the verb ראה "to see" with the noun פנים "face" of YHWH/God in the Psalms. As said earlier, Clements reflects that the dwelling of YHWH/God in the temple was "justified and explained on the basis of his appearing there in a theophany".[9] The temple worship seems to be the continuity of the tabernacle worship (as described in Leviticus-Numbers) in terms of the divine self-revelations. In line with his promise that he would appear in the cloud above the mercy seat, which is upon the ark (Exod 25:22; 40:21; Lev 16:2), YHWH appears and when Moses goes into the tent of meeting to speak with YHWH, he hears the voice of YHWH speaking to him from above the mercy seat that is on the ark of the testimony, from between the two cherubim (Num 7:89); this signifies that YHWH was understood corporeally present above the place of atonement or mercy seat.

Even in the temple, the ark still plays a significant role, and the pattern of the appearance of YHWH's glory in the Psalms is similar to the pattern found in Exodus-Numbers; when the sacrifices are made, the priests bring the ark of the covenant of YHWH into the inner sanctuary of the temple (1 Kgs 8:4–6; cf. Exod 40:35; Lev 9:23–24); and when the ark (with the two tablets in it: v. 9) is taken to the temple, the temple is filled with כבוד־יהוה "the glory of YHWH" (vv. 10–11); YHWH/God is addressed as יהוה אלהי אבתינו "YHWH God of our fathers", and God's dwelling place is understood to be in heaven (1 Kgs 8:49; 2 Chr 20:6); and YHWH's presence is understood to be between the cherubim (Exod 25:22; 1 Kgs 8:6; Pss 80:1; 99:1)— all this seems to indicate that the self-revelations of YHWH/God continued to take place in the temple worship, and perhaps he was understood to be physically present during the worship in the temple.

Given that "'seeing' the 'face' of God" played a significant role among the ancient Israel (as discussed throughout this dissertation), it is possible that the subsequent generations of the Israelites believed that God revealed himself also in the context of temple worship, and that "seeing the face of YHWH/God" is associated with the worship in the Jerusalem

---

9. Chapter 6, 223.

Temple, as the book of Psalms seem to indicate.[10] The psalmist expresses: את־פניך יהוה אבקש "your face, YHWH, I will seek" (Ps 27:8); although the verb בקש is used here, rather than the verb ראה, it is still YHWH who would be sought; and the psalmist's prayer: והאר פניך "cause your face to shine" (Ps 80:4, 8, 20) reflects the worship at the tabernacle (Num 6:25). It was in the belief that God would reveal himself in the temple that people desired to go there with a thirst to see the face of God (Ps 42:3 אראה פני אלהים).

However, some scholars, for example, J. Barton understands that "in early times there may have been an image of YHWH in the temple", and that "later writers edited it out of the text, and changed the phrase 'to see God' into 'appear before (i.e. be seen by) God'".[11] While there is all reason to believe that the self-revelations of YHWH/God had taken place even in the temple, this aspect demands further research in the book of Psalms.

II.3 A Closing Reflection

Previous critical scholarship has not located the Israelite concept of "seeing the face of YHWH/God" within the canonical context of the Hebrew traditions, because of which the noun פנים "face" has not been associated with YHWH/God, whom the Hebrew writers seem to have believed and described as appearing in "human form". As noted throughout this dissertation, even those scholars, who have focussed on the canonical texts (in the final form) have not located the motif of seeing the face of YHWH/God in the context of "the divine self-revelations", but argued for the invisibility/incorporeality of YHWH/God (Exod 33:20, Deut 4:12, 15), rather than taking the immediate canonical context seriously.

When the immediate canonical context is taken seriously in this dissertation, and the motif of "seeing the face of YHWH/God" is located in the context of the divine self-revelations, it helped to draw different conclusions. It is found that any assumption that the concept of an embodied

---

10. See chapter 1, fn. 29.

11. J. Barton expressed this view, when this researcher contacted him on 20 June 2008; Cf. Niehr, "Cult Statue", 91.

God is absent from the HB is not acceptable to the Hebrew traditions; on the contrary, it is observed that whenever God revealed himself to people, he was understood to have appeared in a human form in association with a "body" that was visible to the human eye; and the suggestions, that the expressions פני־יהוה "face of YHWH", פנים אל־פנים "face to face", and לפני יהוה "before YHWH" are to be treated metaphorically, are found inappropriate to the texts studied, as discussed throughout this dissertation. And on the contrary, this study has shown that the noun פנים "face" occurs in association with YHWH/God, whom the Israelite/Hebrew traditions understood as appearing in human form.

The repeated use of פנים "face", in association with the living person of YHWH/God", who revealed himself in a "human form", is a proof that the motif of "face of YHWH/God" had its background in the self-revelations of YHWH/God, and the association of the verb ראה "to see" with the "face of YHWH/God" signifies that he appeared in a "human form" in order to relate himself with humankind. It is more convincing to believe, than not to, that the appearances of YHWH/God were understood to have taken place in a literal/real sense and that they involved physicality and visibility; and all the divine appearances in the Pentateuch are understood to be in human form. There is no textual evidence to establish that "seeing the face of YHWH/God" resulted in the death of anyone in the Pentateuch.

The textual evidence stands in contradiction with the scholarly arguments that the concept of "face of YHWH/God" was influenced from the idol worship in the ANE, since the Hebrew traditions associate פנים "face" with YHWH/God", even in the context where calf-worship was treated as great sin;[12] conversely, the comparison of the motif of "seeing YHWH/God" with "seeing the face of the king" for an audience is found inappropriate, since Hebrew traditions believe that the noun פנים "face" is associated with YHWH/God, who took the initiative to reveal himself and to meet and communicate with different people.[13]

It is unthinkable that Israelites would have imagined their God/YHWH to be non-corporeal or invisible. The readers of that day would have had no difficulty in believing in the physical manifestation of God, since their

---

12. Chapter 5, 122–125.
13. Chapters 2, 63; 3, 93; 4, 113, 117; 5, 143, 184, 190–191; 6, 197.

traditions believed God as the creator of humankind and also believed that he maintained a contact and a relationship with humankind by means of self-revelations.

Bibliography

Aalen, S. "אור". *TDOT*. Vol. 1. Eds. G. J. Botterweck and H. Ringgren. Grand Rapids: Eerdmans, 1974: 147–167.

Aaron, D. H. תנייך *Biblical Ambiguities: Metaphor, Semantics and Divine Imagery*. Leiden: Brill, 2001.

———. "Shedding Light on God's Body in Rabbinic Midrashim: Reflections on the Theory of a Luminous Adam." *HTR* 90 (1997): 299–314.

Ackroyd, P. R. and B. Lindars, eds. "Meaning and Exegesis". *Words and Meanings*. Cambridge: Cambridge University Press, 1968.

Albrektson, B. "On the Syntax of אהיה אשר אהיה". *Words and Meanings*. Eds. P. R. Ackroyd and B. Lindars. Cambridge: Cambridge University Press, 1968.

Albertz, R. *The History of Israelite Religion in the Old Testament Period*. Vol. 1. London: SCM Press, 1994.

Albright, W. F. *From the Stone Age to Christianity*. New York: Doubleday, 1957.

———. "The Names Israel and 'Judah' with an Excursus on the Etymology of Tôdâh and Tôrâh". *JBL* 46 (1927): 154–168.

Allen, R. B. *Genesis–Numbers*. *EBC*. Gen. ed. F. E. Gaebelein. Grand Rapids: Zondervan, 1990.

Alexander, T. D. *From Paradise to the Promised Land*. Carlisle: Paternoster Press, 1995.

Alt, A. "The God of the Fathers". *Essays on Old Testament History and Religion*. Oxford: Blackwell, 1966.

Alter, R. *The Art of Biblical Narrative*. London: Allen & Unwin, 1981.

———. *Genesis: Translation and Commentary*. New York: Norton, 1996.

Andersen, F. I. *The Sentence in Biblical Hebrew*. The Hague: Mouton Publishers, 1980.

———. "2 (Slavonic Apocalypse of) Enoch". *The Old Testament Pseudepigrapha*. Vol. 1. Ed. J. H. Charlesworth. New York: Doubleday, 1985.

Anderson, B. W. *Contours of Old Testament Theology*. Minneapolis: Fortress Press, 1999.

Anderson, G. W. "'Sicut cervus': Evidence in the Psalter of Private Devotion in Ancient Israel." *VT* 30 (1980): 388–397.

Ashby, G. *Exodus. Go Out and Meet God*. ITC. Grand Rapids: Eerdmans, 1998.

Ashley, T. R. *The Book of Numbers*. NICOT. Ed. R. K. Harrison. Grand Rapids: Eerdmans, 1993.

'Assāf, A. A. *Der Tempel von 'Ain Dārā*. Mainz am Rhein: Verlag Philip von Zabern, 1990.

Averbeck, R. E. "שׁלם". *NIDOTTE*. Vol. 4. Gen. ed. W. A. VanGerman. Carlisle: Paternoster Press, 1996: 130–142.

Babut, J. M. *Idiomatic Expressions of the Hebrew Bible*. N. Richland Hills: Bibal Press, 1999.

Baden, J. S. "Hithpael and Niphal in Biblical Hebrew: Semantic and Morphological Overlap". *VT* 60 (2010): 33–44.

Baker, D. W. *Idiomatic Expressions in Hebrew and Akkadian Relating to the Head*. M. Phil. diss., University of London, 1976.

Baker, W. R. "Did the Glory of Moses' Face Fade? A Re-examination of καταργέω in 2 Corinthians 3:7–18." *BBR* 10 (2000): 1–15.

Baldwin, J. *The Message of Genesis 12–50*. BST. Leicester: Intervarsity Press, 1986.

Balentine, S. E. *The Hidden God: The Hiding of the Face of God in the Old Testament*. Oxford: Oxford University Press, 1979.

———. *Prayer in the Hebrew Bible*. Minneapolis: Fortress Press, 1993.

———. *Leviticus*. Interpretation. Louisville: John Knox Press, 2002.

Bandstra, B. *Genesis 1–11. A Handbook on the Hebrew Text*. Waco: Baylor University Press, 2008.

Barkay, G. "The Priestly Benediction on the Ketef Hinnom Plaques." *Cathedra* 52 (1989): 37–76.

_____, et al. "The Challenges of Ketef Hinnom." *NEA* 66 (2003): 161–171.

Barnhouse, D. G. *Genesis: A Devotional Exposition*. Grand Rapids: Zondervan, 1971.

Barr, J. "Theophany and Anthropomorphism in the Old Testament". VTS, 7 (1959): 31–38.

———. *The Semantics of Biblical Language*. Oxford: Oxford University Press, 1961.

———. "Revelation". *DB*. Ed. J. Hastings. Edinburgh: T. & T. Clark, 1963: 847–849.

———. *Holy Scripture: Canon, Authority, Criticism*. Oxford: Clarendon Press, 1983.

———. *The Concept of Biblical Theology: An Old Testament Perspective*. London: SCM Press, 1999.
Barth, C. *God with Us*. Grand Rapids: Eerdmans, 1991.
Barth, K. *The Doctrine of Creation*. CD. Vol. 3. Edinburgh: T. & T. Clark, 1958.
Barthes, R. *Structural Analysis and Biblical Exegesis*. Pittsburgh: Pickwick Press, 1974.
———. *Image-Music-Text*. Oxford: Oxford University Press, 1982.
Barton, J. *Reading the Old Testament*. Philadelphia: Westminster Press, 1997.
Baruch, A. L. *Numbers 1–20*. AB. New York: Double Day, 1993.
Baudissin, W. W. G. "'Gott schauen' in der alttestamentlichen Religion". In F. Nötscher, *Das Angesicht Gottes schauen: nach biblischer und Babylonischer Auffassung*. Darmstadt: Wissenschaftliche Buchgesellschaft, 1969: 193–261. Reprint from *Archiv für Religionswissenschaft* 18 (1915): 173–239.
Bellinger. Jr. W. H. *Leviticus, Numbers*. NIBC. Ed. Peabody: Hendrickson Publishers, 2001.
Beyerlin, W., ed. *Near Eastern Religious Texts Relating to the Old Testament*. Philadelphia: Westminster Press, 1978.
Billings, R. M. "The Problem of the Divine Presence: Source-critical Suggestions for the Analysis of Exodus 33:12–23". *VT* 54 (2004): 427–444.
Botterweck, G. J. "ידע". *TDOT*. Vol. 5. Eds. G.J. Botterweck and H. Ringgren. Grand Rapids: Eerdmans, 1986: 448–481.
Brenton, Sir L. C. L. *The Septuagint with Apocrypha, Greek and English*. Grand Rapids: Zondervan, 1851.
Brown, F., S. R. Driver and C. A. Briggs, eds. *HELOT*. Oxford: Clarendon Press, 2005.
Brown, M. L. "ברך". *NIDOTTE*. Vol. 1. Gen. ed. W. A. VanGemeran. Carlisle: Paternoster Press, 1996: 757–767.
Brown, R. *The Message of Numbers*. BST. Ed. A. Motyer. Leicester: Intervarsity Press, 2002.
Brown, W. P. *The Ethos of the Cosmos*. Grand Rapids: Eerdmans, 1999.
———. *Seeing the Psalms*. London: Westminster John Knox Press, 2002.
Brotzman, E. R. *Old Testament Textual Criticism*. Grand Rapids: Eerdmans, 1996.
Brueggemann, W. "Genesis 17:1–22." *Int* 45 (1991): 55–59.
———. *Theology of the Old Testament*. Minneapolis: Fortress Press, 1997.
———. *Reverberations of Faith*. Louisville: Westminster John Knox Press, 2002.
———. "The Travail of Pardon: Reflections on slh." *A God So Near*, B. A. Strawn, and N. R. Brown, eds. Winona Lake, Indiana: Eisenbrauns, 2003.

———. *Old Testament theology*. Nashville: Abingdon Press, 2008.
Budd, P. J. *Numbers*. WBC. Ed. D. A. Hubbard. Waco: Word Books, 1984.
Burrows, M. *An Outline of Biblical Theology*. Philadelphia: Westminster Press, 1946.
Cairns, I. *Word and Presence: Deuteronomy*. ITC. Grand Rapids: Eerdmans, 1992.
Caird, G. B. *The Language and Imagery of the Bible*. London: Duckworth, 1980.
Campbell, A. F., and M. A. O'Brien. *Sources of the Pentateuch: Texts, Introductions, Annotations*. Minneapolis: Fortress Press, 1993.
Carpenter, E. "שמר". *NIDOTTE*. Vol. 4. Gen. ed. W. A. VanGemeran. Carlisle: Paternoster Press, 1997: 182–183.
Cassuto, U. *The Documentary Hypothesis*. Jerusalem: The Magnes Press, 1961.
———. *Commentary on the Book of Genesis*. Jerusalem: Magnes Press, 1961.
———. *Commentary on the Book of Exodus*. Jerusalem: Magnes Press, 1983.
Childs, B. S. *Memory and Tradition in Israel*. London: SCM Press, 1962.
———. *Biblical Theology in Crisis*. Philadelphia: Westminster Press, 1970.
———. *Introduction to the Old Testament as Scripture*. London: SCM Press, 1979.
———. *The Book of Exodus: A Critical, Theological Commentary*. OTL. Louisville: John Knox Press, 2004.
Chisholm, Jr. R. B. "Theophany". *NDBT*. Eds. T. D. Alexander and B. S. Rosner. Leicester: Intervarsity Press, 2000: 815–816.
Clements, R. E. *Exodus*. CBC. Cambridge: Cambridge University Press, 1972.
———. *God and Temple*. Oxford: Basil Blackwell, 1965.
———. *Old Testament Theology*. London: Marshall, Morgan & Scott, 1978.
Clines, D. J. A. "The Image of God in Man." *TB* 19 (1968): 53–103.
———. ed. *The Dictionary of Classical Hebrew*. Sheffield Academic Press: Sheffield, 1998.
———. *The Theme of the Pentateuch*. JSOTS. Sheffield: Sheffield Academic Press, (1978) 2001.
Cole, R. A. *Exodus*. TOTC. London: Intervarsity Press, 1973.
———. *Numbers*. NAC. Nashville: Broadman & Holman, 2000.
Cooper, A. M., and B. R. Goldstein. "At the Entrance to the Tent: More Cultic Resonances in Biblical Narrative." *JBL* 116 (1997): 201–215.
Coppes, L. J. "קול". *TWOT*. Vol. 2. Ed. R. L. Harris. Chicago: Moody, 1980: 792–793.
Cornelius, I. "The Many Faces of God: Divine Images and Symbols in Ancient Near Eastern Religions". *The Image and the Book*. Ed. K. van der Toorn. CBET. Leuven: Peeters, 1997.

Cross, F. M. *Canaanite Myth and Hebrew Epic: Essays in the History of the Religion of Israel*. Cambridge: Harvard University Press, 1973.

———. "Yahweh and the God of Patriarchs". *HTR* 55 (1962): 256–257.

Culver, D. "חזה". *TWOT*. Vol. 1. Ed. R. L. Harris. Chicago: Moody, 1980: 274–275.

———. "ראה". *TWOT*. Vol. 1. Ed. R. L. Harris. Chicago: Moody, 1980: 823–825.

Cummins, S. A. "The Theological Interpretation of Scripture: Recent Contributions by Stephen E. Fowl, Christopher R. Seitz, and Francis Watson". *CBR* 2 (2004): 179–196.

Cunningham, V. "Roland Barthes (1915–1980): Introduction. Barthes Text: Wrestling with the Angel: Textual Analysis of Genesis 32:23–32". *The Postmodern God*. Ed. G. Ward. Oxford: Blackwell Publishing, 2005.

Danell, G. A. *The Name Israel in the Old Testament*. Uppsala: n.p. 1946.

Davidson, B., ed. *The Analytical Hebrew and Chaldee Lexicon*. New York: Harper & Brothers, n.d.

Davies, E. W. *Numbers*. NCBCS. Ed. London: Marshal Pickering, 1995.

Davies, G. I. "A Note on the Etymology of histahawah." *VT* 29 (1979): 493–495.

Davies, P. R. "The Hebrew Canon and the Origins of Judaism". In *The Historian and the Bible*. Eds. P. R. Davies and D. V. Edelman. T. & T. Clark. London, 2010.

Davis, E. F. *Getting Involved with God*. Cambridge: Cowley Publications, 2001.

Dearman, J. A. "Theophany, Anthropomorphism, and the Imago Dei: Some Observations about the Incarnation in the Light of the Old Testament". Oxfordscholarship Online: *The Incarnation* (2002): 31–35.

De Moor, J. C. *The Rise of Yahwism*. Leuven: Leuven University Press, 1997.

De Vaux, R. *The Early History of Israel*. London: Longman & Todd, 1978.

Dillmann, A. *Genesis*. Vol. 1. Edinburgh: T. & T. Clark, 1897.

Douglas, M. *In the Wilderness: The Doctrine of Defilement in the Book of Numbers*. Sheffield: Sheffield Academic Press, 1993.

Doyle, R., *Faces of Gods: Baal, Asherah and Molek and Studies of the Hebrew Scriptures*. PhD diss., University of Sheffield, 1979.

Dozeman, T. B. *The Book of Numbers. NIB*. Vol 2. Ed. L. E. Keck, Nashville: Abingdon Press, 1998: 3–268.

———. "Masking Moses and Mosaic Authority in Torah". *JBL* 119 (2000): 21–45.

Driver, G. R. *The Book of Exodus*. Cambridge: Cambridge University Press, 1953.

———. *The Book of Genesis*. London: Methuen & Co, 1954.

———. *Treatise on the Use of Tenses in Hebrew and Some Other Syntactical Questions*. Oxford: Oxford University Press, 1998.

Duguid, I. M. *Living in the Gap Between Promise and Reality*. New Jersey: P & R Publishing Company, 1999.

———. *Numbers: God's Presence in the Wilderness*. PW. Gen. ed. R. Kent Hughes. Wheaton: Crossway Books, 2006.

Dumbrell, W. J. "The Prospect of Unconditionality in the Sinaitic Covenant". A. Gileadi, *ed. Israel's Apostasy and Restoration. Essays in Honour of R. K. Harrison*. Grand Rapids: Baker Books, 1988.

Durham, J. I. *Exodus*. WBC. Ed. D. A. Hubbard. Waco: Word Books, 1987.

Dyrness, W. *Themes in Old Testament Theology*. Carlisle: Paternoster Press, 1977.

Eck, D. *Darshan*. Chambersberg: Animal Books, 1985.

Eichrodt, W. "Revelation and Responsibility." *Int* 4 (1949): 386–399.

———. *Man in the Old Testament*. London: SCM Press, 1959.

———. *Theology of the Old Testament*. Vol. 1. OTL. London: SCM Press, 1964.

Elliger, K. "Das JakobsKampf am Jabbok." *ZTK* 48 (1951): 1–31.

———, and W. Rudolph, eds. *Biblia Hebraica Stuttgartensia*. Stuttgart: Deutsche Bibelgesellschaft, 1990.

Emerton, J. A. "Etymology of *histahawah*". *OS* 20 (1977): 41–55.

Engnell, I. *Critical Essays on the Old Testament*. Ed. J. T. Willis. London: SPCK, 1970.

Erdman, C. R. *The Pentateuch: An Exposition*. Grand Rapids: Baker Book House, 1987. Etheridge, J. W. *The Targums of Onkelos and Jonathan Ben Uzziel. Pentateuch*. London: Longman, 1862.

Exell, J. S. *Exodus: A Commentary*. Grand Rapids: Baker Book House, 1996.

Fee, G. D. *God's Empowering Presence*. Peabody: Hendrickson Publishers, 1994.

Fishbane, M. "Form and Reformulation of the Biblical Priestly Blessing." *JAOS* 103 (1983): 115–121.

———. *Biblical Interpretation in Israel*. Oxford: Clarendon Press, 1985.

———. *Judaism: Revelation and Traditions*. New York: Harper San Francisco, 1987.

———. "Arm of the Lord: Biblical Myth, Rabbinic Midrash, and the Mystery of History". *Language, Theology and the Bible*. Eds. S. E. Balentine and J. Barton. Oxford: Clarendon Press, 1994.

Ford, D. *Self and Salvation*. Cambridge: Cambridge University Press, 1999.

Ford, W. A. *God, Pharaoh and Moses*. Bletchley: Paternoster, 2006.

Fowler, M. D. "The Meaning of lipnê YHWH in the Old Testament." *ZAW* 99 (1987): 384–390.

Fretheim, T. E. *The Suffering of God.* Philadelphia: Fortress Press, 1984.

———. *Exodus.* Interpretation. Louisville: John Knox Press, 1991.

———. "*Numbers*". *OBC.* Eds. J. Barton and J. Muddiman. Oxford: Oxford University Press, 2001.

———. *God and World in the Old Testament.* Nashville: Abingdon Press, 2005.

Frolov, S. "The Other Side of the Jabbok: Genesis 32 as a Fiasco of Patriarchy." *JSOT* 91 (2000): 41–59.

Fuhs, H. F. "ראה". *TDOT.* Vol. 13. Eds. G. J. Botterweck and H. Ringgren. Grand Rapids: Eerdmans, 2004: 208–242.

Gane, R. *Leviticus, Numbers. The NIV Application Commentary.* Grand Rapids: Zondervan, 2004.

Gesenius, H. W. F. *HCLOT.* Grand Rapids: Baker Book House, 1979.

Gibson, J. C. L. *Canaanite Myths and Legends.* London: T. & T. Clark, 2004.

Gileadi, A., ed. *Israel's Apostasy and Restoration.* Grand Rapids: Baker Book House, 1988.

Gilchrist, P. R. "יכל" *TWOT.* Vol. 1. Ed. R. L. Harris. Chicago: Moody, 1980: 377–378.

Goldingay, J. *Approaches to Old Testament Interpretation.* London: Intervarsity Press, 1981.

———. *Theological Diversity and the Authority of the Old Testament.* Grand Rapids: Eerdmans, 1995.

Gordon, R. P. *1 & 2 Samuel.* Exeter: The Paternoster Press, 1986.

———. *Hebrew Bible and Ancient Versions.* SOTSM. Aldershot: Ashgate, 2006.

Gray, G. B. *Numbers.* ICC. Edinburgh: T. & T. Clark, 1956.

Grenz, S. J. and R. E. Olson, *20th Century Theology: God and the World in a Transitional Age.* Downers Grove: Intervarsity Press, 1992.

———, and R. E. Olson. *Who Needs Theology?* Leicester: Intervarsity Press, 1996.

———. *Theology for the Community of God.* Grand Rapids: Eerdmans, 2000.

———. *Social God and the Relational Self.* Louisville: Westminster John Knox Press, 2001.

Greenspahn, F. E. "Syncretism and the Idolatry in the Bible". *VT* 54 (2004): 480–494.

Gressmann, H. *Mose und seine Zeit.* Göttingen: Vandenhoeck & Ruprecht, 1913.

Gruber, M. I. "The Many Faces of Hebrew נשא פנים 'lift up the face.'" *ZAW* 95 (1983): 252–260.

Gruenwald, I. "God the 'Stone/Rock': Myth, Idolatry, and Cultic Fetishism in Ancient Israel." *JR* 76 (1996): 428–449.

Gunkel, H. *What Remains of the Old Testament*. London: Unwin Brothers, 1928.

———. *The Legends of Genesis*. New York: Schocken Books, 1964.

———. *The Folktale in the Old Testament*. England: Sheffield Academic Press, 1987.

———. *Genesis: A Commentary*. Macon: Mercer University Press, 1997.

Gutmann, J. "The 'Second Commandment' and the Image in Judaism." *HUCA* 32 (1961): 161–174.

Hafemann, S. J. and P. R. House. *Central Themes in Biblical Theology*. Grand Rapids: Baker Academic, 2007.

Hamilton, V. P. *Handbook on the Pentateuch*. Grand Rapids: Baker Book House, 1982.

———. *The Book of Genesis*. NICOT. Ed. R. K. Harrison. Grand Rapids: Eerdmans, 1995.

Hanson, A. "The Treatment in the LXX of the Theme of Seeing God." *LXX*. Eds. G. J. Brooke and B. Lindars. Atlanta: Scholars Press, 1992.

Hanson, P. D. *The People Called: The growth of Community in the Bible*. San Francisco: Harper & Row, 1986.

Haran, M. *Temples and Temple-Service in Ancient Israel: An Inquiry into the Character of Cult Phenomena and the Historical Setting of the Priestly School*. Oxford: Clarendon Press, 1978.

Haims, L. "The Face of God: Puritan Iconography in Early American Poetry, Sermons and Tombstone Carving". *EAL* 14 (1979), 15–47.

Harper, W. R. *Amos and Hosea*. ICC. Edinburgh: T. & T. Clark, 1979.

Harrison, R. K. *Numbers*. WEC. Gen. Ed. K. L Barker. Chicago: Moody Press, 1990.

Hartenstein, F. "Das 'Angesicht Gottes' in Exodus 32–34". *Gottes Volk am Sinai*. Eds. M. Köckert and E. Blum. Gütersloh: Verlagshaus, 2001.

———. *Das Angesicht JHWHs*. FAT. Tübingen: Mohr Siebeck, 2008.

Hartley, J. E. *Genesis*. NIBCOT. Peabody: Hendrickson, 2000.

Hasel, G. *Old Testament Theology: Basic Issues in the Current Debate*. Grand Rapids: Eerdmans, 1991.

Hayes, J. H. *An Introduction to Old Testament Study*. Nashville: Abingdon Press, 1979.

———, and C. R. Holladay. *Biblical Exegesis*. London: SCM Press, 1999.

Hendel, R. S. "Aniconism and Anthropomorphism in Ancient Israel". *The Image and the Book*. Ed. K. van der Toorn, CBET. Leuven: Peeters, 1997.

Hershon, P. I. *Genesis with a Talmudical Commentary*. London: Bagster & Sons, 1883.

Hertz, J. H., ed. *The Pentateuch and Haftorahs*. London: Soncino Press, 1937.

Heschel, A. *Man is not Alone. A Philosophy of Religion*. New York: Harper Torchbooks, 1951.

Hooke, S. H. *Babylonian and Assyrian Religion*. Oxford: Basil Blackwell, 1962.

Horst, F. "Face to Face." *Int* 4 (1950): 259–70.

House, P. R. *Old Testament Theology*. Downers Grove: Intervarsity Press, 1998.

Houtman, C. *Exodus*. Vol. 1. Kampen: Kok Publishing House, 1993.

———. *Exodus*. Vol. 3. Leuven: Peeters, 2002.

Hubert, G. "The God of Sinai and Jerusalem." *JQR* 17 (1905): 489–513.

Hyatt, J.P. "Yahweh as 'The God of my Father.'" *VT* 5 (1955): 130–136.

———. *Exodus*. NCBCS. Eds. R. E. Clements and M. Black. Grand Rapids: Eerdmans, 1971.

Jacob, B. *Exodus*. Jersey City: KTAV Publishing House, 1992.

Jacob, E. *Theology of the Old Testament*. London: Hodder & Stoughton, 1958.

Jacobson, T. "Formative Tendencies in Sumerian Religion". *The Bible and the Ancient Near East*. Ed. G. E. Wright. London: Routledge & Kegan, 1961.

Janzen, J. G. *Genesis 12–50: Abraham and All the Families of the Earth*. ITC. Eerdmans: Grand Rapids, 1993.

Johnson, A. R. "Aspects of the Use of the Term פָּנִים in the Old Testament". *Festschrift O. Eissfeldt*. Ed. H. J. Fück. Halle an der Saale: Niemeyer Verlag, 1947: 155–159.

Johnstone, W. *Exodus*. Sheffield: Sheffield Academic Press, 1995.

Kaiser, W. C. Jr. *Mission in the Old Testament*. Grand Rapids: Baker Book House, 2000.

———. "שׁם". *TWOT*. Vol. 2. Ed. R. L. Harris. Chicago: Moody, 1980: 934–935.

Kaufman, G. D. "On the Meaning of Transcendence without Mythology." *HTR* 59 (1966): 105–132.

Kautzsch, E., and A. E. Cowley. *Gesenius' Hebrew Grammar*. Oxford: Clarendon Press, 1910.

Keel, O. and C. Uehlinger. *Gods, Goddesses, and Images of God in Ancient Israel*. Edinburgh: T. & T. Clark 1998.

Keil, C. F., and F. Delitzsch. *The Pentateuch*. Vol. 1. Grand Rapids: Eerdmans, 1949.

———. *Pentateuch*. Vol. 2 & 3. Grand Rapids: Eerdmans, 1959.

Kendrick, R. *Does God Have a Body?* London: SCM Press, 1977.

Kidner, D. *Genesis*. TOTC. Illinois: Intervarsity Press, 1982.

Knierim, R. P., and G. W. Coats. *Numbers*. FOT. Grand Rapids: Eerdmans, 2005.

Koch, K. *The Growth of the Biblical Tradition: The Form-Critical Method*. London: Adam & Charles Black, 1969.

———. "אהל". *TDOT*. Vol. 1. Eds. G. J. Botterweck and H. Ringgren. Grand Rapids: Eerdmans, 1974: 118–130.

———. "Saddaj . . ..". *VT* 26 (1976): 299–332.

———. "תמם". *TLOT*. Vol. 3. Ed. E. Jenni and C. Westermann. Peabody: Hendrickson, 1997: 1424–1428.

Köckert, M. and E. Blum, eds. *Gottes Volk am Sinai*. Gütersloh: Verlagshaus, 2001: 157–183.

Koester, C. R. *The Dwelling of God: The Tabernacle in the Old Testament, Intertestamental Jewish Literature, and the New Testament*. Washington: Catholic Biblical Association of America, 1989.

Köhler, L. *Hebrew Man*. London: SCM Press, 1953.

———, and W. Baumgartner. *HALOT*. Vol. 3. Ed. M. E. J. Richardson. Leiden: Brill, 1996.

———. *Old Testament Theology*. Cambridge: James Clarke & Co. Ltd., 2002.

Korpel, M. C. A. *A Rift in the Clouds. Ugaritic and Hebrew Descriptions of the Divine*. Münster: Ugarit-Verlag, 1990.

———. "The Poetic Structure of the Priestly Blessing". *JSOT* 45 (1989): 3–9.

Kuntz, J. K. *The Self-Revelation of God*. Philadelphia: The Westminster Press, 1967.

Larsson, G. *Bound for Freedom*. Peabody: Hendrickson, 2003.

Lasor, W. S., et al., eds. *Old Testament Survey*. Grand Rapids: Eerdmans, 1996.

Leupold, H. C. *Exposition of Genesis*. Ohio: Columbus Press, 1942.

Levine, B. A. *In the Presence of the Lord*. Leiden: Brill, 1974.

———. *Numbers: 1–20*. AB. New York: Doubleday, 1993.

Lisowsky, G., ed. *KZHAT*. Stuttgart: Deutsche Bibelgesellschaft, 1981.

Livingston, G. H. "חטא". *TWOT*. Vol. 1. Ed. R. L. Harris. Chicago: Moody, 1980: 277–279.

Loewenstamm, S. E. "Prostration from Afar in Ugaritic, Accadian and Hebrew". *BASOR* 188 (1967): 41–43.

Lohse, E. "προσωπον" *TDNT*. Vol. 7. Ed. G. Friedrich. Grand Rapids: Eerdmans, 1969: 768–780.

López, G. "שמר". *TDOT*. Vol. 15. Eds. G.J. Botterweck and H. Ringgren. Grand Rapids: Eerdmans, 2006: 279–305.

Long, V. P. "Reading the Old Testament as Literature". *Interpreting the Old Testament*. Ed. C. C. Broyles. Grand Rapids: Baker Books, 2002.

Longman III, T., "Literary Approaches and Interpretation". *NIDOTTE*. Vol. 1. Gen. ed. W. A. VanGerman Carlisle: Paternoster Press, 1997: 103–124.

Lund, J. A. "The Interpretation of the Palestinian Targumic Reading *wqht* in Gen. 32:25." *JBL* 105 (1986): 99–103.

Lundbom, J. R. "God's Uses of the *Idem per Idem* to Terminate Debate." HTR 71 (1978): 193–201.

Mackay, J. L. *Exodus*. Fearn: Christian Focus Publications, 2001.

———. "Helel and the Dawn-Goddess." *VT* 20: 451–464.

Mann, T. W. *Divine Presence and Guidance in Israelite Traditions: The Typology of Exaltation*. Baltimore: Johns Hopkins University Press, 1977.

Marsh, J. *Numbers*. IB. Vol. 2. Gen. Ed. G. A. Buttrick. Nashville: Abingdon, 1952.

Marshall, J. W. *Israel and the Book of the Covenant*. SBLDS, 140. Atlanta: Scholars Press, 1992.

Martens, E. A. *God's Design: A Focus on Old Testament Theology*. Grand Rapids: Baker Book House, 1994.

Mayes, A. D. H., and R. B. Salters, eds. *Covenant as Context: Essays in Honour of E. W. Nicholson*. New York: Oxford University Press, 2003.

McKay, H. A. "Jacob Makes it Across the Jabbok: An Attempt to Solve the Success/Failure Ambivalence in Israel's Self-consciousness." *JSOT* 38 (1987): 3–13.

McKenzie, J. L. "Jacob at Peniel: Gn 32, 24–32." *CBQ* 25 (1963): 71–76.

———. *A Theology of the Old Testament*. New York: Doubleday, 1974.

McKeown, J. *Genesis: Two Horizons Old Testament Commentary*. Grand Rapids: Eerdmans, 2008.

McNeile, A. H. *The Book of Exodus*. London: The Westminster Commentaries, 1908.

Mendenhall, G. E. *The Tenth Generation*. Baltimore: Johns Hopkins University Press, 1973.

———. "Covenant Forms in Israelite Tradition." *BA* 17 (1954): 50–76.

Mettinger, T. N. D. *The Dethronement of Sabaoth: Studies in the Shem and Kabod Theologies*. CBOT 18. CWK Gleerup: Malmö, 1982.

———. *In Search of God*. Philadelphia: Fortress Press, 1987.

———. "The Study of the *Gottesbild*: Problems and Suggestions." *SEÅ* 54 (1989): 135–145.

———. *No Graven Image? Israelite Aniconism in its Ancient Near Eastern Context.* Stockholm: Almquist & Wiksell International, 1995.

Meyers, C. *Exodus.* NCBC. Cambridge: Cambridge University Press, 2005.

Middleton, J. R. *The Liberating Image: The Imago Dei in Genesis 1.* Grand Rapids: Brazos Press, 2005.

Milgrom, J. *Numbers.* JPS. Philadelphia: The Jewish Publication Society, 1990.

Milik, J. T. ed. *The Books of Enoch: Aramaic Fragments of Qumrân Cave 4.* Oxford: Clarendon Press, 1976.

Miller, J. M. "In the 'Image' and 'Likeness' of God." *JBL* 91 (1972): 289–304.

———, and J. H. Hayes, *A History of Ancient Israel and Judah.* London: SCM Press, 1986.

Miller, P. D. "The Blessing of God." *Int* 29 (1975): 240–251.

———. "Prayer and Action". *God in the Fray.* Eds. T. Linafelt and T. K. Beal, Minneapolis: Fortress Press, 1998.

Moberly, R. W. L. *At the Mountain of God: Story and Theology in Exodus 32–34.* Sheffield: JSOT Press, 1983.

———. "Did the Serpent Get it Right?" *JTS* 39 (1988): 1–27.

———. *Genesis 12–50.* Sheffield: Sheffield Academic Press, 1992.

———. *The Old Testament of the Old Testament.* Minneapolis: Fortress Press, 1992.

———. "God is not a Human that He Should Repent." *God in the Fray.* Eds. T. Linafelt and T. K. Beal. Minneapolis: Fortress Press, 1998: 112–123.

———. *The Bible, Theology, and Faith.* Cambridge: Cambridge University Press, 2000.

———. *Old Testament Theology: The Theology of the Book of Genesis.* Cambridge: Cambridge University Press, 2009.

Moore, S. D. "Gigantic God: Yahweh's Body." *JSOT* 70 (1996): 87–115.

Morris, H. M. *The Genesis Record.* Grand Rapids: Baker Book House, 1976.

Motyer, A. *The Message of Exodus.* BST. London: Intervarsity Press, 2005.

Muilenburg, J. "Form Criticism and Beyond." *JBL* 88 (1969): 1–18.

———. "The Intercession of the Covenant Mediator (Exod 33:1a, 12–17)". *Words and Meanings.* Eds. P. R. Ackroyd & B. Lindars. Cambridge: University Press, 1968.

Murtonen, A. L^{c}bårek and b^{c}råkå^h in the Old Testament". *VT* 9 (1959): 168–170.

Nicholson, E. W. *Exodus and Sinai in History and Tradition.* Oxford: Blackwell, 1973.

———. "The Interpretation of Exodus xxiv 9–11." *VT* 24 (1974): 77–97.

———. "The Covenant Ritual in Exodus 24:3–8." *VT* 33 (1982): 74–86.

Niehr, H. "In Search of YHWH's Cult Statue in the First Temple". *The Image and the Book*. Ed. K. van der Toorn. CBET. Leuven: Peeters, 1997.

Niehaus, J. J. *God at Sinai. Studies in Old Testament Theology*. Grand Rapids: Zondervan, 1995.

———. "In the Wind of the Storm: Another Look at Genesis iii: 8", *VT* 44 (1994): 263–267.

Noth, M. *Exodus*. London: SCM Press, 1962.

———. *History of Pentateuchal Traditions*. Englewood Cliffs: Prentice-Hall, 1972.

———. *Numbers: A Commentary*. London: SCM Press, 1968.

Nötscher, F. *Das Angesicht Gottes schauen: nach biblischer und babylonischer Auffassung*. Darmstadt: Wissenschaftliche Buchgesellschaft, 1969.

Oblath, M. "To Sleep, Perchance to Dream': What Jacob Saw at Bethel (Genesis 28:10–22)". *JSOT* 95 (2001): 117–126.

O'Connor, M. P. "יהוה" *TDOT*. Vol. 5. Eds. G. J. Botterweck and H. Ringgren. Grand Rapids: Eerdmans, 1986: 500–521.

Olson, D. T. *Numbers*. Interpretation. Ed. J. L. Mays, et al. Louisville: John Knox Press, 1989.

Orlinsky H. M. "The Treatment of Anthropomorphisms and Anthropopathisms in the Septuagint of Isaiah." *HUCA* 28 (1956): 193–200.

Orlov, A. "Ex 33 on God's Face: A Lesson from the Enochic Tradition." SBLSP 39 (2000): 130–147.

Otto, R. *The Idea of the Holy*. London: Oxford University Press, 1925.

———. *Naturalism and Religion*. London: Williams and Norgate, 1913.

Perdue, L. G. *The Collapse of History: Reconstructing Old Testament Theology*. Eugene: Wipf and Stock, 2002.

———. "Hermeneutics". In *Biblical Theology*. Ed. L. G., Perdue, et al. Nashville: Abingdon Press, 2009.

Patterson C. H. "Can Man Know God?" *JBR* 20 (1952): 176–181.

Peterson, D. L., ed. *Genesis*. *NIB*. Vol. 1. Nashville: Abingdon Press, 1994.

———. "Exodus." *NIB*. Vol. 2. Nashville: Abingdon Press, 1994.

———. *Engaging with God*. Downers Grove: Intervarsity Press, 1992.

Maass, F. "אדם", *TDOT*. Vol. 1. Eds. G. J. Botterweck and H. Ringgren. Grand Rapids: Eerdmans, 1974: 75–98.

Polak, F. "Theophany and Mediator." Ed. M. Vervenne, *Studies in the Book of Exodus*. Leuven: Leuven University Press, 1996.

Porter, S. E. *Dictionary of Biblical Criticism and Interpretation*. London: Routledge, 2009: 371–383.

Preuss, H. D. "השתחוה, חוה". *TDOT*. Vol. 4. Eds. G. J. Botterweck and H. Ringgren. Grand Rapids: Eerdmans, 1980: 249–257.

Pritchard, J. B. *Palestinian Figurines in relation to Certain Goddesses known Through Literature*. New Haven: American Oriental Society, 1943.

———, ed. *The Ancient Near East: An Anthology of Texts and Pictures*. London: Oxford University Press, 1969.

Propp, W. H. *Exodus 19–40*. AB. Vol. 2. New York: Doubleday, 2006.

———. "The Skin of Moses' Face — Transfigured or Disfigured?" *CBQ* 49 (1987): 375–386.

Reindl, J. *Das Angesicht Gottes im Sprachgebrauch des Alten Testaments*. Leipzig: St. Benno-Verlag, 1970.

Reiterer, F. V. "שם". *TDOT*. Vol. 15. Eds. G.J. Botterweck and H. Ringgren. Grand Rapids: Eerdmans, 2006: 128–174.

Rendtorff, R. *The Old Testament: An Introduction*. London: SCM Press, 1985.

———. "Creation and Redemption in the Torah." *The Blackwell Companion to the Hebrew Bible*. Ed. L. G. Perdue, Oxford: Blackwell, 2001.

Reventlow, H. G. "Modern approaches to Old Testament Theology". In *The Blackwell Companion to the Hebrew Bible*. Ed. L. G. Perdue, Oxford: Blackwell, 2001.

Richards, L. *Freedom Road*. Colorado: David C. Cook Publishing, 1976.

Richardson, A., ed. *A Theological Word Book of the Bible*. London: SCM Press, 1950.

Riggans, W. *Numbers*. DSB. Gen. Ed. J. C. L. Gibson. Edinburgh: The Saint Andrew Press, 1983.

Ringgren, H. "כה". *TDOT*. Vol. 7. Eds. G. J. Botterweck and H. Ringgren. Grand Rapids: Eerdmans, 1995: 122–128.

———. "נשא". *TDOT*. Vol. 10. Eds. G. J. Botterweck and H. Ringgren. Grand Rapids: Eerdmans, 1999: 24–40.

Robertson, O. P. *The Christ of the Covenants*. Grand Rapids: Baker Book House, 1980.

Roberts, B. J. "The Old Testament: Manuscripts, Text, and Versions". In *The Cambridge History of the Bible*. Vol. 2. Ed. G. W. H. Lampe. Cambridge: Cambridge University Press, 1969.

Roberts, J. J. M. "The Hand of Yahweh". *VT* 21 (1971): 244–251.

Robinson, H. W. *The Theology of the Old Testament: Record and Revelation*. Oxford: Clarendon Press: 1938.

———. *Inspiration and Revelation in the Old Testament*. Oxford: Clarendon Press, 1946.

———. *Corporate Personality in Ancient Israel*. Philadelphia: Fortress Press, 1964.

Rogerson, J. W., ed. *The Pentateuch*. Sheffield: Sheffield Academic Press, 1996.

———. *Genesis and Exodus*. Sheffield: Sheffield Academic Press, 2001.

Rooy, H. F. "פנים". *NIDOTTE*. Vol. 3. Ed. W. A. VanGemeran. Grand Rapids: Zondervan, 1997: 637–640.

Ross, A. P. *Creation and Blessing*. Grand Rapids: Baker Book House, 1988.

———. *Leviticus: Holiness to the Lord*. Grand Rapids: Baker Academic, 2002.

Ross, B. L. *The Individual in the Community: Personal Identification in Israel*. PhD diss., Drew University, 1979.

Rowley, H. H. *The Faith of Israel*. London: SCM Press, 1956.

———. *The Old Testament and Modern Study*. Oxford: Clarendon Press, 1961.

Runzo, J. "Religious Pluralism". In *Philosophy of Religion*. Eds. P. Copan, and C. Meister, eds. Oxford: Blackwell, 2008.

Ruppert, L. "שחר". *TDOT*. Vol. 14. Eds. G. J. Botterweck and H. Ringgren. Grand Rapids: Eerdmans, 2004: 570–582.

Rylaarsdam, J. C. *Exodus. IB*. Vol. 1. Gen. Ed. G. A. Buttrick. Nashville: Abingdon, 1952: 833–1099.

Ryken, L. *Literary Guide to the Bible*. Ed. T. Longman III. Grand Rapids: Zondervan, 1993.

Sailhamer, J. H. *The Pentateuch as Narrative*. Grand Rapids: Zondervan, 1992.

Sakenfeld, K. D. *Numbers: Journeying with God*. ITC. Grand Rapids: Eerdmans, 1995.

Salvesen, A. *Symmachus in the Pentateuch*. Manchester: Manchester University Press, 1991.

Sanders, S. L. "Old Light on Moses' Shining Face." *VT* 52 (2002): 400–406.

Sarna, N. M. *Genesis. The JPS Torah Commentary*. Philadelphia: Jewish Publication Society, 1989.

———. *Exodus*. Philadelphia: The Jewish Publication Society, 1991.

Satyavani, P. *Israelite Understanding of ירא in the Hebrew Bible and its Implications for Worship*. M.Th. diss., Senate of Serampore, 1999.

———. *The "Face of God" in Genesis and its Significance for Worship*. M.Litt. diss., University of St. Andrews, 2006.

Savran, G. W. *Encountering the Divine*. London: T. & T. Clark, 2005.

Scharbert, J. "ברך". *TDOT*. Vol. 2. Ed. G. J. Botterweck and H. Ringgren. Grand Rapids: Eerdmans, 1988: 279–308.

Schild, E. "On Exodus 3:14—'I am that I am.'" *VT* 4 (1954): 296–297.

Schüle, A. "Made in the 'Image of God': The Concepts of Divine Images in Gen 1–3." ZAW 117 (2005): 1–20.

Sellers, O. R. "Seeking God in the Old Testament." *JBR* 21 (1953): 234–237.

Selman, M. J. "אור". *NIDOTTE*. Vol. 1. Gen. Ed. VanGemeran Carlisle: Paternoster Press, 1997: 324–329.

Seybold, K. *Der aaronitische Segen*. Neukirchener Verlag: Neukirchen-Vluyn, 1977.

Siebesma, P. A. *The Function of the Niphal in Biblical Hebrew*. Assen: Van Gorcum, 1991.

Simpson, C. A. *Genesis. The Interpreter's Bible*. Vol. 1. Gen. Ed. G. A. Buttrick. Nashville: Abingdon, 1952.

Skinner, J. *Genesis*. ICC. Edinburgh: T. & T. Clark, 1956.

Smith, H. P. "The Scriptural Conception of the Glory of God." *OTS* 3 (1884): 325–329.

Smith, M. S. *The Pilgrimage Pattern in Exodus*. JSOT. Sheffield: Sheffield Academic Press, 1997.

Snaith, S. H. *Leviticus and Numbers*. NCB. London: Thomas Nelson, 1967.

Soffer, A. "The Treatment of Anthropomorphisms and Anthropopathisms in the Septuagint of Psalms." *HUCA* 28 (1957): 85–107.

Sommer, B. D. "Revelation at Sinai in the Hebrew Bible and in Jewish Theology." *JR* 79 (1999): 422–451.

———. *The Bodies of God and the World of Ancient Israel*. Cambridge: Cambridge University Press, 2009.

Soskice, J. M. "The Ends of Man and the Future of God." Ed. G. Ward. *Postmodern Theology*, Oxford: Blackwell, 2001.

Sparks, K. L. *God's Word in Human Words*. Grand Rapids: Baker Academic, 2008.

Speiser E. A. *Genesis*. AB. New York: Doubleday, 1964.

———. "The Durative Hithpa'el: A tan-Form." *NY* 15 (1954): 118–121.

Sprinkle, J. M. *Literary Approach to the Book of the Covenant*. JSOTS, 174. Sheffield: JSOT Press, 1994.

Stähli, H.-P. "ראה". *TLOT*. Vol. 2. Eds. E. Jenni and C. Westermann, Peabody, Massachusetts: Hendrickson: 568–578.

Stanley, C. D. *The Hebrew Bible: A Comparative Approach*. Minneapolis: Fortress Press, 2010.

Stendebach, F. J. "שלום". *TDOT*. Vol. 15. Ed. G. J. Botterweck and H. Ringgren. Grand Rapids: Eerdmans, 2006: 13–49.

Stephen, J. *Theophany: Close Encounters with the Son of God*. Surrey: Day One Publications, 1998.

Stern, E. "What Happened to the Cult Figurines? Israelite Religion Purified after the Exile." *BAR* 15 (1989): 22–53.

Stuart, D. *Old Testament Exegesis*. Louisville: Westminster John Knox Press, 2001.

Stubbs, D. L. *Numbers*. TCB. London: SCM Press, 2009.

Sturdy, J. *Numbers*. Cambridge: Cambridge University Press, 1976.

Tov, E. *Textual Criticism of the Hebrew Bible*. Minneapolis: Fortress Press, 1992.

Terrien, S. *The Elusive Presence: Toward a New Biblical Theology*. New York: Harper & Row, 1978.

———. "History and Significance of a Standard Text". In *Hebrew Bible/Old Testament: The History of Its Interpretation*. Vol. 1. Ed. M. Sæbø. Göttingen: Vandenhoeck & Ruperecht, 1996.

Thiselton, A. C. *The Two Horizons*. Carlisle: Paternoster Press, 1993.

Tucker, G. M. *Form Criticism of the Old Testament*. Philadelphia: Fortress Press, 1971.

Turner, L. A. *Genesis*. Sheffield: Sheffield Academic Press, 2000.

van der Toorn, K. "Teraphim". *DDDB*. Leiden: Brill, 1999.

van der Woude, A. S. "פנים". *TLOT*. Vol. 2. Eds. E. Jenni and C. Westermann. Peabody: Hendrickson Publishers, 1997: 995–1014.

Vetter, D. "חזה". *TLOT*. Vol. 1. Eds. E. Jenni and C. Westermann, Peabody: Hendrickson, 1994: 400–403.

———. "ראה". *TLOT*. Vol. 3. Eds. E. Jenni and C. Westermann, Peabody: Hendrickson, 1994: 1176–1183.

Von Rad, G. *Moses*. London: Lutterworth Press, 1960.

———. *Genesis*. OTL. London: SCM Press, 1972.

———. *The Theology of the Old Testament*. Vol. 1 & 2. New York: Harper & Row, 1962.

———. *God at Work in Israel*. Nashville: Abingdon Press, 1980.

Von Soden, W., ed. *Akkadisches Handwörter Buch*. Band II M-S. Wiesbanden: Otto Harrassowitz, 1972.

Wagner, N. E. "רנה in the Psalter." *VT* 10 (1960): 435–441.

Wagner, S. "אמר". *TDOT*. Vol. 1. Ed. G. J. Botterweck and H. Ringgren. Grand Rapids: Eerdmans, 1974: 328–345.

Walker, N. "Do Plural Nouns of Majesty Exist in Hebrew?" *VT* 7 (1957): 208.

Walton, J. H. *Ancient Israelite Literature in its Cultural Context*. Grand Rapids: Zondervan, 1989.

Waltke, B. and M. O'Connor. *Introduction to Biblical Hebrew Syntax*. Winona Lake: Eisenbrauns, 1990.

Watson, F. *Text, Church and World*: Biblical Interpretation in Theological Perspective. Edinburgh: T. & T. Clark, 1994.

Weinfeld, M. *Deuteronomy and the Deuteronomic School*. Oxford: Clarendon Press, 1972.

Wenham, G. J. *Numbers*. TOTC. Gen. Ed. D. J. Wiseman. Leicester: Intervarsity Press, 1981.

———. *The Book of Leviticus*. NICOT. Ed. R. K. Harrison. Grand Rapids: Eerdmans, 1988.

———. *Genesis 16–50*. WBC. Dallas: Word Books, 1994.

Wessner, M. D. *Face to Face:* פנים אל־פנים *in Old Testament Literature*. MA. diss., Regent College, 1998.

Westermann, C. *Genesis 1–11: A Commentary*. London: SPCK, 1984.

———. *Genesis 12–36: A Commentary*. Minneapolis: Augsburg Publishing House, 1985.

———. *Handbook to the Old Testament*. London: SPCK, 1980.

Whybray, R. N. *The Making of the Pentateuch: A Methodological Study*. Sheffield: JSOT Press, 1987.

———. *Introduction to the Pentateuch*. Grand Rapids: Eerdmans, 1995.

———. *The Good Life in the Old Testament*. London: T. & T. Clark, 2002.

Widmer, M. *Moses, God, and the Dynamics of Intercessory Prayer*. Tübingen: Mohr Siebeck, 2004.

Wilson, I. *Out of the Midst of the Fire*: *Divine Presence in Deuteronomy*. SBLDS, 151. Atlanta: Scholar's Press, 1995: 161–197.

Williamson, P. R. *Abraham, Israel and the Nations*. Sheffield: Sheffield Academic Press, 2000.

———. *Sealed with an Oath*. Nottingham: Intervarsity Press, 2007.

Willis, T. M. *Leviticus*. Nashville: Abingdon Press, 2009.

Wolf, H. *An Introduction to the Old Testament Pentateuch*. Chicago: Moody Press, 1991.

Wolf, H. "אור". *TWOT*. Vol. 1. Ed. R. L. Harris. Chicago: Moody, 1980: 25–27.

Wolters, Al. "The Text of the Old Testament". In *The Face of Old Testament Studies: A Survey of Contemporary Approaches*. Ed. D. W. Baker and B. T. Arnold. Baker Books: Grand Rapids, 1999.

Wolterstorff, N. *Inquiring about God*. Ed. T. Cuneo. Cambridge: Cambridge University Press, 2010.

Wright, C. J. H. *Walking in the Ways of the Lord: The Ethical Authority of the Old Testament*. Downers Grove: Intervarsity Press, 1995.

Wright, G. E. *The Old Testament Against its Environment*. London: SCM Press, 1957.

———. *God Who Acts*. London: SCM Press, 1952.

Würthwein, E. *The Text and the Old Testament*. Grand Rapids: Eerdmans, 1995.

Yardeni, A. "Remarks on the Priestly Blessing on Two Ancient Amulets from Jerusalem." *VT* 41 (1991): 176–185.

Yofre, S. "פנים". *TDOT*. Vol 11. Ed. G. J. Botterweck and H. Ringgren. Grand Rapids: Eerdmans, 2001: 589–615.

Young, I. "The Stabilization of the Biblical Text in the Light of Qumran and Masada: A Challenge for Conventional Qumran and Chronology?" *DSD* 9 (2002): 364–390.

Zimmerli, W. *Old Testament Theology in Outline*. Atlanta: John Knox Press, 1978.

Web articles

Frisch, A. *The Priestly Blessing*. Ramat Gran: Bar Ilan University, Last Modified June 11, 2005. http://www.biu.ac.il/JH/Parasha/eng/naso/fri.html.

Calvin, J. *The Institutes of the Christian Religion*. Grand Rapids: Christian Classics Ethereal Library, Accessed 21 August, 2014. http://www.ccel.org/ccel/calvin/institutes.pdf.

Wikipedia. "Brahman." Last modified 18 August, 2014, http://en.wikipedia.org/wiki/Brahman.

Langham Literature and its imprints are a ministry of Langham Partnership.

Langham Partnership is a global fellowship working in pursuit of the vision God entrusted to its founder John Stott –

to facilitate the growth of the church in maturity and Christ-likeness through raising the standards of biblical preaching and teaching.

Our vision is to see churches in the majority world equipped for mission and growing to maturity in Christ through the ministry of pastors and leaders who believe, teach and live by the Word of God.

Our mission is to strengthen the ministry of the Word of God through:
- nurturing national movements for biblical preaching
- fostering the creation and distribution of evangelical literature
- enhancing evangelical theological education

especially in countries where churches are under-resourced.

Our ministry

Langham Preaching partners with national leaders to nurture indigenous biblical preaching movements for pastors and lay preachers all around the world. With the support of a team of trainers from many countries, a multi-level programme of seminars provides practical training, and is followed by a programme for training local facilitators. Local preachers' groups and national and regional networks ensure continuity and ongoing development, seeking to build vigorous movements committed to Bible exposition.

Langham Literature provides majority world preachers, scholars and seminary libraries with evangelical books and electronic resources through publishing and distribution, grants and discounts. The programme also fosters the creation of indigenous evangelical books in many languages, through writer's grants, strengthening local evangelical publishing houses, and investment in major regional literature projects, such as one volume Bible commentaries like *The Africa Bible Commentary* and *The South Asia Bible Commentary*.

Langham Scholars provides financial support for evangelical doctoral students from the majority world so that, when they return home, they may train pastors and other Christian leaders with sound, biblical and theological teaching. This programme equips those who equip others. Langham Scholars also works in partnership with majority world seminaries in strengthening evangelical theological education. A growing number of Langham Scholars study in high quality doctoral programmes in the majority world itself. As well as teaching the next generation of pastors, graduated Langham Scholars exercise significant influence through their writing and leadership.

To learn more about Langham Partnership and the work we do visit **langham.org**

www.ingramcontent.com/pod-product-compliance
Lightning Source LLC
Chambersburg PA
CBHW051537230426
43669CB00015B/2624

This work provides a unique contribution to the growing field of Asian Biblical studies. In viewing "the face of the Lord" and "the glory of the Lord" as referring to the physical, corporeal presence of God, Satyavani presents an intriguing study of the self-revelation of God which challenges received views of divine personhood. Drawing implicitly on her own Hindu background in contesting non-metaphorical readings of divine presence in the Pentateuch, Satyavani offers a highly detailed exegesis of key scriptural readings related to "seeing" God.

Chloe Starr
PhD Assistant Professor
Asian Christianity and Theology, Yale Divinity School

Here, treated together for the very first time, are the texts most relevant for this intriguing subject. Indeed, the virtue of this work is its insistence on situating these texts within the wider narrative sequence of the Pentateuch—an approach long overdue in the long running discussion of this important topic, "Seeing the Face of God".

David Shepherd
PhD Assistant Professor of Hebrew Bible/Old Testament
Loyola Institute Trinity College, Dublin

That the Almighty God has chosen to reveal himself to us is a basic tenet of the biblical faith. This study on the "Face of God" is particularly fascinating because the author relates seeing the face of God to his self-revelation. Besides, the relevance of this study here in South Asia is fairly obvious, for people go to a temple here to have darshana [divine seeing] of a sacred image—that is, they not only go to "see" God, but to be seen by God. So this study is of interest and value from two perspectives—biblical and contextual.

Brian Wintle
Regional Secretary, India, Asia Theological Association